Spatial Databases

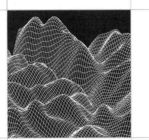

With Application to GIS

Philippe Rigaux

Michel Scholl

Agnès Voisard

MORGAN KAUFMANN PUBLISHERS

AN IMPRINT OF ELSEVIER

SAN FRANCISCO   SAN DIEGO   NEW YORK   BOSTON
LONDON   SYDNEY   TOKYO

Executive Editor	Diane D. Cerra
Publishing Services Manager	Scott Norton
Assistant Publishing Services Manager	Edward Wade
Associate Production Editor	Marnie Boyd
Assistant Editor	Belinda Breyer
Cover Design	Yvo Reizebos Design
Text Design	Side by Side Studios/Mark Ong
Composition	Integre Technical Publishing Co., Inc.
Technical Illustration	Dartmouth Publishing, Inc.
Copyeditor	Daril Bentley
Proofreader	Jennifer McClain
Indexer	Bill Meyers
Printer	Courier Corporation

Designations used by companies to distinguish their products are often claimed as trademarks or registered trademarks. In all instances where Morgan Kaufmann Publishers is aware of a claim, the product names appear in initial capital or all capital letters. Readers, however, should contact the appropriate companies for more complete information regarding trademarks and registration.

Permissions may be sought directly from Elsevier's Science and Technology Rights Department in Oxford, UK. Phone: (44) 1865 843830, Fax: (44) 1865 853333, e-mail: permissions@elsevier.co.uk. You may also complete your request on-line via the Elsevier homepage: http://www.elsevier.com by selecting "Customer Support" and then "Obtaining Permissions".

Morgan Kaufmann Publishers
An imprint of Elsevier
340 Pine Street, Sixth Floor
San Francisco, CA 94104-3205
http://www.mkp.com

Library of Congress Control Number: 200129409
ISBN 1-55860-588-6

This book is printed on acid-free paper.

Spatial Databases

WITH APPLICATION TO GIS

The Morgan Kaufmann Series in Data Management Systems
Series Editor: Jim Gray, Microsoft Research

Spatial Databases: With Application to GIS
Philippe Rigaux, Michel Scholl, and Agnès Voisard

Information Modeling and Relational Databases: From Conceptual Analysis to Logical Design
Terry Halpin

SQL:1999 Understanding Relational Language Components
Jim Melton and Alan R. Simon

Component Database Systems
Edited by Klaus R. Dittrich and Andreas Geppert

Managing Reference Data in Enterprise Databases: Binding Corporate Data to the Wider World
Malcolm Chisholm

Information Visualization in Data Mining and Knowledge Discovery
Edited by Usama Fayyad, Georges G. Grinstein, and Andreas Wierse

Data Mining: Concepts and Techniques
Jiawei Han and Micheline Kamber

Understanding SQL and Java Together: A Guide to SQLJ, JDBC, and Related Technologies
Jim Melton and Andrew Eisenberg

Database: Principles, Programming, and Performance, Second Edition
Patrick and Elizabeth O'Neil

The Object Data Standard: ODMG 3.0
Edited by R.G.G. Cattell and Douglas K. Barry

Data on the Web: From Relations to Semistructured Data and XML
Serge Abiteboul, Peter Buneman, and Dan Suciu

Data Mining: Practical Machine Learning Tools and Techniques with Java Implementations
Ian Witten and Eibe Frank

Joe Celko's SQL for Smarties: Advanced SQL Programming, Second Edition
Joe Celko

Joe Celko's Data and Databases: Concepts in Practice
Joe Celko

Developing Time-Oriented Database Applications in SQL
Richard T. Snodgrass

Web Farming for the Data Warehouse: Exploiting Business Intelligence and Knowledge Management
Richard D. Hackathorn

Database Modeling and Design, Third Edition
Toby J. Teorey

To

Cécile, Simon, Clément
—Philippe

Claire, Julien, P. G.
—Michel

Oliver, Juliette, Amélie
—Agnès

Foreword

Victor Vianu, University of California, San Diego

These are exciting times for the database area. Gone are the days when databases were limited to such mundane tasks as handling payroll records. Today, a database is just as likely to hold web pages, genome collections, chip designs, videos, satellite imagery, music, or maps. The basic functions of a database remain the same: efficient storage and querying. However, they now require a vastly wider range of techniques, integrating classical and specialized approaches to various types of data.

Among the specialized data handled by today's databases, *spatial data* has emerged as central to many applications. These include geographic information systems (GISs), computer-aided design (CAD), robotics, image processing, and VLSI, all of which have at their core spatial objects that must be stored, queried, and displayed. The need for specific techniques geared toward spatial objects gave rise to the area of *spatial databases*. In a relatively short period, spatial databases have developed a comprehensive technology, including representations for spatial objects, spatial access methods for fast retrieval, specific query languages, and algorithms adapted from adjacent areas such as computational geometry.

Spatial Databases: With Application to GIS presents this diverse and intellectually challenging material in a thorough, comprehensive, yet accessible fashion. The focus is on the fundamental technology of spatial databases, with a special eye toward GIS, which remains this technology's foremost application. The presentation strikes the right balance between fundamental concepts of spatial databases and the state of the art in GIS. The book is aimed primarily at computer scientists, but also at geographers who would like to understand the technical issues raised by their field within computer science.

The authors of this book—Philippe Rigaux, Michel Scholl, and Agnès Voisard—have worked for many years in the field of spatial databases as researchers, project leaders, and educators. They have contributed to the foundations of the area, as well as to the development of major prototypes. The book has benefited enormously from their experience, and will be an invaluable resource for anyone interested in this exciting field.

Contents

4   THE CONSTRAINT DATA MODEL   113

Figures

Preface

"In that Empire, the Art of Cartography achieved such Perfection
that the Map of one single Province
occupied the whole of a City, and
the Map of the Empire, the whole
of a Province. In time, those Dis-
proportionate maps failed to satisfy
and the Schools of Cartography
sketched a Map of the Empire
which was of the size of the Empire
and coincided at every point with
it. Less addicted to the study of
Cartography, the Following Generations comprehended that this
dilated Map was Useless and, not
without Impiety, delivered it to the
Inclemencies of the Sun and of the
Winters. In the Western Deserts
there remain piecemeal Ruins of
the Map, inhabited by Animals and
Beggars. In the entire rest of the
Country there is no vestige left of
the Geographical Disciplines."

JORGE LUIS BORGES
*Suarez Miranda, Viajes de
Varones Prudentes, IV*

A few decades ago, paper maps were the principal means to synthetize and represent geographic information. Manipulating this information was limited to a manual, noninteractive process. Since then, the rapid development of new technologies to collect and digitize geographic data, together with an increasing demand for both interactive manipulation and analysis of this data, has generated a need for dedicated softwares, namely geographic information systems (GISs).

A GIS is more than a cartographic tool to produce maps. It stores geographic data, retrieves and combines this data to create new representations of geographic space, provides tools for spatial analysis, and performs simulations to help expert users organize their work in many areas, including public administration, transportation networks, military applications, and environmental information systems.

Due to the ever-increasing volume of geographic data, one of the major tasks of GIS is to efficiently manage huge databases of complex information. In a classical software architecture, this task is usually devoted to a database management system (DBMS). Most DBMSs in practical use are *relational* DBMSs. However, relational DBMSs are strongly geared toward business applications, which manipulate large but simple data sets. It turns out that these systems are unable to manage geographic data, in particular because of its inherent spatial component. There have been considerable efforts to extend and adapt DBMS technology to spatial information. This book aims at reporting on the major achievements in this field. Although there are increasing interdependencies between GIS and DBMS technologies, two different viewpoints can be taken. On the one hand, GISs see database systems as one tool among many that provide facilities for the storage and retrieval of data. In turn, this data is processed by other tools, such as spatial analysis or graphical user interfaces. DBMS designers, on the other hand, see GIS as one important, but not unique, application of their novel ability to handle spatial data. From a database point of view, the emphasis is less on the application itself than on the functionality; namely, the storage of large volumes of spatial information, the application of computational techniques on this information, and the development of efficient access methods to retrieve relevant data from voluminous data sets stored on disk.

This book is mainly influenced by the second perspective. It explores the various techniques (and thus the required extensions of classical

DBMSs) necessary to meet the requirements of spatial data management, both at the user level and at the system level.

In many respects, these requirements go beyond the management of geographic data. Indeed, the ability to manipulate spatial information—which is at the core of the novel features of spatial DBMS—is useful for any application based on large spatial data sets, including computer-aided design (CAD), very large scale integration (VLSI), robotics, and image processing. We chose, however, to take our examples and illustrations from the field of geographic applications, both because this is still the primary target of spatial DBMS and because geographic applications served as the first motivation to develop spatial DBMS and thus strongly influenced its design.

Geospatial information concerns phenomena occurring above, on, and below Earth's surface. Geospatial information is represented in maps. A map contains geographic objects such as land parcels, rivers, and roads that are related to the same geographic area. Any geographic object has the following components:

- The component referred to as *spatial* or *geometric attribute*, or *spatial extent*. This component describes the location, shape, orientation, and size of the object (for instance, a land parcel) in 2D or 3D space.

- The component that describes the object by means of *nonspatial* attributes. These attributes are also referred to as *thematic* or *descriptive* attributes (for instance, the name of a land parcel).

The foregoing characteristics are not exclusive to geographic information. For example, VLSI layout description also deals with objects having an extent in multidimensional space. This is why *spatial databases* should be preferred as a more generic term for information systems dealing with objects having a spatial component. Spatial databases should be distinguished from *image information systems* or *image databases*, which manage collections of 2D or 3D scenes. Medical databases, electronic documents, and cultural heritage collections are examples of potential image sources. Image databases support the search for scenes that contain certain objects or patterns. Location, direction, and size of the object are usually of little importance—a major difference from spatial databases, where these search criteria play an important role. Image databases will not be discussed further here.

Some of the tasks currently handled by GIS existed before GIS technology. These include systematic collection of data about land for census activities, atlases, public administration mapping efforts, public utilities management, new construction planning and engineering, urban and rural planning, and cartography, as well as tasks required by the military and various sciences, such as geography, geology, and geodesy. In addition, many regional and national agencies, as well as other organizations, use geographic data for less traditional tasks that have been influenced by the development of GIS technology, such as forest management, postal services, space applications, socioeconomic studies, and market analysis.

Organization of This Book

This book seeks to explain the major features of a spatial database. It deals with the concepts, techniques, and algorithms that have been developed around the core issues in database management, such as how to represent data, which operations should be supplied by the system to manipulate and retrieve this data, and how to access and retrieve data from secondary storage. The main objective is to identify the challenges raised by the peculiar nature of spatial information, and to describe the specific techniques recently developed to meet these novel requirements.

The book covers basic material and some advanced topics. As far as basic material is concerned, we provide a sound and detailed coverage of several well-established topics—for example, structures for spatial data representation or spatial access methods—that can serve as a reference for practitioners, scientists, and graduate students. Advanced topics and more specialized aspects are also introduced, either because we believe they will soon be adopted in commercial systems (this is the case for query processing techniques, for instance), or because they represent a new and exciting way of thinking about spatial data and its representation in database systems (for example, constraint databases). The presentation style of advanced material is based on intuition and examples, rather than on a meticulous and exhaustive treatment. The interested reader will find, at the end of each chapter, a section devoted to bibliographic notes. The book is organized in eight chapters, whose content is as follows:

◆ Chapter 1 provides *introductory material* toward understanding subsequent chapters. We present the main features of database management systems and GIS, and we introduce the vocabulary used throughout the book.

◆ Chapter 2 concerns *spatial data representation*. It studies the internal or physical representation of *spatial* objects.

◆ Chapter 3 presents *logical models and query languages* for representing and manipulating geographic information. Our discourse relies on common database technology; namely, extended relational and object-oriented database management systems.

◆ Chapter 4 deals with a recent alternative way of modeling and querying geographic information through *constraint databases*.

◆ Chapter 5 introduces algorithmic techniques for implementing the spatial operations presented in Chapter 3. These techniques belong to the field of *computational geometry*.

◆ Chapter 6 is devoted to the study of *spatial access methods* (SAMs), or spatial indices, necessary for accelerating the access to a large number of spatial objects stored on disk.

◆ Chapter 7 is an introduction to *query processing techniques* for evaluating end-user queries on spatial databases. It includes in particular some algorithms for spatial joins.

◆ Chapter 8 presents five products on the market. The first three are GIS platforms; namely, ArcInfo, ArcView, and Smallworld. The fourth is the Oracle relational DBMS spatial extension SDO, and the fifth is an open source DBMS, PostgreSQL.

The book has two potential audiences. The primary audience includes people from the database research community and database people developing tools for spatial applications. A second audience consists of geographers and GIS users interested in understanding the challenges in current and future GIS technology. We tried as much as possible to introduce the technical background necessary for readers with no expertise in databases. It can be anticipated, however, that readers with solid database background (the primary audience previously discussed) will be more interested in Chapters 1, 2, 4, 5, 6, and 7, whereas geographers and GIS users will find information that meets their needs in Chapters 1, 3, 6, and 8.

Acknowledgments

Writing this book would not have been possible without the contribution of many people, whom we wish to thank here. We are indebted to Jean-Paul Peloux and Laurent Raynal, with whom we published a preliminary version of this book in French. Jean-Paul focused on spatial indexing, whereas Laurent was particularly concerned with ArcInfo.

Some of our colleagues provided us with many useful comments on many parts of the manuscript, among them Oliver Günther (Chapter 2), Luc Segoufin (Chapters 4 and 5), Anne Verroust (Chapter 5), and Jean-Marc Saglio (Chapter 6). We are grateful to them.

We wish to thank Dave Abel, Martin Breunig, and Rolf de By, who as formal reviewers of parts of this book made many detailed and constructive remarks. In particular, Dave gave us extremely valuable feedback regarding the organization of the book and pointed to interesting issues, whereas Rolf did a tremendous job getting into the details of three chapters.

It would not have been possible to develop many of the aspects presented here without common reflection with colleagues, some of them being coauthors of publications. We wish to thank Benoît David, Kenn Gardels, Gilles Grangeret, Stéphane Grumbach, Oliver Günther, Gaby Kuper, Yannis Manolopoulos, Apostolos Papadopoulos, Xavier Rhésé, Hans-Jörg Schek, Luc Ségoufin, and Pierangelo Veltri.

Many people indirectly contributed to this book through their technical abilities, among them Günter Feuer, Thomas Klinkski, and Vilim Vesligaj, who provided technical support at the Freie Universität, Berlin; Catherine Breton and Daniel Marcel, who shared their knowledge of ArcView; Steffi Fritz and Cornelia Pester of Smallworld, Germany, who helped us set our Smallworld environment at the Freie Universität, Berlin; Laurent Breton from IGN, who shared his expertise with ArcInfo; and José Moreira and Jean-Marc Saglio, with whom we had many technical discussions about Oracle. We wish to thank them.

We also wish to acknowledge the programs and host institutions who helped us travel and meet each other, despite the distance, during this long process. Michel Scholl visited the Freie Universität many times, thanks in particular to the Berlin-Brandenburg graduate school on distributed information systems (DFG grant no. GRK 316) and the

Procope Franco-German exchange program (DAAD grant no. 312). Agnès Voisard visited CNAM and INRIA for extended periods through the Procope cooperation. We would also like to acknowledge the partial support of the European Network TMR Chorochronos. We are grateful to its members for the stimulating discussions of the past two years. We are indebted to our home institutions for their continuing support: the Vertigo database group in the Cedric lab of CNAM, the Verso database project at INRIA, and the database group at Freie Universität Berlin. We are grateful to our colleagues in these institutions for the warm atmosphere in which this work was carried out, including notably Serge Abiteboul, Helmut Alt, Bernd Amann, Alain Cazes, Vassilis Christophides, Sophie Cluet, Claude Delobel, Daniel Faensen, Lukas Faulstich, Annika Hinze, Marcus Jürgens, Leonid Libkin, Alain Michard, Stéphane Natkin, Andreas Sabisch, Heinz Schweppe, Anne-Marie Vercoustre, Victor Vianu, François-Yves Villemin, Dan Vodislav, Franz Wagner, Gerald Wagner, and Gerald Weber. We owe a great deal to our secretaries Heike Eckart, Danny Moreau, and Virginie Moreau for their constant support in everyday life. We also thank our students Irini Fundulaki, Christophe Gurret, Laurent Mignet, and Cedric Du Mouza.

Finally, we are grateful for the assistance we received from the editorial staff at Morgan Kaufmann. We are especially thankful to Marnie Boyd, Belinda Breyer, and Diane Cerra for their patience during the entire process.

1

An Introduction to Spatial Databases

"Where shall I begin, please your
Majesty?" he asked.

"Begin at the beginning," the King
said, very gravely, "and go on till
you come to the end: then stop."

    LEWIS CARROLL
    Alice in Wonderland

CONTENTS

If we move away from the traditional paper map and the explanation or journal that usually accompanies it, we have to consider a new type of digital information, characterized by its large volume (for instance, the amount of images recorded per day by a satellite is in the terabyte range) and its intrinsic complex structure. In addition, geographic information differs in nature according to the type of application and the way it was obtained. Basically, it may be derived

- *From primary data collection in the field.* Data is directly collected from field surveys. The determination of point locations on Earth is often done with the help of the Global Positioning System (GPS) of satellites. Data is in other ways remotely collected, through various remote sensing techniques, which produce satellite images (usually Landsat and Spot), aerial photographs (with the help of photogrammetry), and other input. The problems in primary data collection include delimiting geographic objects (the boundary may be fuzzy, for example, in the case of soil type) and associating thematic attribute values with spatial objects.
- *From existing maps.* A map may be created by integrating several existing digital data sources (maps). For example, analog maps and other cartographic documents can be digitized using manual, automatic, or semiautomatic techniques. Maps come with a map *scale*. Furthermore, to represent geographic coordinates (longitude, latitude) on a 2D map, you also need a *reference system*, which involves the choice of a map *projection system* (Mercator, Universal Transverse Mercator, and so on.). Integration from various sources often raises problems due to heterogeneous scale and coordinate systems (e.g., data accuracy), as well as problems related to data quality.

The use of computerized maps varies widely, according to the type of application. A site description in archaeology and a fire-truck routing certainly appear to be dissimilar applications. However, they do have in common the need for a system that provides the following functions:

- Data input and verification
- Data storage and management
- Data output and presentation
- Data transformation
- Interaction with end users

A full-fledged geographic information system (GIS) is able to handle all of these tasks. The kernel of a GIS is therefore a database management system (DBMS) handling the storage and management of the data, as well as interaction with users.

Before using such a system, the objects of interest have to be modeled; in other words, the real world needs to be simplified, which leads to a model of it. The next step is to find appropriate structures to store all the data.

This introductory chapter is meant to give the reader some background needed to comprehend the material covered by this book. It provides non-database experts with the DBMS concepts necessary for understanding the subsequent chapters, shows database specialists examples of geographic applications, and illustrates the specific requirements of geospatial applications. This chapter is organized as follows. First (Section 1.1), basic notions on DBMS are given. We then introduce the vocabulary necessary for the subsequent chapters (Section 1.2). Section 1.3 presents operations typically performed while using a GIS. System architecture alternatives to support such operations are discussed in Section 1.4. Section 1.5 covers the requirements of a spatial DBMS. Finally, Section 1.6 provides bibliographic notes in the general areas of database systems and GIS. Pointers to related topics not treated in this book are also given in this last section.

1.1   DATABASE MANAGEMENT SYSTEMS (DBMSs)

This section is devoted to a concise description of databases and DBMSs. The reader interested in more elaborate descriptions will find the information in dedicated books (see Section 1.6, Bibliographic Notes).

1.1.1   Basic Description and Main Features

A *database* is a large collection of interrelated data stored within a computer environment. In such environments, the data is *persistent*, which means that it survives unexpected software or hardware problems (except severe cases of disk crashes). Both large data volume and persistence, two major characteristics of databases, are in contrast with information manipulated by programming languages, which is small enough in volume to reside in main memory and which disappears once the program terminates.

Traditional applications of databases include management of personnel, stocks, travel reservations, and banking. Many "nonstandard" applications have emerged in the past 15 years, among them spatial databases, images, computer-aided design and manufacturing (CAD/CAM), textual databases, software engineering, and bioinformatics.

A database can be seen as one or several files stored on some external memory device, such as a disk. Although it would be possible to write applications that directly access these files, such an architecture would raise a number of problems pertaining to security, concurrency, and complexity of data manipulation. A DBMS is a collection of software that manages the database structure and controls access to data stored in a database. Generally speaking, a DBMS facilitates the process of

- *Defining* a database; that is, specifying the data types, structures, and constraints to be taken into account.

- *Constructing* the database; that is, storing the data itself into persistent storage.

- *Manipulating* the database.

- *Querying* the database to retrieve specific data.

- *Updating* the database (changing values).

Figure 1.1 depicts a simplified database system environment. It illustrates how a DBMS acts as a mediator between users or application programs and the devices where data resides. DBMS software consists of two parts. The upper part processes the user query. The lower part allows one to access both the data itself (denoted "stored database" in the figure) and the metadata necessary to understand the definition and structure of the database.

A DBMS hinges on the fundamental concept of *data independence*. Users interact with a representation of data independently of the actual *physical* storage, and the DBMS is in charge of translating the user's manipulations into efficient operations on physical data structures. Note that this is quite different from file processing, in which the structure

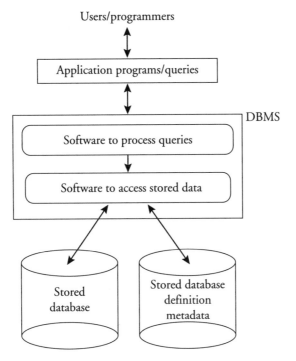

Figure 1.1   A simplified database system environment.

of a file, together with the operations on this file, are embedded in an access program.

This mechanism is achievable through the use of different *levels of abstraction*. It is customary in the database community to distinguish three levels in a database environment. The *physical level* deals with the storage structures, the *logical level* defines the data representation proposed to the user, and the *external level* corresponds to a partial view of the database provided in a particular application.

The distinction between physical and logical representations, made throughout this book, is central to the field of databases. This clearly separates the tasks devoted to the system from the simplified representation and manipulation functionality offered to the user. She can hence focus primarily on the adequate modeling and implementation of her application. The following briefly elaborates on the main issues pertaining to each level.

1.1.2 Modeling Applications

At the logical level, the first task is to define the *database schema* that describes the structure of the information managed by the application, as well as the constraints to be respected by the data in the database. Once the schema has been defined, data can be inserted, updated, deleted, and queried by means of a *query language*.

The particular structures, constraints, and operations provided by a DBMS depend on the *logical data model* supported by this DBMS. Nowadays, the most widely used is the *relational* data model. The following illustrates the development of an application with relational databases.

DATA REPRESENTATION IN A RELATIONAL DATABASE
In a relational environment, data representation is fairly simple. It relies on a single type of structure, the *table* or *relation*. For instance, to represent the name, capital, and population of a collection of countries, a style such as that shown in Table 1.1 is used, containing one *row* or *tuple* per country and one *column* or *attribute* per property represented in each country (namely, its *name, capital,* and *population*). In order to design a *relational schema*—that is, the set of tables necessary to represent the application data—one normally follows a two-step approach.

♦ *Conceptual modeling (step 1).* This step is independent from any possible implementation. It allows one to generically describe the objects of interest, often called *entities* at this stage, together with the relationships among them. Entities are instances of *entity types*, and relationships are instances of *relationship types*. For instance, in the sentence "Paris is the capital of France," Paris (France) is an entity

Table 1.1 Example relation: Countries.

Country

name	capital	population
Germany	Berlin	78.5
France	Paris	58
. . .	. . .	. . .

that belongs to an entity type called city (respectively, country), and "is the capital of" is a relationship type. The fact that the city of Paris is the capital of France is a relationship; that is, a particular instance of the previous relationship type. Relationships between entities can be generic, such as composition, aggregation, or inheritance. Other relationships apply to particular situations (such as "A road *connects* cities"). Entities and relationships are usually depicted graphically within diagrams such as entity-relationship (ER), UML (Unified Modeling Language), or OMT (object modeling techniques) diagrams. Once such a diagram has been designed, one obtains a *conceptual schema*.

◆ *Logical level (step 2)*. At this stage, the conceptual schema is translated into the data model of a particular DBMS. In the context of relational databases, one follows some simple transformation rules, and describes the relational schema with the *data definition language* (DDL).

DATA MANIPULATION

Generally speaking, within a DBMS environment, manipulating data is done through expressing queries and other operations (updates, inserts, and so on) in the *data manipulation language* (DML). One of the reasons for the success of relational DBMS is the existence of a widely accepted query language named SQL, uniformly used in all relational systems. SQL enjoys fundamental properties that are worth mentioning. First, SQL is *declarative*, which means that the user expresses what he expects as a result, without specifying how the system must operate to compute this result. The language is simple, and is accessible to nonexpert users, who do not need to be aware of how the result is obtained. This also gives the system the freedom (and the responsibility) to choose an appropriate execution.

Second, SQL relies on sound mathematical foundations. The set of data manipulations expressible by the language is precisely defined by two equivalent, formal languages; namely, *relational calculus* and *relational algebra*. The first is essentially first-order logic. The second is a small set of operators that describes how relations can be manipulated to evaluate a query.

However, there is a counterpart to SQL simplicity. The expressive power of SQL is not sufficient, as it does not match that of complete programming languages such as C. Recursion, for instance, cannot be expressed, nor can arithmetic computations. Although this is the price to be paid for simplicity and efficiency, it entails some strong limitations with respect to the computations required to manipulate spatial objects. These issues—in particular those that relate to declarativeness and expressiveness—are considered in the discussion on spatial query languages (in Section 3.3).

1.1.3 Physical Data Management

The following is a partial list of the tasks handled by any DBMS at the physical level. All of these functionalities are hidden to the end user.

- *Storage.* A DBMS manages an efficient organization of data on a persistent secondary storage unit (typically one or many disks). The representation used at this level might be completely different from that shown to the user according to the logical data model. A table, for instance, might be stored in several files, possibly distributed over many disks.

- *Access paths.* A DBMS provides data access methods or *access paths* that accelerate data retrieval. A typical data structure or *index* that accelerates data retrieval is the B-tree.

- *Query processing.* Processing (*evaluating*) a query usually involves several operations. To efficiently evaluate the query, these operations must be properly combined. An important issue in query processing is the design of efficient *join* algorithms.

- *Query optimization.* Because the user query is purely declarative (at least with SQL), it is the responsibility of the system to find an acceptably efficient way to evaluate a query.

- *Concurrency and recovery.* The DBMS manages concurrent access to data and resources from several users, and guarantees the security and consistency of the database, as well as the recovery of the database to a consistent state after a system failure.

It should be noted that many of these functionalities (with the exception of concurrency control and recovery) are geared toward an efficient evaluation of queries. The foregoing tasks must also be handled in spatial databases. However, with spatial data, many of these tasks require a specific solution. In particular, the relational data model turns out to be too poor to represent and manipulate geometric data. This gives rise to some exciting challenges regarding both the extension of existing logical data models and the development of new query processing techniques.

1.2   VOCABULARY IN GEOSPATIAL DATABASE APPLICATIONS

This section reviews vocabulary used throughout the book.[1] The main terms defined here are *theme, map,* and *geographic object*. The section ends with the main issues to be addressed in geospatial modeling.

1.2.1   *Theme*

In a GIS, the geospatial information corresponding to a particular topic is gathered in a *theme*. A theme is similar to a relation as defined in the relational model. It has a schema and instances. Rivers, cities, and countries are examples of themes. When a theme is displayed on paper or on-screen, what the user sees is a *map* as it is commonly displayed, with colors, a particular scale, a legend, and so on. Topographic maps, railway maps, and weather maps are examples of maps commonly used. Figure 1.2 shows a typical map. The first step when using a GIS is to construct a conceptual schema for all themes of interest (step 1 of Section 1.1.2).

1.2.2   *Geographic Objects*

The major objects to be considered at a conceptual level are *geographic objects*. A theme is a collection of geographic objects. A geographic object corresponds to an entity of the real world and has two components:

♦ A *description*. The object is described by a set of *descriptive attributes*. For instance, the name and population of a city constitute its description. These are also referred to as alphanumeric attributes.

---

1. Apart from a few terms, the vocabulary is one widely used by the GIS community, and in particular by ArcInfo (ESRI).

Europe

Figure 1.2   A typical map.

♦ A *spatial component*, which may embody both geometry (location
   in the underlying geographic space, shape, and so on) and topology
   (spatial relationships existing among objects, such as adjacency). For
   instance, a city might have as a geometric value a polygon in 2D
   space. The isolated spatial component of a geographic object is what
   we call *spatial object*. It may be considered separately; for instance,
   when it is shared by many geographic entities (typically, a border
   between two countries).

Given the complexity of geographic entities in the real world and
the intrinsic composition relationships that exist among many such
entities, we introduce the notion of *atomic geographic object* and *complex geographic object*. Complex geographic objects consist of other
geographic objects, which may in turn be atomic or complex (note the
many possible levels in the composition hierarchy). For example, in the

theme that corresponds to American administrative units, the (complex) geographic object "State of California" consists of the (atomic) geographic objects "Counties of California." During the modeling phase, this type of composition relationship must be taken into account. The following abstract definition, whose syntax is meant to be intuitive, summarizes the notions of atomic and complex geographic objects.

theme = {geographic-objects}
geographic-object = (description, spatial-part)   // atomic object
* | (description, {geographic-object}) // complex object*

A theme is hence a set of homogeneous geographic objects (i.e., objects having the same structure or *type*). It can be seen as a particular abstraction of space with a single type of object. Consider the example of the city theme. Each city is described by the same collection of attributes, which constitute its *schema*: name, population, and geometry. A theme has to be represented according to the GIS logical data model (step 2 of Section 1.1.2). This model is here called a *geographic model;* it represents a way to describe and manipulate themes and their objects in a DBMS environment.

The spatial attribute of a geographic object does not correspond to any standard data type, such as string or integer, in a computer programming environment. The representation of the geometry and topology requires powerful modeling at the theme or object level, which leads to *spatial data models.* Usually, the following basic data types are used in spatial data models: *point* (zero-dimensional object), *line* (one-dimensional), and *region* (2D object). For instance, the spatial object associated with a river is a line, whereas the object associated with a city is a region (polygon). In some geographic applications that take into account punctual elevation (e.g., height of buildings), it is customary in the GIS jargon to refer to dimension "2.5." A third, and possibly a fourth, dimension is introduced if volume or time is considered.

1.3   GEOSPATIAL DATA MANIPULATION

This section discusses simple operations that take one or many themes as input and give as a result a theme. The section then moves to more

complex operations and ends with typical GIS operations, such as allocation and location of resources.

1.3.1 Simple Operations on Themes

Suppose the existence of the following themes: (1) *Countries*, with the
descriptive attributes *name, capital, population*, and with a geometric
attribute referred to as *geo*, and (2) *Languages*, representing the distribution of main spoken languages (or families of languages, to be more
precise), with the descriptive attribute *language* and spatial attribute
geo. This is summarized in the following two-theme schema:

- *Countries (name, capital, population, geo:region)*
- *Languages (language, geo:region).*

The following are a few common manipulations of these themes. They
rely on operations from the relational algebra, such as *projection, selection, join*, and *union*.

THEME PROJECTION
Theme projection with signature[2] *theme* $\times \{A_1, \ldots A_n\} \rightarrow$ *theme*,
where $\{A_1, \ldots A_n\}$ is a subset of the descriptive attributes of *theme*, returns a theme whose description is made of the attributes in $\{A_1, \ldots A_n\}$
and whose spatial part is unchanged. If *geo* denotes the spatial type,
and T denotes an instance of the theme schema (i.e., a collection
of geographic objects of this theme), this operation is denoted by
$\pi_{A_1,\ldots An,geo}(T)$ (projection in the relational algebra).

   Consider this operation and theme of western European countries
with their respective names and populations. Each country is a geographic object, and the name of the country together with its population represents its description (Figure 1.3a). By applying a *theme projection* to the population, we eliminate the country names (Figure 1.3b).
The resulting theme has as a schema (*population, geo*).

---

2. An operation *signature* describes the type of the argument(s) and the type of the
result. Here projection takes as an input (i) a theme (*theme* is a shortcut for the set of
attributes of the input theme) and (ii) a subset of attributes of this theme.

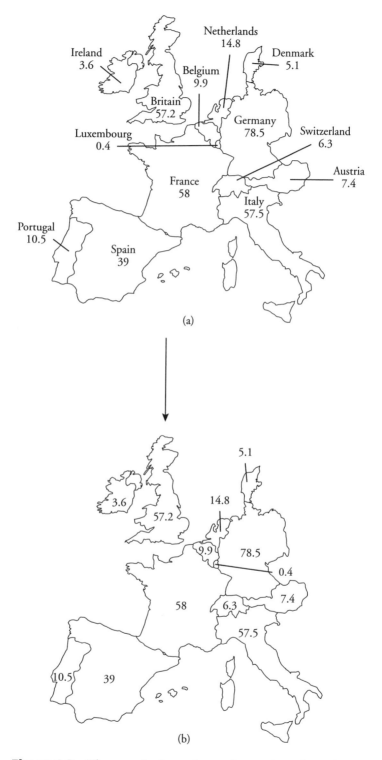

Figure 1.3 Theme projection: a theme of countries and population of western Europe (a) and projection on the attribute *population* (b).

THEME SELECTION

Theme selection (*theme*× p_{A_i} → *theme*), where p_{A_i} is a predicate on the descriptive attributes, is similar to relational selection and is denoted by $\sigma_{p_{A_i}}(T)$. Consider the query *Name and population of countries of 50 million inhabitants or more*. After the selection of the countries whose population is greater than 50 million inhabitants, in Figure 1.4a, we obtain the theme of Figure 1.4b.

THEME UNION

The (relational) union of two themes (*theme* × *theme* → *theme*) consists in performing the union of sets of geographic objects having the same schema. It is similar to the relational union. Hence if T_1 and T_2 are two theme instances, the result is denoted $T_1 \cup T_2$. Figure 1.5 depicts the union of two themes.

THEME OVERLAY

Overlaying two themes (*theme* × *theme* → *theme*) is common in GIS applications. This operation generates a new theme from overlaid themes. New geographic objects are created in the resulting theme. Their geometry is computed by applying the intersection operation to the geometry of the involved geographic objects. Their description is a combination of the participating descriptions.

There exists a variety of map overlay operations. The one previously described can be expressed as a *spatial join*. An object of one theme is *joined* with an object of the other theme if their geometries intersect. The resulting object has the descriptive attributes of both participating objects, and its geometry is the intersection of the participating objects' geometry (see Chapter 6). If $\bowtie_G$ denotes a spatial join, and T_1 and T_2 are themes, then the overlay is expressed as $T_1 \bowtie_G T_2$. Figure 1.6 gives an example of the overlay of *Countries* and *Languages*. The new theme has as descriptive attributes (country) name and language. An example object of the new theme is the northern part of Switzerland whose descriptive attributes are "Switzerland" and "Anglo-Saxon."

GEOMETRIC SELECTION

Geometric selection includes operations such as the following.

◆ *Windowing (window query)*. By *windowing* a theme, one obtains another theme, which includes only those objects of the input theme

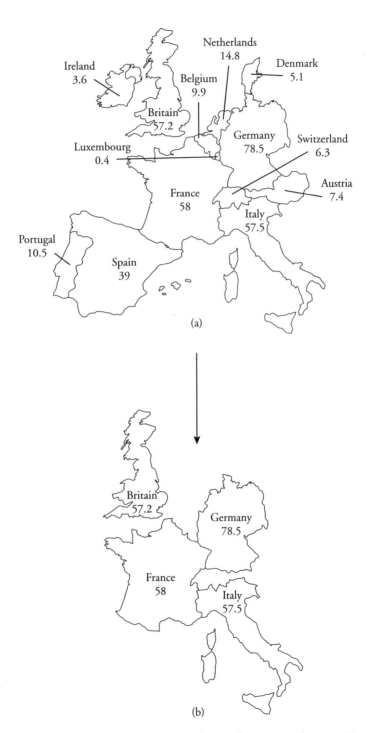

Figure 1.4 Theme selection: a theme of countries of western Europe (a) and selection for countries of more than 50 million inhabitants (b).

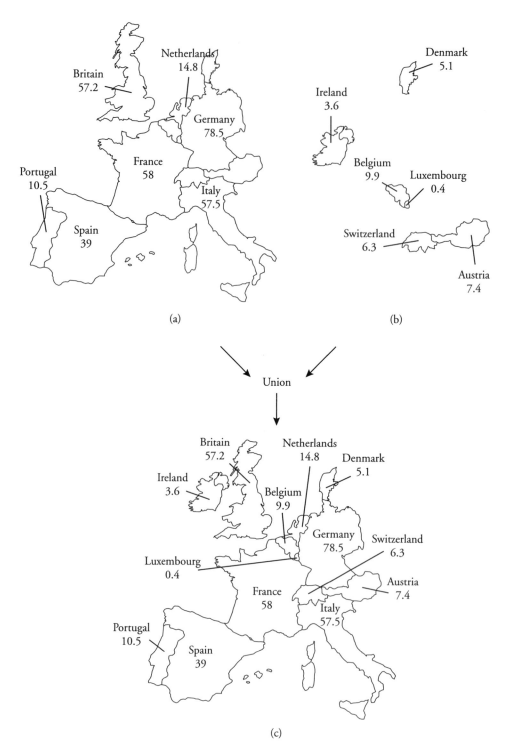

Figure 1.5 Theme union: a theme of countries of western Europe with more than (or exactly) 10 million inhabitants (a), theme of countries and population of western Europe with less than 10 million inhabitants (b), and the union of these two themes (c).

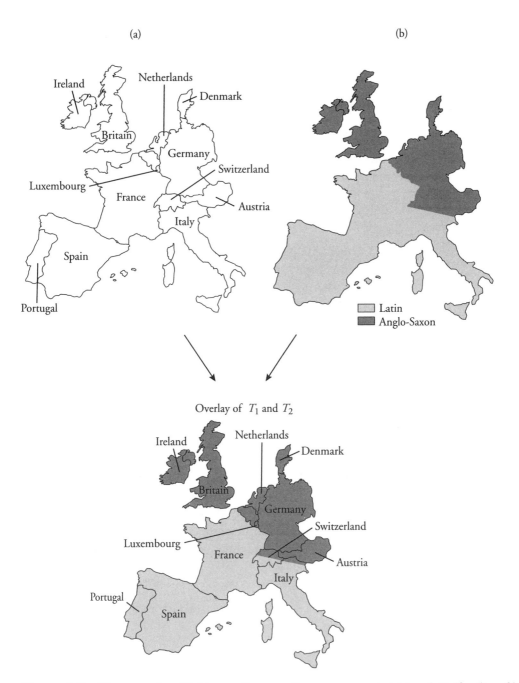

Figure 1.6   Theme overlay: T_1 (theme of western European countries) (a) and T_2 (families of languages spoken all over western Europe) (b).

that overlap a given area or *window*, which is usually rectangular (Figure 1.7).

◆ *Point query.* A similar operation, denoted *point query*, is the query that retrieves all objects whose geometry contains a given point.

◆ *Clipping.* Clipping extracts the portion of a theme located within a given area (Figure 1.8). As opposed to windowing, the geometry of an object in the result corresponds exactly to the intersection of the geometry of the geographic objects and the geometry of the area.

MERGER

The merger operation performs the geometric union of the spatial part of *n* geographic objects that belong to the same theme, under a condition supplied by the end user (Figure 1.9). As it operates within a single theme, its signature is *theme × condition → theme* (observe the difference with the theme union, which takes as arguments two themes and gathers them into a single theme). Merger relies on the concept of object aggregation.

1.3.2   Further Theme Operations

The operations previously described belong to what might be considered *theme algebra*. Each operation takes one or more themes as input and returns a theme. However, not all operations on themes give as a result a theme. For instance, some operations based on metrics will return a number (e.g., the distance operation). Other operations on themes are more complex. Examples of operations of these categories are

◆ *Operations using a metric.* Examples of queries include, *What is the distance between Paris and Berlin?*

◆ *Topological operations.* These operations are related to the (topological) relationships existing among data. A query that uses such an operation is, for instance, *What are the countries adjacent to Belgium?* Another topological query on networks is, *What cities can I reach by train from Berlin without any stop?*

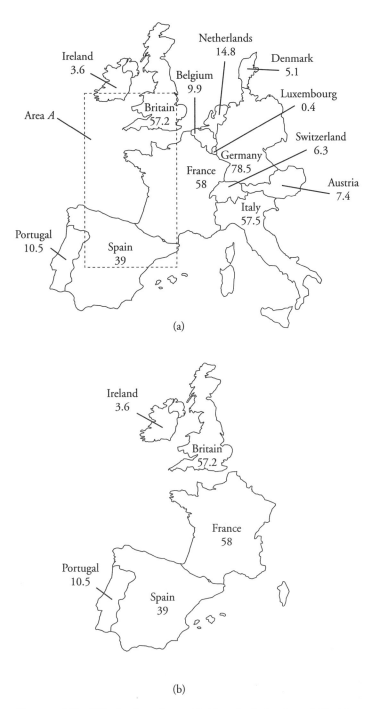

Figure 1.7 Windowing: theme T (a) and windowing of T with area A (b).

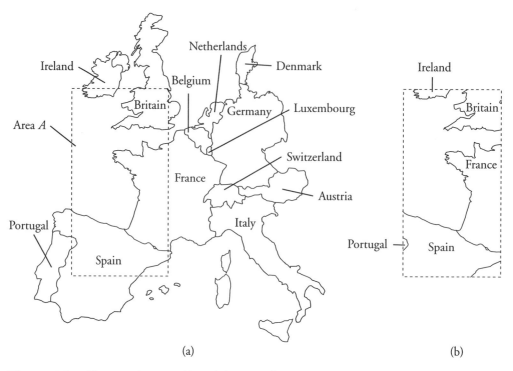

(a)   (b)

Figure 1.8   Clipping: theme T (a) and clipping of T with area a (b).

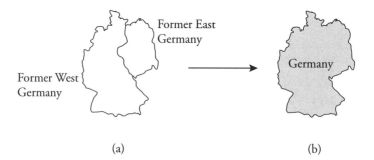

(a)   (b)

Figure 1.9   Merging two geographic objects in a theme: theme with two geographic objects (a) and theme with one geographic object (b).

1.3.3   Other Typical GIS Operations

There exist a large number of other operations that are very common in GISs. They occur in many situations, such as map or theme creation or geospatial data analysis. These operations are not detailed here. The following are examples.

- *Interpolation/extrapolation.* The need for such operations occurs in situations with limited information (e.g., samples), and when new values have to be estimated. Many techniques exist for that purpose, such as *spatial autocorrelation* (nearby data points receive the highest weight in averaging) or so-called *modeling technique* (e.g., kriging, developed by mining geologists).

- *Location.* In the location problem, there is a known finite set of possible locations to which resources are allocated. The question is to choose the location that corresponds to a certain amount of resources. For instance, the input can be a known set of customer locations, a known transportation system, or a known set of available plots on which to build. The output is the best location to maximize sales.

- *Allocation.* This problem (dual with the location problem) deals with the allocation of quantities (resources) among supply and demand points. Typical applications are geomarketing applications and urban planning.

- *Location/allocation combination.* The location and allocation functions are often used simultaneously in many GIS applications. For instance, one might want to find out the location of schools and the precise schools to which pupils may be assigned.

1.4   DBMS SUPPORT FOR GEOSPATIAL DATA

The previous section points out the need for a system that allows one to perform the following on geospatial and alphanumeric data:

- Input and store
- Retrieve and analyze
- Display and select

A GIS needs to store (in files) both spatial and alphanumeric data. Storage can be controlled either directly by the application or by a database management system.

Early GISs were built directly on top of proprietary file systems. Some off-the-shelf current GISs still follow this approach. Geospatial and alphanumeric data are both stored in files controlled by the application, and functions are defined on this data. This, however, does not respect the important data independence principle, and leads to many problems regarding, for instance, data security and concurrency control.

The section that follows investigates the possible approaches when using a DBMS in a GIS environment. The section first explains why pure relational databases are not suitable for handling spatial data. Two alternatives are considered; namely, the coupled approach and the use of an extensible DBMS.

1.4.1   Use of a Relational DBMS

The major features of this approach are

- A representation of themes by relations (tables). A geographic object is one tuple (row) of such a relation. Each column is an attribute.
- Attributes that have alphanumeric types (e.g., string and real).
- SQL-based querying.

Figure 1.10 shows an example for theme Country with schema (attributes) *name, capital, population,* and *geo* (as in Section 1.3). It is stored in relation *Country*. Representing spatial objects is achieved as follows. The geometric attribute *geo* corresponds to the boundary of the country. Assuming a country possibly consists of several parts, we consider a relation *Boundary* made of contours. A contour is characterized by an identifier (e.g., C1) and a list (relation) of points, one per polygon vertex, each listed in the *Point* table.

Because there is no notion of ordered list in the relational model, a trick needs to be used to describe a list of ordered points in a contour. Here the attribute *point-num* is intended to represent an ordering of the points along the boundary of a region. Contour C1, for instance, is represented by the sequence {P2, P1, P3}, although the points are not stored in this order. Similarly, one can define tables for other spatial types, such as lines consisting of points, and regions, whose contour consists of lines.

Querying themes that are defined in this way is performed via SQL. Consider the query *Return the contours of France.* Solving this query implies getting the set of coordinates of the vertices that correspond to the polygons approximating the boundaries of France; that is, getting the boundaries of all objects constituting France (i.e., the mainland and the islands). This query can be expressed in SQL as follows:

Country

name	capital	population	id-boundary
Germany	Berlin	78.5	B1
France	Paris	58	B2
...	...	...	...

Boundary

id-boundary	id-contour
B1	C1
B2	C2
B2	C3
B3	C4
B3	C5
...	...

Contour

id-contour	point-num	id-point
C1	2	P1
C1	1	P2
C1	3	P3
C1	...	...
C2	1	P4
C2	2	P5
C2	...	...
...	...	...

Point

id-point	x	y
P1	452	1000
P2	365	875
P3	386	985
P4	296	825
P5	589	189
...	...	...

Figure 1.10 A relational representation of countries.

select	*Boundary.id-contour, x, y*
from	*Country, Boundary, Contour, Point*
where	*name* = 'France'
and	*Country.id-boundary = Boundary.id-boundary*
and	*Boundary.id-contour = Contour.id-contour*
and	*Contour.id-point = Point.id-point*
order by	*Boundary.id-contour, point-num*

The major advantage of this approach is that it hinges on a standard (SQL). On the other hand, it suffers from drawbacks that make it inappropriate for handling geospatial applications, among them:

♦ A violation of the data independence principle, as formulating queries on themes requires a knowledge of the spatial objects' structure. Changing this structure implies a deep reorganization of the database and changing the query formulation.

- The bad performance of this approach, which requires in particular a considerable amount of relational tuples to represent spatial information.
- Its lack of user friendliness, as one has to manipulate tables of points.
- The difficulty in defining new (spatial) types.
- The impossibility of expressing geometric computations such as adjacency test, point query, or window query.

1.4.2 Loosely Coupled Approach

Many current GISs separate descriptive data management from geospatial data management. ArcInfo (ESRI), MGE, and TiGRis (Intergraph) are well-known GISs that follow this approach. In such architectures, two systems coexist (see Figure 1.11):

- A (relational) DBMS, or some components of it for descriptive (alphanumeric) data
- A specific module for spatial data management

However, this approach also suffers from drawbacks. Among them, the most important are

- The coexistence of heterogeneous data models, which implies difficulties in modeling, use, and integration
- A partial loss of basic DBMS functionality, such as recovery techniques, querying, and optimization

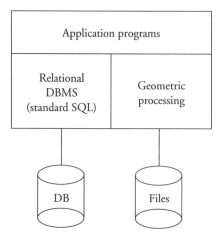

Figure 1.11 Loosely coupled architecture.

1.4.3   Integrated Approach Based on DBMS Extensibility

To circumvent many of the problematic aspects previously described, DBMS extensibility has been receiving a growing interest in the past years in many new application domains. The basic concept is the ability to add new types and operations to a relational system. In the case of geospatial applications, a current trend is to extend relational DBMS as follows:

◆ The query language SQL is extended to manipulate spatial data as well as descriptive data. New spatial types (point, line, region) are handled as base alphanumeric types.
◆ Many other DBMS functions, such as query optimization, are adapted in order to handle geospatial data efficiently.

Most relational off-the-shelf DBMSs offer such a spatial extension (see bibliographic notes of Chapter 8). Two of these systems, Oracle8*i* and Postgres, are studied in detail in Chapter 8 in the context of spatial data modeling, querying, and indexing.

1.5   REQUIREMENTS FOR A SPATIAL DBMS

In this book we are mostly interested in the integrated approach, although we shall also present in Chapter 8 the coupling architecture with an example of commercial GIS. We suppose the existence of a DBMS devoted to spatial applications. As explained in the previous section, this database system should (1) integrate the representation and manipulation of geometric information with traditional data at the logical level, and (2) provide an efficient support at the physical level to store and process this information. The following is a list of requirements for an extended DBMS to fulfill these objectives.

◆ The logical data representation must be extended to geometric data, while satisfying the data independence principle and keeping as much as possible its simplicity and its closeness to the user's vision of reality.
◆ The query language must integrate new functions in order to capture the rich set of possible operations applicable to geometric objects.
◆ There should exist an efficient physical representation of the spatial data.

♦ Efficient data access is essential for spatial databases as well as for classical ones. Unfortunately, B-trees are no longer appropriate for spatial data access. We hence need new data structures for indexing spatial databases.

♦ Finally, some of the most important achievements in the field of relational query processing, such as join algorithms, cannot be used in geospatial databases. Here, again, some new algorithms are needed.

1.6 BIBLIOGRAPHIC NOTES

As far as database books are concerned, there are many, from theoretical viewpoints to practical aspects. For a comprehensive survey on general as well as practical aspects, we will retain the classic work of [Ull88, Ull89], as well as [EN94] (where we borrowed most of the introductory material of this chapter and Figure 1.1), [O'N94], and [Ram97]. More specialized textbooks include [AHV95], which gives an in-depth presentation of the theoretical aspects of database models, and [P86] and [BHG87], which cover database concurrency control.

Regarding general books on GIS and spatial information systems, an introduction to early GIS can be found in [ABCK91, Tom90]. The two volumes [MGR99] give a thorough overview of principles and applications of GIS. The book [LT92] studies many aspects of spatial information systems, from data description to practical techniques. It gives in particular (Chapter 7) examples of typical GIS operations, such as location/allocation. [Wor95] is a comprehensive study of the kernel of current GISs and their relationship with databases. In addition to its large scope, from conceptual levels to representational levels, it provides a thorough list of references in the field. The book [BD98] provides a thorough overview of techniques currently in use in GIS to handle geographic data, as well as a large panorama of GIS applications. The definition of a spatial database system given here is borrowed from [Güt94], which gives an introduction to spatial database systems and shows the major challenges from a database perspective. More information on the topic can be found in the proceedings of the biannual Symposium on Spatial Databases [BGSW89, GS91, AO93, HE95, SV97, GPL99] and in survey articles [GB90, MP94], which explain the peculiarity of databases for spatial information. The book

[Gün98] studies issues related to environmental information handling. The theme operations found in Section 1.3 are described in [VD01], whose first part describes informally common operations on themes. Material on the modeling tools UML, OMT, and Rational Rose can be found in [Qua98, RBP$^+$91].

Some database topics are neglected in this book. A first reason is that these topics are not necessarily major challenges in the context of spatial-based applications. The most notable examples are concurrency control and recovery. A second reason for the absence of such topics is the relative immaturity of the field. Web interfaces to GIS [Ple97] and interoperability [GEFK99, Vko98, Lau98, Vck99] are examples of topics not yet well established. Issues in conceptual representation of space and conceptual modeling of GIS are investigated in, for example, [Peu84, BW88, CL93, HT97, SEM98]. Recent work on conceptual modeling of spatio-temporal applications can be found in [TJ99]. As far as GIS-related topics not treated in this book are concerned, the interested reader will find a comprehensive list of themes in [Ber97], and the description of typical GIS techniques such as map production, data capture, and spatial data analysis in the general GIS books previously cited. The periodical reports of the U.S. National Center for Geographic Information and Analysis (NCGIA) [NCG00] represent an excellent source of information on specialized areas. Other GIS features that will not be addressed include accuracy [GG89, Bur94], spatial data quality and update [GM95, SL95, Ege97, FB97, GJ98, SUPL00], representation of spatial knowledge [PS94], spatial reasoning for uncertainty handling (see, for example, [JM95, Jea99]), direction modeling [Fra92, PE97], integration from multiple sources [DPS98], visual languages and visualization techniques [MP90, BTAPL99, Ege96, PS95, DSS98], and specific urban planning techniques [Lau00].

These topics raise interesting challenges in terms of modeling and querying. In particular, in the field of cartography we would need to represent spatial data, together with toponyms identifying it, using symbolized cartographic representation at different degrees of detail [LP86]. Other sources of challenging issues are spatial data mining [NH94, KH95, KN96, XEKS98, EKS97], network modeling (see, for example, [Mai95]), map generalization [BW88, BM91, MLW95, LPL97, WJ98, PBR98, Rua98], and multiscale representation (see, for instance, [FT94, RS95, Dum97, SPV00]). With a smaller map scale, less information is shown on the map. Some information is removed, whereas other information is simplified. Most current GIS systems include tools for spatial analysis, among which statistical analysis and modeling play a central role. These are, for instance, classification, exploratory analysis, and detection of patterns; testing hypotheses or estimating formal models; and so on.

The importance of time in GIS (i.e., the evolution of geographic information with time) has been a topic of interest for more than a decade [Lan92, Wor94, YdC95]. More recently, spatio-temporal databases and, more particularly, moving objects have received considerable attention. It is an emerging topic not addressed in this book, except for a short development in Chapter 4, because of its relative immaturity. A recent book [GKS00] covers the most promising research results in this area. More specific references will be given in the appropriate chapters. Last, it is worth mentioning the management of multimedia documents, a related area whose spatial and spatio-temporal requirements are similar to those of GIS. We shall not address these here. [MPS+00, VTS98] are references on related issues.

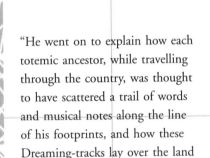

2

Representation of
Spatial Objects

"He went on to explain how each totemic ancestor, while travelling through the country, was thought to have scattered a trail of words and musical notes along the line of his footprints, and how these Dreaming-tracks lay over the land as 'ways' of communication between the most far-flung tribes.

'A song,' he said, 'was both map and direction-finder. Providing you knew the song, you could always find your way across country...'
...In theory, at least, the whole of Australia could be read as a musical score. There was hardly a rock or creek in the country that could not or had not been sung. One should perhaps visualise the Songlines as a spaghetti of Iliads and Odysseys, writhing this way and that, in which every 'episode' was readable in terms of geology."

BRUCE CHATWIN
The Songlines, Chapter 3

CONTENTS

This chapter describes the various ways of modeling and representing geometric and topological information in GIS. This modeling process relies on mathematical foundations that would deserve a rigorous development. However, we limit ourselves to a few basic concepts of geometry sufficient to our needs. They are summarized thereafter.

First, the space of interest is $\mathbb{R}^d$, together with the Euclidean distance. We refer to it as the *Euclidean space*, and, unless otherwise specified, we assume that dimension d is 2.

Points are elements of this space. A point has a pair of (Cartesian) coordinates that, according to common use, we denote as x (the abscissa) and y (the ordinate). Although points in the Euclidean plane are quite useful to represent the location and shape of objects of the Earth's surface, it should be underlined that the latter is a globe (hence a curved surface), and that we need a conversion, called a *map projection*, to map geographic entities onto a planar representation. We ignore this process in this book.

Finally, we usually restrict our attention to the region of $\mathbb{R}^2$ that contains the relevant objects. This region is bounded, and for the sake of convenience we assume that it is a sufficiently large rectangle whose edges are parallel to the axes of the coordinate system. We call it the *embedding space* in the following, and sometimes the *search space* whenever a search operation is to be performed.

This chapter is organized as follows. Section 2.1 describes entity-based models and field-based models as the main approaches in geographic space modeling. In Section 2.2, we present three representation modes commonly used to support these models. They are namely the tessellation modes (regular and irregular), the vector mode, and a half-plane representation. This section focuses on the representation of single objects in the plane. Section 2.3 studies the representation of *collections* of spatial objects, including their interrelationships.

Section 2.4 provides an illustration of the basic concepts through the description of spatial data exchange formats. In particular, we present the widely used TIGER/Line (*Topologically Integrated Geographic Encoding and Referencing data*) format and the geometry feature of the Open GIS consortium. We end the section with the study of some commonly used formats for exchanging data, with emphasis on ongoing efforts for standardizing spatial data exchange (OpenGIS, TC/211, and TC/287). Finally, bibliographic entries are found in Section 2.5.

2.1   GEOGRAPHIC SPACE MODELING

This section first describes *entity-based models*, also referred to as *object-* or *feature-based models*. It then briefly reviews another view, in which embedding space is the main focus. In this approach, points in space are associated with attribute values, such as temperature. This latter approach is called *space based* or *field based*.

2.1.1   Entity-Based Models

In Chapter 1, we saw that a geographic object has two components: (1) a description and (2) a spatial component, also referred to as *spatial object*, or *spatial extent*, which corresponds to the shape and location of the object in the embedding space.

This view of geographic information gathers within a spatial object points of the embedding space sharing several common properties (i.e., having the same description). In order to distinguish an object from others, an explicit *identity* is assigned to it. The entire set (identity, spatial object, and common description) constitutes a *geographic object*, also called in the literature an *entity* or *feature*.

The interpretation of space depends on the semantics associated with the geographic territory. Consider, for instance, the territory of France. If we adopt an administrative point of view, France is partitioned into several administrative units. According to a geologist viewpoint, we obtain a completely different organization of space into geologic areas. If one is interested in traffic control, the focus is on the road network. In each case, we choose a new interpretation of space and define a new collection of entities describing this space. This collection was called a *theme* in Chapter 1. Moreover, although the definition of a spatial object as a set of points is quite general, in practice one uses one of the following types of spatial objects:

- *Zero-dimensional objects* or *points*. Points are used for representing the location of entities whose shape is not considered as useful, or when the area is quite small with respect to the embedding space size. Cities, churches, and crossings are examples of entities whose spatial extent might be reduced to a point on a large-scale map.
- *One-dimensional objects* or *linear objects*. These objects are commonly used for representing networks (roads, hydrography, and so on). The basic geometric type considered throughout this book is the *polyline*.

A polyline is defined as a finite set of *line segments* or *edges*, such that each segment endpoint (called a *vertex*) is shared by exactly two segments, except for two endpoints (called the *extreme points*), which belong to only one segment. We shall occasionally consider the following variants:

- A polyline is *closed* if the two extreme points are identical.
- A *simple* polyline is such that no pairs of nonconsecutive edges intersect at any place.
- A polyline is *monotone* with respect to a line $\mathcal{L}$ if every line $\mathcal{L}'$ orthogonal to $\mathcal{L}$ meets the polyline at one point at most.

Figure 2.1 depicts one-dimensional objects, as previously described. The last polyline in this figure is non-monotone. We shall often use the term *line* instead of *polyline* when there is no ambiguity.

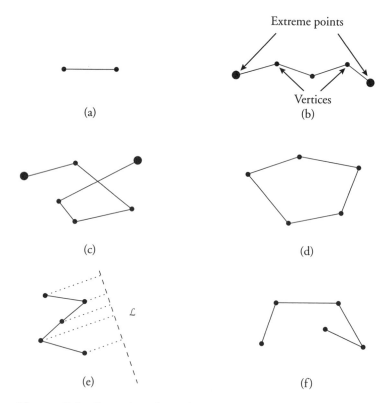

Figure 2.1 Examples of one-dimensional objects: line segment (edge) (a), polyline (b), non-simple polyline (c), simple closed polyline (d), monotone polyline (e), and non-monotone polyline (f).

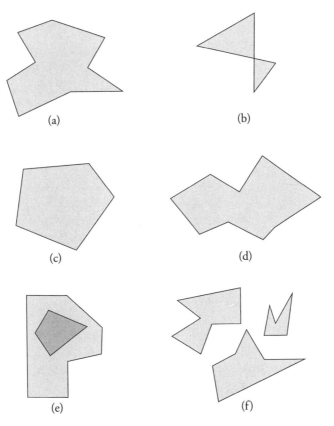

Figure 2.2   Examples of 2D objects: simple polygon (a), non-simple polygon (b), convex polygon (c), monotone polygon (d), polygon with hole (e), and region (f).

◆ *Two-dimensional objects* or *surfacic objects* are mostly used for representing entities with large areas, such as parcels or administrative units. *Polygons* constitute the main geometric type for such objects. A polygon is a region of the plane bounded by a closed polyline, called its *boundary*. It is customary to distinguish the following types of polygons (Figure 2.2).

  • A polygon is *simple* if its boundary is a simple polyline.

  • A *convex* polygon P is such that for any pair of points A and B in P the segment AB is fully included in P.

  • A *monotone* polygon is a simple polygon such that its boundary δP can be split into exactly two monotone polylines MC_1 and MC_2. The monotonicity is usually expressed with respect to the axes. For instance, the monotone polygon of Figure 2.2(d) is monotone with respect to the x axis.

2D objects are not necessarily connected. Consider, for example, a country and its islands. A *region* is defined as a set of polygons.

Two remarks are noteworthy. First, the choice of geometric types is arbitrary. More precisely, it depends on the future use of the collection of entities. Many factors may influence this choice, an important one being the *scale* of interest for the intended applications. For instance, an airport may either be viewed as a point (if interested in air links), or as an area, if the focus is the inner organization of the airport. It might be interesting to store the representation of objects at various scales and to derive the proper representation on demand. This topic is beyond the scope of this book, and we will assume that a single appropriate geometric type has been chosen for our entities.

A second remark is that the description of linear and surfacic objects is based on line segments. In other words, we use only a linear approximation of entities, which could be more precisely represented with higher-order polynomials in x and y. Such an approximation simplifies the design of spatial databases and leads to efficient ways of modeling and querying spatial information. However, there is a trade-off between a faithful approximation and the number of segments for representing the curve. The larger the number of segments in the linear approximation, the more faithful the representation, but the larger the memory space required to store the objects.

2.1.2 Field-Based Models

In a *field-based* (or *space-based*) approach, with each point in space is associated one or several attribute values, defined as continuous functions in x and y. The altitude above sea level is an example of function defined over x and y, whose result is the value of a variable h for any point in the 2D space. The measures for several phenomena can be collected as attribute values varying with the location in the plane. These are, for example, precipitation, temperature, and pollution. This view of space as a continuous *field* is in contrast with the entity-based model, which identifies a set of points (region, line) as an *entity* or *object*. The concept of object is not relevant in the field-based approach.

2.2   REPRESENTATION MODES

So far, spatial objects have been represented at a rather abstract level, using primitives such as points or edges. We now study the practical implementation of geometric information. To state it briefly, the difficulty to overcome is the representation of infinite point sets of the Euclidean space in a computer.

There exist different representation *modes* to solve the problem, either by approximating the continuous space by a discrete one (*tessellation mode*) or by constructing appropriate data structures (*vector mode* and half-plane representation). For instance, in a tessellation mode a city is represented as a set of *cells* that cover the city's interior, whereas in the vector mode it will be represented as a *list of points* describing the boundary of a polygon.

2.2.1   *Tessellation*

A cellular decomposition of the plane (usually, a grid) serves as a basis for representing the geometry. The partitioning of the embedding space into disjoint cells defines a *discrete model*, sometimes called *spatial resolution model*, tiling, or *meshes* in the field of computer graphics.

The approach can be further divided into *fixed* (or regular) and *variable* (or irregular) tessellation modes. A fixed representation model uses a regular grid or *raster*, which is a collection of polygonal units of equal size. A variable spatial resolution model handles units of decomposition of various sizes. The size of the units may also change according to the level of resolution. Figure 2.3 depicts two cases of regular tessellation,

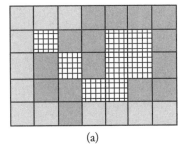
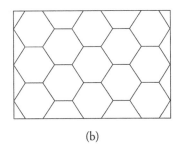

(a)   (b)

Figure 2.3   Regular tessellations: grid squares (a) and hexagonal cells (b).

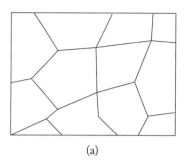
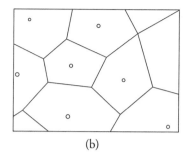

(a)   (b)

Figure 2.4 Irregular tessellations: cadastral zones (a) and Thiessen polygons (b).

one with square cells and one with hexagonal cells. Figure 2.4 shows two examples of irregular tessellations. The first (Figure 2.4a) considers a cadastral partitioning of the plane into various zones, whereas the second (Figure 2.4b) shows a partitioning into Thiessen polygons.[3]

In a raster representation, the rectangular 2D space is partitioned into a finite number of elementary *cells*. Usually the space is decomposed according to a regular 2D grid of $N \times M$ rectangular cells, whose sides are parallel to the space coordinate axes. The cells are called *pixels*. A pixel has an address in the plane, which usually is a pair (x, y) where $x \leq N$ is the column of the cell in the grid, and $y \leq M$ is the row.

FIELD-BASED DATA IN TESSELLATION MODE

In practice, a regular tessellation may be encountered in applications that process image data coming from remote sensing (satellite images), such as weather or pollution forecast. Then field-based data is still represented as a function from space to a range such as temperature or elevation. However, the function domain is no longer the infinite set of points but a finite set of pixels. In other words, space is no longer seen as a continuous field, but as a discrete one, which permits an explicit representation of data.

An irregular tessellation is used, for instance, in zoning (a typical GIS function) in social, demographic, or economic data. Other applications include surface modeling using triangles or administrative and political units.

---

3. Given a set of points P, partitioning into Thiessen polygons associates with each $p \in P$ a polygon that is the set of points whose closest point in P is p. The resulting partitioning is also called a Voronoi diagram.

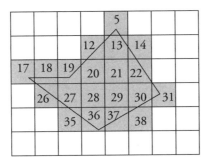

Figure 2.5   Discrete representation of polygon P.

ENTITY-BASED DATA IN TESSELLATION MODE

A spatial object in 2D space is represented by the smallest (finite) sub-set of pixels that contains it. A point is described as a single pixel. Its location is described as the pixel address; that is, a pair of integer coordinates. A polyline, polygon, or region is represented by a finite number of pixels. In Figure 2.5, the following list of pixels is a representation of polygon P.

$$< 5, 12, 13, 14, 17, 18, 19, 20, 21, 22, 26, 27, 28,$$
$$29, 30, 31, 35, 36, 37, 38 >$$

For the sake of simplicity, instead of using the (x, y) coordinate nota-tion we referenced cells by an integer identifier.

DISCUSSION

The tessellation mode makes it possible to approximate a spatial ob-ject by a finite number of cells. The larger the grid resolution (i.e., the smaller the pixel size), the better the approximation but the higher the number of cells for representing an object.[4] A faithful object represen-tation has as a consequence that objects occupy much memory space. In addition, operations on objects are then more time consuming. This is a clear drawback to this approach. Nevertheless, information may sometimes be compressed to lead to a more compact form.

To conclude this section, the tessellation mode is of prime impor-tance because of the exponentially growing volume of data coming from satellite (raster) sources and because of the increasing use of it in specific applications, such as environmental fields (pollution, weather,

---

4. An A4 formatted image, with 12 pts/mm, occupies 9 million pixels.

and so on). However, most of the analysis, storing, and querying in many applications (and hence in commercial GIS) is made on spatial data stored under vector format, as described in material to follow.

2.2.2   *Vector Mode*

In vector mode, objects are constructed from points and edges as primitives. A point is represented by its pair of coordinates, whereas more complex linear and surfacic objects are represented by structures (lists, sets, arrays) on the point representation. In contrast to a raster representation, a vector representation is not eager in memory. In particular, a polygon is represented by the finite set of its vertices.

ENTITY-BASED DATA IN VECTOR MODE
There exists a large number of variants to represent polylines and regions in a vector mode. The following is a simple representation.

- A polyline is represented by a *list* of points $< p_1, \ldots p_n >$, each p_i being a vertex. Each pair (p_i, p_{i+1}), with $i < n$, represents one of the polyline's edges.
- A polygon is also represented as a list of points. The notable difference is that the list represents a *closed* polyline, and therefore the pair (p_n, p_1) is also an edge of the polygon.
- A region is simply a set of polygons.

STRUCTURE NOTATION
In the following, tuples are denoted by *[ ]*, lists by $<>$, and sets by { }. Using this notation, the structure of points, polylines, polygons, and regions can be summarized as follows:

- *point : [x: real, y: real]*
- *polyline : < point >*
- *polygon : < point >*
- *region : { polygon }*

A few remarks are noteworthy. First, a polygon with n vertices has $2n$ possible representations. There are n ways of choosing where to start the boundary description; once the starting vertex has been chosen, there are two ways of scanning the vertices, called *clockwise* and *counterclockwise* orders.

Second, there is no apparent distinction between a polyline structure and a polygon structure. It is up to the software that manipulates geometric data to interpret properly the structure, and to check that the representation is valid; that is, to verify that the polyline is closed for the polygon.

This remark holds for other possible constraints on the polygon type, such as convexity. Neither can we guarantee that a polygon is *simple*, in that the foregoing data structure does not prevent two nonconsecutive edges to intersect. The structure is unfortunately not powerful enough to ensure the correctness of the representation (i.e., the satisfiability of such constraints).

The same situation holds for regions. Again, the structure is relatively permissive. A polygon can be contained in another, and two polygons can be adjacent, overlapping, or disconnected.

Figure 2.6 shows the representation of polygon P in vector mode. It is described by an ordered list of pairs of coordinates, such as the following:

$$< [4, 4], [6, 1], [3, 0], [0, 2], [2, 2] >$$

Figure 2.7 shows examples of polylines using this vector representation. For the sake of simplicity, we use a slightly different notation, referred to as "vertex notation" in the following. We index vertices with integers instead of giving their coordinates, as previously. We can see the following in Figure 2.7.

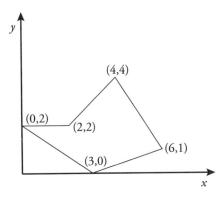

Figure 2.6 Vector representation of polygon P.

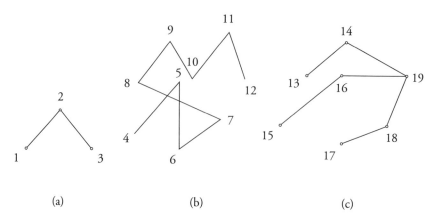

Figure 2.7 Examples of polylines: L_1 (a), L_2 (b), and L_3 (c).

- $L_1 = < 1, 2, 3 >$ is a polyline consisting of two line segments.
- $L_2 = < 4, 5, 6, 7, 8, 9, 10, 11, 12 >$ illustrates the freedom of non-consecutive edges to intersect: L_2 is a non-simple polyline.
- Finally, L_3 is *not* a polyline according to our (somewhat restrictive) definition, in that vertex 19 is an endpoint for three edges. Then L_3 should be represented as a set of polylines. If we add a set constructor in order to represent sets of polylines, L_3 can be represented as the set of lines $\{< 13, 14, 19 >, < 15, 16, 19 >, < 17, 18, 19 >\}$.

The foregoing examples show a clear trade-off between the power of representation and the complexity of the structures used to represent spatial objects. Figure 2.8 shows examples of surfacic objects (polygons and regions) with this vector representation, using the "vertex" notation. The region consisting of adjacent polygons P_2 and P_3 can be described as

$$\{< 5, 6, 12, 10, 11 >, < 6, 7, 8, 9, 10, 12 >\}$$

where each polygon is described by a list of vertices. The region consisting of the single polygon P_4 is described by the singleton $\{< 13, 14, 15, 16 >\}$. Similarly, the region consisting of polygon P_1 is described as the singleton $\{< 1, 2, 3, 4 >\}$.

In summary, this representation allows one to represent a variety of polyline and region objects. Compared to the raster mode, it is a very concise representation, because the memory space required to represent the objects is proportional to the number of vertices of the linear ap-

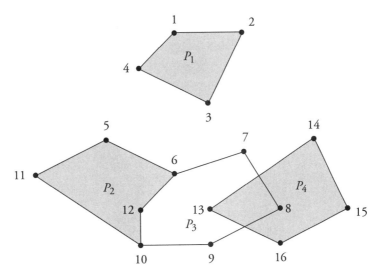

Figure 2.8   Examples of polygons.

proximations of the objects. The more precise the approximation, the larger the number of points and, of course, the larger the space required for storing the objects.

Again, this representation is loose and cannot check on a large number of constraints. For instance, there is no way to distinguish a simple polygon from a non-simple one, a convex polygon from a nonconvex one, a polygon from a polyline, or a set of adjacent polygons from a set of disjoint or intersecting polygons.

FIELD-BASED DATA IN VECTOR MODE
We now informally describe a couple of structures for representing field-based data in vector mode. Because the focus of this book is not on field-based applications, the presentation is deliberately concise and concentrates on *Digital Elevation Models* (DEMs).

DEMs provide a digital (and thereby finite) representation of an abstract modeling of space. Although the term *elevation* refers to the altitude above sea level, DEMs are useful to represent any natural phenomenon that is a continuous function of the 2D space (e.g., temperature, pressure, moisture, or slope).

Generally speaking, the function of x and y is not represented at all points in 2D space. Instead, DEMs are generally based on a finite collection of sample values, from which values at other points are obtained by *interpolation*. There are various ways to define the interpolation, which mostly depend on the sampling policy. Among them, Triangulated Irregular Networks (TINs) are widely used.

A TIN is based on a triangular partition of 2D space. No assumption is made on the distribution and location of the vertices of the triangles. The elevation value is recorded at each vertex, and inferred at any other point P by linear interpolation of the three vertices of the triangle that contains P (see Figure 2.9).

Data structures for TINs require an intensive use of pointers. Apart from the set of sample points P, a set V of edges and a set T of triangles need to be stored. Each edge points to its endpoints and to its incident triangles (four pointers). Each triangle points to its edges (three pointers). For a detailed description of the structure, the reader is referred to the representation of TINs in the ArcInfo GIS in Section 8.2.

2.2.3 Half-Plane Representation

Compared to the loose and implementation-dependent vector mode previously described, the alternative in the following presents the advantage of relying on sound bases. All spatial objects are defined with a single primitive; namely, *half-planes*. Although proposed a long time ago, this simple model has only recently gained considerable attention, with the advent of constraint databases and their use for modeling and querying geographic objects (see Chapter 4). A half-space H in the d-dimensional space $\mathbb{R}^d$ can be defined as the set of points $P(x_1, x_2, \ldots x_d)$ that satisfy an inequation of the form

$$a_1 x_1 + a_2 x_2 + \cdots + a_d x_d + a_{d+1} \leq 0$$

Therefore, a representation of H is the vector $[a_1, a_2, \ldots a_{d+1}]$. A *convex d-dimensional polytope P* is defined as the intersection of some finite number of closed half-spaces. If H is part of the half-spaces defining P, $H \cap P$ is a *face* of P.

The union of a finite number of polytopes is a d-dimensional *polyhedron Q* in $\mathbb{R}^d$. Q is not necessarily convex, and its components are not necessarily connected. Furthermore, they may overlap. Each polyhedron divides the space into its *interior*, its *boundary*, and its *exterior*.

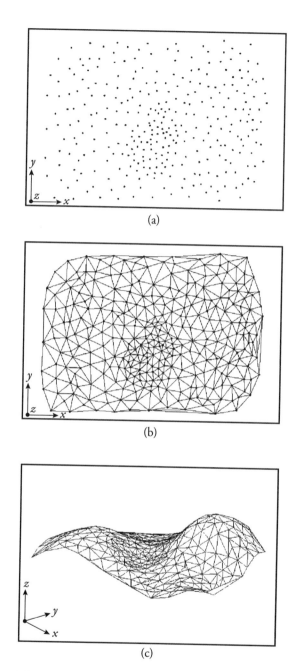

(a)

(b)

(c)

Figure 2.9 Progression of a triangulated irregular network (TIN): point sample (a), triangulation (b), and TIN (c).

One way of defining regions, polylines, and points is to consider polyhedra of respective dimensions 2, 1, and 0. A convex polygon with n edges (n vertices) is defined as the intersection of n half-planes delimited by lines. A *region* is then a union of convex polygons. This definition enables the definition of non-simple polygons, regions with holes, and simple nonconvex polygons.

A line segment is a convex polytope of dimension 1, defined by the intersection of two *half-lines* or *rays*, each delimited by an endpoint of the segment. A polyline is a polyhedron of dimension 1, obtained by performing the union of some number of line segments. A set of (possibly disconnected) polylines is also a polyhedron of dimension 1. Finally, a point is a zero-dimensional polytope, and a set of points is a zero-dimensional polyhedron.

Figure 2.10 shows the construction of polygon P_1 (a triangle), which is defined as the intersection of three half-planes; namely, H_1, H_2, and H_3. These are delimited by lines L_1, L_2, and L_3. Similarly, Figure 2.11 shows that polygon P_2 is built using half-planes H_4, H_5, H_6, and H_7.

A nonconvex polygon cannot be represented by a 2D polytope; that is, it cannot be built using intersections of half-planes only. Instead, it is divided into convex pieces and represented by a polyhedron that is the union of its adjacent convex pieces.

Figure 2.12 shows polygon P of Figure 2.6 split into two polygons, P_1 and P_2, whose common boundary is line L_3 containing points $(2, 2)$ and $(3, 0)$. P is then the geometric union of P_1 and P_2. To decompose

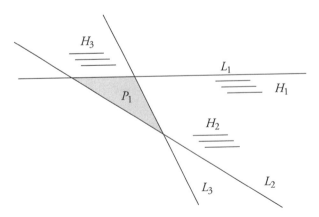

Figure 2.10   Definition of polygon P_1.

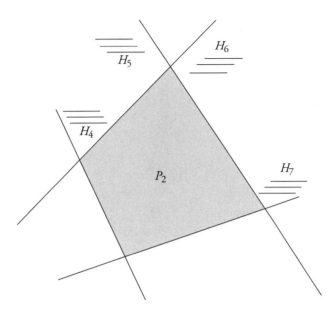

Figure 2.11 Definition of polygon P_2.

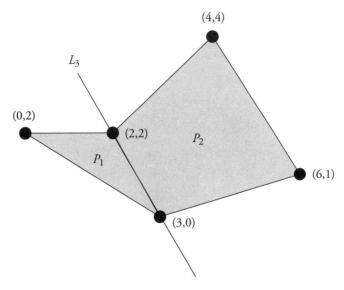

Figure 2.12 Building a nonconvex polygon.

a nonconvex polygon, convex components are isolated on both parts of concavities. The decomposition into convex components is not unique. P might have been represented as the union of two convex polygons adjacent along the line containing points (0, 2) and (2, 2). Algorithms for polygon decomposition are presented in the chapter devoted to computational geometry (Section 5.4).

The homogeneous definition of convex objects as a conjunction of linear constraints in the plane enables a representation of heterogeneous collections mixing points, lines, and polygons. This is achieved by performing the union of intersections of half-planes. Moreover, nonbounded objects (straight lines, for instance) can easily be represented. The representation extends without modification to arbitrary dimensions. The ability to represent a large class of point sets with linear (in) equations is one of the underlying motivations of the *constraint data model*, presented in Chapter 4.

2.3   REPRESENTING THE GEOMETRY OF A COLLECTION OF OBJECTS

From this point, the text focuses on entity-based models and on their vector-based representation (see first part of Section 2.2.2). The previous section showed the possible representations of *single* objects in a plane. This section is devoted to the representation of *collections* of spatial objects. By considering collections and no longer individual objects, we become interested in the *relationships* among objects of the same collection.

There are three commonly used representations of collections of spatial objects, respectively called *spaghetti*, *network*, and *topological* models. They mainly differ in the expression of *topological relationships* among the component objects. Topological relationships among spatial objects are those relations that are invariant under topological transformations. In other words, they are preserved when the spatial objects are, for instance, translated, rotated, or scaled in the Euclidean plane. Topological relationships include *adjacency*, *overlapping*, *disjointness*, and *inclusion*, and constitute therefore an important class of spatial relationships. The *explicit* representation of such relationships in the spatial data model provides more knowledge and is helpful during the evaluation of queries. These three models are described in the following.

2.3.1 Spaghetti Model

In this model, the geometry of any spatial object of the collection is described independently of other objects. It corresponds to the representation provided in Section 2.2.2. No topology is stored in such a model, and all topological relationships must be computed on demand. This structure also implies representation redundancy. For instance, the boundary between two adjacent regions is represented twice. This simple model enables the heterogeneous representation that would mix points, polylines, and regions with no restrictions. In particular, polylines might intersect in the plane without the intersection points of these lines being stored explicitly in the database.

The main advantage of this approach is its simplicity. In addition, because all objects are stored independently, it provides the end user with easy input of new objects into the collection. On the other hand, the drawbacks of this model are mainly due to the lack of explicit information about the topological relationships among spatial objects, such as adjacency or inclusion. There is no straightforward way to find out whether the boundaries of two polygons share a point. Second, as there is no sharing of information, data is stored with some redundancy, which may be a problem as the data sets already tend to be large. For instance, the common boundary between two polygons is represented twice. In addition to replication, a risk of inconsistency is incurred. As an example, the replicated boundary of two adjacent countries might have slightly different coordinates due to different sources of information.

2.3.2 Network Model

The *network* spatial model was first designed for representing networks in network (graph)-based applications such as transportation services or utility management (electricity, telephone, and so on). In this model, topological relationships among points and polylines are stored. The

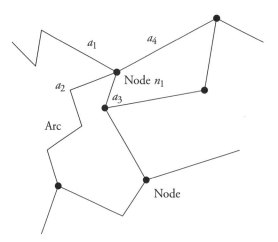

Figure 2.13   A network.

set of geometric types to consider is slightly more complex than in the spaghetti model. We need to introduce two new concepts: *nodes* and *arcs*. A node is a distinguished point that *connects* a list of *arcs*. An arc is a polyline that starts at a node and ends at a node.

The corresponding structure is depicted in Figure 2.13. As we can see from the figure, node n_1, for instance, connects arcs a_1, a_2, a_3, and a_4. Given this information, it becomes possible to *navigate* through the network, by choosing, whenever a node is encountered, the arc to follow. Nodes allow efficient line connectivity tests and network computations (e.g., shortest paths).

Hence, there are two types of points; namely, *regular point*s and *nodes*. A node is either an arc endpoint (extreme) or an isolated point in the plane. Other line and polygon vertices are regular points.

Depending on the implementation, the network is either planar or nonplanar. In a planar network, each edge intersection is recorded as a node, even though the node does not correspond to a geographic object; that is, to a tangible entity from the real world. In a nonplanar network, edges may cross without producing an intersection. Examples of nonplanar networks include ground transportation with tunnels and passes.

As in the spaghetti model, a region is described by the ordered list of vertices of its polygon boundaries. To summarize, in the network model, the objects of interest are

- ◆ *point: [x: real, y: real]*
- ◆ *node: [point, < arc >]*
- ◆ *arc: [node-start, node-end, <point>]*
- ◆ *polygon: <point>*
- ◆ *region: {polygon}*

One advantage of this approach is its intrinsic description of a net-worked topology, with the notion of connectivity useful for optimal-paths search. No information on the relationships between 2D objects is stored in this model.

2.3.3   *Topological Model*

The *topological model* is similar to the network model, except that the network is planar. This network induces a planar subdivision into adjacent polygons, some of which may not correspond to actual geographic objects. The objects of interest in this model are the following:

- ◆ *point: [x: real, y: real]*
- ◆ *node: [point, < arc >]*
- ◆ *arc: [node-start, node-end, left-poly, right-poly, < point >]*
- ◆ *polygon: < arc >*
- ◆ *region: {polygon}*

As in the network model, a node is represented by a point and the list of arcs starting (or ending) at this node. If the list is empty, this corresponds to a point isolated from the network. Isolated points are used for identifying the location of point features or area features collapsed to a point, such as towers, squares, and so on. In addition to its ending points and the list of its vertices, an arc also features the two polygons having the arc as a common boundary.

A polygon is represented by a list of arcs, each arc being shared with a neighbor polygon. Some redundancy exists for efficiency reasons while accessing objects. For instance, polygons can be accessed through either polygons or arcs. However, there is no redundancy in the stored geometry, as each point/line is stored only once.

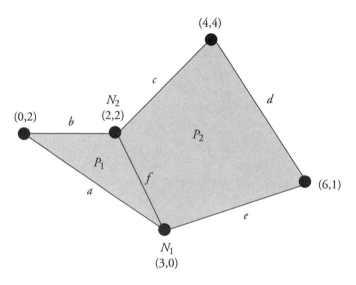

Figure 2.14 Representation of polygons in the topological model.

Regions are represented by one or more adjacent polygons. A representation of polygons P_1 and P_2 of Figure 2.12 is shown in Figure 2.14. One can extract the following objects:

- $P_1 :< a, b, f >$
- $P_2 :< c, d, e, f >$
- $f : [N_1, N_2, P_1, P_2, <>]$
- $N_1 : [[3, 0], < a, f, e >]$

In this example, the plane contains two polygons, P_1 and P_2. Each polygon is represented by a list of arcs, each having, for simplicity, a single edge. We have illustrated the representation of one arc and one node: arc f consists of two nodes (one for each endpoint), followed by its left adjacent polygon, its right adjacent polygon, and the list of coordinates of the intermediate points (in our example, the list is empty because there is no intermediate vertex). Node N_1 is represented by its coordinates, followed by arcs a, f, and e, which have the node as an endpoint.

One advantage of the topological model is the efficient computation of topological queries. For example, looking for polygons adjacent to a given polygon P is straightforward. P is scanned. Accessing each of its arcs provides a polygon adjacent to P. Another advantage is related to update consistency. Because of object sharing, consistency maintenance and updates are easier with the topological model than with the spaghetti model. With the spaghetti model, an edge common to two adjacent polygons is stored in the two polygons' representations. Each edge update should be propagated to the other edge instance. This contrasts with the topological model, in which each edge geometry is stored once.

However, this approach suffers from a few drawbacks. First, some spatial objects in the database may have no semantics in a real-world application. Second, the complexity of the resulting structure may slow down some operations. For example, displaying a subset of a map requires scanning a set of lines. With the topological model, scanning is much slower than with a set of "spaghetti" lines. Indeed, navigating through complex data structures a large number of times might lead to significant overhead. Note also that displaying a region might require scanning several adjacent polygons and erasing their common boundary. In addition, the input of a new object requires the precomputation of part of the planar graph.

2.4   SPATIAL DATA FORMATS AND EXCHANGE STANDARDS

Government agencies and other organizations collect geographic data (e.g., base maps, elevation data, and satellite imagery) and georeferenced socioeconomic data (e.g., demographic census and health surveys) in their own areas of responsibility. Along with international standardization committees, these organizations also help define geospatial data standards, whose data formats have very strict rules about the content (elevation, political boundaries, and so on) and characteristics (e.g., precision and projection) of the data they contain.

As far as the vector representations are concerned, we can distinguish those that were defined or acknowledged by official organizations from those defined by private institutions and that sometimes lead to de facto standards.

Data is also available in formats specific to particular GIS or CAD packages. For example, the DXF format was intended as a data transfer format between CAD software data and became a popular GIS data format.

One comparison criterion between spatial data formats is the richness of their underlying spatial model. Most of the commonly used data formats defined for geographic or CAD/CAM applications enable a representation of complex topological relationships among their spatial objects. Only a few of them allow the description of attributes associated with spatial objects and a description of relationships different from topological ones, such as the composition of objects. This section first provides a panorama of current spatial data formats. We then study the TIGER/Line format, widely used in the United States (e.g., by the Census Bureau). Finally, we present the solutions advocated in the context of an open GIS framework, as defined by the Open GIS worldwide consortium (OGC) and by the International Organization for Standards (ISO).

2.4.1 Overview of Current Spatial Data Formats

Among prominent official organizations, we can cite national institutions of standards—such as the *American National Standards Institute* (ANSI), the *Association Française de Normalisation* (*AFNOR*), and the *British Standard Institution* (BSI)—as well as international working groups, such as ISO and the *Digital Geographic Information Working Group* (DCWIG), which gathers the army ministries from 10 countries in the NATO framework.

De facto standards include DXF, DIGEST, TIGER, NTF, and SDTS. *Drawing Interchange Format* (DXF) is a standard for CAD/CAM applications that was influenced by the software AutoCAD. The *Digital Geographic Information Exchange Standard* (DIGEST) was developed for military applications by the DCWIG. DIGEST is used in military applications within many NATO countries. It defines a large variety of formats, such as raster models, spaghetti models, and simple and complex topological models. Finally, the *Spatial Data Transfer Standard* (SDTS) was introduced by the U.S. Geological Survey (USGS) and is used by many U.S. national agencies. Similar to DIGEST, SDTS allows description of geographic objects in a separate catalog and offers a complex topological model.

An SDTS *profile* may be defined as a (limited) subset of the SDTS, in order to be used with a specific type of data. The first profile was the topological vector profile, intended for use with geographic vector data with planar graph topology. Another profile is the raster profile, which can accommodate image data, digital terrain models, and gridded geographic data.

SDTS has been for a long time the reference as a formal attempt to develop a standardized list of terms, controlled by the American Federal Geographic Data Committee (FGDC). The FGDC coordinates the development of the American National Spatial Data Infrastructure (NSDI). The NSDI encompasses policies, standards, and procedures for organizations to cooperatively produce and share geographic data. The 16 federal agencies that make up the FGDC are developing the NSDI in cooperation with organizations from state, local, and tribal governments; the academic community; and the private sector.

Many GISs have their proprietary formats. Many countries also have their own data format officially in use by public institutions as well as by GIS software companies. We cannot cite all of them. The following are a few of these standards. In France, EDIGéO[5] is a standard acknowledged in 1992 by the AFNOR. It is a French civilian application of the DIGEST format. In Germany, the *Amtliches Topographisch-Kartographisches Informationssystem* (ALK/ATKIS) format was developed between 1985 and 1989 and became a standard. It is based on an object-oriented data model for describing the modeling of landscapes. In Switzerland, INTERLIS is sponsored by the Swiss Directorate of Cadastral Surveying. It is meant to be a "data exchange mechanism for land information systems (LIS)." In the United Kingdom, the *National Transfer Format* (NTF) is the standard adopted by BSI since 1987. The *Spatial Archive and Interchange Format* (SAIF) is a recent Canadian standard. Most of these standards allow the description and transfer of raster and vector data with an underlying topological model.

Several standards were defined for discrete (*raster*) representation exclusively, such as GIF and JPEG (Joint Photographic Experts Group). However, only a few of them were conceived for spatial data. Among them, the *Tagged Image File Format* (TIFF) is the most widely used. Its popularity is mainly due to the fact that it is based on tags and that various compression methods can be applied on its objects. *Computer Graphic Metafile* (CGM) is another common raster format. Among

---

5. *EDI: Echange de Données Informatisé* (i.e., *Electronic Data Interchange*).

the standards defined for spatial applications, we can cite *Arc Standard Raster Product* (ASRP).

2.4.2   *The TIGER/Line Data Format*

TIGER is an acronym for *Topologically Integrated Geographic Encoding and Referencing*. It is the name for the system and digital database developed at the U.S. Census Bureau in order to support its mapping needs for both the decennial census and other Bureau programs.

We present the data model and file organization of TIGER as a practical implementation of the topological data model presented in Section 2.3. The model also resembles the spatial model of ArcInfo (see Section 8.2). In the following, we give an overview of the concepts before describing the spatial objects TIGER handles.

OVERVIEW

In regard to information stored in the census TIGER database, the Census Bureau releases periodic extracts of the database to the public. These include TIGER/Line files. The most recent version is TIGER/Line 1998. TIGER/Line files are a database of geographic entities such as roads, railroads, rivers, lakes, political boundaries, and census statistical boundaries covering the entire United States. In TIGER, these objects are referred to as *features*. The database contains information about these features, such as their location in latitude and longitude, the name, the type of feature, address ranges for most streets, geographic relationships to other features, and other related information. TIGER data sets provide support for the following:

◆ Creation and maintenance of the geographic database that includes complete coverage of the United States, Puerto Rico, and the Virgin Islands, among others

◆ Production of maps from the TIGER database for all Census Bureau enumeration and publication programs

◆ Ability to assign individual addresses to geographic entities and census blocks based on polygons formed by features such as roads and streams

The topological structure of the TIGER database defines the location and relationships of streets, rivers, railroads, and other features to each other and to the numerous geographic entities for which the Census Bureau tabulates data from its censuses and sample surveys. It is designed to ensure no duplications of these features or areas.

SPATIAL OBJECTS

The spatial objects in TIGER/Line obey a spatial model that resembles the topological model of Section 2.3.3. They belong to the Geometry and Topology (GT) class of the standard SDTS, and they embody both geometry (coordinate locations and shape) and topology. We use the terminology from the TIGER documentation. The reader can easily make the correspondence with the vocabulary of Section 2.3.

The description of spatial objects is distributed over a collection of 17 files, each file storing a specific type of record. We refer to them as record type 1, record type 2, and so on, in the following. There is a collection of files for each county in the United States. The process of data extraction is rather complex. In order to reconstruct a spatial object, one has to fetch a set of records from several files, before linking these records via common identifiers. In TIGER terminology (derived from STDS), the spatial object types are

- *Node:* A zero-dimensional object that is a topological junction of two or more links or chains, or an endpoint of a link or chain.
- *Entity point:*[6] A point used for identifying the location of point features (or areal features collapsed to a point), such as towers, buildings, or places.
- *Chain:* A simple polyline described by a start node, an end node, and a list of intermediate points called *shape points*. Chains intersect each other only at nodes. The term *chain* in TIGER corresponds to what we called an "arc" in Section 2.3.3. One can further distinguish the following types of chains:
    - A *complete chain* explicitly references left and right polygons and start and end nodes. Such chains are said to be complete because they form polygon boundaries.
    - A *network chain* does not reference left and right polygons (above network model).

---

6. An isolated node in the model of Section 2.3.3.

◆ *GT-polygon:* An area described by the list of complete chains that form its boundary. GT-polygons are mutually exclusive, and their union forms a partition of the space.

All spatial objects are mixed in a single layer that includes roads, hydrography, railroads, boundary lines, and miscellaneous features. All are topologically linked. This defines a very detailed decomposition of space, and introduces many spatial objects that do not correspond to geographic objects. For instance, nodes mark the intersection of roads and rivers. Subsurface features (e.g., tunnels) or above-surface features (e.g., bridges) also create nodes when they cross surface features, even though there is no real-world connection.

Figure 2.15 shows an example of TIGER objects. Space is organized as (decomposed by) *chains.* Chain intermediate points or *shape points* describe the geometry of the chain. For instance, chain$_1$ features two shape points, whereas chain$_4$ has a single shape point.

An area enclosed by a list of *complete chains* constitutes a *GT-polygon.* The figure contains three polygons, denoted as GT-polygon$_1$, GT-polygon$_2$, and GT-polygon$_3$. The latter is described by five chains that meet only at their endpoints to form the boundary of the polygon. A polygon features a "polygon interior point." Such a point P is useful, for example, for computing distances. The distance between an external point P' and the polygon is interpreted as the distance between P

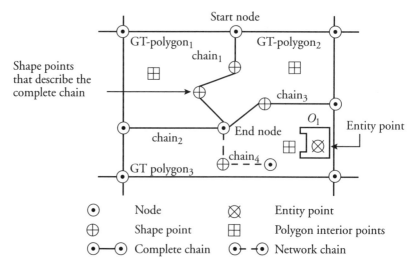

Figure 2.15 TIGER objects (after TIGER documentation).

and P'. Note that, by construction, the set of GT-polygons partitions the space.

Chain$_4$ is an example of a *network chain*, which serves primarily as a network description, and is not part of the boundary of a GT-polygon. It represents a cul-de-sac.

Finally, the representation of some objects might be reduced to their location, which does not embody their geometric description. Object O_1 in Figure 2.15 is represented by an *entity point*.

Extracting the representation of spatial objects from the TIGER files takes several steps. The basic building blocks are the complete chains, described by record type 1 and record type 2.

- Record type 1 contains the main fields of a chain; namely, its ID, denoted as TLID (TIGER/Line ID), and its start and end nodes. A node is represented by its longitude and latitude. We focus here on the geometric description, so we leave apart for the moment several other attributes that link the chain to geographic objects.
- Record type 2 describes the shape points of the chains. Each record may contain up to 10 points, and there can be as many records as necessary for a given chain.

Table 2.1 shows a few examples of record type 1 instances (actually, a small subset of the attributes of record type 1). Two chains, respectively identified as TLID 8086 and 8087, feature the start (FR) and end (TO) nodes, in longitude (LONG) and latitude (LAT). For example, FRLAT stands for the latitude of the start node.

As soon as the chain is not a line segment, we need additional information on intermediate (shape) points, found in record type 2. Table 2.2 shows the record type 2 instances associated with the complete chain 8086. Each record has 22 fields; namely, (1) the TLID, (2) a record sequence number RTSQ, and (3) a list of 10 pairs (latitude,

Table 2.1 Examples of record type 1 (chains).

TLID	FRLONG	FRLAT	TOLONG	TOLAT
...	...	...	...	...
8086	−72156546	+41957498	−72161936	+41958117
8087	−72197129	+41957206	−72197197	+41957669
...	...	...	...	...

Table 2.2 Examples of record type 2 (shape points).

TLID	RTSQ	LONG1	LAT1	...	...	LONG10	LAT10
...	...	...	...	...	...	...	...
8086	1	−72156638	+41957658	...	...	−72157985	+41958184
8086	2	−72161599	+41958117	0	0	0	0
...	...	...	...	...	...	...	...

longitude). A zero (0) indicates a NULL coordinate. Assuming that chain 8086 has 11 shape points, it needs two records of record type 2, with sequence numbers 1 and 2, and the second record contains only one non-null point. By "joining" the two files on the TLID field, one obtains a full description of complete chains.

The next step is to construct GT-polygons by assembling the complete chains that form the boundary of the polygon. Recall that in a topological model each chain (or arc) references its left and right polygons. The record type P lists all polygons, identified by a pair (CENID, POLYID). CENID (Census Bureau Identifier) is a polygon identifier, not unique over the entire database. Then the number POLYID allows us to distinguish polygons with the same CENID.

Each complete chain that forms a part of a polygon's boundary (in other words, all chains except network chains) corresponds to one record in the record type I file. This record gives the identifiers of the left and right polygons. Table 2.3 displays an example of a record of type I (again, we show only a part of the record's fields). Chain 8086 has polygon (PO123, 1) on the left, and polygon (PO1987, 1) on the right.

Computing the boundary of a polygon is done in two steps. First, one finds the chains sharing the polygon identifier, either on the left or on the right. Then one has to find the nodes connecting adjacent chains. This involves numeric comparisons, because the TIGER model

Table 2.3 Examples of record type I (link chains/polygons).

TLID	CENIDL	POLYIDL	CENIDR	POLYIDR
...	...	...	...	...
8086	PO123	1	PO1987	1
...	...	...	...	...

Table 2.4 Examples of record type 7 (landmarks).

LAND	STATE	COUNTY	CFCC	LANAME	LALAT	LALONG
...	...	...	...	...	...	...
9735	NJ	Salem	D61	Monroe	−7216159	+4195811
...	...	...	...	...	...	...

does not identify nodes by an ID, and thus provides no support for an automatic connection of chains.

With complete chains and GT-polygons (i.e., with record types 1, 2, and I), information related to the spatial data model is almost complete. It remains to add entity points, which can be found in record type 7. The Census Bureau calls these isolated points *landmarks*, and identifies them with a LAND attribute. Record type 7 files contain all landmarks, together with their point coordinates (LALAT, LALONG) and some descriptive attributes (see Table 2.4). STATE and COUNTY give the state code and county name, and CFCC is the *Census Feature Class Code* (i.e., a code that gives the type of landmark). For instance, D51 is an airport, D61 a shopping center, D62 an office building, and so on. Finally, LANAME is the landmark name.

Descriptive attributes can be associated with polygon, chain, and landmark spatial objects, and sometimes grouped to form geographic objects. We outline how the TIGER model handles descriptive information in material to follow.

GEOGRAPHIC OBJECTS

The Census Bureau uses the term *features* to refer to what we have called geographic objects. This encompasses objects whose geometry is linear, such as streets and rivers, as well as objects with surfacic geometry, such as states, counties, and school districts. The following are the major types of features that can be found.

◆ Lines features
  • Roads
  • Railroads
  • Hydrography
  • Transportation features, power lines, and pipelines
  • Boundaries

- ◆ Landmark features
  - Point landmarks (e.g., schools and churches)
  - Area landmarks (e.g., parks and cemeteries)
  - Office buildings and factories
- ◆ Polygon features
  - Census statistical areas
  - School districts
  - Voting districts
  - Administrative divisions: states, counties, county subdivisions
  - Blocks

It is important to note that in most cases the TIGER files do not list features as such, with their descriptive attributes, an identifier, and a link to their geometric representation. Rather, descriptive information is recorded together with spatial data (chains, polygons, landmarks), and features are constructed on demand from the spatial objects. The following are two examples that illustrate the process.

- ◆ *Boundaries of voting districts.* The process is similar to the construction of a GT-polygon. Record type 3 provides some additional information on complete chains, including the voting district codes (VTD) on the left and right of the chain. This VTD acts as an identifier of the voting district. The boundary of a voting district can be reconstructed by taking all chains that have the same VTD on either the left or the right side, *but not both.* As in the case of GT-polygons, these chains must then be linked to form a ring.
- ◆ *Rivers.* Rivers are linear geographic objects that consist of one or several chains. Record type 1 includes, with the geometric description of the chain, the *feature name* and the *feature type.* By grouping and linking all chains with feature type "river" and feature name "Mangosteen," one might expect to get a correct description of the Mangosteen River. However, there is no guarantee that this pair of values uniquely identifies a river (there might be several rivers with the same name), nor that the naming will be consistent enough to get *all* chains involved in the geometric description of an object.

The existence of a feature identifier eases the reconstruction of a feature whose description is distributed in many records. This is the case for voting districts, as well as for counties, states, and so on. When this identifier does not exist (the name of a river is not reliable as a unique identifier), the Census Bureau does not provide the additional support that would be necessary to associate without ambiguity an object with its geometric description.

We will not detail further the record linkage that allows the building of features (geographic objects) from spatial objects. Essentially, the two examples previously cited cover the techniques, with many possible variants, and a somewhat complicated file structure when several objects share the same geometric description. The same chain C, for instance, can be part of a state boundary and of a county boundary. It can also be a highway section. The same highway section may be part of a state and interstate highway, and so on. This information is associated with C, due to its TLID, in the TIGER files. In addition, there sometimes exist several ways to obtain the same geometric information; that is, instead of linking complete chains, one can, for example, group GT-polygons to form the area of counties. Many other aspects are not cited here, including the support for address location, an important characteristic of the TIGER data sets.

In summary, the TIGER files constitute a practical example of a topological data model. The data representation is oriented toward the soundness and consistency of the spatial representation. This yields a collection of spatial objects that are strongly interrelated with topological relationships. From these spatial objects, the description of a feature can be obtained, but in several situations there is only a loose support for creating geographic objects, as the information that would permit unique identification of entities is missing.

2.4.3 Recent Standardization Initiatives

With the objective of improving interoperability between GISs, many institutional bodies have been working in the past few years on the standardization of exchange formats and spatial data models. In the following, we briefly present three recent initiatives.

THE OPENGIS CONSORTIUM (OGC)

The OpenGIS Consortium was created in 1994 to foster communication among GISs in order to ensure interoperability. The idea of an open GIS is to move away from a GIS as a monolithic system toward a modular system that would encompass different softwares. The OGC is a consensus-based association of public and private sector organizations dedicated to the creation and management of an industry-wide architecture for interoperable geoprocessing. The technical goals of OGC are

- A universal spatio-temporal data and process model that will cover all existing and potential spatio-temporal applications, called the OGC data model
- A specification for each of the major database languages to implement the OGC data model
- A specification for each of the major distributed computing environments (DCEs) to implement the OGC process model

The OGC's technical activities fall into three categories: the development of an *abstract specification*, the development of an *implementation specification*, and the *specification revision* process.

Following the OGC agenda, the purpose of the abstract specification is to create and document a conceptual model sufficient to allow for the creation of implementation specifications. The abstract specification consists of two models: the *essential model*, which establishes the conceptual linkage of the software to the real world, and the *abstract model*, which defines the eventual software system in an implementation-neutral manner (i.e., without defining the exact protocols that need to be used). This enables data servers and processing clients to communicate in various environments, such as on the Internet, across a local area network, or even on the same machine. Technical specifications implementing the abstract requirements in each of the common distributed computing environments—for example, the Common Object Request Broker Architecture (CORBA), DCOM, and Java—are now available.

The formalism for all models included in OGC abstract specification and implementation specification documents is the Unified Modeling Language (UML). The main entity considered in the OGC model is a *feature*, which has a type and a *geometry* defined by the OGC under "Well-Known Structures."

ISO TC/211

The ISO Technical Committee 211 (TC/211), *Geographic Information/Geomatics*, is at the forefront of global standardization issues related to GIS. TC/211 is currently preparing a family of geographic information standards in cooperation with other ISO technical committees working on related standards such as IT standards. The standards currently under study may specify, for geographic information, methods, tools, and services for data management and transfer between different users, systems, and locations.

For many years, OGC and ISO were working independently to reach overlapping goals related to interoperability in geospatial data processing. Since 1997, both bodies (whose intersection in terms of members is not empty) seek to converge toward a common solution. The TC/211 committee is divided into several groups:

◆ Working group 1: Framework and reference model
◆ Working group 2: Geospatial data models and operators
◆ Working group 3: Geospatial data administration
◆ Working group 4: Geospatial services
◆ Working group 5: Profiles and functional standards

Project No. 19107, *Geographic Information: Spatial Schema*, aims at defining a conceptual model of geometry and topology related to geospatial entities.

SPATIAL DATA ON THE INTERNET AND THE FUTURE
OF EXCHANGE FORMATS

The Open Geospatial Datastore Interface (OGDI) is meant to offer a solution that leverages and accelerates standardization efforts. OGDI is an application programming interface (API) that resides between an application and various geodata products in order to provide standardized geospatial access methods. It is a client/server architecture for delivering spatial data over the Internet. OGDI is the result of a research-and-development partnership between the Canadian Department of National Defense (DND) and Global Geomatics, Inc., whose goal is to implement a simple feature interface for Java in OGDI as soon as OpenGIS issues the specifications. OGDI handles important geodata integration needs, such as

◆ The distribution of geodata products via the Internet/intranet. This reduces the space needed to store geographic data, and ensures that all users have access to the same, up-to-date data.

- Access to data in native format. There is no need to keep multiple versions of geographic data in order to accommodate different GIS software packages.
- The adjustment of coordinate systems and cartographic projections, done on the fly such that original data is unaltered.
- The retrieval of geometric and alphanumeric data.

Current map servers usually transfer GIF, JPEG, and other static images of geospatial information using the HyperText Transfer Protocol (HTTP), which is based on a stateless connection (i.e., no memory of previous connections and data transmitted once the communication ends). The static-image format in which the data is transferred does not allow the subsequent modification of image scaling or the printing of scaled maps. The Geographic Library Transfer Protocol (GLTP) is a new Internet protocol for the transfer of geospatial data. It is a stateful replacement for HTTP that allows easy exchange of geospatial data over the Internet. The OGDI server uses GLTP to maintain a continuous connection between the server and the application—allowing native data to be used for analysis at the needed resolution—and to print scaled maps.

2.5 BIBLIOGRAPHIC NOTES

The concepts introduced in the first three sections—in particular, the distinction between entity-based and field-based models; raster and vector modes; and spaghetti, network, and topological models—are discussed in a large number of references on GIS. See, for example, [LT92, MGR99, Wor95, AG97].

The book by Michael Worboys [Wor95] provides a survey on basic and more elaborate spatial notions. It contains a succinct although comprehensive description of algorithms for conversion from raster to vector ("vectorization"), and vice versa ("rasterization"), together with pointers to the relevant literature. Important aspects not described here and underlying GIS applications (transformations in the Euclidean plane and topology of space, among others) can also be found in that source, as well as in [Arm90, LT92].

Several parts of the course material of [Fra95] are relevant to the topics presented in this chapter, and provide more detailed information to the interested reader. Among the aspects surveyed in the preceding, it is worth mentioning [Num95], an introduction to the concepts of space and time; [Mol95], where a discussion on raster and vector modes can be found; and [KPJE95], which covers the numerous data acquisition sources and techniques for GIS (detailed description of GPS, remote sensing and image interpretation, and photogrammetry techniques).

The simple spaghetti structure is widely used in many areas that need to consider single geometric objects and not collections of objects. In order to support the analysis of topological relationships among objects, more involved structures are required. We have presented the network and topological model as two structures widely used in geospatial applications and GIS. The mathematical foundations of these structures are mostly graph theory and topology; see [Arm90, Kir95]. The structure is not directly suitable for the management of topological information for polygons and regions, and several variants or extensions have been proposed, as in [MP78, FK86, Kin93, MKB94].

In particular, DCEL [MP78] is a well-known variant of the topological structure. DCEL stands for *doubly connected edge list.* The principle is the same as in the topological model, but the main object of interest is a line segment instead of an arc, as we defined it. With each line segment (or edge) is associated two pointers: one to the next segment and one to the previous segment. DCEL adds information on the planar orientation of arcs around their extremes (there is still information about the areas located to their left- and right-hand sides).

The *winged-edge* representation [Bau72, Wei85] is closely related to DCEL structural schemes. It associates with each edge the start and end nodes, pointers to the left and right faces adjacent to the edge, and finally to edges adjacent to the two vertices in a clockwise and counterclockwise manner. This representation is mainly used in computer graphics.

Another interesting approach for modeling spatial objects is that of [GS93]. It is based on user-defined structures, called *realms,* as geometric domains underlying spatial data types (points, lines, and regions). A realm is defined as a planar graph over a discrete domain, as illustrated in Figure 2.16. Realm objects (points and segments) are defined not in abstract Euclidean space but in terms of finite representations.

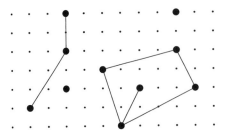

Figure 2.16   Examples of a realm.

The data model in [GS93] is an entity-based model, in which a *spatial object* is defined as an object with a spatial attribute of a data type, such as *point, line,* or *region.* All points, lines, and regions associated with objects, called *spatial attribute values,* can be defined in terms of points and line segments present in the realm. In a database, spatial attribute values are never created directly but by selecting realm objects. The algebraic operations for the spatial types are defined so as to construct only geometric objects that are realm based. All geometric primitives and realm operations, such as updates, are defined in error-free integer arithmetic. For mapping an application's set of intersecting line segments into a realm's set of nonintersecting segments, the concepts of redrawing and finite resolution geometry from [GY86] are used. Although intersection points computed with finite resolution in general move away from their exact Euclidean position, this concept ensures that the unavoidable distortion of geometry (the numerical error) remains bounded and very small, and that essentially no topological errors occur. See also [Wor95] for a discussion on the Green-Yao algorithm [GY86] and the problems arising from discretization. Section 2.2.3 is based on [GW87], which provides one of the first attempts to use the half-plane paradigm to define spatial objects in a database context. More information on the topic can be found in [Gün88].

The presentation of DEMs is based on [vK97]. Another relevant source on DEMs is the survey of [FPM00]. The authors place a strong emphasis on data structures for representing DEMs and on algorithms to manipulate them. The course material in [Fra95] also includes a section on terrain modeling. Other representations of DEMs have been proposed. For instance, *contour lines* are a representation of isolines for a sample set of elevation values. Hierarchical triangulation for multi-resolution surface description is studied in [FP95].

Tessellation is perhaps the simplest way to specify a DEM. The space is partitioned into rectangular cells. One value is recorded per cell (usually associated with the center of the cell). Unlike the representations with TIN or contour lines, this imposes as an input a predefined set of cells. It can therefore not adapt to situations in which the density of information is not uniform.

Some exchange formats and standards are described in [Buc94]. For more information on TIGER, see [TIG00]. [OGI00, TC200, ISO00] are references on recent standardization initiatives. Information regarding OGDI can be found in [OGD00]. [Ple97] is a comprehensive book on issues in defining on-line GIS, which provides in particular many hints on distributed geographic data and exchange formats for spatial information on the Internet.

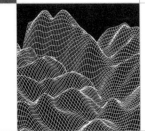

3

Logical Models and Query Languages

"'Would you tell me, please, which way I ought to go from here?'

'That depends a good deal on where you want to get to,' said the Cat.

'I don't much care where—' said Alice.

'Then it doesn't matter which way you go,' said the Cat.

'—so long as I get SOME-WHERE,' Alice added as an explanation.

'Oh, you're sure to do that,' said the Cat, 'if you only walk long enough.'"

LEWIS CARROLL
Alice in Wonderland

CONTENTS

This chapter is devoted to logical models and query languages for spatial database systems. Chapter 2 concerns the internal representation of the *spatial* objects. Conversely, we deal here with the representation of *geographic* objects. Hence, both descriptive and spatial characteristics of an object are simultaneously taken into account.

We consider in this chapter how the representation and querying of geographic objects can be supported by the main categories of DBMS; namely, relational and object-oriented systems. In contrast, although the trend in the most recent systems is to rely on DBMS, GISs use more dedicated models for representing and querying geographic information. This is the topic of Chapter 8.

Take the example of the relational model. In order to serve as a support for geospatial applications, it needs to be extended taking into account non-built-in types (such as integer or real). Introducing these types in the DBMS requires not only defining their structure but the operations that can be performed on them. For instance, a type "polygon" can be introduced with operation PolygonArea (which computes the area of a polygon). Combinations of such data types and their operations are referred to as *abstract data types* (ADTs). An important point is that ADTs are encapsulated in the sense that they are accessible only through the operations defined on them. In addition, the DBMS need not have any knowledge on the ADT implementation (i.e., on the code corresponding to the operations). For instance, the way PolygonArea is implemented is not relevant. This crucial notion of *encapsulation* is detailed further in this chapter.

The concept of ADT is also useful in the context of object-oriented database systems, in which objects of a certain type are gathered in classes on which operations are defined.

Designing spatial ADTs is a challenging task. Many definitions make sense, and there is a trade-off between the simplicity of ADT definitions and their richness of representation. These points are discussed in depth in this chapter, and alternative definitions are noted. However, ADT definitions are application driven and do not hinge on a sound formalism. A related topic is the study of the possible topological relationships existing among geographic objects.

Because this chapter intends to provide the reader with a precise idea of modeling and querying geospatial information in a DBMS environment, we chose to illustrate our discourse using an extended case study.

Hence we introduce reference themes and sample queries, which are respectively modeled and performed in relational and object-oriented contexts.

The organization of this chapter is as follows. Sections 3.1 and 3.2 introduce, respectively, the reference schemas and a set of representative queries of our case study. Section 3.3 presents spatial abstract data types; that is, the possible spatial types, together with their operations. We discuss important issues related to the design of spatial ADTs, and describe a systematic approach to handling topological relationships among objects.

Section 3.4 studies the representation of geographic objects using an extended relational model as a support. A list of representative queries extracted from Section 3.2 is expressed in an SQL-like language. Section 3.5 presents the same concepts in the object-oriented framework; namely, the representation of geographic objects and their manipulation. The latter point is again illustrated by expressing queries from Section 3.2 in OQL, the standard query language for object-oriented DBMS. Finally, Section 3.6 provides bibliographic notes.

3.1 REFERENCE SCHEMAS

A conceptual schema describes at an abstract level one or many themes necessary for representing the set of geographic objects existing in a geographic application, as well as relationships among them. Three conceptual schemas are presented in the material that follows. They serve as a reference throughout the chapter. The topics we are interested in are American administrative units, the American highway network, and land use. For each of them, we represent the relevant entities according to the OMT formalism, independent of a DBMS.

3.1.1 Administrative Units (Schema 1)

We consider a hierarchy of partitions in 2D space, which follows the U.S. administrative scheme of units. A *country* (e.g., the United States or Germany) consists of *states*, and a single *state*, in turn, consists of *counties*. Finer subdivisions of the space exist, such as the subcounty division in the United States, as defined by the Census Bureau. However,

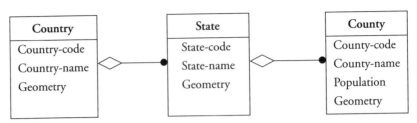

Figure 3.1   Administrative units in the United States (schema 1).

these finer subdivisions of the plane are not our concern here. To make things simpler, a country has as attributes a name and a geometry. A state also has a *name* and a *geometry*. A county has as attributes *name*, *population*, and *geometry*. Countries, states, and counties are uniquely identified by their administrative code.

These three themes are summarized in Figure 3.1. The diamond-shaped symbol (◇) between two entity types expresses an aggregation relationship (e.g., a **State** consists of **Counties**). The solid circle symbol (●) is used to denote a *one-to-many* relationship.

3.1.2   Highway Network Among Cities (Schema 2)

The second schema we consider, independently of schema 1, is a simple highway network among cities. Three themes are defined in this schema. A *highway* entity has a name and a type (such as U.S. Highway, State Highway, or Interstate), and consists of *sections*, each of which has a name, a certain number of lanes, and a geometric part. Highways and sections are identified by a code. A section may be shared by several highways; hence, the many-to-many relationship. The sections of highways connect *cities* to each other. This is summarized in Figure 3.2. Note the use of the named associations *starts-at* and *ends-at* between entities **Section** and **City**. A section starts in a given city and ends in another. Via these two relationship types, a highway connects many cities to one another, and cities are connected by many highways (*many-to-many* relationship).

3.1.3   Land Use (Schema 3)

Finally, our third schema of interest has one theme only; namely, land use. Within this theme, a particular area in the plane is associated with

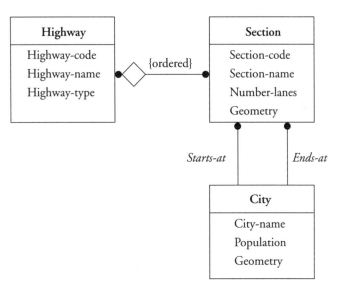

Figure 3.2 Highway network among cities (schema 2).

a type of use, such as *housing, agricultural area,* and *forest*. Such an area is represented by a 2D geometric object (region).

3.2 REFERENCE QUERIES

This section explores a set of representative queries posed against a spatial database based on the schemas previously introduced. Some queries are simple and involve only the description of geographic objects. Other queries are more complex, and more difficultly handled in a DBMS, as they require the existence of spatial operations (e.g., intersection, difference, or adjacency). These queries are studied in further detail in this chapter, according to different DBMS data models and query languages.

We list the reference queries according to the following classification: (1) queries with alphanumeric criteria, (2) queries with a spatial criterion (i.e., an operation that applies to the spatial part of one or several geographic objects), and (3) interactive queries, which require participation from the end user (e.g., to select a particular area by drawing it on a display device using a mouse). For later reference, each query is assigned a name. Queries with alphanumeric criteria

are prefixed by **ALPHA-**, whereas queries with spatial criteria are prefixed by **SPAT-** and interactive queries by **INTER-**. Reference(s) to the
schema(s) involved follow the prefix. These are **ADM** for schema 1
(administrative units), **R** for schema 2 (roads), and **LU** for land use,
followed by a counter of reference (e.g., **ALPHA-ADM2** for the second
alphanumeric query on administrative units).

Queries with alphanumeric criteria are as follows:

- **ALPHA-ADM1.** Number of inhabitants in the County of San Fran-
  cisco.
- **ALPHA-ADM2.** List of the counties of the State of California.
- **ALPHA-ADM3.** Number of inhabitants in the United States.
- **ALPHA-R1.** Number of lanes in the first section of Interstate 99.
- **ALPHA-R2.** Name of all sections that constitute Interstate 99.

Queries involving spatial criteria are as follows:

- **SPAT-ADM4.** Counties adjacent to the County of San Francisco in
  the same state.
- **SPAT-ADM5.** Display of the State of California.
- **SPAT-ADM6.** Counties larger than the largest county in California.
- **SPAT-R3.** Length of Interstate 99.
- **SPAT-ADMR1.** All highways going through the State of California.
- **SPAT-ADM-LU1.** Display of all residential areas in the County of
  San Jose.
- **SPAT-ADM-LU2.** Overlay of the themes of administrative units and
  land use.

Interactive queries are as follows:

- **INTER-ADM7.** Description of the county pointed to on the screen.
- **INTER-ADM8.** Counties that intersect a given rectangle on the
  screen.
- **INTER-ADM9.** Parts of counties within a given rectangle on the
  screen.
- **INTER-R5.** Description of the section pointed to on the screen.
- **INTER-R6.** Description of the highway of which a section is
  pointed to on the screen.

3.3   SPATIAL ABSTRACT DATA TYPES

ADTs were introduced as a way to circumvent the lack of modeling power—as far as nonstandard database applications are concerned—inherent in the basic relational database model. An ADT is an abstract functional view of objects: a set of operations is defined on objects of a given type. The idea behind this concept is to hide the structure of the data type to the user (or programmer), who can access it only through the operations defined on it. From the external world, the interface to an ADT is a list of operations.

This type of split between use and implementation, called *encapsulation*, enables us to extend a query language with geometric functionality independently of a specific representation/implementation. More precisely, it becomes possible to define a list of spatial data types that provides a convenient and simple interface to the user. How these types are implemented is vendor dependent, and remains transparent to the end user.

This section first introduces the definition of spatial ADT by considering the requirements of our reference schemas. We define a set of ADTs that permits us to express all of our reference queries. This set of ADTs is by no means fully complete and general enough to be used in a broad range of applications. Instead, it is simple, and thus useful for illustrating how geographic objects can be queried in an extended DBMS environment. We end this section by showing some limits of the use of ADTs for representing and querying spatial information. We investigate some issues in spatial data type design, and discuss some of the problems that render the design of a sound and well-accepted set of types for geographic applications a difficult task.

3.3.1   *Extending Data Models with Spatial ADTs*

We begin with a quite intuitive approach. Starting from the requirements of our geographic schemas, we define a set of operations sufficient for expressing the reference queries.

SPATIAL ADTS: BASIC CONCEPTS

With a spatial ADT approach, a spatial object, say, a region, is considered as the list of operations that one can perform on it, independently

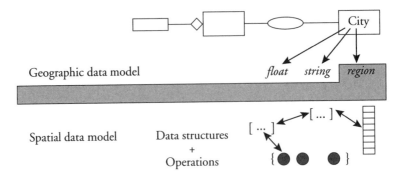

Figure 3.3   Hiding the spatial data model.

of its internal representation. Examples include *testing of intersection* with other objects (two objects intersect if they have at least one point in common), computation of the *intersection* (with other objects), and *area size* calculation. The underlying philosophy is one of layered development, as known in the software engineering area: the less visible the details of a layer are, the easier its update is, and, to a certain extent, the more general its use is.

The concept can be directly related to the distinction already made between *geographic data models* and *spatial data models*. This is illustrated in Figure 3.3, taking as an example a *region* data type. The spatial data model constitutes a first layer at the bottom. It provides data structures for representing a region (see Chapter 2), as well as operations on these structures (the implementation of which is described in Chapter 5).

These mechanisms are hidden to the upper layer, which deals with geographic objects. Here, *region* appears as a type at the same level as *float* or *string*. A geographic object, such as an instance of **City**, can now be described with values whose types belong to the type system of the DBMS, extended with *region* and possibly other spatial data types.

The abstraction of the region in the geographic data model (its independence from the spatial data model) allows for any choice of spatial data model (e.g., spaghetti, network, or topological), as described in Chapter 2. In Figure 3.4, objects o_1, o_2, and o_3 are stored either with a topological representation (left-hand side) or a spaghetti representation (right-hand side). As long as the proposed operations are the same, this makes no difference from the user's point of view. Note, however,

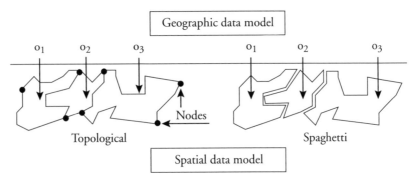

Figure 3.4   Type support with topological or spaghetti structures.

that the operation implementation depends on the representation and that the first choice provides a better support to topological operations. Asking, for instance, whether o_2 is adjacent to o_3 is easily answered, whereas it requires a complex, costly, and less robust computation with spaghetti structures.

CHOOSING APPROPRIATE TYPES

Figure 3.5 depicts a (non-exhaustive) set of possible choices for geometric types. There is a trade-off between the modeling power captured by a definition and the constraints imposed on the chosen representation.

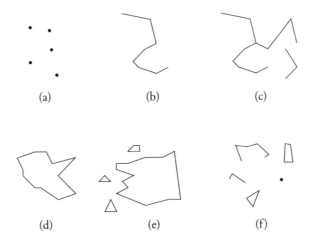

Figure 3.5   Candidates for geometric types: points (a), polyline (b), complex polyline (c), polygon (d), polygon set (e), and mixed (f).

For instance, considering the "polyline" of Figure 3.5, the endpoint of a segment is part of, *at most*, two segments. In addition, each segment is connected to at least one other segment. It might be important to know that such constraints are satisfied. On the other hand, with this definition and constraints, we are unable to represent the "complex polyline" shown in Figure 3.5.

Given the requirements of our schemas, we make the following simple choices in representing spatial objects.

◆ Type *point* (zero-dimensional). A point is an instance of this type.
◆ Type *polyline*, *line* in short (one-dimensional). An instance of this type is a list of pairwise connected segments (a segment is part of a line limited by two points). We add the constraint that an endpoint can be shared by, at most, two segments.
◆ Type *region* (two-dimensional). An instance of this type is any set of nonoverlapping polygons. In some situations, choosing a *polygon* type for surfacic objects may be too restrictive, as some geographic objects (such as states or counties) might consist of several non-connected components. In the following, for the sake of simplicity, we do not consider polygons with holes.

The next step is to define, for each of the spatial types, the operations needed to express (and evaluate) our reference queries.

DEFINING SPATIAL ADT OPERATIONS

Choosing a set of operations to assign to an ADT is not simple. In particular, the result of the operation must be either any atomic type (e.g., real or integer) provided by the DBMS or one of the three abstract types.

Examine Figure 3.6. It depicts the intersection of two polygons. Each polygon represents the infinite set of points lying both inside and on its frontier. If we choose for the intersection of two polygons "all points common to both polygons," the result can be (1) two polygons, in which case it can be represented as an object of type *region*; (2) two polygons and a line; or (3) two polygons, a line, and a point. In the latter cases, we have no types to represent these combinations.

For the sake of simplicity, we adopt here the first semantics. The result is a set of polygons, and we ignore points and lines. Observe that this does not exactly match the point set semantics of intersection.

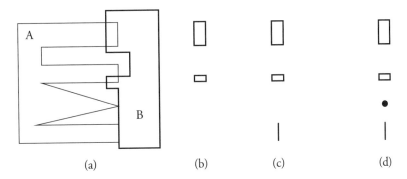

Figure 3.6   The result of an intersection: $A \cap B$ (a) might be two polygons (b); two polygons and a line (c); or two polygons, a line, and a point (d).

However, the result is enforced to be of one of the chosen types. The other operations have also been chosen to comply with the type system.

Each operation in the following has a name and a *signature*. An operation signature states the type of each of its arguments and of its result. A short description of the operation is provided after each operation signature. We assume the existence of a fourth ADT, *rectangle*, which is not detailed here. The *region* ADT includes the following operations.

◆ *PointInRegion: region × point → bool* (Tests whether a point belongs to a region.)
◆ *Overlaps: region × region → bool* (Tests whether two regions intersect.)
◆ *OverlapsRect: region × rectangle → bool* (Tests whether a region intersects a rectangle.)
◆ *Clipping: region × rectangle → region* (Computes the intersection of a region and a rectangle: a region, possibly empty.)
◆ *Intersection: region × region → region* (Returns the intersection of two regions: a region, possibly empty.)
◆ *Meets: region × region → bool* (Tests the adjacency of two regions.)
◆ *Area: region → real* (Returns the area size of a region.)
◆ *RegionUnion: {region} → region* (Takes a set of regions and returns a region, the union of the input regions. This function can be viewed as an *aggregate* function in SQL terminology, similar to *min, max,* and *sum,* among other functions.)

The *line* ADT includes the following operations.

- *PointInLine: line × point → bool* (Tests the intersection between a point and a line.)
- *Length: line → real* (Computes the length of a line.)
- *OverlapsLR: line × region → bool* (Tests the intersection between a line and a region.)

The *point* ADT includes the following operation.

- *Distance: region × point → real* (Computes the distance between a point and the boundary of a region.)

Although this list is clearly not exhaustive, it is meant to provide the reader with a simple set of operations sufficient for answering the reference queries. It is worth mentioning that several intuitive and useful operations cannot be defined, due to our type restrictions. For instance, the union of regions yields a region, but this would not be the case for the union of lines (see the example of a complex polyline in Figure 3.5). Similarly, we do not define the intersection of a line and a rectangle or a region, as the result is not always a list of pairwise connected segments. In a real implementation, we should consider these limitations, but this makes the type system more intricate.

The rest of this section further explores these issues in spatial data type design. Notice that the material presented so far is already sufficient for understanding the queries in Sections 3.4 and 3.5.

3.3.2 Designing Spatial ADTs

The previously listed type definitions are strongly application driven. We considered the need for specific database schemas, as well as a restricted list of queries on the database. However, a spatial database system should propose a much more general set of types and operations, capable of providing a wide range of functions for data representation and data manipulation. We illustrate this with a list of operations.

DEFINING AN EXHAUSTIVE LIST OF OPERATIONS
Functional requirements for GIS and other spatial applications are vast, and go far beyond database functionality. For example, market analysis requires displaying data at different levels of resolution, car navigation systems need path-finding operations, applications dealing with terrain

modeling need interpolation (deriving elevation for points where there is no data measure), and so on. We focus here on the basic spatial operations for querying geographic information, and illustrate their use in the functional requirements of the aforementioned GIS applications.

The list that follows neither claims to be exhaustive, nor to have well-founded grounds, nor to be minimal (some of the operations might be expressed by others of the same list). Its purpose is to informally illustrate the large variety of functional requirements, as well as their complexity. We chose a conventional classification of the spatial operations into seven classes, depending on the operation's signature (i.e., on the type of its arguments). We assume, of course, that at least one of the arguments is spatial.

- *Unary operations with Boolean result.* These operations test a spatial object for a given property. Examples include the *convex* and *connected* tests.

- *Unary operations with scalar result.* The most often used operations are computing the length, area size, and perimeter of a spatial object.

- *Unary operations with spatial result.* There are a large number of operations of differing natures in this class. *Topological transforms* are the operations (homeomorphisms) that preserve topological relationships; that is, all of the continuous, bijective applications $\mathbb{R}^2 \to \mathbb{R}^2$. These include rotation, translation, scale change, and symmetry. Other operations transform a d-dimensional object into an object of another, lower or higher, dimension. The most important operation is *boundary*, mapping a d-dimensional object into a $(d-1)$-dimensional one, where $d > 0$. The third important subclass is *object extraction*. This category includes operations such as *minimal bounding rectangle* and region centroid. Another interesting operation is the *buffer operation*, which extends an object by means of a *buffer*.

- *N-ary operations with spatial result.* A variety of operations are part of this general category, among them *Voronoi diagram* construction of a set of points and convex hull.[7]

---

7. For a definition of a convex hull, see Chapter 5.

◆ *Binary operations with spatial result.* The most frequently used operations for spatial queries are the *set operations*. These operations apply to objects represented as (infinite) sets of points: intersection, union, and difference. They are used in queries when computing a new spatial object. For example, intersection is used in the query "Part of highways inside the State of California." Intersection is also the basis for *map overlays*, a central query for applications handling map layers.[8] New layers are created by *overlaying* two or more layers; for example, land use can be overlaid with altitude. In this example, map overlay is the intersection between two sets of regions.

◆ *Binary operations with Boolean result.* Also called *spatial predicates*, they are the basis for spatial querying and more particularly for *spatial selection* and *spatial join*. One commonly distinguishes among the following:

• *Topological predicates* invariant with respect to topological transforms, such as *intersects, contains, adjacent,* or *is enclosed by. Point queries* and *region queries* are examples of spatial selection queries that use, respectively, the *contains* and *intersects* predicates. Point queries (e.g., "Who is the owner of the land parcel in a cadastre containing a point drawn on the screen?") test whether each spatial object of a collection (e.g., each parcel) contains a given point. Region or *range* queries test whether an object intersects a given region (e.g., which roads intersect a given county). *Windowing* is a region query in which the region argument is a rectangular window, useful for interactively selecting on the screen a set of objects.

• *Direction predicates* such as *above* or *North of.*

• *Metric predicates,* a typical example of which is testing whether the distance between two objects is less than a given number of units.

◆ *Binary operations with scalar result. Distance* (e.g., between a road and a county) is a typical operation in this class.

SEMANTICS OF OPERATIONS

An operation may have different meanings, depending on the dimension considered. Take, for example, the intersection operation. As de-

---

8. From this point, unless there is an ambiguity, we use the expressions "map overlay" and "theme overlay" interchangeably.

scribed in Section 3.3.2, the intersection operation does not preserve
the dimension of its operands. One can circumvent this problem by
defining a different intersection operation such that it preserves the dimension of its operands (sometimes called *"regularized" intersection*).
We adopted this interpretation in our type system. A summary of the
possible cases is illustrated in Figure 3.7.

The result of the (regularized) intersection of two polygons depends
on the definition of the arguments of the intersection operation. Convex polygons are closed under intersection; that is, the intersection of
two convex polygons (Figure 3.7a) is always a *single* convex polygon.
The intersection of two nonconvex polygons may generate many polygons (Figure 3.7b). In addition, the semantics of the intersection operation may vary from one application to another. This is mainly a matter
of the dimension considered, according to the following:

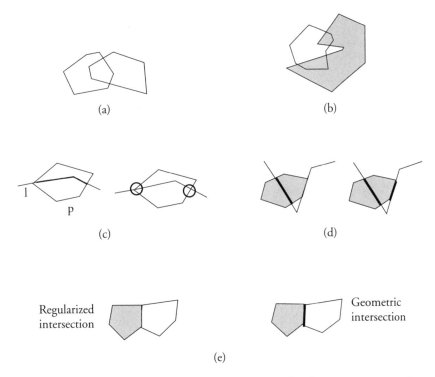

Figure 3.7   Many possible cases for intersection in the plane: two convex polygons (a), two nonconvex polygons (b), line and polygon (c), line and polygon
having a line segment in common (d), two adjacent polygons (e), leading to regularized intersection (left) and geometric intersection (right).

- The intersection of a line and a polygon may be understood either as the part of the line inside the polygon or as the intersection points between the line and the boundary of the polygon, as depicted in Figures 3.7c and 3.7d.
- Similarly, the intersection of two lines is either (1) a segment or the set of segments common to the two lines given as argument or (2) the set of points of intersection between the two lines.
- The intersection of two adjacent polygons or regions can be understood either as a (2D) *regularized intersection,* which means, for instance, that the intersection of two adjacent parcels is empty, or as a *geometric intersection,* in which case the returned value is their common boundary (Figure 3.7e).

STRONG VERSUS WEAK TYPING

As previously stated, the result of spatial operations should satisfy one of the existing types. The rationale behind such a design choice is that in common situations the result of an operation is reused in the following operation of the same query (functional view of queries as a composition of operations). As an example, regions defined as sets of polygons in our type system are closed under intersection: the intersection of two sets of polygons is a set of polygons. We could not have chosen for a region a single polygon because, as shown in Figure 3.7, unless polygons are convex the intersection of two polygons in the general case is not a polygon but a *set* of polygons. It is easy to find other examples that show the limits of our simple type system (*point, line, region*), such as the following:

- The intersection of a line and a region returns many points (i.e., neither a single point nor necessarily a line).
- The union of two (poly)lines is not a (poly)line according to our definition of a polyline as a set of pairwise connected segments.
- The difference of two polygons (without holes) may be a polygon with a hole.

Defining a *larger* type system seems appropriate in some cases, provided it at least incorporates the notion of set (see our type *region*). One therefore chooses a type large enough to remain closed under a set of common operations. We refer to this approach as a *weak type*–based approach. In this case, one defines, for instance, one type *geometry*, which is a set of either points (or lines) or polygons.

However, having a type that is too general means encompassing a large number of cases and not taking advantage of the power of *strong typing* (e.g., control on the operations). For instance, modeling a line by a set of segments enables us to perform a union of lines. However, *any* collection of segments will then be accepted, whatever their position and relationships.

To conclude this issue, the ADT definition must be rich enough that many applications can access an object having this type without frequently "disencapsulating" the type. Indeed, if a type is not appropriately defined, it might be necessary to access its internal structure (i.e., to violate its encapsulation). A typical example is the access to holes of polygons in applications dealing with objects of such types (e.g., lakes on islands, with a lake defined as a polygon).

3.3.3 *Exploring Relationships Between Spatial Objects: Topological Predicates*

Exploring spatial relationships is a challenging task that involves multidisciplinary effort (geography, cognitive sciences, and so on.). Predicates such as "far from" or "meets" are not as clear as relationships that exist between, for instance, reals. A formal definition of spatial relationships is needed in order to clarify the various understandings of spatial relationships among users, and to infer relationships among spatial objects.

A computational method is introduced for reasoning about binary topological relations between spatial regions and to deduce the consistency of complete and incomplete topological information. The method can be used to refine incomplete topological information. It applies to query processing, for detecting unsolvable queries before their execution. Another goal of this method is to distinguish among many topological relationships by other than intuitive means. Topological relations are only a subset of the large variety of spatial relationships and are preserved under topological transformation such as translation, rotation, and scaling.

Hence we focus here on topological relationships between two objects in the plane. A rather intuitive and common formalism is based on pure set theory. Using (1) function *point* (x), which denotes the set of points that belongs to a spatial region x, and (2) the collection of set operations $=$, $\neq$, $\subseteq$, and $\cap$, we can write the following definitions for the relations *equal, not equal, inside, outside*, and *intersects*:

- $x = y$ corresponds to *point*$(x) = $ *point*(y)
- $x \neq y$ corresponds to *point*$(x) \neq $ *point*(y)
- x *inside* y corresponds to *point*$(x) \subseteq $ *point*(y)
- x *outside* y corresponds to *point*$(x) \cap $ *point*$(y) = \emptyset$
- x *intersects* y corresponds to *point*$(x) \cap $ *point*$(y) \neq \emptyset$

This approach may be criticized as being neither minimal nor complete. Predicates *equal* and *inside*, for instance, are both included in the *intersects* definition. Predicates *overlaps* (non-empty intersection of two spatial regions) and *meets* ("two spatial regions touch each other") are also covered by the definition of *intersects*.

The point set approach was hence augmented with the notion of *boundary* and *interior* of spatial objects, such that relations *overlap* (non-empty intersection of boundaries and non-empty intersection of interiors) and *meets* (non-empty intersection of boundaries and empty intersection of interiors) can be distinguished. By comparing whether or not boundaries and interiors of two spatial regions intersect, four relations can be identified. This is referred to as the *4-intersection* scheme, or 4-intersection, to be shorter. More formally, to describe topological relations, the common concepts of point set topology with open and closed sets are used.

- A point set S in $\mathbb{R}^2$ is *open* if for each of its points p there exists an $\epsilon \in \mathbb{R}$, $\epsilon > 0$, such that the disk with radius ϵ and center p is contained in S.
- S is *closed* if $\mathbb{R}^2 - S$ is open.

Let us assume the existence of a non-empty set of points A, previously denoted as *spatial region* or *spatial object*. The *interior* of A, denoted by A^o, is the union of all open sets in A. In other words, it is the largest open set contained in A. The *closure* of A, denoted by $\bar{A}$, is the intersection of all closed sets that contain A. The *complement* of A with respect to the embedding space $\mathbb{R}^2$, denoted by $\mathbb{R}^2 - A$ or C_A, is the set of all points of $\mathbb{R}^2$ not contained in A. The *boundary* of A, denoted by δA, is the intersection of the closure of A ($\bar{A}$) and the closure of the complement of A, $\overline{C}_A$. A^o, δA, and C_A are mutually exclusive. The union $A^o \cup \delta A \cup C_A$ is $\mathbb{R}^2$. Interior, boundary, and complement are sometimes referred to as the three-object part. Given two spatial regions considered as closed point sets, the idea is to find out what can be deduced about the topological relationships between them from the relationships existing among their interiors and boundaries. More precisely, if A and B are spatial regions, and if their respective boundaries and interiors are known, to find out about their relationship we only need to test whether possible intersections are empty or not. There are 16 (2^4) different combinations. Each possibility is a condition on the boundaries and interiors of the two participating sets. It leads to a relationship between the two sets that is preserved under topological transformations. For general sets in a point set topology, all possible combinations are listed in Table 3.1, where *name* r_n denotes the name of the topological relationship of the corresponding 4-tuple.

Because a set cannot be both empty and non-empty, the 16 relations in Table 3.1 are mutually exclusive, which means that for any pair (A, B) in a topological space X, exactly one relation holds. Notice that according to different topological spaces in which A and B lie (the "setting"), a same configuration may show different relations among spatial regions, as the notions of boundary and interior may vary. For instance, the interior of a line is empty in the plane, whereas it is non-empty in a one-dimensional space.

Not all of the sixteen relations of Table 3.1 exist between two point sets in $\mathbb{R}^2$. For instance, the spatial relations r_2, r_4, r_5, r_8, r_9, r_{12}, and r_{13} cannot occur. This is proven by the fact that if the boundary-interior or interior-boundary intersection is not empty, then the interior-interior intersection between the same two regions is also non-empty.

Look at relation r_{14} (intersection interior-interior non-empty; intersection boundary-boundary empty; and one boundary intersects an interior, whereas the other one does not). r_{14} is similar to relation r_6, except that the intersection between the interior of A and the boundary of B is not empty. It implies that one of the two spatial regions (the larger region) contains holes. Under the hypothesis that spatial regions do not contain holes, only eight intersections can occur between two spatial regions embedded in the Euclidean plane. These, together with their customary names, are shown in Table 3.2, where we can also see

Table 3.1   The 16 specifications of binary topological relations between interiors and boundaries of spatial objects.

Name	$\delta A \cap \delta B$	$A^o \cap B^o$	$\delta A \cap B^o$	$A^o \cap \delta B$
r_0	$\emptyset$	$\emptyset$	$\emptyset$	$\emptyset$
r_1	$\neg\emptyset$	$\emptyset$	$\emptyset$	$\emptyset$
r_2	$\emptyset$	$\neg\emptyset$	$\emptyset$	$\emptyset$
r_3	$\neg\emptyset$	$\neg\emptyset$	$\emptyset$	$\emptyset$
r_4	$\emptyset$	$\emptyset$	$\neg\emptyset$	$\emptyset$
r_5	$\neg\emptyset$	$\emptyset$	$\neg\emptyset$	$\emptyset$
r_6	$\emptyset$	$\neg\emptyset$	$\neg\emptyset$	$\emptyset$
r_7	$\neg\emptyset$	$\neg\emptyset$	$\neg\emptyset$	$\emptyset$
r_8	$\emptyset$	$\emptyset$	$\emptyset$	$\neg\emptyset$
r_9	$\neg\emptyset$	$\emptyset$	$\emptyset$	$\neg\emptyset$
r_{10}	$\emptyset$	$\neg\emptyset$	$\emptyset$	$\neg\emptyset$
r_{11}	$\neg\emptyset$	$\neg\emptyset$	$\emptyset$	$\neg\emptyset$
r_{12}	$\emptyset$	$\emptyset$	$\neg\emptyset$	$\neg\emptyset$
r_{13}	$\neg\emptyset$	$\emptyset$	$\neg\emptyset$	$\neg\emptyset$
r_{14}	$\emptyset$	$\neg\emptyset$	$\neg\emptyset$	$\neg\emptyset$
r_{15}	$\neg\emptyset$	$\neg\emptyset$	$\neg\emptyset$	$\neg\emptyset$

Table 3.2   The eight possible spatial relationships between two spatial regions.

Inst. name	$\delta A \cap \delta B$	$A^o \cap B^o$	$\delta A \cap B^o$	$A^o \cap \delta B$	Rel. name
r_0	$\emptyset$	$\emptyset$	$\emptyset$	$\emptyset$	A disjoint B
r_1	$\neg\emptyset$	$\emptyset$	$\emptyset$	$\emptyset$	A meets B
r_3	$\neg\emptyset$	$\neg\emptyset$	$\emptyset$	$\emptyset$	A equals B
r_6	$\emptyset$	$\neg\emptyset$	$\neg\emptyset$	$\emptyset$	A inside B
r_7	$\neg\emptyset$	$\neg\emptyset$	$\neg\emptyset$	$\emptyset$	B covers A
r_{10}	$\emptyset$	$\neg\emptyset$	$\emptyset$	$\neg\emptyset$	B inside A
r_{11}	$\neg\emptyset$	$\neg\emptyset$	$\emptyset$	$\neg\emptyset$	A covers B
r_{15}	$\neg\emptyset$	$\neg\emptyset$	$\neg\emptyset$	$\neg\emptyset$	A overlaps B

that the relations *meets* and *overlaps* are topological refinements of the (set-oriented) *intersection* operation.

3.4   RELATIONAL MODELS EXTENDED WITH ADT

Within extended relational systems, end users manipulate values whose types are basic, such as integer or real types, but also abstract data types accessible through the operations defined on them. To represent and query our reference geographic application with such a relational system, we now consider the spatial abstract data types defined in the previous section. This section starts with a description of the schemas presented at the beginning of this chapter. We then express a few queries extracted from Section 3.2.

3.4.1   *Representation of the Reference Schemas*

The conceptual schema presented in Section 3.1 can easily be translated into a relational schema. Each entity type corresponds to a relation whose attributes are those of the entity considered. The composition links among entities—such as the fact that a state belongs to a country, or a section to a highway—also have to be taken into account. To do this, the composed theme (e.g., *Country*) is mentioned in the component (e.g., *State*) by means of a foreign key. The key of *Country* becomes an attribute[9] of *State*. The mechanism is standard in relational schemas, and the SQL2 data definition language (DDL), used in the following, provides a specific clause (**Foreign Key**) to declare that one or several attributes reference a tuple in another relation.

ADMINISTRATIVE UNITS (SCHEMA I)
In the relational schema that follows, a reference to a country is made in a *State* relation. The same reasoning applies to states and counties. This leads to the relations of the following. For each relation, we provide its name and its attribute list (attribute name and type).

Create Table *Country*
  (country_code **integer**,
  country_name **varchar (30)**,
  geometry region,
  Primary Key *(country_code))*

Create Table *State*
  (state_code **integer**,
  state_name **varchar (30)**,

---

9. A *key* attribute is an attribute whose value identifies a tuple. Two tuples of a given relation cannot have the same key value. Sometimes the key consists of several attributes. The key attribute(s) of a relation is called the primary key. A foreign key is an attribute whose value is that of a primary key of another relation.

country_code **varchar (30)**,
geometry region,
Primary Key *(state_code),*
Foreign Key *(country_code)* **References** *Country)*

Create Table *County*
    (county_code **integer**
    county_name **varchar (30)**,
    state_code **varchar (30)**,
    population **integer**,
    geometry region,
    Primary Key *(county_code),*
    Foreign Key *(state_code)* **References** *State)*

Note that, similar to the schema provided in Section 3.1, the spatial attribute appears at all levels; that is, attribute *geometry* is in relations *Country*, *State*, and *County*. The geometry could have appeared only at the lowest level in the administrative hierarchy, and then propagated to the higher levels, given the partitioning of the plane at all administrative levels. However, even though the base objects, such as counties, form a partition, computing the geometry of a state from the union of the geometry of all counties turns out to be extremely costly. In addition, such geometries are assumed not to change over time, or rarely, so it is certainly more time efficient to compute them only once.

Choosing to represent such attributes (or not) at all levels depends on their use in a given application. On the other hand, an attribute such as *population* is easily computed from base objects (counties). We hence chose to have a *population* attribute only at the *County* level, and not at the *Country* or the *State* level. Sometimes attributes form a foreign key; that is, a key to another relation. They are used to maintain referential integrity. This means in particular that if they make a reference to a tuple of another relation, this tuple must exist. The only difference between this schema and a pure relational schema is the existence of a spatial abstract data type *region*, to represent the geometric part of a country, a state, and a county.

HIGHWAY NETWORK AND CITIES (SCHEMA 2)
Using the same principle, we can define a schema on highway networks. The geometry of a highway, a polyline, does not appear in the *Highway*

relation. In fact, as opposed to the administrative units discussed previously, it appears only at the highway section level. The geometry of a highway is obtained by applying the geometric union to all sections that constitute it. Thus, we avoid here the redundancy of the previous schema. The main reason for not storing the geometry at the highway level is the relative frequency of change in the geometry of highway sections.

There is a many-to-many relationship between highways and their sections, which means that a highway has many sections and that a section may be shared by many highways. To express this in the relational model, we use three relations: (1) *Highway* represents a highway with basic information, (2) *Section* represents a piece of highway, and (3) *HighwaySection* makes the correspondence between a section and a highway. The existence of the three relations allows us to eliminate the redundancies that would exist if only two relations (for example, *Highway* and *Section*) were present. Because such a section may belong to many highways, and because the section order may be useful to consider, relation *HighwaySection* keeps track of the section number for a particular highway. The *starts-at* and *ends-at* relationship between *Section* and *City* are expressed through the introduction of *City_start* and *City_end*, respectively.

Independently, the geometric part of a city appears in the *City* relation as a *region*. We suppose that *city_name* is a key attribute of relation *City*. Consider the following schema.

Create Table *Highway*
  (highway_code **integer**,
  highway_name **varchar (4)**,
  highway_type **varchar (2)**,
  Primary Key *(highway_code))*

Create Table *HighwaySection*
  (section_code **integer**,
  section_number **integer**,
  highway_code **integer**,
  Primary Key *(section_code,highway_code)*,
  Foreign Key *(section_code)* **References** *Section*,
  Foreign Key *(highway_code)* **References** *Highway)*

Create Table *Section*
 (section_code **integer**,
 section_name **varchar (4)**,
 number_lanes **integer**,
 city_start **varchar (30)**,
 city_end **varchar (30)**,
 geometry line,
 Primary Key *(section_code)*,
 Foreign Key *(city_start)* **References** *City*,
 Foreign Key *(city_end)* **References** *City)*

Create Table *City*
 (city_name **varchar (30)**,
 population **integer**,
 geometry region,
 Primary Key *(city_name))*

LAND USE (SCHEMA 3)

The only relation to be considered is *Land_Use*, as shown in the following.

Create Table *Land_Use*
 (region_name **varchar (30)**,
 land_use_type **varchar (30)**,
 geometry region,
 Primary Key *(region_name))*

3.4.2   Reference Queries

This section examines queries of Section 3.2 using a relational language extended with the manipulation of ADT. This means in particular that the system is supposed to know the operations on spatial data types described above. Each query is written as an SQL "**select from where**" clause. The keyword **select** is followed by one or many attributes that belong to the relation(s) to be considered, or by an operation defined on the spatial ADTs; **from** is followed by the name of this (these) relation(s). The keyword **where** gives the conditions for selecting tuples.

All queries are presented with classifications and definitions in Section 3.2.

QUERIES WITH ALPHANUMERIC CRITERIA

ALPHA-ADM1. Number of inhabitants in the County of San Francisco.

This is a relational selection/projection. The only relation to be considered is *County*. The tuples of the *County* relation are selected such that their value for attribute *county_name* is "San Francisco."

select   *population*
from   *County*
where   *county_name* = 'San Francisco'

ALPHA-ADM2. List of the names of the counties in the State of California.

First, all counties with California as the state name have to be listed. To do this, a join is performed between relations *County* and *State*, restricted to the tuple such that *state_name* is 'California.' Finally, there is a projection on attribute *county_name*. The attribute for the join is *state_code*.

select   *county_name*
from   *County, State*
from   *State.state_code* = *County.state_code*
and   *state_name* = 'California'

This involves two relations, and these relations share an attribute having the same name, *state_code*. In order to indicate which attribute is meant, SQL allows us to put the relation name in front of it. Thus, *State.state_code* refers to the attribute *state_code* of relation *State*. Where there is no ambiguity, prefixing an attribute is not necessary.

A common alternative form of the query uses *aliases* to relation names. In the **from** clause, expression *R* **as** *A* allows one to use *A* as a synonym for relation *R* anywhere in the query. As previously stated, this prefix is not compulsory when there is no ambiguity.

select   *county_name*
from   *County* **as** *c, State* **as** *s*
where   *s.state_code* = *c.state_code*
and   *state_name* = 'California'

This is particularly useful when a query involves two or more tuples from the same relation. In the following, we do not use the keyword **as**, which is optional in the standard for SQL2.

ALPHA-ADM3. Number of inhabitants of the United States of America.

Because the population of a country cannot be accessed directly, to answer this query, the population of a country is computed by summing up the population of all its counties (obtained through the states that belong to a country). The join between *County* and *State* is performed as in query **ALPHA-ADM2**. A second join is needed between *Country* and *State*. The total population is computed by applying the aggregate function *sum* on all population values coming from the *County* relation.

select	*sum (c2.population)*
from	*Country c1, State s, County c2*
where	*c1.country_name =* 'USA'
and	*s.state_code = c2.state_code*
and	*c1.country_code = s.country_code*

ALPHA-R1. Number of lanes in the first section of Interstate 99. The three relations to consider when expressing this query are *HighwaySection, Highway,* and *Section.* The two joins between relations (1) *Highway* and *HighwaySection* and (2) *HighwaySection* and *Section* are performed such that the name of the highway is I99 and the section number of the section for this highway is 1. Finally, the projection on attribute *number_lanes* coming from relation *Section* is performed.

select	*s.number_lanes*
from	*HighwaySection h1, Highway h2, Section s*
where	*h2.highway_code = h1.highway_code*
and	*h1.section_code = s.section_code*
and	*h2.highway_name =* 'I99'
and	*h1.section_number =* 1

ALPHA-R2. Names of sections that constitute Interstate 99.

All sections that constitute the highway having name I99 have to be retrieved. To do this, the join between *Highway, HighwaySection,* and *Section* is performed such that the highway considered is I99.

```
select    section_name
from      HighwaySection h1, Highway h2, Section s
where     h2.highway_name = 'I99'
and       h2.highway_code = h1.highway_code
and       h1.section_code = s.section_code
```

QUERIES INVOLVING SPATIAL CRITERIA

As opposed to the previous queries, queries of this category involve functions and predicates defined on spatial ADTs. Predicates are used as selection criteria (**where** clause in SQL). Spatial functions can be applied on the tuples of a resulting relation (**select** clause), exactly like aggregate functions. They can also be used as arguments of a predicate (**where** clause, such as in query **SPAT-ADM6**).

SPAT-ADM4. Counties adjacent to the County of San Francisco in the same state.

Because an inner join between County and itself has to be performed in this case, using aliases is mandatory. Two variables are used to denote the two tuples of relation *County* that need to be considered. *County c1* denotes a tuple of the first one, and *c2* represents the county of San Francisco (*c2.county_name* = 'San Francisco'). Counties *c1* that are in the same county as San Francisco (this is verified by the first two conditions of the **where** clause) are kept in the result only if they are adjacent to the county of San Francisco, which is found out through the adjacency test *Meets (c1.geometry, c2.geometry)*.

```
select    c1.county_name
from      County c1, County c2
where     c2.county_name = 'San Francisco'
and       c1.state_code = c2.state_code
and       Meets (c1.geometry, c2.geometry)
```

SPAT-ADM5. Display of the State of California.

Because the geometry attribute appears at all levels in the administrative hierarchy in the proposed schema, expressing this query is straightforward.

```
select    geometry
from      State
where     state_name = 'California'
```

However, if the geometry had been stored at the county (bottom) level only, this query would have been expressed as follows:

select	*RegionUnion (c.geometry)*
from	*County c, State s*
where	*s.state_code = c.state_code*
and	*s.state_name =* 'California'

With a join between relations *State* and *County*, we get all counties that belong to the state of California. We project on their geometric attribute and we apply a geometric union on all the values (aggregate function). Function *RegionUnion* takes as an argument a set of regions and returns the region that contains all polygons of the input. It could be useful in such a case to eliminate the possible common boundaries in the result. In this case, another operator, *Fusion*, is required.

SPAT-ADM6. Counties larger than the largest county in California.

This query is expressed as follows:

select	*county_name*
from	*County*
where	*Area (County.geometry) >*
	(**select** *max (Area (c.geometry))*
	from *County c, State s*
	where *s.state_code = c.state_code*
	and *s.state_name =* 'California')

In the nested **select** clause, all counties of California are selected. Their area size is computed (spatial function *Area*), and the largest is determined (SQL aggregate function *max*). Finally, the outer clause checks all counties for area size and returns those whose area size is greater than that selected in the inner clause.

SPAT-R3. Length of Interstate 99.

This query is expressed as follows:

select	*sum (Length (s.geometry))*
from	*Highway h1, HighwaySection h2, Section s*
where	*h1.highway_name =* 'I99'
and	*h1.highway_code = h2.highway_code*
and	*h2.section_code = s.section_code*

On each section of Highway I99, function *Length* defined on type *Line* is applied. Again, there is a join between relations *Highway*, *Highway-Section*, and *Section*. The SQL operator *sum* is applied on the list of values (length of the various sections), which computes the sum.

SPAT-ADMR1. All highways going through the State of California.

All sections that intersect the state of California have to be returned (spatial predicate *OverlapsLR* applied on the geometry of a section and the geometry of a state). The name of the highway they belong to is returned. Note the elimination of duplicates with the use of **distinct**.

select	**distinct** *h1.highway_name*
from	*State s1, Highway h1, HighwaySection h2, Section s2*
where	*s1.state_name* = 'California'
and	*h1.highway_code* = *h2.highway_code*
and	*h2.section_code* = *s2.section_code*
and	*OverlapsLR (s2.geometry, s1.geometry)*

SPAT-ADM-LU1. Display of all residential areas in the County of San Jose.

This query is expressed as follows:

select	*Intersection (l.geometry, c.geometry)*
from	*County c, Land_Use l*
where	*c.county_name* = 'San Jose'
and	*l.land_use_type* = 'residential area'
and	*Overlaps (l.geometry, c.geometry)*

We make a selection of both the residential areas in the *Land_Use* relation and the county of San Jose from the *County* relation. Only residential areas whose geometry intersects with the geometry of the county of San Jose are retained (*Overlaps* predicate defined on type *region*). The area that is exactly within the county of San Jose is computed (*Intersection* operation defined in the *region* ADT). This query can be simplified by removing the spatial intersection test, which is supposed to be made when the intersection itself is computed (**select** clause).

SPAT-ADM-LU2. Overlay of the themes of counties and land use.

This query is expressed as follows:

select	*county_name, land_use_type,*
	Intersection (c.geometry, l.geometry)
from	*County c, Land_Use l*
where	*Overlaps (c.geometry, l.geometry)*

This query corresponds to a map (theme) overlay operation, which builds a new relation whose schema is created from (1) the set of descriptive attributes of the two relations considered, *County* and *Land_Use*, and (2) a spatial attribute that comes from the intersection of the two sets of regions. Each tuple of this relation corresponds to the intersection between a land parcel and a county. Its description is built from both the one of the county and the one of the parcel. Note that for the sake of simplicity we did not keep all the descriptive attributes of the original relations in the query expression above.

INTERACTIVE QUERIES

INTER-ADM7. Description of the county pointed to on the screen.

This query is expressed as follows:

select	*county_name, population*
from	*County*
where	*PointInRegion (geometry, @point)*

This is a point query. The *PointInRegion* spatial predicate makes a first selection of the counties that contain the point clicked on the screen (with parameter *@point*). The name and population of the county chosen are retrieved from the database and returned to the end user.

INTER-ADM8. Counties that intersect a given rectangle on the screen.

This query is expressed as follows:

select	*county_name*
from	*County*
where	*OverlapsRect (geometry, @rectangle)*

This is an example of windowing. The rectangle drawn on the screen is stored in *@rectangle*. The *OverlapsRect* predicate takes a region and a rectangle as arguments.

INTER-ADM9. Parts of the counties that are within a given rectangle on the screen.

This query is expressed as follows:

select   *Clipping (geometry, @rectangle)*
from   *County*
where   *OverlapsRect (geometry, @rectangle)*

Clipping returns the part of a region contained in a rectangle given as argument. As for queries **SPAT-ADM-LU1** and **SPAT-ADM-LU2**, the expression of the previous query can be simplified by removal of the **where** condition, provided the intersection test is made when the clipping operation is performed.

INTER-R5. Description of the section pointed to on the screen.

This query is expressed as follows:

select   *section_name, number_lanes*
from   *Section*
where   *PointInLine (geometry, @point)*

This point query is similar to **INTER-ADM9**. *@point* is the point clicked on the screen.

INTER-R6. Description of the highway(s) of which a section is pointed to on the screen.

This query is expressed as follows:

select   *h2.highway_name, h2.highway_type*
from   *HighwaySection h1, Highway h2, Section s*
where   *h1.highway_code = h2.highway_code*
and   *h1.section_code = s.section_code*
and   *PointInLine (s.geometry, @point)*

To express this point query, the highway the argument section belongs to has to be retrieved. Compared to query **INTER-R5**, two joins have to be performed: one to retrieve the *HighwaySection* of the section, and another to get the corresponding highways.

3.5   OBJECT-ORIENTED MODELS

Object-oriented database systems were born in the 1980s from the merger of two technologies: database systems and object-oriented programming languages (mainly Simula and Smalltalk). This merger brought to databases many advantages, from a design viewpoint as well as a development viewpoint: new modeling power, extensibility of systems, code reuse, and easy maintenance of programs. We present in the following how an object-oriented DBMS can be used to provide support for spatial data handling.

3.5.1   A Brief Overview of Object-Oriented DBMS

Object-oriented database systems do not always rely on a unique model, but they now follow, more or less closely, a standard proposed by the Object Database Management Group (ODMG) in 1993. The common characteristics of these systems are described in the sections that follow.

OBJECT IDENTITY
An object is denoted in a unique way in the database system, using an identifier or *oid* (*object identifier*) that the object keeps during its entire lifetime, independently of its attributes value.

TYPES, CLASSES, AND METHODS
The type of an object corresponds to its structure and to the operations that can be performed on it. Atomic types such as *string* and *integer* are distinguished from more complex types that are defined using constructors (e.g., the tuple or the set constructor). Note that as opposed to relational environments, the attribute of an object *o* can have as atomic value not only a string or real but the *oid* of another object *o'*. Object *o* is said to consist of (or to reference) object *o'*. Objects with the same type are grouped into classes. Classes encompass objects having the same structure and behavior, which is expressed by the set of *methods* (or operations) applicable to the objects they contain.

ENCAPSULATION
A *class* corresponds to the implementation of an abstract data type. As opposed to relational systems for which an ad hoc extension needs to be

provided, ADTs are part of the object-oriented model. Encapsulation means that neither the structure of an ADT nor its implementation is visible from the outside world. Instead, one accesses objects only via the methods defined on the class they belong to, without any knowledge of their detail of implementation. Only the signature of methods is known from the outside world. In other words, from a programming language viewpoint, an object has a specification and an implementation, but whereas designers know the implementation, only the specification is known by end users. The concept of encapsulation allows one to abstract from the internal view of the manipulated objects. It then guarantees a certain modularity, together with separated code development. In particular, one can modify the implementation of an ADT (or a class) without having to modify the implementation of the other ADTs (or classes).

INHERITANCE

It is possible to define a (sub)class from an existing (super)class with a refinement of its structure. Starting with a type *Person*, for instance, with attributes *name* and *address*, one can define a new type of person (for instance, *Student*) with all the attributes of *Person*, and new attributes, such as *major, grade*, and *year*. A student being a person, all methods defined on class *Person* can be used in class *Student*. Class *Student* is said to *inherit* methods and structure from class *Person*. However, a method defined on a superclass such as *Person* (as opposed to a subclass such as *Student*) can be redefined in a subclass. This is called *overriding*. Such a method keeps the name it has in the superclass, but the piece of code that corresponds to it may change. In addition, methods can be defined on a subclass only, such as *compute-grade* on class *Student*. Class *Person* is said to be a *generalization* of class *Student*, and class *Student* is a *specialization* of class *Person*. Note that in principle a class can inherit from many superclasses. This is called *multiple inheritance*.

3.5.2 *Representation of Reference Schemas*

In an object-oriented environment, spatial and geographic objects are represented by objects in a homogeneous way. Each theme and each spatial ADT is materialized by a class. We define in the following the structure of each class. To do this, we use as a support the model and syntax defined in the object-oriented DBMS O$_2$. A basic type, such as real or integer, is written in lowercase letters. A type name starting with an uppercase character corresponds to a class. We start with the classes representing geographic themes. We then show the classes representing the spatial types: *Region*, *Line*, and *Point*.

ADMINISTRATIVE UNITS (SCHEMA I)

In the following, note the difference with the relational representation. In particular, we no longer need to introduce an explicit key to identify objects, because this is done automatically by the system. For instance, in class *County*, a state is not referenced by its code anymore, but by its *oid*. Attribute *state_in_county* is an object of class *State*.

Class *Country*
    tuple *(country_name: string,*
        geometry: Region,
        states: **set***(State))*

Class *State*
    tuple *(state_name: string,*
        country_in_state: Country, // Composition reference
        geometry: Region,
        counties: **set***(County))*

Class *County*
    tuple *(county_name: string,*
        population: integer,
        state_in_county: State, // Composition reference
        geometry: Region)

In this schema, we also defined a link from an object to its components (e.g., object of class *Country* composed of a set of objects of class *State*). Attribute *states* in class *Country* has for a value a set of objects of class *State*, or more precisely, a set of references to objects (*oid*s) of class *State*. In the same way, the counties of a state are referenced in attribute *counties* in class *State*. Note also the references to upper classes in the hierarchy. Class *State* has a reference to *Country* via attribute *country_in_state*, and class *County* makes a reference to *State* through attribute *state_in_county*. We refer to such links as *composition references*. As with the previous relational representation, we chose to represent the geometry at all levels in the hierarchy (attribute *geometry: Region*), and not only in atomic objects of class *Country*.

HIGHWAY NETWORK (SCHEMA 2)

As for the administrative units previously discussed, note that each attribute of a class is either atomic (descriptive attribute), is a reference to an object or to a set of objects (component objects), or is a spatial attribute whose value is a reference to a spatial object that belongs to class *Region, Line*, or *Point*.

The schema is simplified in comparison to the relational representation because it is not necessary to use an intermediate structure *HighwaySection* to represent the link between highways and sections. The **list** constructor allows us to describe the ordered sequence of sections that constitute a highway.

Class *Highway*
   tuple *(highway_name:* **string**,
            highway_type: **string**,
            sections: **list***(Section))*

Class *Section*
   tuple *(section_name:* **string**,
            number_lanes: **integer**,
            city_start: City,
            city_end: City,
            geometry: Line)

Class *City*
   tuple *(city_name:* **string**,
            population: **integer**,
            geometry: Region)

LAND USE (SCHEMA 3)

Again, the only class to consider is Land Use.

Class *Land_Use*
   tuple *(region_name: string*,

land_use_type: string,
geometry: Region)

3.5.3 Spatial Classes

Chapter 2 described many possible structures for representing lines and regions, from a simple vector spaghetti model to complex topological models. For instance, the spaghetti model is implemented by the following classes:

Class *Point*
   tuple *(x:* **real***, y:* **real***)*

A line is an arc. That is, it is a list of pairwise connected segments represented by the coordinate list of its vertices.

Class *Line*
   list   **(tuple** *(x:* **real***, y:* **real***))*

As opposed to the relational model, the object-oriented model enables the representation of complex structures by the composition of constructors. For instance, a line of this class is a list of tuples. A region is implemented as a set of polygons whose list of vertex coordinates is given.

Class *Region*
   set *(***list** *(***tuple** *(x:* **real***, y:* **real***)))*

The topological model of Chapter 2 can be implemented by the following classes. First, either a node is an endpoint of one or many arcs, or it is an isolated node.

Class *Node*
   tuple *(x:* **real***, y:* **real***,*
         endpoints: **list***(Arc))*

An arc has origin and destination nodes, a left face, a right face (faces are objects of class *Polygon*), and a list of vertices. Intermediate vertices have no meaning and are hence stored as coordinates, contrary to the begin and endpoints, which belong to class *Node* and which can be shared by many arcs.

Class *Arc*
> **tuple** *(origin: Node, destination: Node,*
> *left: Polygon, right: Polygon,*
> *vertices:* **list** *(***tuple** *(x:* **real***, y:* **real***))*

A (poly)line is a list of *Arc.* The class implementation must check that these arcs are pairwise connected.

Class *Line*
> **list**   *(Arc)*

A polygon is a list of connected arcs, and references the region to which it belongs. Each arc corresponds to the boundary with another polygon (possibly in another region).

Class *Polygon*
> **tuple** *(boundary:* **list** *(Arc),*
> *in_region : Region)*

Finally, a region is a set of polygons.

Class *Region*
> **set**   *(Polygon)*

Even though the implementation of classes must be carefully chosen (mainly for efficiency reasons), only methods of classes *Point, Line*, and *Region* need to be known by end users. The structure of the classes shown previously are hidden to end users.

Spatial operations are implemented via methods of the foregoing spatial classes. Except for the syntax, these operations are similar to those defined in a relational model extended with ADTs. A method is always applied to an object of the class on which it is defined, which is called the *receiver* of the method. In the following expressions, between the parentheses that follow method names are the possible arguments, together with their type. A method returns an instance of a certain type (**boolean**, **string**) or of a class (i.e., an object). The following are methods in class *Region:*

- **method** *pointInRegion (p: Point)* **in class** *Region:* **boolean** (Tests whether a given region contains point *p*.)

- **method** *overlaps (r: Region)* **in class** *Region:* **boolean** (Tests whether two regions intersect.)
- **method** *overlapsRect (r: Rectangle)* **in class** *Region:* **boolean** (Tests whether a region intersects a rectangle.) We suppose here the existence of class *Rectangle.*
- **method** *clipping (r: Rectangle)* **in class** *Region: Region* (Computes the part of the region that is inside rectangle *r.*)
- **method** *intersection (r: Region)* **in class** *Region: Region* (Computes the intersection of two regions: a region, possibly empty.)
- **method** *meets (r: Region)* **in class** *Zone:* **boolean** (Tests the adjacency between the receiver region and region *r.*)
- **method** *area* **in class** *Region:* **real** (Computes the area size of a region.)

The following are methods in class *Line:*

- **method** *pointInLine (p: Point)* **in class** *Line:* **boolean** (Tests whether the line contains point *p.*)
- **method** *length* **in class** *Line:* **real** (Computes the length of a line.)
- **method** *overlapsLR (r: Region)* **in class** *Line:* **boolean** (Tests whether the (receiver) line intersects region *r.*)

The following is a method in class *Point:*

- **method** *distance (r: Region)* **in class** *Point:* **real** (Computes the distance of a receiver point to region *r,* i.e., to its boundary.)

3.5.4 *Reference Queries*

Most object-oriented database management systems provide end users with a powerful query language OQL, whose syntax is similar to SQL. OQL, proposed by the Object Database Management Group (ODMG), allows the end user to access complex structures, to run methods, and to return a result that may be structured in a complex way. It also considers elaborate type constructors such as sets, lists, bags, and arrays.

In the following, we express queries from Section 3.2 using OQL. As the reader will see, queries are expressed in a manner similar to that of the previous section (relational model extended with ADT). We hence express two queries only. Other queries from Section 3.2 are left as exercises. All queries are presented with classifications and definitions in Section 3.2.

ALPHA-ADM1. Number of inhabitants in the County of San Francisco.

This query is expressed as follows:

select	*c.population*
from	*c* **in** *Counties*
where	*c.county_name* = 'San Francisco'

Access to the database is done from entry points called *persistence roots* or *roots of persistence*. In the relational model, this query was concerned with tuples from relation *County*. In the O_2 model, this query is applied to an object collection (persistence root) in a similar way. In this example, the entry point is *Counties* of type **set** (*County*), which contains a set of references to objects of class *County*. Variable *c* denotes a county (object of class *County*) taken from the set of counties in *Counties*. Notation *c.county_name* refers to the name of such a county. Apart from the **from** clause, the query is formulated in an SQL-like fashion. The county of San Francisco is selected, and all attributes are projected out except its population.

In the O_2 environment, objects of a class are not necessarily persistent. The only persistent objects are those that are part of a persistence root and the objects that are reachable from a persistent object by following reference links. For instance, if we define *All_countries:* **set**(*country*) as an entry point to the database, the countries in *All_countries* are persistent, as well as each state of such a country, and each county of such state is also stored in the database. If *All_countries* were the only persistence root (i.e., if entry point *Counties* did not exist), the previous query would be expressed as follows:

select	*c2.population*
from	*c1* **in** *All_countries, s* **in** *c1.states, c2* **in** *s.counties*
where	*c2.county_name* = 'San Francisco'

In order to get an object of class *County*, we have to describe the path from the persistence root through the objects of the database following reference links. For each country *c1* in the persistence root, each object of class *state* is accessed, and for each (referred to as *s*), all of its counties are accessed (*s.counties*).

QUERIES INVOLVING SPATIAL CRITERIA

OQL allows the use of methods in a query formulation. If *x* is a variable representing an object of class *c* on which method *m* is defined, $x \rightarrow m$ denotes the result of applying method *m* of class *c* to *x*. Methods can be used in both **select** and **where** clauses.

SPAT-R3. Length of Interstate 99.

This query is expressed as follows:

sum (**select** *s.geometry* $\rightarrow$ *length()*
            from *h* **in** *All_highways, s* **in** *h.sections*
            where *h.highway_name* = 'I99')

We suppose the existence of one root of persistence, *All_highways*. The sum of the length of all sections that constitute Highway I99 is performed with the use of method *length* defined on lines (geometric type of a section).

3.6   BIBLIOGRAPHIC NOTES

Abstract data types were introduced in the late 1970s and early 1980s. For a study on the topic, see [SRG83, Sto86]. The extension of the relational model to abstract data types is covered by general database textbooks such as [EN94, Ram97]. The object-oriented standard defined by the ODMG is described in [Cat95]. [BDK92] is a collection of papers describing the object-oriented database system O_2. The OQL variant used in this chapter is the one used by the O_2 system, initially called O_2SQL. For a more comprehensive study on OQL, see [Clu98]. [Ash99] describes the current effort toward an extension of SQL called SQL/MM Spatial, for querying spatial data.

As far as the definition of ADTs is concerned, [Til80] defines "regularized" operations for circumventing possible ambiguities in the semantics of some spatial operations (see Section 3.3.2). The idea is to make a clear distinction between operations (e.g., geometric and geographic intersections) according to the various dimensions of the considered entities. This is achieved by taking the closure of interiors (see

Section 3.3.3). The concept of "regularized" operations was reused in many attempts to define geospatial types.

Regarding topological relationships, the 4-intersection, which consists of the (four) set intersections of boundaries and interiors only, is introduced in [Ege89, EH90]. The 4-intersection concept can be extended to higher-dimensional spaces, as described in [EF91]. In addition to the dimension of the space considered, a parameter called *co-dimension* may also be taken into account. A co-dimension represents the difference between the dimension of the space and the dimension of the embedded spatial object. For instance, the co-dimension of a line in 2D space is 1. Moreover, in addition to the notions of interior and boundary used in the 4-intersection, we now use the notion of *complement* or *exterior* of a spatial region, as described previously.

Given two 2D point sets *A* and *B*, the topological relationship r_n between them can also be described by the nine set intersections (I_9) of *A*'s boundary, interior, and *complement* with the boundary, interior, and *complement* of *B*. This is called the 9-intersection and can be represented as the following 3×3 matrix.

$$I_9(A, B) = \begin{pmatrix} A^o \cap B^o & A^o \cap \delta B & A^o \cap C_B \\ \delta A \cap B^o & \delta A \cap \delta B & \delta A \cap C_B \\ C_A \cap B^o & C_A \cap \delta B & C_A \cap C_B \end{pmatrix}$$

The principle is the same as in the 4-intersection case. The distinction between values empty ($\emptyset$) and non-empty ($\neg\emptyset$) for the three concepts (boundary, interior, and complement) gives 2^9 possible combinations.

Depending on restrictions on sets *A* and *B* (e.g., whether they may contain holes) and the underlying topological space, the actual set of existing topological spatial relations may be a subset of the 2^9 (512) possible combinations. In $\mathbb{R}^2$, there are eight relations between two connected spatial objects without holes: *disjoint, contains, inside, equal, meet, cover, coveredBy,* and *overlap*. The eight relations that provide a mutually exclusive complete coverage are given, together with their corresponding 9-intersection matrices, in Figure 3.8 (in the figure, 0 corresponds to $\emptyset$, and 1 to $\neq \emptyset$).

Note that for objects of co-dimension 0, the 4-intersection and the 9-intersection provide the same result. However, when the objects have a co-dimension greater than 0, the 9-intersection provides more detail

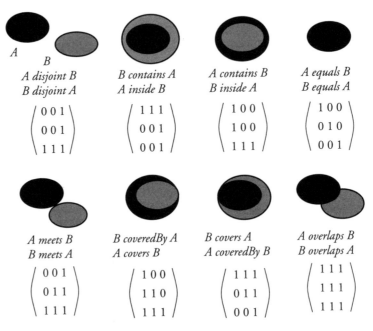

Figure 3.8 Eight topological relations between two spatial regions and their 9-intersection matrices.

than the 4-intersection, which can be utilized to find out whether two objects are equal. Modeling topological relationships has also been investigated in [MKB94, ZC95].

The database approach to modeling and querying spatial information has a long history. General references on geographic modeling are [SE89, Fra95, LT92, MGR99]. [Güt94] and [VD01] describe various approaches for modeling database objects with spatial attributes, as well as some of the algebras for manipulating sets of such objects. [VD01] also establishes categories of operators in extended and object-oriented DBMSs, which are necessary in performing spatial queries. Mapquery, explored in [Fra82], is a pioneering extension of SQL to spatial data. [SV89] defines an algebra on maps, based on an algebra on regions. GeoTropics [BDQV90, LPV93] and GEOQL [SDMO87, OSDD89] are also extensions of the relational model that uses a spatial domain. [Abe89] presents a database toolkit for handling geospatial information. GRAL [Güt89] is an implementation of the Geo-Relational algebra defined in [Güt88], which is a set of basic operators on geospatial types. Spatial SQL [Ege94] is a more complete extension of SQL for spatial data. Spatial SQL also takes into account graphical aspects by adding clauses to SQL to specify a layout on the screen. The Rose algebra [GS95], based on the Realm foundation for spatial types [GS93, Sch97b], is also noteworthy. GeoSal is another proposal for a spatial database language [HS93]. The Concert prototype database system [RSHN97] provides a generic framework for physical database design of external objects; in particular, for spatial and spatio-temporal objects. The recent work [FGNS00] is an extension of the ADT approach to moving object modeling. An interesting pioneer work on modeling and querying moving objects can be found in [SWCD97]. [MO86, vOvdB89, GR93, SV92] describe spatial database research prototypes based on object-oriented models and DBMS.

Many aspects of Section 3.5 are discussed in [SV92], which is the description of an implementation of the thematic map model of [SV89] using the O_2 system. [DRSM93] is also the implementation of the kernel of a GIS using O_2. The spatial model is a topological model defined at the French National Geographic Institute (IGN). Worboys et al. [WHM90] is a first attempt to truly take advantage of object-oriented features in the modeling of GIS objects, such as class composition and class hierarchies. This is described thoroughly in [Wor95].

The reference schema and queries are adapted from those used in [SVP+96] for a French geographic application. The classification of spatial operations is mostly from [Gün98], which also discusses the lack-of-closure property.

The Constraint Data Model

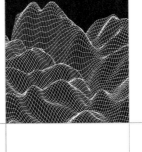

"We do not inherit earth from our parents, we borrow it from our children."

KENYAN PROVERB

CONTENTS

This chapter presents an alternative approach to the logical modeling of spatial objects. It is based on a database model called a *constraint data model*. Although this approach has until now been assessed only by research prototypes, it deserves an in-depth presentation because of its promising features. The basic idea is quite different from that of adding new data types to relational DBMSs. Indeed, the constraint data model is based on the belief that the main limitation of relational databases with respect to spatial data is their inability to represent and manipulate *infinite relations*. If we had a model capable of handling the infinite set of points in space, we would model spatial data in a simple way. Constraint databases mainly aim at extending the relational paradigm in order to handle infinite relations.

As a result, one obtains a data model that encompasses classical and spatial data (seen, respectively, as *finite* and *infinite* relations), and that allows one to express spatial queries with pure relational languages. Another strong feature is the ability to represent and manipulate data in arbitrary dimension within a uniform framework.

In this chapter, we give the intuition behind the concept of constraint databases and illustrate the querying features with two types of applications. First, we examine some queries on the *entity-based* database presented in Chapter 3. We then study how the constraint approach can be used to handle higher-dimensional data, and provide examples pertaining to *spatio-temporal data* (moving objects) and *field-based data* (elevation data). We also examine simple SQL queries on these objects.

4.1   SPATIAL DATA MODELING WITH CONSTRAINTS

As previously mentioned, the data model aims at keeping the essential features of the database relational model. A spatial object in 2D space is considered as a potentially infinite set of points, each point being represented as a tuple of a relation $Spat(x, y)$, where the x and y attributes are naturally interpreted as the coordinates of the points in Euclidean space.

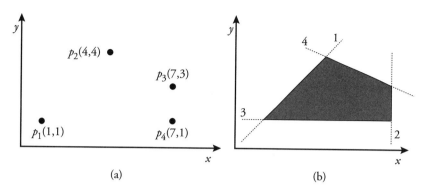

Figure 4.1 Modeling spatial data as a set of points in $\mathbb{R}^2$: a finite set of points (a) and an infinite set of points (b).

4.1.1 Point Sets as Infinite Relations

Consider the two examples of Figure 4.1. The set of four points in Figure 4.1a is represented by the finite relation *Spat*, shown in Table 4.1a. On the other hand, the points inside the polygon in Figure 4.1b consist *also* of a set of points, which is infinite (if we consider an embedding space based on a dense domain such as the rationals or the reals).

Conceptually, one can represent this instance as a relation, but in this case an infinite number of tuples has to be stored, as suggested in Table 4.1b, in which all pairs of rational coordinates contained in the convex polygon are enumerated. Obviously, one cannot store an infinite set in a finite memory computer. We will see later how to overcome this shortcoming. Suppose, for the time being, that all spatial objects are stored in infinite relations. In this case, spatial queries are easily

Table 4.1 Instances of *Spat*: a finite instance (a) and an infinite instance (b).

Spat

x	y
1	1
7	3
4	4
7	1

(a)

Spat

x	y
1	1
1.001..	1
1.002..	1
1.003..	1

Spat (cont.)

x	y
...	...
3	2
3.001..	2
...	...

(b)

expressed with the relational query language SQL. For example, *clipping*—where the rectangle argument *Rect* is represented as an infinite relation as well—is expressed in SQL as follows:

select	*x, y*
from	*Spat, Rect*
where	*Spat.x = Rect.x*
and	*Spat.y = Rect.y*

This query is a simple join or intersection. It returns the (infinite) set of points that belongs to both the rectangle and the spatial object. Let *Road* denote the infinite relation storing a road. The intersection between *Spat* and *Road* can be expressed by an SQL query similar to the previous query, as follows:

select	*x, y*
from	*Spat, Road*
where	*Spat.x = Road.x*
and	*Spat.y = Road.y*

This query language is purely declarative; that is, it avoids burdening the user with technical or geometric issues. Two of its advantages follow.

◆ One does not need to worry about the type of the objects (lines, rectangles, or polygons). In fact, any spatial feature is seen at an abstract level as a set of points, which simplifies reasoning about queries.
◆ No geometric skills are required. For instance, there is no need to think about the specific operation to be applied (e.g., clipping or line-polygon intersection).

Returning to the main issue, *How can we represent and manipulate infinite relations in a database?* The spatial data type approach yields a solution to the problem by representing a polygon by its boundary. Such a representation relies on geometric data structures that do not integrate easily with the relational data model. As a result, the set of points represented by its boundary can no longer be queried with relational languages. In contrast, the constraint approach does not introduce new data structures, but smoothly extends the relational paradigm to permit the representation of infinite instances.

4.1.2   *Finitely Representing Infinite Relations*

A starting point to capture the intuition behind the constraint data model is to adopt a new point of view on the classical relational representation. Instead of viewing a relation as a set of tuples (rows), one can view it as a simple logical formula interpreted exactly as the relation's extension. The logical representation of the finite set of four points of Figure 4.1a is, for instance:

$$\phi_{Spat} \equiv (x = 1 \wedge y = 1) \vee (x = 7 \wedge y = 3)$$

$$\vee (x = 4 \wedge y = 4) \vee (x = 7 \wedge y = 1)$$

The semantics of ϕ_{Spat} consists of those pairs of values for $[x, y]$ such that ϕ_{Spat} is true. Obviously, we obtain the original set of four points. In this representation, a tuple $[a, b]$ in $Spat(x, y)$ is a conjunction $x = a \wedge y = b$, whereas a *set* of tuples (a relation) is equivalently replaced by a *disjunction*.

This apparently complex point of view provides the key to the constraint data model. In the logical framework previously stated, the constraint representation is close in spirit to the "relation" and "tuple" concepts. The syntax of the formulas can be generalized by allowing new predicates (such as $\leq$), as well as some arithmetic operations (such as $+$ or $\times$). The polygon of Figure 4.1b is then represented as follows:

(1) $\qquad\qquad\qquad y \leq x$

(2) $\qquad\qquad\qquad \wedge\ x \leq 7$

(3) $\qquad\qquad\qquad \wedge\ y \geq 1$

(4) $\qquad\qquad\qquad \wedge\ x + 3y - 16 \leq 0$

This logical formula describes the polygon as a conjunction of four *constraints*. The interpretation of this formula is natural. It corresponds to all pairs of values $[x, y]$ in $\mathbb{R}^2$ such that the formula is true.

There exists actually a simple geometric interpretation of such formulas, where each constraint of the form $\alpha x + \beta y + \gamma \leq 0$ defines a half-plane in Euclidean space (see Chapter 2). Moreover, a *conjunction* of such constraints corresponds to an *intersection* of half-planes. In the previous example, this intersection defines a compact set of points (i.e., a convex polygon). There is a one-to-one correspondence between the four constraints 1, 2, 3, and 4 in the formula above, and the four half-planes that are shown in Figure 4.1b.

Polylines can be represented by constraints as well. Figure 4.2 illustrates a polyline L, which can be represented, in vector mode, as a list of points:

$$L =< [4, 3], [6, 5], [8, 2], [10, 5] >$$

Unlike the previous polygon, because this object is not convex (only its line segment components are convex), we use disjunction in the constraint representation. Intuitively, this consists of modeling a non-convex object as a union of convex components. The following is the constraint representation of the polyline.

$$(4 \leq x \leq 6 \land 3 \leq y \leq 5 \land x - y - 1 = 0)$$

$$\lor$$

$$(6 \leq x \leq 8 \land 2 \leq y \leq 5 \land 3x + 2y - 28 = 0)$$

$$\lor$$

$$(8 \leq x \leq 10 \land 2 \leq y \leq 5 \land 3x - 2y - 20 = 0)$$

We obtain a *disjunction* of *conjunctions* of constraints. Such a formula is said to be in *disjunctive normal form* (DNF). Take, for example, the first

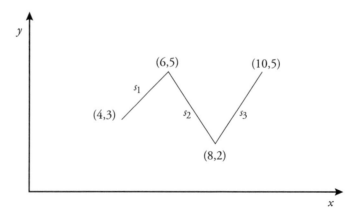

Figure 4.2 Representation of polylines in constraint databases.

conjunction interpreted as the line segment ([4, 3], [6, 5]). The constraint $x - y - 1 = 0$ is interpreted as a straight line, and the constraints $4 \leq x \leq 6$ and $3 \leq y \leq 5$ define a rectangle that clips the line so as to obtain a segment. Thus, each conjunction represents a segment, and the disjunction ($\vee$) of conjunctions represents the polyline as a union of segments.

A nonconvex polygon (Figure 4.3) is also defined as a union of convex components (convex polygons). The constraint representation of the polygon

$$P = < (1, 1), (9, 1), (9, 6), (7, 3), (4, 4) >$$

is as follows:

$$(y \leq x \wedge y \geq 1 \wedge x + 3y - 16 \leq 0 \wedge 3x - 2y - 15 \leq 0)$$

$$\vee$$

$$(x \leq 9 \wedge y \geq 1 \wedge 3x - 2y - 15 \geq 0)$$

This formula presents the same structure as the finite relation representing four points, except that we now build a "tuple" from a conjunction of constraints; that is, arithmetic expressions involving $+$ and $\leq$. Actually, such a "tuple" is a finite representation of an infinite set of points. It is referred to as a *symbolic tuple* in the following. The "relation" (i.e., the set of symbolic tuples) is also a finite representation of an infinite set of points, called a *symbolic relation*.

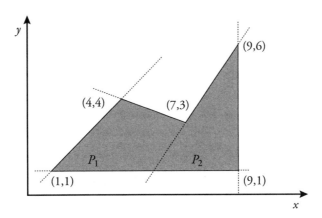

Figure 4.3   Nonconvex polygons in constraint databases.

4.1.3   Evaluating Queries on Infinite Instances

Returning to the query that computes the intersection of a road *Road* and a polygon *Spat*, assume that the instances of each relation are respectively the line of Figure 4.2 and the polygon of Figure 4.3. This query is expressed as follows:

select	*x, y*
from	*Spat, Road*
where	*Spat.x = Road.x*
and	*Spat.y = Road.y*

The evaluation of this query, whose result is the set of points common to both relations, raises some problems, namely:

- Each relation being infinite, we cannot use classical access methods, such as scanning a relation.
- The result itself is an infinite set of points, and must be finitely represented.

Regarding the first issue, we must use the finite representation with constraints. As for the second, we must be able to represent the result with constraints as well. Furthermore, given two constraint relations and a relational query, there must exist an algorithm that computes the result of the query. For example, for the previous query, a simple algorithm is to take the conjunction of the formulas that represent *Road* and *Spat*.

$$[(4 \leq x \leq 6 \wedge 3 \leq y \leq 5 \wedge x - y - 1 = 0)$$

$$\vee$$

$$(6 \leq x \leq 8 \wedge 2 \leq y \leq 5 \wedge 3x + 2y - 28 = 0)$$

$$\vee$$

$$(8 \leq x \leq 10 \wedge 2 \leq y \leq 5 \wedge 3x - 2y - 20 = 0)]$$

$$\wedge$$

$$[(y \leq x \wedge y \geq 1 \wedge x + 3y - 16 \leq 0 \wedge 3x - 2y - 15 \leq 0)$$

$$\vee$$

$$(x \leq 9 \wedge y \geq 1 \wedge 3x - 2y - 15 \geq 0)]$$

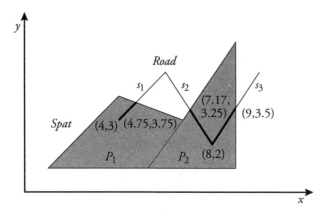

Figure 4.4   The intersection of *Road* and *Spat*.

This new formula represents exactly the intersection of *Road* and *Spat* shown in Figure 4.4 (thick segments). The computation is trivial, in that we just concatenated the two initial formulas, separating them with an $\wedge$. It is possible to apply a standard transformation of the formula to put it in disjunctive normal form with six symbolic tuples (conjunctions of constraints). Each of these tuples represents one of the pairwise intersections between the segments $\{s_1, s_2, s_3\}$ of the polyline and the convex components $\{P_1, P_2\}$ of the polygon.

It is worth noting that of the six symbolic tuples in the result, only three represent actual line segments: the result of the intersection is a set of three line segments (see Figure 4.4). Indeed, the intersection of s_1 and P_2, for instance, is empty. This means that some symbolic tuples represent an empty set of points, and can be removed from the constraint representation. One then obtains a more compact representation, such as the following:

$$(4 \leq x \leq 4.75 \wedge 3 \leq y \leq 3.75 \wedge x - y - 1 = 0)$$

$$\vee$$

$$(7.17 \leq x \leq 8 \wedge 2 \leq y \leq 3.25 \wedge 3x + 2y - 28 = 0)$$

$$\vee$$

$$(8 \leq x \leq 9 \wedge 2 \leq y \leq 3.5 \wedge 3x - 2y - 20 = 0)$$

A fundamental requirement is that for *any* query and any instance, there must exist an algorithm that allows one to obtain a finite representation of the result. Moreover, this algorithm should be reasonably efficient. The *linear constraint model*, presented below, satisfies these requirements.

4.1.4   Summary of the Constraint Data Model

The basic intuition behind the constraint data model is summarized in Figure 4.5. Recall that several layers exist in a classical DBMS architecture. In particular, there is a fundamental distinction between the *logical level*—which proposes simple structures and query languages to the end user—and the *physical level*, where the actual storage and query processing take place (see Chapter 1).

In the constraint framework, the decomposition into layers is slightly more complex. Consider the following:

- The *abstract level* is that of *abstract relations*, which can be finite or infinite. The user is not concerned with the finiteness of a relation. He can uniformly see the database as a set of tables storing tuples (points).
- The *symbolic level* supports the finite representation of infinite relations. This level is no longer of interest to the user. It is purely intended to provide a technological means of representing and manipulating data.
- Finally, the *physical level* stores the relations and performs queries by accessing the database. This aspect is not discussed in this chapter.

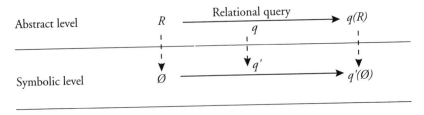

Figure 4.5   Abstract, symbolic, and physical levels.

Given that at the abstract level the database is seen as purely relational, one can consistently use relational queries. Of course, the evaluation of a query is peculiar. An infinite relation, say, R, is finitely represented in a symbolic form, say, ϕ (see Figure 4.5). Therefore, query q must be evaluated with q', where the computation q' upon the constraint representation is equivalent to the relational expression q. One then obtains $q'(\phi)$, which must be a finite representation of $q(R)$.

The class of geometric objects that can be represented depends on the type of constraint(s) allowed in the data model. The foregoing examples were built on the *linear constraint* data model, which uses only the $+$ operation in the expression of constraints. Introducing the multiplication allows one to represent high-order curves (e.g., circles and disks). Note that the choice of constraint data model (linear versus higher order) also has an impact on the cost of the algorithms used during query evaluation. In the following we limit the presentation to the linear constraint model, which turns out to be sufficient for representing and manipulating the spatial objects considered throughout this book.

The next section presents the linear constraint model. It precisely defines what is a symbolic relation under this model, and how these relations are manipulated. Two query languages are presented, which have equivalent expressive power.

4.2   THE LINEAR CONSTRAINT DATA MODEL

A constraint is a polynomial on variables x and y. The keyword *linear* suggests that the polynomial is linear in x and y. More precisely, we focus on geometric objects in the d-dimensional space $\mathbb{R}^d$, which can be represented with constraints using only the $+$ operation and the $\leq$ predicate. Any of the spatial objects considered so far in this book can be represented in this model.

We cannot handle high-order curves represented by a polynomial with degree larger than 1 because the $\times$ operation is not available. For instance, the unit disk (defined as $x^2 + y^2 \leq 1$) is not representable in the linear constraint data model. Adding the multiplication is possible, but this increases the complexity of evaluating queries (see the bibliographic notes).

In the following, we successively study the data representation, as well as the associated query languages. It is assumed that the reader is familiar with first-order logic.

4.2.1 Data Representation

As informally presented in the previous section, infinite sets of points are represented by formulas in a first-order language. Linear constraints are the atomic formulas of this first-order language $\mathcal{L}$. They consist of equations and inequalities of the form

$$\sum_{i=1}^{p} a_i\, x_i \Theta a_0$$

where Θ is a predicate among $=$ or $\leq$, x_i denotes variables, and a_i denotes integer constants. Note that a constraint can have rational coefficients. However, rationals can always be replaced by integer coefficients in such constraints. Further, the term $a_i x_i$ stands for $x_i + \cdots + x_i$ (a_i times). This implies that for constructing an atomic formula (a constraint) with this language one needs only variables taking their value in $\mathbb{R}$, integers, the $+$ operation, and the predicates $=$ and $\leq$.

Let $S \subseteq \mathbb{R}^k$ be a potentially infinite set of points in $\mathbb{R}^k$ space; that is, a relation at the abstract level with k variables (see Figure 4.5). Relation S is a *linear constraint relation* if there exists a formula $\varphi(x_1, \ldots, x_k)$ in $\mathcal{L}$ with k distinct free variables $x_1, \ldots, x_k$ such that $\varphi(p_1 \cdots p_k)$ is true iff point $P(p_1 \cdots p_k)$ is in S. φ is called a *constraint representation* of S. Equivalently, S is the interpretation of φ. In other words, the model can represent all point sets S such that there exists a first-order formula in our language whose interpretation is exactly S.

There exist several (actually, an infinite number of) possible representations for a same set of points S; namely, all equivalent first-order formulas whose interpretation is exactly S. We adopt in the following a specific form based on two features:

- *The formula is quantifier free.* This restriction is harmless, in that any formula in the language $\mathcal{L}$ where the variables take their values in $\mathbb{R}$ has an equivalent quantifier-free formula.
- *The formula is in DNF.*

All examples cited in the previous section gave a constraint representation based on a DNF, quantifier-free formula. A DNF formula $\varphi \equiv \bigvee_{i=1}^{k} \bigwedge_{j=1}^{\ell_i} \varphi_{i,j}$ is a constraint representation or *symbolic relation* of a set of points in $\mathbb{R}^k$ space. A symbolic relation is a finite set of *symbolic tuples*, which are conjunctions of atomic formulas $\varphi_{i,j}$.

$$\left\{ t_i \mid 1 \leq i \leq k, \quad t_i = \bigwedge_{j=1}^{\ell_i} \varphi_{i,j} \right\}$$

The representation in terms of DNF formulas enforces a specific view of spatial objects. Indeed, each symbolic relation is the union (disjunction) of a finite set of convex objects (symbolic tuples). In terms of 2D applications, this implies, for example, that the polygons are decomposed into convex component polygons (see Chapters 2 and 5).

The convexification does not restrict the class of spatial objects that can be represented. However, it imposes a decomposition of the objects into convex components prior to their manipulation. Other forms have been proposed (see the bibliographic notes).

4.2.2   Query Languages: First-Order Queries

We now consider the query languages for manipulating the (symbolic) relations previously introduced. Recall that we aim at generalizing the relational data model. The relational standard query language SQL is founded on two equivalent paradigms: *first-order queries* and *relational algebra*. We successively study two equivalent languages, also based on first-order queries and on an algebra of operations. The objective is to show that the result of a query applied to a linear constraint relation is always a linear constraint relation and can be evaluated at a reasonable cost.

Consider first-order queries. In the context of the traditional relational data model, this approach yields a language called *relational calculus*. A large subset of the SQL language can actually be seen as a user-friendly syntax of the relational calculus. For instance, the following query asks for the names of the states that contain County 94220, using the relational schema of Chapter 3.

$$\{state\text{-}name \mid \exists \ scode \ (State \ (scode, \ state\text{-}name)$$

$$\wedge \ County(94220, \ scode, \ \_))\}$$

The query defines a "pattern" to be satisfied by tuples of tables *State* and *County*. We look for pairs of tuples in *State* and *County*, respectively, such that

- Attribute *state-code* is identical in both tuples. This is simply expressed by using the same variable, *scode*.
- Attribute *county-code* in *County* is the constant value 94220.

The "anonymous variables" symbol (_) is used for attributes of no concern to the query. The result is a set of state names.

We can use first-order queries on DNF quantifier-free representations of linear constraint (infinite) relations, as previously defined. Consider again the relations *Road* and *Spat* of Figures 4.2 and 4.3. The following are first-order queries on these two relations, where $Spat(x, y)$ and $Road(x, y)$ denote the first-order formulas representing the relations.

- Query 1. *Intersection of Spat and Road*:

$$\{x, y \mid Spat(x, y) \wedge Road(x, y)\}$$

  The result was shown in Figure 4.4.
- Query 2. *Points in Road that are not in Spat*:

$$\{x, y \mid Road(x, y) \wedge \neg Spat(x, y)\}$$

  The result is shown in Figure 4.6 (thick segments).
- Query 3. *Points p_1 in Spat such that there exists a point p_2 in Road that is above p_1 along the y axis*:

$$\{x, y \mid \exists y' \ Spat(x, y) \wedge Road(x, y') \wedge y \leq y'\}$$

  The result is shown in Figure 4.7 (dark polygon).

This query language allows one to express various operations in a simple and natural way. However, two questions remain: (1) Can we always evaluate these queries? and (2) How much does evaluation cost? In answering the first question, consider the following issues:

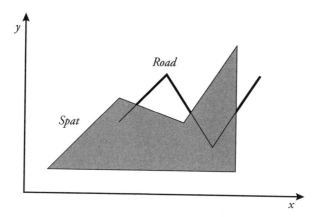

Figure 4.6   The difference between *Road* and *Spat*.

- *Closure:* Is the result of a query on linear constraint relations a linear constraint relation? As previously discussed in regard to the ADT approach, this property is crucial. Recall, for instance, that any relational query yields a relation.
- *Computability:* Is there an algorithm for evaluating any query expressible in the language?

Evaluating a query means producing a first-order formula in $\mathcal{L}$ as a finite representation of the result. The formula must be in DNF, and the quantifiers, if any, eliminated. Let's examine query evaluation in regard to the three previous example queries.

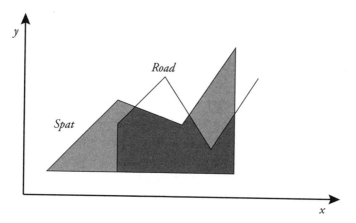

Figure 4.7   Points of *Spat* south of *Road*.

♦ *Query 1.* Replacing *Spat* and *Road* with their finite representations, φ_1 and φ_2, one obtains the formula

$$\psi \equiv \varphi_1(x, y) \land \varphi_2(x, y)$$

The result of the query is the interpretation of ψ; that is, the pair of points $[x, y]$ such that ψ is true. ψ is quantifier free. Hence, computing the result is reduced to transforming ψ in DNF.

♦ *Query 2.* The same technique (as for query 1) holds, except that the transformation of $\psi' \equiv \varphi_1 \land \neg\varphi_2$ in DNF is more complex.

♦ *Query 3.* The formula obtained by substituting the constraint representation for the relation's symbols contains an existential quantifier:

$$\exists y' \, \varphi_1(x, y) \land \varphi_2(x, y') \land y \leq y'$$

The query evaluation involves two steps: (1) apply the quantifier elimination algorithm (any formula ϕ has an equivalent quantifier-free formula ϕ', and there exists an algorithm to compute ϕ' from ϕ) and (2) transform the result in DNF.

The quantifier elimination property of the linear constraint data model guarantees that any first-order query can be evaluated in closed form; that is, that the query result is a DNF quantifier-free formula. It can also be shown that the cost of this procedure is polynomial in terms of the size of the database, which implies that efficient algorithms exist for evaluating queries.

4.2.3   *Query Languages: Algebraic Queries*

First-order languages (SQL can be seen as such a language) provide a declarative way to express queries. The user defines *what* she wants to obtain, not *how* the result is to be computed. The system is in charge of solving the "how" problems, such as access to data, operations on data, and the sequencing order of operations. A first step toward the evaluation of a declarative query is its transformation in a more procedural language, which provides a description of the operations that must be carried out. Operations belong to a predefined set such as that defined by the *relational algebra,* which allows one to express the same queries as the relational calculus (both languages have the same *expressive power*) but relies on a small set of operations on sets.

Let's now turn our attention to the algebraic counterpart of the first-order query language described for manipulating linear constraint relations. The relational algebra for manipulating (at the abstract level) finite or infinite relations consists of the classical *set operations* (*union* $\cup$, *intersection* $\cap$, and *set difference* $-$), as well as other important operations; namely, *selection* σ_F, where F is an atomic constraint, *projection* π, *join* $\bowtie$, and *Cartesian product* $\times$.

The definition of the operations on symbolic relations must match the semantics of the classical relational operations at the abstract level (infinite relations). Let R_1 and R_2 be two relations and e_1 and e_2 their respective constraint representation in the form of a symbolic relation (i.e., a set of symbolic tuples). The following are the semantics of each operation. The left-hand side denotes the operation at the abstract level; the right-hand side shows the semantics of the operation in terms of the symbolic representation e_1 of the input(s), and possibly e_2.

- $\sigma_F(R_1) = \{t_1 \wedge F, t_1 \in e_1\}$
- $R_1 \times R_2 = \{t_1 \wedge t_2 \mid t_1 \in e_1, t_2 \in e_2\}$
- $R_1 \bowtie R_2 = \{t_1 \wedge t_2 \mid t_1 \in e_1, t_2 \in e_2\}$
- $R_1 \cap R_2 = \{t_1 \wedge t_2 \mid t_1 \in e_1, t_2 \in e_2\}$
- $\pi_{\bar{x}}(R_1) = \{\pi_{\bar{x}}(t) \mid t \in e_1\}$, where $\pi_{\bar{x}}(t)$ denotes the projection on the variables in $\bar{x}$ of the conjunction of constraints t. It is obtained by an algorithm that eliminates variables from a formula defining a convex polyhedron. Recall that a symbolic tuple t has for an interpretation a convex polyhedron.
- $R_1 \cup R_2 = e_1 \cup e_2$
- $R_1 - R_2 = \{t_1 \wedge t_2 \mid t_1 \in e_1, t_2 \in (e_2)^c\}$, where $(e_i)^c$ is the set of tuples or disjuncts of a DNF formula corresponding to $\neg e_i$.

As can be seen from these definitions, the purpose of the algebraic operators on the constraint representation is to simulate standard relational operators applied to infinite relations, and therefore to deliver a correct mathematical representation of the result that complies with the constraint representation.

The expressions for $\bowtie$, $\cap$, and $\times$ are identical. Nevertheless, they correspond to different operations. They differ according to the variables of tuples in each relation. Variables are identical (respectively, partly distinct and pairwise distinct) in the case of intersection (respec-

	φ_1	
x	$\geq$	4
x	$\leq$	6
y	$\geq$	3
y	$\leq$	5
$x \;-y$	$=$	1
x	$\geq$	6
x	$\leq$	8
y	$\geq$	2
y	$\leq$	5
$3x \;+2y$	$=$	28
x	$\geq$	8
x	$\leq$	10
y	$\geq$	2
y	$\leq$	5
$3x \;-2y$	$=$	20

	φ_2	
$x \;-y$	$\geq$	0
y	$\geq$	1
$x \;+3y$	$\leq$	16
$3x \;-2y$	$\leq$	15
x	$\leq$	9
y	$\geq$	1
$3x \;-2y$	$\geq$	15

Figure 4.8 The finite representations of *Road* and *Spat*.

tively, join, Cartesian product). The join operator generalizes both the intersection and Cartesian product.

The following are examples of selection, intersection, and projection processed on the *Road* and *Spat* relations. Included are the finite representations φ_1 and φ_2 of these relations. φ_1 has three tuples, whereas φ_2 has two tuples. Each tuple is represented in a separate box, where the $\wedge$ between atomic constraints has been omitted (see Figure 4.8).

The result of $\sigma_{y \leq 5}(Spat)$ is shown in Figure 4.9.

	φ_2	
$x \;-y$	$\geq$	0
y	$\geq$	1
$x \;+3y$	$\leq$	16
$3x \;-2y$	$\leq$	15
x	$\leq$	9
y	$\geq$	1
$3x \;-2y$	$\geq$	15

$\sigma_{y \leq 5}(Spat) \Rightarrow$

	φ_2	
$x \;-y$	$\geq$	0
y	$\geq$	1
$x \;+3y$	$\leq$	16
$3x \;-2y$	$\leq$	15
y	$\leq$	5
x	$\leq$	9
y	$\geq$	1
$3x \;-2y$	$\geq$	15
y	$\leq$	5

Figure 4.9 The result of $\sigma_{y \leq 5}(Spat)$.

The computation of the result is trivial. The constraint $y \leq 5$ is simply added to each symbolic tuple. The formula in the result defines all pairs of $[x, y]$ values that satisfy *both* the constraints defining *Spat* and $y \leq 5$.

The result of the intersection between *Spat* and *Road* is shown in Table 4.2. It consists of all possible pairs of symbolic tuples from *Spat* and *Road*. The σ and $\cap$ operations are purely symbolic. They create

Table 4.2 The intersection of *Road* and *Spat*.

Road $\cap$ *Spat*

x		$\geq$	4
x		$\leq$	6
	y	$\geq$	3
	y	$\leq$	5
x	$-y$	$=$	1
x	$-y$	$\geq$	0
	y	$\geq$	1
x	$+3y$	$\leq$	16
$3x$	$-2y$	$\leq$	15

x		$\geq$	6
x		$\leq$	8
	y	$\geq$	2
	y	$\leq$	5
$3x$	$+2y$	$=$	28
x	$-y$	$\geq$	0
	y	$\geq$	1
x	$+3y$	$\leq$	16
$3x$	$-2y$	$\leq$	15

x		$\geq$	8
x		$\leq$	10
	y	$\geq$	2
	y	$\leq$	5
$3x$	$-2y$	$=$	20
x	$-y$	$\geq$	0
	y	$\geq$	1
x	$+3y$	$\leq$	16
$3x$	$-2y$	$\leq$	15

Road $\cap$ *Spat*

x		$\geq$	4
x		$\leq$	6
	y	$\geq$	3
	y	$\leq$	5
x	$-y$	$=$	1
x		$\leq$	9
	y	$\geq$	1
$3x$	$-2y$	$\geq$	15

x		$\geq$	6
x		$\leq$	8
	y	$\geq$	2
	y	$\leq$	5
$3x$	$+2y$	$=$	28
x		$\leq$	9
	y	$\geq$	1
$3x$	$-2y$	$\geq$	15

x		$\geq$	8
x		$\leq$	10
	y	$\geq$	2
	y	$\leq$	5
$3x$	$-2y$	$=$	20
x		$\leq$	9
	y	$\geq$	1
$3x$	$-2y$	$\geq$	15

$$
\begin{array}{c}
\underline{\qquad\qquad E_1 \qquad\qquad} \\
\begin{array}{rll}
y & \leq & x \\
y & \geq & 1 \\
y & \leq & -x/3 \;+16/3 \\
y & \geq & 3x/2 \;-15/2 \\
\hline
0 & \leq & -x \quad +9 \\
y & \geq & 1 \\
y & \leq & 3x/2 \;-15/2
\end{array}
\end{array}
$$

Figure 4.10   First step of $\pi_x(Spat)$: isolation of y.

tuples by concatenating constraints from the inputs without modifying the constraints themselves.

The computation of the projection is more complex. The following is the computation of the projection $\pi_x(Spat)$ in two steps (see Figures 4.10 and 4.11). First, y is isolated in each constraint, as shown in Figure 4.10. In the second step, y is eliminated, as shown in Figure 4.11.

An important observation is that tuples in the result of an operation might be inconsistent. Indeed, it is possible that the conjunction of constraints in a tuple is not satisfiable by any pair $[x, y]$. This is the case, for example, for the second tuple of the intersection between *Road* and *Spat* (Table 4.2): there is no intersection between the first line segment of *Road* and the second polygon of *Spat* (Figure 4.4). Such inconsistent tuples are also said to be empty. It may also happen that tuples in the result are redundant. The result of the previous projection contains a symbolic tuple $(x \leq 15 \wedge x \leq 13 \wedge x \leq 7)$, which reduces

$$
\begin{array}{ccc}
\underline{\qquad\qquad\qquad \pi_x(E_1) \qquad\qquad\qquad} & & \underline{\qquad \pi_x(E_1) \qquad} \\
\begin{array}{rcl}
1 & \leq & x \\
3x/2 \;-15/2 & \leq & x \\
1 & \leq & -x/3 \;+16/3 \\
3x/2 \;-15/2 & \leq & -x/3 \;+16/3 \\
\hline
0 & \leq & -x \quad +9 \\
1 & \leq & 3x/2 \;-15/2
\end{array}
& \Rightarrow &
\begin{array}{rcl}
x & \geq & 1 \\
x & \leq & 15 \\
x & \leq & 13 \\
x & \leq & 7 \\
\hline
x & \leq & 9 \\
x & \geq & 17/3
\end{array}
\end{array}
$$

Figure 4.11   Second step of $\pi_x(Spat)$: elimination of y.

$$\frac{\pi_x(E_1)}{\begin{array}{ccc} x & \leq & 7 \\ x & \geq & 1 \end{array}}$$

x	$\leq$	7
x	$\geq$	1
x	$\leq$	9
x	$\geq$	17/3

Figure 4.12   The result of $\pi_x(Spat)$ after simplification.

to $(x \leq 7)$. Therefore, a semantic evaluation, denoted *simplification*, must be carried out at some point in the query execution process in order to eliminate redundancies and to detect inconsistencies (empty tuples). This operation, applied to the result of $\pi_x(Spat)$, would yield that shown in Figure 4.12.

The result consists of two intervals, $[1, 7]$ and $[17/3, 9]$, on the x axis, whose union is $[1, 9]$. The *simplify* operation can be implemented by algorithms whose complexity depends on the number of variables. In dimension 2 (two variables), there exist simple and efficient algorithmic techniques, which are presented in Chapter 5.

In summary, because of the evaluation technique previously outlined, it becomes possible to express queries upon spatial data with purely relational query languages. This approach permits one to "see" a geographic object at a high level of abstraction. It is no longer necessary for the end user to worry about the spatial type of objects or about the specific function that must be used to carry out an operation. An intersection query, for instance, is expressed the same way on lines, points, polygons, and so on. In addition, as illustrated in the following, the model extends naturally to higher dimensions.

However, the representation with constraints presents some limitations. One of them is the necessity of representing spatial data as first-order formulas, which entails a noncompact representation with respect to the common vector data structures. For instance, when the DNF normal form is adopted, polygons need to be decomposed into convex components in the database (performing such a decomposition at run time would be prohibitively costly).

A more important shortcoming arises from the limitation in the expressive power of first-order queries in the aforementioned language, denoted $\mathcal{L} = \{\leq, +, 0, 1\}$. The distance operation, for instance, is not expressable in the language because we cannot use the multiplication. In addition, some topological relationships are expressible, but with somewhat complex expressions. Extending the language by adding common topological operators leads to some theoretical issues still under investigation. In the following section, we illustrate the application of the linear constraint data model to the two main approaches in geographic data modeling: *entity based* and *field based*.

4.3 MODELING ENTITY-BASED DATA

Recall (Chapter 1) that in this approach we focus on *geographic entities*. With each spatial object is associated an alphanumeric description (descriptive attributes) and a geometric attribute. Actually, this has been our view of spatial data from the outset, and in particular throughout Chapter 3.

We develop in this section the modeling of geographic entities with a constraint-based approach. We first describe the extension of relational tables to *non–first normal form* relations, which allow one to "nest" the relation that represents the geometric attribute as an attribute of the tuple that corresponds to a geographic entity. We provide schemas and queries based on this modeling, using examples found in Chapter 3.

4.3.1 Nested Relations

In the entity-based approach, one usually makes a clear distinction between the geographic data model used for modeling geographic entities and the spatial data model used for modeling geometric information. The constraint model treats both representations uniformly. Sets of homogeneous entities, as well as sets of points, are represented as *relations*.

A geographic entity corresponds to a (potentially infinite) set of points. We would like to be able to gather all points of an entity and to represent this set of points as the value of the geometric attribute. Unfortunately, with the relational model, a tuple would correspond to a single point. This is because the model is restricted to "flat" tuples, where the value of each attribute is an atomic value and therefore cannot be a *set*. We need to break this limitation by introducing the possibility of representing an attribute value as a set (a relation). We therefore

Table 4.3 The *Land_Use* relation with nested point sets.

Land_Use

region_name	land_use_type	geometry
R1	forest	$\{(1, 1), (1, 1.0001), (1, 1.0002), \ldots$ $(3, 2), (3, 2.0001), \ldots (4, 4) \ldots\}$
R2	grass	$\{(12, 3), (12, 3.0001), \ldots$ $(15, 6), \ldots (15, 6.0006), \ldots\}$

introduce the possibility of nesting a relation as a value of an attribute. Such relations are called *nested relations*.

Table 4.3 depicts an instance of the *Land_Use* relation, where the geometric attribute is represented, according to the constraint paradigm, as an enumeration of an infinite set of points. As for spatial abstract data types, we "integrate" geometric data in the "flat" tuple that lists the attributes of a given entity. The difference is that we do not require new types, but simply use another relation, which is "nested" within the first.

The extension of the relational data model with nested relations has been studied for a long time. A nested relation can itself contain sub-nested relations, and there is a priori no limit to the number of nesting levels. In the following, we restrict the number of nesting levels to 1, which is sufficient for the modeling of most geographic entities. The nested relation holds a possibly infinite set of tuples, one per point of the geographic entity. The actual internal representation must in fact use the finite representation by constraints of infinite point sets, as illustrated in Table 4.4.[10] This is, however, transparent to the user.

A geographic relation can now be defined as a standard relation, except that we can use the additional type $\mathcal{R}(x_1, x_2, \ldots x_d)$, which denotes a nested relation with d attributes, each representing a coordinate in $\mathbb{R}$. The nested relation holds the set of points in the d-dimensional space. For example, the following is the definition of the *Land_Use* relation.

---

10. In the example of the table, for each tuple, the set of constraints is a singleton: the geometry of the entity is a single convex polygon. However, there could be several tuples in the nested relation (several conjunctions of constraints), implying that the geometry is made of several convex components.

Table 4.4   The *Land_Use* relation with nested point sets.

Land_Use

region_name	*land_use_type*	*geometry*
R1	forest	$\{x \leq 1 \wedge x \geq -1$ $\wedge y \leq 1 \wedge y \geq -1\}$
R2	grass	$\{x \geq 1 \wedge y \geq -1$ $\wedge x + y - 2 \leq 0\}$

Create Table *Land_Use*
  (region_name **varchar (30)**,
  land_use_type **varchar (30)**,
  geometry $\mathcal{R}(x, y)$,
  Primary Key *(region_name))*

The specification of the schemas of Chapter 3 with nested constraint relations is similar to that proposed in the context of extended relational models. Hence, we omit the full list of table definition commands, and skip directly to the expression of queries.

4.3.2   Queries

The query language must be capable of expressing queries that simultaneously filter the entities on descriptive attributes and nested relations. We use a variant of SQL, the syntax of which has been slightly modified. The language features are illustrated by a sample of queries on the example database.

SPAT-ADMR1. All highways going through the State of California.

A relational expression for this query includes a selection (State of California) and several joins, as follows:

♦ Two joins between, respectively, *Highway* and *HighwaySection*, and *HighwaySection* and *Section*. These are standard relational joins on descriptive attributes.

♦ A join (actually an intersection) between the nested relations *Section.geometry* and *State.geometry* to keep the highway sections overlapping a state. This is also a relational join, but it concerns infinite extensions and must therefore be evaluated with constraint manipulations, as described in the previous section.

In the SQL variant that follows, we use variables that represent tuples ranging over a relation, whether finite or infinite. The difference with SQL syntax comes from the introduction of the keyword **in**. Expression *s1* **in** *State* defines the variable *s1*, which ranges over *State* (a tuple of relation *State*). In the standard SQL, it would be expressed as *State s1*; expression *p1* **in** *s1.geometry* denotes a point (*p1*) in *s1* geometry. More precisely, this expression defines a tuple (a variable) *p1*, which ranges over the nested relation *s1.geometry*. Conceptually, point *p1* ranges over the set of points of the entity referred to by *s1*. The last two **and** clauses select the highways' sections that share at least one point in their respective geometric extensions.

select	**distinct** *h1.highway_name*
from	*s1* **in** *State*, *h1* **in** *Highway*, *h2* **in** *HighwaySection*,
	s2 **in** *Section*, *p1* **in** *s1.geometry*, *p2* **in** *s2.geometry*
where	*s1.state_name* = 'California'
and	*h1.highway_code* = *h2.highway_code*
and	*h2.section_code* = *s2.section_code*
and	*p1.x* = *p2.x*
and	*p1.y* = *p2.y*

Apart from the use of the keyword **in** with variables on relations, the syntax is standard SQL, as are the semantics. We qualify a highway to the result if it is possible to instantiate variables *s1, s2, p1, p2, h1,* and *h2* to some tuple in their respective ranges such that the **where** clause is true.

SPAT-ADM-LU1. Display of all residential areas in the County of San Jose. The query is expressed as a relational selection and a join on nested relations. The result consists of all points common to both the geometry of a *County* object and the geometry of a *Land_Use* object. Hence, we simply have to keep in the **select** clause one of the variables that ranges on the nested relations.

```
select    p1
from      c in County, l in Land_Use, p1 in c.geometry,
          p2 in l.geometry
where     county_name = 'San Jose'
and       land_use_type = 'living area'
and       p1.x = p2.x
and       p1.y = p2.y
```

SPAT-ADM-LU2. Overlay of the themes of counties and land use.
This query is expressed as follows:

```
select    county_name, land_use_type, {p1}
from      c in County, l in Land_Use, p1 in c.geometry,
          p2 in l.geometry
where     p1.x = p2.x
and       p1.y = p2.y
```

The expression $\{p1\}$ denotes a nested point set for the geometry of each parcel resulting from the overlay.

INTER-ADM7. Description of the county pointed to on the screen.
This query is expressed as follows:

```
select    county_name, population
from      c in County, p in c.geometry
where     p.x = @point.x
and       p.y = @point.y
```

INTER-ADM8. Counties that intersect a given rectangle on the screen.
This query is expressed as follows:

```
select    county_name, population
from      c in County, p in c.geometry
where     p.x = @rect.x
and       p.y = @rect.y
```

The query syntax is the same for point and window queries. Indeed, as mentioned previously, we do not bother about the type of the point sets manipulated. Compare this to the version in Chapter 3 in which the appropriate function has to be chosen, depending on whether the argument is a point or a rectangle.

INTER-ADM9. Parts of the counties that are within a given rectangle on the screen.

This query is expressed as follows:

select $\{p\}$
from c **in** *County, p* **in** *c.geometry*
where $p.x = @rect.x$
and $p.y = @rect.y$

INTER-R5. Description of the section pointed to on the screen.
This query is expressed as follows:

select   *section_name, number_lanes*
from s **in** *Section, p* **in** *s.geometry*
where $p.x = @point.x$
and $p.y = @point.y$

4.4   MODELING FIELD-BASED DATA AND MOVING OBJECTS

Although all examples from the previous section were based on 2D data, a nice feature of the constraint data model is to permit the representation and manipulation of geometric objects in arbitrary dimension. For instance, a convex polytope in dimension three with n faces is represented by the intersection of n half-spaces (this is actually a generalization of the definition of a convex polygon with half-planes). A half-space is a constraint over three variables—say, x, y, and z—expressed as follows:

$$\alpha x + \beta y + \gamma z + \theta \leq 0$$

The ability to represent and manipulate objects embedded in a 3D space turns out to be useful in modeling *field-based data* (see Chapter 2), which considers phenomena as a continuous function defined on space. Under this point of view, there is no longer an identity associated with a set of points. Instead, an attribute value is associated with each point: the function value at this point.

To illustrate how such data can be modeled with constraints, we study in this section two applications: *elevation data* and *moving objects*.

We describe how such objects can be directly modeled with the linear constraint data model as infinite, flat relations.

4.4.1 Elevation Data

Digital elevation models (DEMs) (see Chapter 2) can be simply and elegantly formalized with the constraint data model. The representation of an object as a point set P in a d-dimensional space can take advantage of the fundamental property that one of the attributes (coordinates) can be defined as a function of a subset of the other attributes. Moreover, this function is a *linear* interpolation based on some finite set of sample values.

Consider the example of a tile (triangle) in a triangulated irregular network (TIN), as shown in Figure 4.13. It can be represented as follows:

$$c_i(x, y) \wedge h = f(x, y),$$

where c_i denotes a conjunction of inequalities on (x, y) representing the triangle (a convex polygon), and $h = f(x, y)$ is an equality constraint among the variables h, x, and y, f being a linear function of x and y. As depicted in Figure 4.13, this tile can be seen as consisting of two parts. First, a conjunction of inequalities in 2D space (the c_i) defines a "cylinder" in 3D space. Second, this cylinder is "cut" by a hyperplane [equality $h = f(x, y)$].

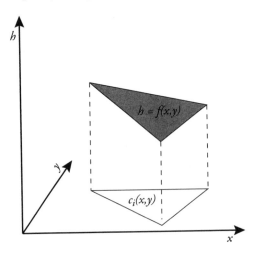

Figure 4.13   The tile of a TIN.

More generally, a TIN defines a partition of the 2D plane into triangles T_i, a height being given to each of the triangle vertices. The interpolated height h of an arbitrary point p in the plane is usually computed by first finding T_i such that T_i contains p. The h value is linearly interpolated from the heights of the three vertices of T_i. This latter function depends only on i, and can be defined as a linear function $f_i(x, y)$, valid only for points in T_i. Hence, the natural and simple symbolic representation of the 3D point set (relation) *TIN* in the linear constraint model is

$$TIN(x, y, h) = \bigvee_i t_i(x, y) \wedge h = f_i(x, y),$$

where $t_i(x, y)$ is the symbolic representation of the triangle T_i (as a conjunction of three inequalities).

4.4.2   *Moving Objects*

Moving objects in 2D space are objects whose location depends on time. Consider points moving in 2D space. If their location is only known at some instant in time, the trajectory can be approximated by a sequence of connected segments in 3D space whose axes are respectively the x and y coordinates of Earth's surface and the time dimension t. Although originated from a quite distinct area, the case of moving objects shares some mathematical properties with TINs; namely, one or several of the variables can be expressed as linear functions of the others.

A trajectory of a moving point in 2D space can be represented by a sample of points in 3D space (x, y, t). The full trajectory can be approximated from these points using linear interpolation. The trajectory of the moving point, depicted in Figure 4.14, can be represented in the following way:

$$x = 10t \; \wedge \; y = 5t \; \wedge \; 0 \leq t \leq 1$$

$$\vee$$

$$y = 5t \; \wedge \; x = 10 \; \wedge \; 5 \leq y \leq 10$$

$$\vee$$

$$3x = 10t + 10 \; \wedge \; 3y = 5t + 20 \; \wedge \; 2 \leq t \leq 5$$

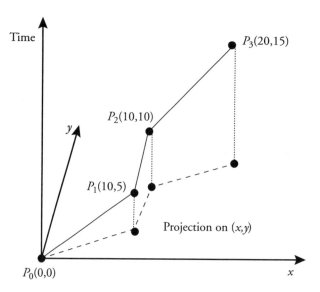

Figure 4.14   A trajectory.

At time $t = 0$, the moving point is located at point P_0. It then moves from P_0 to P_3, where it arrives at a time $t = 5$, via P_1 ($t = 1$) and P_2 ($t = 2$). More generally, assume that the position of the object is known at finitely many time instants. This defines finitely many time intervals T_i. If the speed of the object is assumed to be constant during each time interval,[11] its position at any time t has for coordinates $x = v_i t + x_i$ and $y = v_i t + y_i$, where i is the index of the interval T_i that contains t and v_i is the speed of the object during that interval, and where (x_i, y_i) are chosen appropriately so that the position of the object is correct at both the beginning and end of the interval. Thus, the trajectory $Traj(x, y, t)$ can be symbolically represented in the linear constraint model as follows:

$$Traj(x, y, t) = \bigvee_i t_i(t) \wedge x = f_i(t) \wedge y = g_i(t),$$

where $t_i(t)$ are the constraints defining the time interval T_i and f_i, g_i are the linear equations previously defined.

---

11. This simplifying assumption leads to the representation of spatial objects with piecewise linear functions, a feature that, as seen throughout this book, serves to reduce the complexity of manipulating such objects.

4.4.3   *Queries on Field-Based Data and Moving Points*

The use of constraints leads to a simple logical data model for field-based data and moving objects, based on infinite sets that can be manipulated via definition using constraints. We conclude this presentation in illustrating the power and simplicity of the constraint data model from an end-user point of view with some examples of queries.

Let the *interpolation key* (*ikey*, for short) of a relation be the subset of attributes used as a basis for computing the interpolated values: (x, y) for terrain modeling and t for trajectories. We consider a database schema with the following relations:

- A map *Map* $(x, y, name)$ gives the ground occupancy or land use (attribute *name*), such as "forest" or "pasture" at location (x, y). The *ikey* of the relation is (x, y).
- The trajectories $Traj_1(t, x, y, a)$ and $Traj_2(t, x, y, a)$ of two airplanes, which give the location (x, y) and the altitude a of the airplanes as a function of t, which is the *ikey*.
- $TIN_h(x, y, h)$ for the altitude above sea level. Its *ikey* is (x, y).

It is important to observe that as end users, we need not worry about constraints, first-order formulas, query evaluation techniques, or even the dimension of spatial data. We can simply consider the relations in the schema as storing finite or infinite extensions, and use a classical relational query language such as SQL. In other words, the database can be queried in a purely declarative way. As illustrated by the following queries, this yields a language that is easy to use and to understand. We start with some basic queries on trajectories.

- *Query 1.* Which location was airplane 1 flying over at time t_1? This query is expressed as follows:

  select x, y
  from $Traj_1$
  where $t = t_1$

- *Query 2.* When was airplane 2 flying over point (a, b)? This query is expressed as follows:

  select t
  from $Traj_2$
  where $x = a$ **and** $y = b$

♦ *Query 3.* When and where were the airplanes in the same position at the same time? This can be expressed as a join on x, y, and t. Hopefully the planes do not share the same altitude, so there is no join on a. This query is expressed as follows:

select $T1.t,\ T1.x,\ T1.y$
from $Traj_1\ T1,\ Traj_2\ T2$
where $T1.x = T2.x$ **and** $T1.y = T2.y$
and $T1.t = T2.t$

The previous queries are easily expressed, mainly because the internal mechanisms are not of our concern. *Point location* and *windowing* are standard operations that can both be expressed with a selection. We now switch to the slightly more complex case of TIN.

♦ *Query 4.* Give the trajectory of airplane 1 and its altitude with respect to ground level. Here we make a join on (x, y) in order to obtain, for each point of the trajectory, the elevation h of the ground above sea level. By substracting h from the altitude of the plane (which is recorded with respect to sea level), we get the required information.

select $t1.x,\ t1.y,\ a - h$
from $TIN_h\ t1,\ Traj_1\ t2$
where $t1.x = t2.x$ **and** $t1.y = t2.y$

♦ *Query 5.* Give the contour line on the ground for $h = 1000$ (isoline with altitude 1000). This query is expressed as follows:

select x, y
from TIN_h
where $h = 1000$

♦ *Query 6.* Show the trajectory of airplane 1 with the elevation h of each point the airplane is flying over. This query is expressed as follows:

select x, y, t, h
from $TIN_h\ t1,\ Traj_1\ t2$
where $t1.x = t2.x$ **and** $t1.y = t2.y$

This query is a natural join on x and y, $Traj_1 \bowtie TIN_h$. Observe that it naturally defines a function $h = f(t)$.

- *Query 7.* Show the forests whose altitude ranges between 1000 and 2000 meters. This query is expressed as follows:

select	*m.x, m.y*
from	*TIN$_h$ t, Map m*
where	*t.x = m.x* **and** *t.y = m.y*
and	*h* **between** *1000* **and** *2000*
and	*name =* 'forest'

4.5 BIBLIOGRAPHIC NOTES

The constraint data model was first introduced by Kanellakis, Kuper, and Revesz [KKR90], a more complete version of which can be found in [KKR95]. The use of half-spaces as a single primitive for representing multidimensional data has been suggested by many authors. For example, Günther [GW87, Gün88] uses convex polygons to represent spatial data in any dimension. A consistent and exhaustive presentation of constraint databases and of the research being currently conducted in this area is given in [KLP00].

[KKR90] introduced first-order formulas without quantifiers for data representation. The semantics of a formula is naturally defined as the set of values for which the formula is true. As explained in this chapter, this provides a finite representation to infinite extensions. The vocabulary used to construct the formulas has a strong impact on the class of spatial objects that can be represented. [KKR90] studies several classes of constraints, among which the following are of particular interest to spatial data:

- *Dense linear constraint* formulas are built with the language $FO(<, +, 0, 1)$, interpreted in a dense domain such as $\mathbb{Q}$ or $\mathbb{R}$. This allows the representation of *semilinear sets*.
- *Dense polynomial constraint* formulas are built with the language $FO(<, +, \times, 0, 1)$, interpreted in $\mathbb{Q}$ or $\mathbb{R}$. This allows the representation of *semialgebraic sets*.

In [KKR90], as well as in most succeeding proposals [PVV94, GS97b, GS97a], the normal form of formulas is DNF without quantifiers. This has an impact on the size of the database and on the complexity of the query languages. This is not a prerequisite, and some other forms might be of interest. [GRS98b] proposes, for instance, the *convex normal form with holes* as a practical means of representing polygons with holes.

[KKR90] also investigates the classical formalisms for relational query languages, mainly *first-order queries* (which yield the relational calculus in the classical relational setting), and *fixpoint logic* (which introduces recursion). A fundamental result is that first-order queries on semilinear or semialgebraic instances can always be evaluated in polynomial time in the size of the database (data complexity). The property is essential, because it guarantees that there exists an algorithm for evaluating queries at a reasonable cost.

However, if we measure the complexity with respect to the size of the query (query complexity), the semialgebraic case gives rise to a doubly exponential complexity, which means that in practical situations only very simple queries can be asked. Therefore, the linear constraint model with first-order queries constitutes the most promising model for practical applications.

As in the traditional approach, there exist algebraic languages equivalent to first-order queries, presented, for instance, in [GK96]. The algebra used in this chapter is from [GST94].

The constraint paradigm offers a convenient mathematical framework for studying some of the fundamental issues related to spatial logical database modeling and spatial query languages. One of these issues is the complexity of query evaluation, which, as previously discussed, is tractable in the case of the linear constraint model. A second important issue is *expressive power* of the query language. First-order queries are somewhat limited because common operations might not be easily expressible, or expressible at all. Adjacency, for example, is definable, but the expression is quite complex. The *distance* operator relies on multiplication and thus cannot be expressed. As a simple solution, one might add the *distance* operation to the language, but this way one loses the closure property; that is, for example, computing the part of a region that is less than 100 m from a given point is likely to yield an object that cannot be represented by linear constraints. The extension of constraint query languages to useful operations for spatial data is ongoing work [VGV95, VGV96, DGVV97]. Some other aspects of spatial modeling that have been revisited with the constraint paradigm are topological information and topological queries [KPV95, KPV97, KV99, PSV99, SV98].

Most of the material published so far in the area of constraint databases addresses some of the theoretical issues previously outlined. Recently, the practical applications of the model (in particular, for GIS) have been investigated, and some prototypes have started to emerge. The need to introduce nesting for entity-based data has been independently acknowledged in [GRSS97] and [BBC98]. The DEDALE prototype, based on the nested data model, is presented in [GRS98b, GRS00]. Among other constraint-based prototypes, it is worth mentioning C^3 [BS97] and COSMOS [KRSS98], which also rely on nesting.

The model is also a candidate for spatio-temporal data modeling, a topic of growing interest in the database community [SWCD97, EGSV98, EGSV99, Kou97, GKS00]. Spatio-temporal data models based on constraints have been proposed in [GRS98a, CR99]. The constraint-based modeling of field-based data is from [GRS00]. Spatio-temporal and field-based data illustrate the ability of the constraint model to extend to higher dimensions while keeping the same representation and query languages.

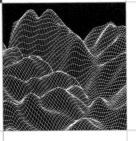

5

Computational Geometry

"Then addressing Herbert—'Do you know the first principles of geometry?' he asked.

'Slightly, captain,' replied Herbert, who did not wish to put himself forward.

'You remember what are the properties of two similar triangles?'

'Yes,' replied Herbert; 'their homologous sides are proportional.'

'Well, my boy, I have just constructed two similar right-angled triangles; the first, the smallest, has for its sides the perpendicular pole, the distance which separates the little stick from the foot of the pole and my visual ray for its hypotenuse; the second has for its sides the perpendicular cliff, the height of which we wish to measure, the distance which separates the little stick from the bottom of the cliff, and my visual ray also forms its hypotenuse, which proves to be prolongation of that of the first triangle.'"

JULES VERNE
Mysterious Island, Part I, Chapter 14

CONTENTS

5.1   AN INTRODUCTION TO COMPUTATIONAL GEOMETRY

This chapter introduces algorithmic techniques for implementing the spatial database operations presented in Chapter 3. These techniques belong to the field of *computational geometry*, a branch of algorithmics dealing with computation on geometric objects. Due to the growth of applications involving such objects in the past two decades, many efforts have been devoted to design new algorithms for emerging problems and to improve existing ones. Spatial databases for GIS are only one example of the application of computational geometry. Other applications include graphical user interfaces (GUIs), robotics, and computer-aided design and manufacturing (CAD/CAM).

We focus here on computational geometry for spatial operations as required in spatial databases (see Chapter 3). The interested reader will find in the bibliographic notes information on other topics from computational geometry.

This chapter is organized as follows. Section 5.2 introduces the necessary concepts and notations from algorithmics. Algorithm description and analysis are introduced, as well as an example of data structure for geometric algorithms. Section 5.3 reviews some well-known general strategies for computational geometry algorithms. Section 5.4 studies polygon partitioning, a fundamental problem in spatial databases. The second part of the chapter is dedicated to algorithms for spatial database operations (Section 5.5). A variety of useful algorithms are reviewed, such as checking whether a point is enclosed in a given polygon, computing the intersection of two polygons, and computing the area of a polygon.

5.2   BACKGROUND

Algorithmics is the branch of computer science that consists of *designing* and *analyzing* computer algorithms. The design of an algorithm involves (1) its description at an abstract level by means of a pseudo-language, and (2) the proof that the algorithm is correct (i.e., that it solves the given problem in all cases). Analysis deals with evaluating the performance of an algorithm; for example, its cost in time, a task called *complexity analysis*.

Roughly speaking, an algorithm is a sequence of operations performed on data that have to be organized in *data structures*. A careful
design of data structures is required for optimizing the operations for a
given algorithm.

5.2.1   Basic Concepts of Algorithms

The following components are the cornerstones of algorithms: the
model of computation, the language used for describing the algorithm,
and the performance evaluation. An algorithm is an abstraction of a
program to be executed on a physical machine. Any algorithm must
therefore be described with respect to a convenient abstraction of this
physical machine. Such an abstraction, or *model of computation*, allows
one to describe what type of information a machine can handle, as well
as the operations available.

It is customary to use the *Random Access Machine* (RAM) model,
where each unit of information is assumed to be accessed in constant
time, independently of location. Real numbers, with the usual arithmetic and comparison operations ($+$, $-$, $/$, $\times$, $<$, $=$), are usually
chosen.

Once the model of computation has been defined, an algorithm can
be described using the primitive operations. One gives a high-level (yet
equivalent) description using a simple language (or pseudo-language)
whose syntax is close to a programming language such as PASCAL or
C. The reader is assumed to be familiar with the usual constructions of
such languages, such as **while** and **for** loops or **if-then-else** tests.

The performance evaluation of an algorithm is obtained by totaling
the number of occurrences of each operation when running the algorithm. For the sake of simplicity and ease of expression, one gets rid of
unnecessary details in the computation. Some operations are neglected,
whereas a cost constant with respect to the input size is assumed for
other operations (denoted *key operations*). Algorithm evaluation is a
function $f(n, c_1, c_2, \ldots, c_m)$, whose arguments are (1) the size n of
the input and (2) the cost c_i of each key operation. The focus is on the
dependence of computation time on input size rather than on the cost
of each operation, which is implementation and machine dependent.
Therefore, the performance is evaluated as a function of the input size
n and is to be considered modulo a multiplicative constant. Given these
conventions, the following notations are commonly used:

- ◆ *Upper bound.* A function $g(n)$ of the input size is said to be $O(f(n))$ (reads "O of f of n") if there exist a constant C and an integer n_0 such that $g(n) \leq Cf(n)$ for all $n > n_0$.
- ◆ *Lower bound.* A function $g(n)$ is said to be $\Omega(f(n))$ if there exist C and n_0 such that $g(n) \geq Cf(n)$ for all $n > n_0$.
- ◆ *Same order.* A function $g(n)$ is said to be $\Theta(f(n))$ if there exist C_1, C_2, and n_0 such that $C_1 f(n) \leq g(n) \leq C_2 f(n)$ for all $n > n_0$.

These notations are used to characterize the complexity of an algorithm, as explained in the following section and illustrated in Section 5.2.3.

5.2.2 Algorithm Analysis

The complexity of an algorithm is a function $g(n)$ that gives the upper bound of the number of operations performed by an algorithm when the input size is n. The number of operations is also called algorithm "running time." However, two interpretations of upper bounds can be made:

- ◆ *Worst-case complexity.* In this case, the running time for any input of a given size will be lower than the upper bound, except possibly for some values of the input where the maximum is reached.
- ◆ *Average-case complexity.* In this case, $g(n)$ is the average number of operations over all problem instances for a given size.

The average-case complexity is more representative of the actual behavior of an algorithm. Unfortunately, it is quite difficult to estimate, as the statistical behavior of the input is not easily predictable. Most of the analyses give, therefore, a worst-case complexity. It is important to keep in mind that the practical behavior of an algorithm may turn out to be better than the value estimated from a worst-case analysis.

Most of the time, the complexity $g(n)$ is approximated by its family $O(f(n))$, where $f(n)$ is one of the following functions: n (linear complexity), $\log n$ (logarithmic complexity), n^a, $a \geq 2$ (polynomial complexity), a^n (exponential complexity). An algorithm whose complexity is linear (logarithmic, and so on) with the input size is referred to as a linear algorithm.

However, even though this approximation provides a useful classification of algorithms, it leads to a loose estimate of the actual complexity because it does not take into account the multiplicative constant C and the fact that the complexity is true for $n > n_0$. Thus, two algorithms with the same asymptotic complexity may lead to quite different computation times.

5.2.3 Optimality

Once the complexity of an algorithm has been estimated, the question arises whether this algorithm is *optimal*. An algorithm for a given problem is optimal if its complexity reaches the lower bound over all the algorithms solving this problem. Hence, estimating a lower bound is an essential task, and unfortunately a difficult one.

A trivial lower bound is given by the output size. Consider, for example, the problem of computing the intersection of n segments (see the examples in Figure 5.1). The output size is $O(n^2)$.

Any algorithm solving this problem will execute at least n^2 operations in the worst case (even if it does nothing but print the output). This is abbreviated by saying that the problem is $\Omega(n^2)$. If one finds an $O(n^2)$ algorithm that solves this problem, it will be optimal and of complexity $\Theta(n^2)$. Indeed, such an algorithm exists: a simple nested loop.

Another useful technique for estimating the complexity of a problem is the *transformation of problems*, also called *problem reduction*. Suppose that we know a lower bound for a problem A, and that we want to estimate a lower bound for a problem B. If we can transform A in B by

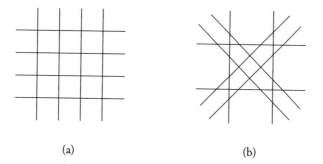

(a)   (b)

Figure 5.1 Segment intersection, instances showing $O(n^2)$ complexity: $\frac{n}{2} \times \frac{n}{2} = 16$ points (a) and $(\frac{n}{2})(\frac{n}{2}) + 2(\frac{n}{4})(\frac{n}{4}) = \frac{3n^2}{8}$ points (b).

a *transformation* step whose cost is less than that for solving A, then B has the same lower bound as A.

A nice illustration of this technique is given in the computational geometry area by the ConvexHull problem. The convex hull of a set of points S is the smallest convex polygon that encloses S. A lower bound is established by reducing the *sorting problem*—whose complexity is known to be $\Theta(n \log n)$—to the *convex-hull problem.*[12]

Let $\{x_1, x_2, \dots, x_n\}$ be a set of n numbers. We can compute in linear time $O(n)$ the pairs (x_i, x_i^2) for all i in $\{1, \dots, n\}$, and interpret these pairs as points that belong to a parabola (see Figure 5.2). We can compute the convex hull of this set of points. Once this has been done, we obtain in linear time the leftmost point of this convex hull, that is, the point with the lowest abscissa. The key observation is that the convex hull is a polygon whose vertices are stored according to an order $\{\dots, x_{i-1}, x_i, x_{i+1}, \dots\}$ such that the vertex with abscissa x_i is adjacent to the vertices with abscissas x_{i-1} and x_{i+1}. Therefore, by scanning in order the convex-hull boundary, we obtain the x_i sorted. Figure 5.2 gives an example of this process with $x_1 = 4$, $x_2 = 1$, $x_3 = 2$. We first reach the leftmost vertex with abscissa x_2 (linear time). We then scan the vertices sequentially. They are sorted according to their abscissas.

Therefore, we have sorted a set of numbers by requiring only a convex-hull computation. Assume that ConvexHull has a complexity

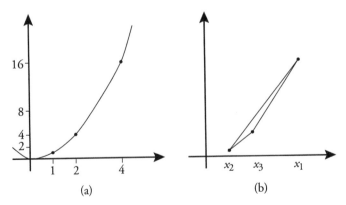

Figure 5.2 Transformation of sorting to ConvexHull: the parabola (a) and the convex hull and the sorted x_i (b).

---

12. Unless otherwise specified, log denotes $\log_2$.

lower than $n \log n$. In this case, the sorting algorithm would have the same complexity, which leads to a contradiction. It follows that ConvexHull is $\Omega(n \log n)$. Note that this is true only because the transformation can be processed in linear time, and thus can be neglected compared to sorting. We show in the next section that computing the convex hull is actually $\Theta(n \log n)$, by exhibiting $O(n \log n)$ algorithms.

5.2.4   Data Structures

A naive way of searching through a collection of n information chunks to find those that satisfy a given criterion is to scan the entire collection and to check the criteria for each chunk. Such algorithms are linear. A fundamental way of obtaining efficient algorithms is to organize the data with *data structures* capable of supporting the basic operations on these structures (namely, searching, inserting, and deleting) in sublinear time. Height-balanced binary search trees such as the AVL trees or the 2-3-4 trees allow one to perform search and update operations in $O(\log n)$. Another structure, quite useful to a wide range of geometric problems, is the *interval tree*.

As suggested by its name, this structure stores a set of intervals in the set of real numbers R. It supports insertions and deletions in $O(\log n)$ and allows one to retrieve all intervals that contain a given point, an operation often called a *stabbing query*.

The interval tree structure is illustrated in Figure 5.3. Each node N in the tree is labeled with a split value $N.v$, and each node stores a set of intervals. Any interval $I = [x_1, x_2]$ is stored in the highest node in the

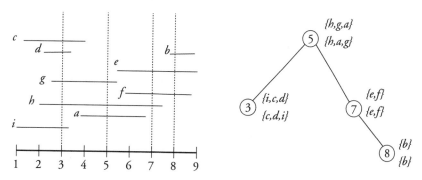

Figure 5.3   An example interval tree.

tree whose split value is contained in I. Its position in the tree can be determined by examining the nodes as follows, starting from the root:

- $x_2 < N.v$. Then the interval is stored in the left subtree of N.
- $x_1 > N.v$. Then the interval is stored in the right subtree of N.
- $x_1 \leq N.v \leq x_2$. Then the interval is stored in N.

A set of intervals in a node is actually represented twice: (1) a list L_1 sorted in increasing order of the interval left endpoint, and (2) a list L_2 sorted in decreasing order of the right endpoint. For instance, in Figure 5.3, the split value of the root (5) is contained in each of the three intervals a, g, and h. The list L_1 sorted on the left endpoint is $\{h, g, a\}$, and the list L_2 sorted on the right endpoint is $\{h, a, g\}$.

Assume now that we want to retrieve all intervals that contain a value w. The algorithm works as follows. Starting from the root, a path down the tree is followed by applying recursively one of the following steps to each visited node N:

- If $w < N.v$, one first scans the list $N.L_1$ and reports all intervals until one meets the first interval $[x_1, x_2]$ with $x_1 > w$. The search continues with the left subtree of N.
- If $w > N.v$, one first scans the list $N.L_2$ and reports all intervals until one meets the first interval $[x_1, x_2]$ with $x_2 < w$. The search continues with the right subtree of N.

To illustrate the algorithm, assume that we search for the intervals that contain value 6. We start with the root. Because $6 > 5$, we scan $L_2 = \{h, a, g\}$ and report successively h and a. The scan stops at g because, given that L_2 is sorted in decreasing order, there is no chance that any remaining interval in L_2 contains 6. We then skip to the right node, whose split value is 7. This time, we scan the list L_1 and report intervals e and f.

The cost of a stabbing query on an interval tree consists of two parts. First, the tree traversal counts for $O(\log n)$. Second, the scan of the lists for each node counts for $O(k)$, where k is the number of intervals in the result. This analysis shows that the overall complexity is $O(\log n + k)$. The algorithm is said to be *output sensitive*, that is, its complexity is expressed with respect to the size of the output. The interval tree is useful in many situations, and in particular during sweep-line algorithms, a technique described in the following section.

5.3   USEFUL ALGORITHMIC STRATEGIES

Most algorithms (being in the computational geometry field or not) rely on well-known general (algorithmic) strategies. In this section, we illustrate the application of three of these general strategies to computational geometry.

The first strategy, known as *incremental algorithms*, is illustrated with the convex-hull problem in two dimensions. The second one, known as *divide and conquer*, is illustrated with the problem of computing the intersection of a set of half-planes. A third technique, denoted *sweep line*—which is quite specific to the geometric nature of problems—is described with the computation of the pairwise intersections in a set of rectangles.

5.3.1   *Incremental Algorithms: The Convex-Hull Example*

An incremental algorithm uses a straightforward strategy that works as follows. The idea is to first take a subset of the input small enough so that the problem is easily solved, and then to add, one by one, the remaining elements of the input while maintaining the solution at each step.

This is well illustrated by the following two algorithms, which incrementally construct the convex hull of a set of points. The first one is a naive algorithm that leads to an $O(n^2)$ complexity. A slight improvement leads to the second algorithm, which achieves the $O(n \log n)$ optimality.

NAIVE ALGORITHM

Let $S = \{p_1, p_2, \ldots, p_n\}$ denote the set of points to be considered for the convex hull. We begin, as previously suggested, by constructing the convex hull for a subset of S such that the solution is straightforward. Clearly, we only have to consider as an initial convex hull the triangle consisting of the three points $\{p_1, p_2, p_3\}$.[13] We now have to deal with the problem of adding a point p_i to an existing convex hull H_{i-1}.

---

13. When describing an algorithm, it is customary to assume that the input does not contain degenerated cases. For instance, we assume here that there is no subset of three collinear points. This simplifies the analysis and delays the tedious task of handling special cases to the programmer.

Two cases may occur:

♦ $p_i \in H_{i-1}$. This means, given our hypothesis of nondegenerated cases, that p_i is inside H_{i-1}. It is easy to detect this in linear time by scanning the points of H_{i-1} in clockwise order and checking that p_i is always on the right of an edge.[14] In this case, $H_i = H_{i-1}$.
♦ $p_i \notin H_{i-1}$ (p_i is outside H_{i-1}). Then $H_i = H_{i-1} \cup p_i$. As shown in Figure 5.4, this operation consists of finding the two tangency lines from p_i to H_{i-1}. Due to our hypothesis regarding nondegeneracy, a line of tangency meets H_{i-1} at a single vertex p_t. The question is how to find such points p_t.

If we scan H_{i-1} in clockwise order, p_t is such that p_i is on the right of the directed edge $p_{t-1} p_t$ and on the left of $p_t p_{t+1}$. The same holds for the other tangency point, replacing "right" by "left" in the previous proposition. Only tangency points have this property. Hence, a scan of H_{i-1} is sufficient to find in linear time both tangency points p_{t1} and p_{t2}. H_i is finally obtained by replacing the sublist $(p_{t1} \ldots p_{t2})$ by $(p_{t1} p_i p_{t2})$ in the description of H_{i-1}.

The analysis of the algorithm is simple. Each step i ($i \in \{1, \ldots, n\}$) involves a scan of H_{i-1}. The complexity is therefore $3 + \cdots + (n-1) = O(n^2)$.

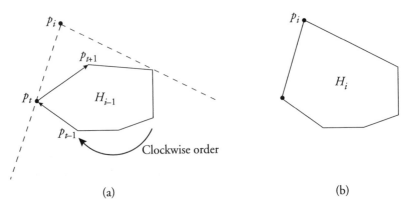

(a)   (b)

Figure 5.4 Looking for tangency points in the incremental hull algorithm: lines of tangency for p_i (a) and the new convex hull (b).

---

14. A point p is "on the right" of a directed segment ab if the cross product $ab \times ap$ is negative (see Section 5.5).

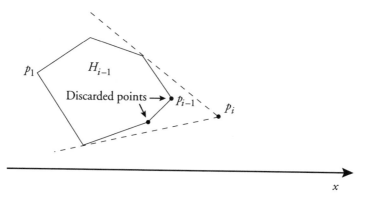

Figure 5.5   The improved incremental hull algorithm.

Although this is not optimal, a nice feature of this algorithm is that it does not require a prior knowledge of the entire input. Such an algorithm is well suited to "dynamic" applications, where the convex hull has to be maintained and updated each time a new point is added.

IMPROVEMENT OF THE NAIVE CONVEX-HULL ALGORITHM

The previous algorithm can be improved to reach the optimal $\Theta(n \log n)$ by presorting the input. Assuming the points in S sorted on their abscissas, consider the problem of adding a point p_i to an existing hull (Figure 5.5).

Because of the initial sorting of points, some new properties appear. Using a strategy similar to the previous, we first construct the triangle with the first three points. When constructing the hull from this triangle and the fourth point p_4, p_4 is on the right of this triangle, because the points are sorted on their abscissas in increasing order. Because a point to be inserted cannot belong to the hull, the scan used in the naive algorithm for detecting this situation is no longer necessary.

Sorting leads to a second property. Because a point to be inserted could be located anywhere around the hull in the naive algorithm, we were forced to perform a "blind" scan for selecting the points of tangency. In other words, a same point on the boundary of the hull was likely to be considered at each step, a feature that leads to the non-optimal $O(n^2)$ complexity.

Consider again Figure 5.5. The hull consists of two monotonic chains with respect to the x abscissa.[15] The first chain extends from

---

15. See Section 2.1.1 for a definition of a monotonic chain or monotone (poly)line.

p_1 to p_{i-1}, and the second one from p_{i-1} to p_1. Clearly, each of these chains contains exactly one point of tangency for p_i, denoted the upper (resp. lower) tangent point.

The following describes the process for finding the upper tangent point (a similar process holds for the lower one). Starting with p_{i-1}, check whether it is a point of tangency. If yes, the algorithm terminates, and p_i will be inserted between the lower tangency point and p_{i-1}. Otherwise, two actions take place. The upper monotonic chain is updated by eliminating p_{i-1} (which will not belong to the final hull); the upper tangency point is checked on the next point in the upper chain. Note that *Point p_{i-1} can be permanently eliminated as a candidate for being an upper point of tangency*; that is, it will not be considered again for the insertion of the next point p_{i+1}.[16]

The following is the pseudo-code of the second algorithm. Note that (1) the boundary of any convex hull H_i is assumed to be stored in clockwise order, and (2) if n is the number of points describing H, point indices are to be computed modulo n ($p_{n+1} = p_1$). The jth point on the boundary of H is denoted h_j.

ALGORITHM   INCREMENTALCONVEXHULL (S: set of points): the hull H

```
begin
    Sort the n points in S by their x coordinate.
    H = triangle (p₁, p₂, p₃)
    for (i = 4 to n) do
    begin
        j = index of the rightmost point of H
        // Find the upper tangency point
        u = j
        while (pᵢhᵤ is not tangent to H) do
        begin
            if (u ≠ j) remove hᵤ from H
            u = u − 1
        end while
        // Find the lower tangency point
        l = j
```

---

16. There is a slight inaccuracy here. Point p_{i-1} belongs to both chains and thus will be eliminated only after the scan of the lower chain. This has a minor impact on algorithm design.

```
   while (p_i h_l is not tangent to H) do
   begin
      if (l ≠ u), remove h_l from H
      l = l + 1
   end while
   Insert p_i in H between h_u and h_l
end for
end
```

Each step of the incremental algorithm consists of eliminating some points. Because we cannot eliminate more than n points, this gives a bound on the cost of the computation. Hence, the overall work for the entire process of inserting the n points is $O(n)$, and the complexity of the algorithm is $O(n \log n)$, due to the dominating cost of the initial sorting phase. In summary, the incremental algorithm computes the convex hull in $\Theta(n \log n)$.

5.3.2   Divide-and-Conquer Strategy: The Half-Plane Intersection Example

The divide-and-conquer strategy has for a long time proved effective in many situations. It relies on a recursive approach and has two steps. In the first step (top-down), the input is recursively divided until the sub-problems are small enough in size to be solved easily. The second step (bottom-up) consists of recursively merging the solutions. This strategy is also used in sorting algorithms such as merge-sort and quicksort.

We illustrate the divide-and-conquer strategy with the problem of reporting the intersection of a set of half-planes.[17] For simplicity, we assume that the result is a compact convex polygon. In addition, we suppose the knowledge of the search space R, which is a rectangle. The resulting polygon is supposed to be always contained in R. The three-step strategy can be sketched as follows:

♦ *Building the structure.* The set of n half-planes in the input is re-cursively halved until one obtains n singleton half-planes. This yields a binary tree.

---

17. This algorithm is of interest, for instance, in the context of constraint databases as it can be used to evaluate the set of points represented by a conjunction of constraints over two variables (see Chapter 4).

- *Solving an atomic problem.* The half-plane in each leaf singleton is intersected with rectangle R. This yields a convex polygon in each leaf.
- *Merging the results.* Compute recursively the intersection of the convex polygons (going up in the structure defined in the first item in this list.).

During the merging phase, the tree is processed bottom-up, as follows. At each node of the binary tree, the intersection of two convex polygons is computed. If p and p' are the number of vertices of the two polygons to be intersected, as we will see later (Section 5.5.4), convex polygon intersection is $O(p + p')$; that is, linear. The merging step eventually delivers a convex polygon that is the intersection (if any) of the n half-planes. The algorithm follows. Due to its recursive structure, the code is quite simple.

ALGORITHM

HALFPLANEINTER (S: set of half-planes): a convex polygon

```
begin
  if (Card(S) > 2) then
    return HALFPLANEINTER (S/2) ∩ HALFPLANEINTER (S − S/2)
  else
    return S ∩ R
  end if
end
```

Figure 5.6 illustrates the process previously described. Starting from five half-planes, one obtains a convex polygon (i) with four edges. Meanwhile, half-plane c, which is redundant with a, has been eliminated.

Let $T(n)$ be the time complexity of the HALFPLANEINTER algorithm. We show in the following that $T(n)$ is $O(n \log n)$.

A divide-and-conquer algorithm can be thought of as a binary tree,[18] where the leaves correspond to "atomic" operations and the nodes to merge operations. If we split the problem of size n into two problems of size $\frac{n}{2}$, and if we assume that the merge step can be done in linear

---

18. The word *binary* holds, of course, only for half-divisions. When the division splits a problem into more than two subparts, the analysis is slightly more complex.

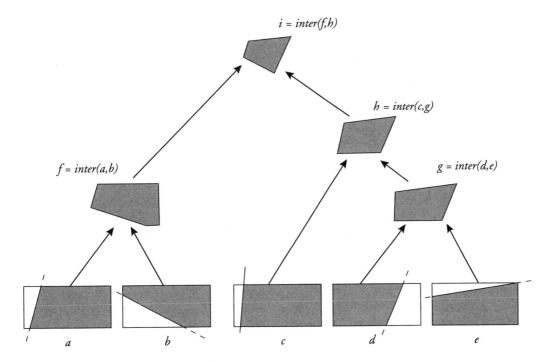

$i = inter(f,h)$

$h = inter(c,g)$

$f = inter(a,b)$

$g = inter(d,e)$

a b c d e

Figure 5.6   The half-plane intersection algorithm.

time $O(n)$ [recall that the convex polygon intersection is $O(n)$], we
have

$$T(n) = 2T\left(\frac{n}{2}\right) + cn,$$

where c is a constant cost factor. If the divide-and-conquer strategy
takes i steps, its cost is

$$T(n) = 2^i T\left(\frac{n}{2^i}\right) + cni$$

Now, let $k = \log n$ be the number of times n can be halved before
reaching 1 (k is the depth of the binary tree). The previous recurrence
relation leads to the following expression at step k:

$$T(n) = 2^k T\left(\frac{n}{2^k}\right) + cnk = nT\left(\frac{n}{2^k}\right) + cn\log n$$

We assume that once the size is small enough so that the problem can
be solved (atomic solution), it is carried out in constant time in the
size of the problem. Therefore, $T(\frac{n}{2^k})$ is $O(1)$. The final complexity

of $T(n)$ is $O(n \log n)$ because of the merge cost, which dominates the $O(n)$ leaves processing cost.

As a matter of fact, this analysis holds for any algorithm following the divide-and-conquer framework, such that the merge step can be carried out in linear time. This is, for instance, the case of the classical sort/merge algorithm. Incidentally, one can show that the algorithm for half-plane intersection is optimal, in that sorting can be reduced to the half-plane intersection problem.

5.3.3   *Sweep-Line Method: The Rectangle Intersection Example*

The sweep-line (or *plane-sweep*) technique is intensively used in computational geometry. It consists of decomposing the geometric input into vertical strips, such that the information relevant to the problem is located on the vertical lines that separate two strips. Therefore, by "sweeping" a vertical line from left to right, stopping at the strip boundaries, we can maintain and update the information needed for solving a given problem.

Even though algorithms based on sweep-line techniques may widely vary, they have in common the use of two data structures:

♦ A structure called the state of the sweep or *sweep-line active list*, denoted in the following $\mathcal{L}$. This structure is updated as the line goes through a finite number of positions, called *events*.

♦ A structure called *event list* and denoted in the following $\mathcal{E}$, which can be known beforehand or discovered step-by-step as the sweep goes on. In the first case, a chained list is used to store the information, whereas in the second case, another structure that supports searching, inserting, and possibly deleting is necessary (e.g., a priority queue).

To illustrate the method, we will consider a classical example. Given a set S of rectangles with sides parallel to the axes, report all their pairwise intersections (Figure 5.7a). Note first that the problem can be solved by a simple nested loop algorithm, which works as follows. First, scan all rectangles and, for each of them, test its intersection with all other rectangles. As pointed out in Section 5.2, there can be up to $O(n^2)$ intersections, and thus this simple nested loop algorithm is optimal!

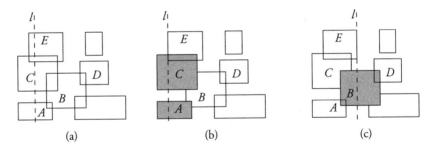

Figure 5.7   Plane sweep.

There is a case, however, where the usual worst-case analysis as a function of the input size is a loose estimate of the actual behavior of the algorithm. It is worthwhile in such cases to design an *output-sensitive algorithm*, which expresses the complexity with respect to the output size, k, more representative of a particular instance of a problem. The sweep-line algorithm relies on two key observations:

♦ First, if we consider a vertical line l and the set S_l of all rectangles cut by l, reporting the pairwise intersections in S_l is reduced to testing the overlapping of the projections of the rectangles on the y axis: the y intervals. For instance, in Figure 5.7a, $S_l = \{A, C, E\}$. Two rectangles in S_l intersect if their y intervals overlap (C and E in Figure 5.7a).

♦ The second observation is that when sweeping line l from left to right, S_l content changes at a finite number of locations of l, called *event points*; namely, when l reaches the left and right vertical edges of each rectangle in S.

Hence, the event points are the $2 \times |S|$ left and right x coordinates of the rectangles, ordered in a list $\mathcal{E}$. We maintain in a data structure $\mathcal{L}$ a list of the active rectangles; that is, those that intersect sweep line l. Now we only have to perform the following operations at each event point:

♦ When the left edge of a rectangle r is reached in $\mathcal{E}$, r is inserted in $\mathcal{L}$. We know that its x interval intersects the x interval of the rectangles currently in $\mathcal{L}$. Hence, the problem is reduced to searching in $\mathcal{L}$ for the rectangles whose y interval intersects the y interval of r. This is a one-dimensional problem.

♦ When the right edge of a rectangle r in $\mathcal{L}$ is reached by the sweep line, we know that r does not overlap with any of the remaining rectangles in $\mathcal{E}$. Hence, r can be removed from $\mathcal{L}$.

This is illustrated in Figure 5.7b. Sweep line l reaches the left edge of E. E is inserted in $\mathcal{L}$, and we must search $\mathcal{L}$ for the active rectangles whose y interval intersects $[E.y_{min}, E.y_{max}]$ (in this case, C). In Figure 5.7c, the sweep line reaches the right edge of E. We know that E can be removed from $\mathcal{L}$ because it cannot intersect any rectangle not yet encountered (for instance, D). The only rectangle remaining in $\mathcal{L}$ at this point is B.

ALGORITHM   RECTANGLEINTERSECTION (S: set of a rectangle)

```
begin
    Sort the 2n xmin and xmax values of S and place them in E
    L = ∅
    while (E ≠ ∅) do
    begin
        p ← MIN(E) // extract the next event from E
        if (p is left edge of a rectangle r) then
        begin
            INSERT (r, L)
            Search and report the rectangles in L intersecting r
        end if
        if (p is right edge of a rectangle r) then DELETE (r, L)
    end while
end
```

The efficiency of the algorithm depends on the data structure $\mathcal{L}$. Such a data structure must support operations of insertion, deletion, and interval search in $O(\log n)$. One can use, for instance, the interval tree of Section 5.2.

The pseudo-code helps to give a straightforward analysis of the previous algorithm. The initial step (sorting) is carried out in $O(n \log n)$. The main loop is executed $2n$ times. Therefore, one must perform $2n$ traversals of the interval tree, for a total cost, which is again $O(n \log n)$. Finally, one must count the cost of scanning the lists in the interval tree. As seen previously, this cost is in $O(k)$, where k is the number of rectangle intersections. Finally, one obtains a complexity in $O(n \log n + k)$, which is one of the fundamental bounds for plane-sweep algorithms.

The worst case is still n^2, because the number of intersections can be up to n^2. However, this algorithm performs better than the nested loop strategy when k is small compared to n^2.

5.4   POLYGON PARTITIONING

Polygon decomposition, an important issue of computational geometry, is central to spatial databases because polygons are the most complex objects to be dealt with in 2D applications. Then, partitioning a polygon in simpler elements often simplifies algorithm design and implementation.

The definition of polygons was given in Chapter 2. We review the main types of polygons in Figure 5.8. Recall in particular that a *monotone polygon P* is a simple polygon such that its boundary δP consists of exactly two monotonic chains MC_1 and MC_2. Stronger constraints imply easier algorithms. It is far simpler to deal with convex polygons than with monotone polygons, and again easier to design algorithms on monotone polygons than on simple polygons. It follows that a key strategy for solving problems on simple polygons is to decompose them into simpler polygons. This section focuses on such a decomposition.

First, we show how to compute the trapezoidalization of a polygon. A simple $O(n \log n)$ algorithm is described thereafter. We then discuss *polygon triangulation*. An intermediate and useful technique is the triangulation of a monotone polygon. Based on this material, an algorithm for simple polygon triangulation is outlined, and a short discussion

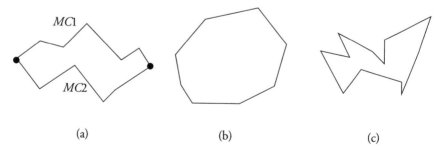

Figure 5.8   Polygons: monotone (a), convex (b), and simple (c).

reports the issue of partition in convex components. For the sake of legibility, we chose to present here simple, although non-optimal, algorithms.

5.4.1   *Trapezoidalization of a Simple Polygon*

A *trapezoid* is a quadrilateral with at least two parallel edges. A triangle can be viewed as a degenerated trapezoid with a null-length edge.

The trapezoidalization algorithm relies on the sweep-line technique. First, the vertices of polygon P are sorted according to their x coordinate. Then a vertical line l scans the sorted vertices. For each vertex v, we compute the maximal vertical segment on l, internal to P and containing v (see Figure 5.9).

This implies looking for the nearest edges of P, above or below v, with the constraint that a vertical segment (called the *visibility segment*) drawn from v to such an edge lies entirely within P. There may be two such edges (Figure 5.9, vertex v_1), only one (vertex v_2), or none (vertex v_3).

The visibility segments define the trapezoidalization. The polygon is decomposed into trapezoids with vertical parallel edges (visibility segments). It remains to describe how we can compute them quickly. We can use the RECTANGLEINTERSECTION algorithm of Section 5.3.3 with the following changes. The *event list* $\mathcal{E}$, where the vertical sweep line stops, is the list of vertices sorted by x coordinate. The *active list* $\mathcal{L}$ must contain the list of edges of P currently intersected by $\mathcal{L}$, ordered by y coordinate. Hence, each segment should be inserted in (respectively,

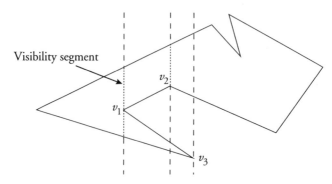

Figure 5.9   Trapezoidalization of a simple polygon.

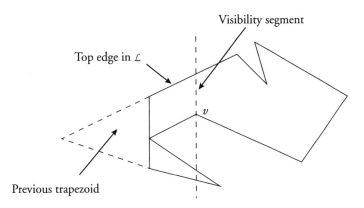

Figure 5.10   Extraction of a trapezoid.

removed from) $\mathcal{L}$ when its leftmost (respectively, rightmost) vertex is encountered in the *event list* $\mathcal{E}$.

At each event, a new vertex v is introduced. Incident edges are either inserted or removed from $\mathcal{L}$, and $\mathcal{L}$ is searched for the edges above and below v. Whenever a nearest edge e above (below) v has been found in $\mathcal{L}$, the visibility segment from v to e defines a vertical edge of a trapezoid. This trapezoid is extracted from P as follows. The visibility segment from v to the intersection point with e, say, i, is the first vertical edge of the trapezoid. Then e from i to its leftpoint is the second edge. The second vertical edge of the trapezoid is the visibility segment of the previous event, and so on (see Figure 5.10).[19]

With an appropriate tree-like structure for $\mathcal{L}$, the edge search can be carried out in $O(\log n)$, and the entire scan requires $O(n \log n)$. The overall complexity of the algorithm is then $O(n \log n)$.

To obtain a triangulation, we could just cut nondegenerated trapezoids. This has the great disadvantage of increasing the complexity because of the introduction of new vertices (i.e., the points i where edges are split to create a trapezoid). There are better algorithms for triangulating a polygon.

---

19. As usual, this description does not take into account the degenerate cases (edges with the same x coordinate), which should be carefully handled at the implementation level.

5.4.2   Triangulation of Simple Polygons

Triangulating a polygon P from scratch consists of finding *diagonals* within this polygon. A diagonal is a segment $v_i v_j$ between two vertices of P whose interior does not intersect the boundary of P. v_i and v_j are said to be *visible* from each other. The triangulation is not deterministic, but one can show that every triangulation of a polygon P of n vertices has $n - 3$ diagonals and results in $n - 2$ triangles.

Algorithms that directly triangulate a simple polygon exist, but they are rather slow. We show in the next section that *monotone polygons* can be linearly triangulated, and thus that partitioning a simple polygon into monotone polygons is the key to efficient triangulation algorithms.

Assume now that the polygon P to be triangulated is monotone with respect to the x axis. An important feature is that the vertices of each monotonic chain of P are x sorted. Thus, a merge of the two monotonic chains gives in linear time a fully sorted list of P vertices.

The triangulation algorithm works as follows: (1) scan in order the sorted vertices of P, (2) maintain a list $\mathcal{L}$ of the points already scanned for which a triangle has not yet been created, and (3) eliminate points within $\mathcal{L}$ when a triangle has been created.[20] For concreteness, we illustrate this process using the example of Figure 5.11. The first three steps are as follows:

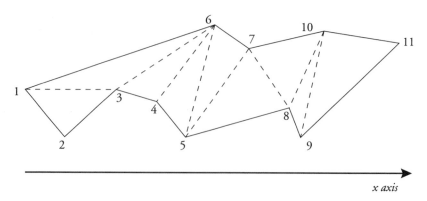

Figure 5.11   Triangulation of a monotone polygon.

---

20. Algorithms that adopt this "as soon as possible" (ASAP) strategy are often denoted "greedy" algorithms.

- *The first three points are on the same chain.* Fortunately, the angle $\widehat{1, 2, 3}$ is convex, which allows points 1 and 3 to be connected with a diagonal. We then get a first triangle. Point 2 is removed from list $\mathcal{L}$, which now contains $(1, 3)$.

- *Add point 4.* Contrary to the previous step, angle $\widehat{1, 3, 4}$ is reflex. Hence, triangle $(1, 3, 4)$ is *outside* the polygon and nothing can be done but to add point 4 to $\mathcal{L}$. The same holds for point 5. $\mathcal{L}$ becomes $(1, 3, 4, 5)$.

- *Point 6 is the next candidate.* Note that (1) it lies on a different chain than the points contained in $\mathcal{L}$, and (2) the points in $\mathcal{L}$ form a reflex chain. Then point 6 can be successively connected to points 3, 4, and 5. We get three triangles and eliminate points 1, 3, and 4, reducing $\mathcal{L}$ to $(6, 5)$.

ANALYSIS

As can be shown from a careful analysis, the three previous cases summarize all situations likely to occur. Note that the points in $\mathcal{L}$ always belong to the same chain. Indeed, as soon as a point p from the opposite chain is introduced, at least one triangle can be created.

On the other hand, the creation of a triangle with points of the same chain depends on the convexity of the new angle in $\mathcal{L}$ (see cases 1 and 2 in the previous example). As a matter of fact, p is introduced in $\mathcal{L}$ only if it forms a reflex angle with the last point of $\mathcal{L}$.

Thus, diagonals are created without an explicit test for visibility between the two points. The pseudo-code follows.

ALGORITHM | MONOTONETRIANGULATION (P: monotone polygon): set(triangles)

```
begin
    Sort the n vertices of P by x coordinate and store them into V
    L = a list with the first two points of V
    while (V ≠ ∅) do
    begin
        p ← MIN(V) // Extract the next vertex from V
        if (p is opposite to points in L) then
        begin
            while ((Card (L) > 1) do
                Output triangle {First(L), Second (L), p}
```

```
                    REMOVE (First(L))
                end while
                Add p to L
            end
            else
            begin
                while (angle (Last(L), Previous(Last(L)), p) is convex
                        and Card(L) > 1) do
                    Output triangle {Last(L), Previous(Last(L)), p}
                    REMOVE Last(L)
                end while
                // The angle is reflex, or Card(L) = 1
                Add p to L
            end
        end while
    end
```

Sorting the vertices of P is carried out in $O(n)$, due to the motonone nature of P. In the last step, triangles are produced during a simple scan of the sorted list of vertices. It follows that the monotone polygon triangulation problem is $\Theta(n)$.

Although monotone polygons are not common in most applications, algorithms exist for partitioning a simple polygon into monotone components. They are examined in the following section.

TRIANGULATION OF SIMPLE POLYGONS

We outline an algorithm that triangulates a simple polygon P with complexity $O(n \log n)$. The solution relies on the material previously presented, which can be sketched as follows:

- Partition P into monotone polygons.
- Triangulate each monotone polygon resulting from the previous step.

Partitioning a simple polygon into monotone components is quite similar to the trapezoidalization process. Consider the example of Figure 5.12. We partition the polygon in monotone components at the "return" vertices. These vertices are *notches* for which both incident edges are on the same side of the vertical line that passes through their common vertex.

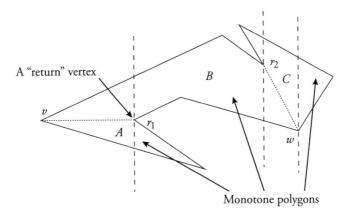

Figure 5.12   Partitioning a polygon into monotone polygons.

We now apply a "virtual" trapezoidalization (i.e., without any output of trapezoids). Consider, for example, Figure 5.12, which has a virtual trapezoid at the left-hand side of notch r_1 and a trapezoid at the right-hand side of notch r_2 (the left trapezoid is actually degenerated into triangles). We obtain the monotone components by creating diagonals in these trapezoids.

By drawing a diagonal between v and r_1, we get one monotonic component; namely, A, which is extracted from the polygon. Then, by drawing a diagonal between the second "return" vertex, r_2, and vertex w, we split the rest of the polygon into two monotone components, B and C.

The monotone partitioning algorithm is in $O(n \log n)$, and the subsequent triangulation of monotone polygons is processed in linear time. Therefore, the simple polygon triangulation is carried out in $O(n \log n)$. This is not optimal because a linear algorithm exists (see bibliographic notes).

5.4.3   Convex Partitioning

We conclude the presentation of polygon partitioning by adopting a somewhat different point of view than previously, where simple polygons were partitioned into trapezoids or triangles. These are examples of convex components. If the initial simple polygon is complex and large, there might be a large number of components after the partition.

Thus, instead of partitioning into basic components (such as trapezoids or triangles), one might be interested in minimizing the number of elements in the partition, while keeping the (strong) constraint that those elements be convex. This is useful, for instance, in constraint databases where infinite data is represented with half-spaces (see Chapter 4).

It can be shown that the number of convex components Φ is bounded by a function of the number r of reflex angles (notches) of the simple polygon: $\lceil r/2 \rceil + 1 \leq \Phi \leq r + 1$. Indeed, in the best case, each of the diagonals that partition the polygon removes two notches (one at each end), whereas in the worst case each removes only one notch.

There exists an algorithm that gives the optimal decomposition; that is, a decomposition for which the number of components is minimal. However, this algorithm is both complex and time consuming. Hence, one might prefer an algorithm suboptimal in terms of number of components if it is simple to implement and if its time complexity is better. We describe in the following such an algorithm, which, assuming the polygon has been triangulated during a pre-processing phase, runs in $O(n)$.

The algorithm requires that the triangulation phase delivers some information about the adjacency relationships between triangles in the partition. An appropriate structure is the *dual graph* of the triangulation. Each node in the graph represents a triangle. There is an edge between nodes n_1 and n_2 if the corresponding triangles are adjacent (i.e., have a common edge, as in Figure 5.13).

The algorithm is now fairly simple. Starting from a set of triangles and its dual graph obtained by triangulating the initial polygon, we take one triangle t_1 and compute the union of t_1 with another adjacent triangle t_2. This consists of removing the edge $e_{1,2}$ common to both triangles. We test whether this union is still convex. This can be done in $O(1)$ because we just have to check whether the boundary is locally convex at the two vertices of $e_{1,2}$.

We continue merging with adjacent triangles until the resulting object can no longer be augmented by adjacent triangles while staying convex. The convex component is output, and the process is then initialized with another triangle. Because the number of triangles is in $O(n)$, the entire process is linear.

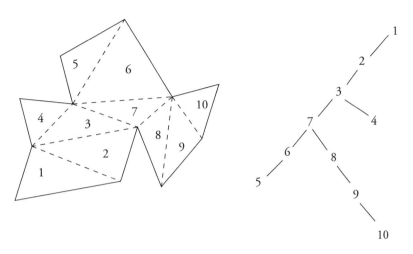

Figure 5.13   A triangulation and its dual graph.

It can be shown that the number of convex pieces obtained by this algorithm is never worse than four times the optimal. This can be considered a satisfying trade-off between the two conflicting goals; namely, minimizing the number of components and the time complexity.

5.5   ALGORITHMS FOR SPATIAL DATABASES

This section addresses the design and analysis of geometric algorithms that can be used for spatial database operations. Most of these algorithms rely on techniques described in previous sections. The classical geometric primitives that we deal with in the context of spatial databases are

- *Points.* Points are represented by a pair of coordinates.
- *Lines.* The term *line* refers actually to a *polyline;* namely, a list of pairwise connected segments.
- *Polygons.* These are *simple polygons* and are represented by the (closed) polyline of their boundary; that is, a circular list of points, one per polygon vertex.

We do not consider polygons with holes or *region* objects consisting of several nonconnected polygons, as these particularities have only a minor impact on the design of algorithms.

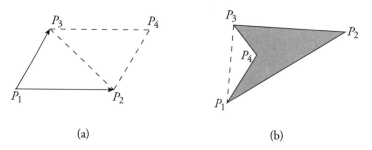

(a)   (b)

Figure 5.14 Computing the area of a polygon: area of a triangle (a) and area of a polygon (b).

5.5.1   Area Size of a Polygon and Related Operations

One of the simplest functions on spatial objects is the computation of the area of any polygon. This computation relies on a basic function that computes the area of a triangle. Consider Figure 5.14a. The area of parallelogram (P_1, P_2, P_3, P_4), which is equal to the cross product $\overrightarrow{P_1P_2} \times \overrightarrow{P_1P_3}$, is twice the area of triangle $T(P_1, P_2, P_3)$. The area of T is given by the formula

$$area_T(P_1, P_2, P_3) = \frac{x_1y_2 - x_2y_1 + x_3y_1 - x_1y_3 + x_2y_3 - x_3y_2}{2}$$

Note that this formula may return a negative value, depending on the order in which the vertices are scanned. Scanning the triangle in counterclockwise order gives a positive value. Scanning the vertices the opposite way returns the same value multiplied by -1. Using negative values turns out to be interesting in withdrawing areas from a polygon.

The area of a polygon can now simply be obtained by choosing a vertex v and by summing up the areas of the triangles formed by v and all the pairs of adjacent vertices, scanned in counterclockwise order. Consider, for instance, polygon P, drawn in gray in Figure 5.14b. The area of polygon P is obtained by the formula

$$area(P) = area_T(P_1, P_2, P_3) + area_T(P_1, P_3, P_4)$$

One subtracts from (P_1, P_2, P_3) the portion that lies in (P_1, P_3, P_4). The second triangle is scanned in clockwise order, and this associates a negative value with the formula.

$$area(P) = \frac{x_1 y_2 - x_2 y_1 + x_3 y_1 - x_1 y_3 + x_2 y_3 - x_3 y_2}{2}$$
$$+ \frac{x_1 y_3 - x_3 y_1 + x_4 y_1 - x_1 y_4 + x_3 y_4 - x_4 y_3}{2}$$

$$area(P) = \frac{x_1 y_2 - x_2 y_1 + x_2 y_3 - x_3 y_2 + x_3 y_4 - x_4 y_3 + x_4 y_1 - x_1 y_4}{2}$$

More generally, the area of a polygon P with vertices $P_1, P_2, \ldots P_n$, scanned in counterclockwise order, is computed as

$$area(P) = \frac{1}{2} \sum_{i=1}^{n} (x_i y_{i+1} - x_{i+1} y_i),$$

where $x_{n+1} = x_1$ and $y_{n+1} = y_1$. From an implementation point of view, the previous functions provide some quite useful primitives. For instance, a point C is located on the left-hand side of the oriented segment AB if $area_T(ABC)$ is positive, or the three points A, B, and C are collinear if $area_T(ABC) = 0$. The function also permits one to determine whether an angle is reflex or convex, and is therefore useful in the various algorithms presented so far.

In addition, function $area_T$ gives a means to test whether two segments AB and CD intersect, in which case A must be located on one side of CD and B on the other, with the same holding for C and D with respect to AB.

5.5.2 Point in Polygon

Testing whether a point p lies within a (simple) polygon P is a quite common operation in spatial applications (as well as in graphical user interfaces). The usual algorithm is based on the following simple remark. If we draw a half straight line (or *ray*) l starting from p, and if we count the number of segments of P that intersect ray l, this number will be even if p is outside P, and is otherwise odd (see Figure 5.15).

This suggests a straightforward algorithm, which works as follows. First, scan the boundary of P and test each edge for intersection with the half straight line drawn from p. Because the direction does not matter, a simple choice is to use the x axis for the ray. The list of edges has to be scanned once only. Thus, the resulting algorithm is $O(n)$.

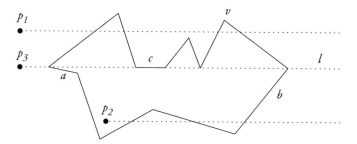

Figure 5.15   Point in polygon.

Some special cases (which cannot be avoided) deserve special attention. Consider, for instance, point p_3 in Figure 5.15. A naive counting would result in nine edge intersections with l. That is, each edge of P, starting from a and ending with b (scanned as usual in counterclockwise order), might be considered to intersect with l. Therefore, we would deduce that p_3 is actually *inside* P. The strategy to handle such cases is not trivial. For instance, interpreting each edge as being a half-closed segment by excluding the final vertex would nevertheless result in this example in five intersections.

To overcome these problems, a first method consists of applying the following rules: (1) do not count edges collinear with l, and (2) count an edge e as a crossing edge only if there exists at least one endpoint of e strictly above l. By applying these rules, edges a, b, and c in Figure 5.15 are not counted when testing for inclusion of point p_3. The number of crossings is then six, leading to the correct conclusion that p_3 is outside P.

This solves most of the special cases, but not all of them. For instance, vertex v in Figure 5.15 would fail the point-in-polygon test, as previously described. It follows that a preliminary scan to test whether the point lies on the boundary is necessary to achieve the final algorithm.

ALGORITHM   POINTINPOLYGON (P: polygon, p: point): Boolean

begin
  if (p is on one edge of P), p is inside P
  else
    count = 0

```
      l = horizontal ray containing p
      for (i = 1 to n)
      begin
        if (INTERSECT(edge(i), l) and not COLLINEAR(edge(i), l)) then
        begin
          if (one endpoint of edge(i) is strictly above l) count = count + 1
        end
      end for
      if (count is odd), p is inside P
    endif
end
```

The algorithm analysis is straightforward. Each edge is subject to a constant number of intersection tests. Therefore, the point-in-polygon problem is $\Theta(n)$. For convex polygons, the point-in-polygon test can be carried out in $\Theta(\log n)$ with a binary search strategy.

5.5.3   Polyline Intersections

In the following sections, we distinguish between *Boolean* operations that *detect* intersection between objects and operations that *compute* a new geometric object (possibly with many components) as being the intersection of two objects. We begin with the following problem.

DETECTION OF LINE SEGMENTS INTERSECTION
Given a set S of line segments, detect whether any two segments intersect. Once more, we could consider the simple nested loop algorithm that runs in $O(n^2)$, stopping as soon as an intersection is found. However, there exists a plane-sweep algorithm, $O(n \log n)$, which can be easily customized to the polyline intersection test.

Sweep-line techniques can be used for detecting an intersection in a set of segments because of the following property. Suppose that we draw a vertical line intersecting some segments of S (Figure 5.16). We can store a list of its intersections with the segments, which is ordered by the y coordinate and called, as usual, the *active list*. This defines a total order $>_x$ over S for a given position x of the line. For instance, at position l_2, we have $s_2 >_{l_2} s_3 >_{l_2} s_1$.

If we now consider the intersection between two segments s_1 and s_2, we note that the closer the vertical line is to this intersection point,

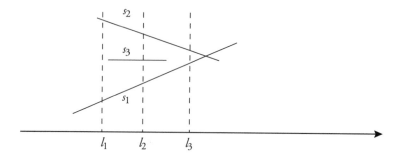

Figure 5.16   The sweep-line algorithm.

the more likely s_1 and s_2 are consecutive in the active list. Hence, if the vertical line is "close enough" from this intersection point (position l_3, for example), s_1 and s_2 are consecutive in the active list.

This property suggests that we do not have to test a segment against all others. By sweeping the line from left to right and maintaining a list of the segments that currently intersect the line, we only have to test the intersection between segments *when they happen to be consecutive in the list*.

As usual in plane-sweep algorithms, we maintain two structures; namely, the *active list* $\mathcal{L}$ and the *event list* $\mathcal{E}$, which stores the x coordinates of the segment endpoints. Two cases may occur:[21]

◆ *The line meets the leftmost point of a segment s.* Then s must be inserted in $\mathcal{L}$, and at most two segments, neighbor segments above and below s in $\mathcal{L}$ after insertion must be tested for intersection with s.
◆ *The line meets the rightmost point of a segment s.* Then s must be deleted from $\mathcal{L}$, and the two previous neighbors of s, which are now adjacent in the list, must be tested for intersection.

ALGORITHM   SEGMENTINTERSECTIONTEST ($S:$ set of segments): Boolean

---

begin
    Sort the $2n$ endpoints of segments in S and place them in $\mathcal{E}$
    for ($i = 1$ **to** $2n$) **do**

---

21. As usual, we eliminate degeneracy cases from the discussion. We thus assume that S contains no vertical segment.

```
begin
    p = E[i]
    if (p is left of a segment s) then
    begin
        INSERT (s, L)
        if (ABOVE (s, L) intersects s), return true
        if (BELOW (s, L) intersects s), return true
    end if
    if (p is right of a segment s) then
    begin
        if (ABOVE (s, L) intersects BELOW (s, L)) return true
        DELETE (s, L)
    end if
    end for
end
```

In this algorithm, function ABOVE (respectively, BELOW) considers the segment located just above (below). The event list $\mathcal{E}$ can be implemented as a simple array. As for the active list $\mathcal{L}$, it must support insertions, deletions, and the ABOVE and BELOW functions in $O(\log n)$. This can be easily achieved with a tree-like structure.

Therefore, detecting whether two line segments intersect can be done in $\Theta(n \log n)$, and this is optimal. This method applies to the polygon intersection test as well, discussed in the following.

COMPUTING THE INTERSECTION OF LINE SEGMENTS

The simplest algorithm for computing the pairwise intersections of line segments of a given set relies on a nested loop, which runs in $O(n^2)$. As previously discussed, this is optimal (under the worst-case viewpoint) because there can be up to $O(n^2)$ intersections. However, n^2 tests are performed even if there is no intersection at all.

If the application is such that the expected number of intersections is small, an output-size-sensitive algorithm is probably a better choice. We present the following two algorithms. The first algorithm is a direct extension of the previous sweep-line algorithm. It applies to a set of segments and runs in $O((n + k) \log n)$, where k is the number of intersections.

The second algorithm computes the intersections existing between two sets of segments, which is often denoted the *red-blue intersection problem*. The segments within a set do not intersect each other. The algorithm is optimal and runs in $\Theta(n \log n + k)$. This important bound in computational geometry was already encountered for the rectangle intersection problem.

FIRST ALGORITHM

In order to generalize the segment intersection test algorithm, we must introduce the following two additional features:

♦ An intersection point is considered an *event* because it triggers a change in the active list. Therefore, each time an intersection is found, it must be inserted in $\mathcal{E}$ (which is therefore a *dynamic* structure). This intersection will be processed as the line sweeps further right.

♦ When the line meets an intersection point between s_1 and s_2, s_1 and s_2 invert their positions in $\mathcal{L}$. Any segment of $\mathcal{L}$ that is now a neighbor either of s_1 or of s_2 must be tested for intersection with its neighbor.

The pseudo-code for this first algorithm is the following.

ALGORITHM   SEGMENTINTERSECTION (S: set of segments): set of points

---

```
begin
    Sort the 2n endpoints of segments in S and place them in E
    L = ∅
    while (E ≠ ∅) do
    begin
        p MIN (E) // extract from E
        if (p is left of a segment s) then
        begin
            INSERT (s, L); s₁ = ABOVE (s, L); s₂ = BELOW (s, L)
            if (s₁ intersects s), ADDINTER(s ∩ s₁, E)
            if (s₂ intersects s), ADDINTER(s ∩ s₂, E)
        end
        if (p is right of a segment s) then
        begin
            s₁ = ABOVE (s, L); s₂ = BELOW (s, L); DELETE (s, L);
            if (s₁ intersects s₂ to the right of p), ADDINTER(s₁ ∩ s₂, E)
        end
        if (p is the intersection of s₁ and s₂) then
        begin
```

```
           s₃ = ABOVE (MAX(s₁, s₂), 𝓛); s₄ = BELOW (MIN(s₁, s₂), 𝓛)
           if (s₃ intersects MIN(s₁, s₂)), ADDINTER(s₃ ∩ MIN(s₁, s₂), 𝓔)
           if (s₄ intersects MAX(s₁, s₂)), ADDINTER(s₃ ∩ MAX(s₁, s₂), 𝓔)
           Swap s₁ and s₂ in 𝓛
      end
           if (s₃ intersects s₂), ADDINTER(s₃ ∩ s₂, 𝓔)
           if (s₁ intersects s₄), ADDINTER(s₄ ∩ s₁, 𝓔)
           Swap s₁ and s₂ in 𝓛
      end
end
```

It may happen that two segments s_1 and s_2 are tested more than once for intersection. This is the case, for instance, in Figure 5.16, when the sweep line reaches the leftmost and rightmost points of s_3. Therefore, we must test in the ADDINTER function whether an intersection point is not already a member of the event list.

The initial step (sorting) is carried out in $O(n \log n)$. The main loop is executed $2n + k$ times, where k denotes the number of intersections. Within this loop, each operation is $O(\log n)$. For achieving this bound, $\mathcal{E}$ is implemented as a specific data structure, called a *priority queue*.

Therefore, the cost of the entire algorithm is $O((n + k) \log n)$. This algorithm is better than the nested loop strategy for small output size k. This is the case, for instance, when one wants to compute the intersection of two complex polylines that do not cross too often.

However, there is still a gap between the complexity of this algorithm and the lower bound, which can be shown to be $\Theta(n \log n + k)$. The second algorithm, outlined in the following, reaches this optimal complexity in the specific case of two sets of nonintersecting segments (the "blue" set and the "red" set).

SECOND ALGORITHM: THE RED-BLUE INTERSECTION PROBLEM
The problem is now to report all intersections between a blue set of segments and a red set. A first obvious modification to the previous algorithm is to maintain two active lists: one (denoted $\mathcal{L}_b$) for the blue segments and one (denoted $\mathcal{L}_r$) for the red ones. Because there is no possible blue-blue or red-red intersection, these lists change only when the right or left endpoint of a segment is encountered. This means that, as in the segment intersection test, the event list can be managed as a simple static array of the $2n$ sorted endpoints, with a cost reduced to

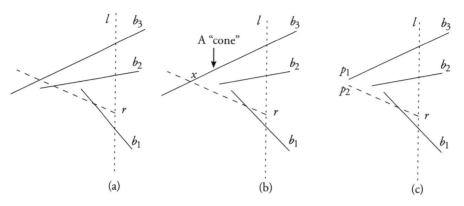

Figure 5.17   A red segment r tested against the blue active list: a safe case (a), a problematic case (b), and breaking the cone (c).

the initial $O(n \log n)$ sort. It remains to show that the intersections can be reported in $O(n \log n + k)$ by using these structures.

A first approach is to compute the intersections between a segment (for instance, a red segment r) and the other set (in this case, the blue set) when the sweep line l reaches the right endpoint of r. This is illustrated in Figure 5.17. Before removing r, we seek in $\mathcal{L}_b$ for the blue segments that intersect r. Two cases must be considered:

- *Case 1* (Figure 5.17a). All blue segments b_1, b_2, and b_3 that intersect r are *consecutive* in $\mathcal{L}_b$. It is then sufficient to find the position of r in $\mathcal{L}_b$ and to scan the list upward and downward until a nonintersecting segment is found. Each step in this scan reports an intersection, and thus the $O(n \log n + k)$ complexity holds.
- *Case 2* (Figure 5.17b). All segments intersecting r are *not* consecutive in $\mathcal{L}_b$. This is the case for b_2, which does not intersect r but is located between r and b_3 in $\mathcal{L}_b$. b_2 is said to hide the intersection of r with b_3. If such cases occur, we must scan all of the list in order to report all intersections.

Case 2 entails a quadratic complexity, even if there are no intersections. Therefore, an important part of the design of this algorithm is to eliminate the situations where this second case may occur. The principles of this method are outlined in the following.

It can be shown that an intersection p between a blue segment u and a red segment v is hidden only when either a left endpoint is above one segment (u or v) or below the other one and to the right of x. The region defined by (p, u, v) is denoted a *cone*. For instance, the left endpoint of b_2 is below b_3, above r, and to the right of x in Figure 5.17; (x, b_3, r) defines a cone. The idea is to detect a cone when a segment s is inserted in an active list and to "break" the cone (p, u, v). By breaking the cone, it is meant that both u and v are cut into two component segments with p as an endpoint. Then the new segments on the left have to be removed and the intersections reported. In particular, the intersection p between u and v is reported at that time.

Once the cone has been broken, s can be safely inserted in its active list. s will not anymore hide a possible intersection between a red segment and a blue segment already inserted. This is illustrated in Figure 5.17c. When b_2 is inserted, one detects the cone (x, b_3, r) and cut b_3 and r at p_1 and p_2, respectively. p_1 and p_2 are just to the right of x. The intersection point x is reported.

When breaking a cone, one must be careful in order to report *all* intersections that involve the fragments of u and v located on the left-hand side of intersection p. For instance, when removing the left fragment of b_3 and r for breaking the cone in Figure 5.17, we must check whether these left fragments intersect another red or blue segment, respectively.

Fortunately, it can be shown that such an intersection, if it exists, involves a segment that is a neighbor of b_3 or r in the active lists. Therefore, we just have to move locally [with $O(1)$ cost] in the structure to test for new intersections, and we can avoid repeated traversals [with $O(\log n)$ cost]. Moreover, each move (except the last one) allows us to report an intersection. Hence, the cost of breaking a cone is proportional to the number of intersections found. In summary

- When a segment is inserted (left endpoint), we must break each cone and report the intersections related to the cones.
- When a segment is to be removed (right endpoint), we search in the proper active list and report the intersections. Because there are no cones, case 1 holds, and the $O(n \log n + k)$ complexity holds.

Indeed, each operation consists of first traversing an active list with an $O(\log n)$ cost, and second in moving downward or upward in the structure, reporting an intersection at each move. Thus, the cost of the entire algorithm is $\Theta(n \log n + k)$.

POLYLINE INTERSECTION

Until now we have only considered the intersection of line segments. The previous algorithms are easily customized to the intersection of two polylines, each line being considered a set of line segments. For instance, with the nested loop $O(n^2)$ algorithm, an outer loop scans the segments of one line, say, l_1. For each segment s_i of l_1, one scans all segments of the other line (inner loop), looking for intersections. Each polyline being a set of nonintersecting segments, the red-blue algorithm can be used without any customization to the intersection of two polylines.

5.5.4   Polygon Intersections

Computing the intersection of two polygons is a most useful operation, not only in spatial databases but in computer graphics and CAD/CAM applications. In the following, we first discuss the detection problem ("Do two polygons intersect?"), which can be solved with algorithms seen in the previous section. We then present the computation problem, first for convex polygons and then for simple polygons. The *windowing* and *clipping* operations (intersection against a rectangle) are addressed last.

DETECTION OF POLYGON INTERSECTION

Two simple polygons P and Q intersect if one of the following cases occurs:

- One edge of P intersects one edge of Q.
- P is inside Q.
- Q is inside P.

This suggests the following algorithm, which calls procedures implementing algorithms previously discussed.

ALGORITHM   POLYGONINTERSECTIONTEST $(P, Q:$ polygons$)$

---

begin
    if (no edge of P intersects any edge of Q) **do** // Line intersection test
    begin
        p = any point of the boundary of P

```
      if (p lies in Q) // Point-in-polygon test
        P ⊂ Q
      else
      begin
        q = any point of the boundary of Q
        if (q lies in P) // Point-in-polygon test
          Q ⊂ P
        else P and Q do not intersect
      end if
    end if
    else P intersects Q
end
```

To detect the edges' intersection, we use the LINEINTERSECTIONTEST algorithm. The cost is dominated by the LINEINTERSECTIONTEST algorithm. Therefore, detecting whether two simple polygons intersect is $\Theta(n \log n)$. This is optimal. In the following, we introduce the computation of intersection through the simple case of convex polygons.

CONVEX POLYGON INTERSECTION

Convexity is a strong constraint that allows us to design efficient algorithms. We present a simple algorithm for computing the intersection of two convex polygons, which achieves the optimal $O(n)$ complexity.

The algorithm relies on a simple idea, illustrated in Figure 5.18, which depicts the steps of the algorithm for intersecting polygons A and B. We assume that the boundary is stored in counterclockwise order. Notice first that the intersection (in gray in Figure 5.18a) is a convex polygon whose boundary is constructed by alternating fragments of the boundary of A and fragments of the boundary of B. We skip from one polygon to another when an intersection point is found.

The basic idea is to perform a synchronized scan on the boundaries of A and B such that (1) all intersection points are eventually found and (2) we know at each step the "inner" boundary that participates in the construction of the result. The algorithm starts with a pair of (oriented) edges from each polygon (denoted a and b in the following) and advances, at each step, the edge that "aims" toward the other. Informally, an edge u "aims" toward v if, by going on the convex boundary containing u, an intersection with v may be found. We provide a more precise definition later.

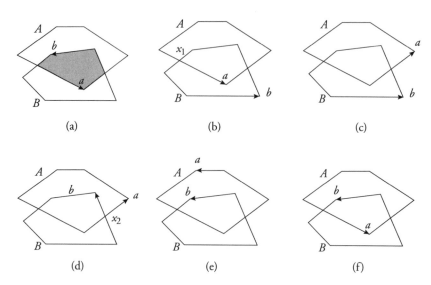

Figure 5.18 Intersection of convex polygons: initial step (a), advance on B (report x_1) (b), advance on A (c), advance on B (report x_2) (d), advance on A then B (e), and final step (f).

Let us examine Figure 5.18. The initial pair of edges is (a, b), as shown in Figure 5.18a. It appears that b "aims" toward a because, by advancing on the boundary of B, we might find an intersection with a. Therefore, we advance on B and report the intersection x_1. Now we know that the part of the boundary of A starting at x_1 belongs to the boundary of $A \cap B$.

We keep going forward on the edge b on boundary B until we are sure that no further intersection with a can be found (Figure 5.18b). We advance then a on A only one step because we are sure there is no intersection possible with b (Figure 5.18c), and again on B (Figure 5.18d), which gives the second intersection x_2. From now on, the boundary of $A \cap B$ is described by the part of the boundary of B starting at x_2. The process continues until both polygons have been scanned. At each step we report either an intersection point or a point on the "inner" boundary. As a result, we construct the result $A \cap B$ in $O(|A|+|B|)$. The corresponding algorithm follows.

ALGORITHM   CONVEXPOLYINTER (A, B): a convex polygon

---

begin
    Let a and b be the first edges of A and B, respectively

```
repeat // Begin the synchronized scan
    if (a intersects b) then
        Report the intersection a ∩ b
        Memorize which boundary is "inside"
    endif
    Advance on A or B (report the points on the inner boundary)
    until (A and B have been scanned)
    if no intersection has been found, test A ⊂ B and B ⊂ A
end
```

We must now set up precise rules for advancing along edges. It turns out that only four cases must be considered. They are summarized in Figure 5.19, where the edge that must be chosen is labeled in boldface.

◆ *Case 1.* Both edges "aim" toward each other. In this case, we can follow any of them (here, b was chosen).

◆ *Case 2.* Neither a nor b aim toward the other. Given the conventional counterclockwise order, we must follow edge b.

◆ *Cases 3 and 4.* The two cases are symmetric. We follow the edge that points toward the straight line containing the other.

More precisely, the four cases can be characterized by two criteria: (1) the sign of the cross product $a \times b$ and (2) the containment of the head of one of the edges [say, $head(a)$] in the half-plane on the left of the other edge [say, $H(b)$]. For instance, case 2 is characterized by $a \times b < 0$ *and* $head(a) \in H(b)$. It is relatively easy to handle the case of collinear edges. In summary, this algorithm provides an optimal solution to the convex polygon intersection problem.

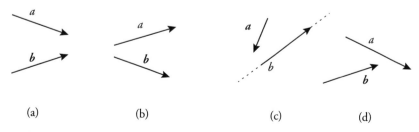

(a)   (b)   (c)   (d)

Figure 5.19   The advance rules: case 1 (a), case 2 (b), case 3 (c), and case 4 (d).

SIMPLE POLYGON INTERSECTION

Establishing a lower bound on the performance of the intersection of two simple polygons is easy. Each edge of polygon P can intersect all edges of polygon Q. Recall (Section 5.2) that the output size is a lower bound for an algorithm. The simple polygon intersection is therefore $\Omega(n^2)$.

The polygon intersection between two simple polygons P and Q[22] is carried out in two steps. First, a *classification* process is applied to the edges and to the vertices of each polygon. The boundary of P (respectively, Q) is consequently divided in *inside, outside,* and *common boundary* components with respect to Q (respectively, P). For instance, a vertex of P is marked with value *inside (outside, boundary)* if it is inside (outside, on the boundary of) polygon Q. In the second step (denoted *construction* stage), these components are extracted to construct the resulting polygons.

The detailed list of the steps performed by the algorithm is provided in the following. For concreteness, we illustrate this process using the instances of Figure 5.20.

◆ *Classification of vertices.* Each vertex is assigned the value *inside* (**i**), *outside* (**o**), or *boundary* (**b**), depending on its position with respect to the other polygon. The classified points are inserted into two lists, P_v and Q_v, one for each polygon. Vertices are marked with values **i**,

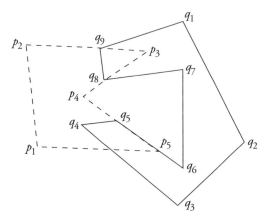

Figure 5.20 Classification algorithm for simple polygon intersection.

22. In the following, we assume that P and Q are stored in counterclockwise order.

o, or **b** in the lists P_v and Q_v.

$$P_v = \; < (p_1, \mathbf{o}), (p_2, \mathbf{o}), (p_3, \mathbf{i}), (p_4, \mathbf{o}), (p_5, \mathbf{b}) >$$

$$Q_v = \; < (q_1, \mathbf{o}), (q_2, \mathbf{o}), (q_3, \mathbf{o}), (q_4, \mathbf{i}), (q_5, \mathbf{b})(q_6, \mathbf{o}),$$

$$(q_7, \mathbf{o})(q_8, \mathbf{b}), (q_9, \mathbf{b}) >$$

- *Finding the intersection points.* Each edge of P is tested for intersection against each edge of Q. Each reported intersection point is inserted in the proper place in P_v or Q_v, and marked **b** (*boundary*). We obtain two lists of so-called *fragment edges*, denoted P_{ef} and Q_{ef}, whose instances (Figure 5.20) are provided in the following.

  For the sake of clarity, Figure 5.21 shows the intersection points introduced in the list. Note that (1) there are exactly the same intersection points in P_{ef} and Q_{ef} and (2) because both polygons are represented in counterclockwise order, the lists of intersection points are stored in inverse order in each fragment edge list. The following is the list P_{ef}:

$$P_{ef} = \; < (p_1, \mathbf{o}), (p_2, \mathbf{o}), (p_1', \mathbf{b}), (p_3, \mathbf{i}), (p_2', \mathbf{b}), (p_4, \mathbf{o}),$$

$$(p_3', \mathbf{b}), (p_5, \mathbf{b}), (p_4', \mathbf{b}), (p_5', \mathbf{b}) >$$

- *Edge fragment selection.* A fragment edge (1) is a part of an original polygon edge and (2) lies entirely within or outside the other polygon. Hence, this step consists of selecting each *inside* edge fragment. This can be deduced easily from the type of the edge fragment endpoints. If one of them is *inside*, so is the edge. If both points are

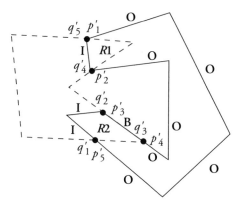

Figure 5.21   Intersection points and edge fragment classification.

boundary, we have to test the edge middle point for inclusion in the relevant polygon. If this is the case, the edge fragment is *inside*. Figure 5.21 shows the edge fragment classification for polygon Q, where each edge fragment is labeled with **O**, **I**, or **B**.

♦ *Extraction of resulting polygons.* Now we only have to extract, one by one, the resulting polygons. We take any edge fragment marked by **I** or **B**, and then seek in both lists another edge fragment whose first endpoint matches the last endpoint of the previous edge. We continue until the first edge is found again. The extracted list constitutes one component of the result. Each edge found must be extracted from the edge fragment list. We can iterate the same process until the list is empty. For instance, we can initiate the process with edge fragment (p_1', p_3). Then we search for an edge fragment (still labeled **I** or **B**) with p_3 as the first endpoint, and we find (p_3, p_2'). Finally, starting from p_2', we find in Q_{ef} the edge fragment $q_4'q_5'$, which closes the result polygon $R1$. The second component of the result, $R2$, can be extracted the same way.

Each step is subject to a separate analysis. Step 2 is the most expensive, as it requires finding the intersection points [in $O(n^2)$] and inserting each of them in the list [in $O(k^2)$] where k is the output size. This gives an $O(n^2 + k^2)$ worst-case analysis and, because k may be up to n^2, this might be $O(n^4)$! However, the algorithm is simple and may be easily generalized to handle other set operations (e.g., union and difference).

5.5.5   Windowing and Clipping

Both operations described in Section 1.3 involve a rectangle as a parameter. They can be defined as follows:

♦ WINDOWING (g,r) is the Boolean operation that consists in testing whether a geometric object g intersects a rectangle r.

♦ CLIPPING (g,r) is the operation that computes the part of the geometric object g that lies inside rectangle r.

Because a rectangle is among the simplest objects to draw on a screen using a mouse, both operations are intensively used in graphical interfaces. In particular, the windowing operation is the usual method of selecting spatial objects.

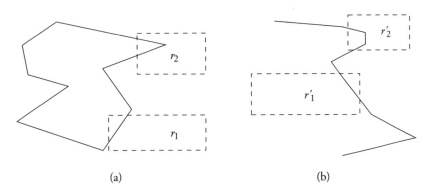

       (a)   (b)

Figure 5.22   The windowing operation: windowing on a polygon (a) and windowing on a polyline (b).

WINDOWING

This operation is trivial in the case of a point. It relies on the same algorithm in the case of lines and polygons, because a polygon is viewed as a closed polyline. Figure 5.22 shows a few cases that may occur.

Note that testing whether one vertex belongs to the rectangle is not sufficient, as a rectangle may intersect a polygon or a polyline without containing any endpoint (rectangles r_1 and r_1' in Figure 5.22). Therefore, the algorithm simply consists in scanning the edges (respectively, the segments) of the polygon boundary (the polyline) and in testing whether the edge (the segment) intersects one of the rectangle edges.

However, this does not solve all possible cases. The geometric object g might be entirely covered by (or might entirely contain) rectangle r. Therefore, when no edge intersections have been detected, we must perform two inclusion tests.

ALGORITHM   WINDOWING (l : line, r : rectangle): Boolean

begin
  for (each edge l_i of l) **do**
    for (each edge r_i of r) **do**
      if (l_i intersects r_i) **then return** true
    end
  end
  // Compute a point-in-rectangle test
  p = any vertex of l
  if (p is in r) **return** true // The geometric object is in r

```
        else // Point-in-polygon test, if l is a polygon's boundary
            p = any vertex of r
            if (p is in l) return true // r is contained in the geometric object
        else return false
    end
```

The analysis of the algorithm is trivial. In the worst case, we test each edge of l against each edge of r, thus performing $4 \times n$, an operation whose cost is constant (n denotes the number of edges of l). The *point-in-rectangle* test is $O(1)$. The final point-in-polygon test is $\Theta(n)$. (See Section 5.5.2). Hence, the windowing operation is $\Theta(n)$.

CLIPPING

Due to its importance in computer graphics, the clipping operation was studied a long time ago. A linear-time (and thus optimal) algorithm was proposed in 1974, which seems to be the most widely implemented today. A detailed description of this algorithm follows.

At first glance, scanning the polyline (or the boundary of the polygon), keeping the part of each edge that lies inside the rectangle, seems to be sufficient. Although this might be true for simple cases (Figure 5.23a) and for polylines, this naive strategy fails to handle intricate situations, such as that shown in Figure 5.23b.

The correct strategy is to consider each edge of the clipping rectangle as defining a half-space, and to clip the polygon against each of these four half-spaces, one at a time. Assume that the polygon P and the clipping rectangle r are stored in counterclockwise order. Keeping

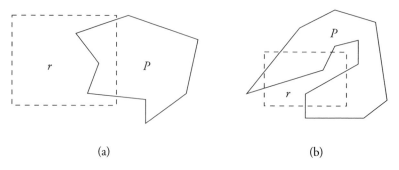

(a)   (b)

Figure 5.23 The clipping operation: a simple case (a) and a complex case (b).

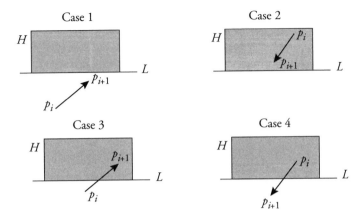

Figure 5.24   Clipping an edge against a half-plane H.

the part of the polygon P that is inside a half-space H defined by a borderline L consists of scanning the directed edges $e_i = p_i p_{i+1}$ of P, and testing the position of each e_i with respect to H. Four cases may occur (Figure 5.24).

◆ Edge e_i is outside H. Then point p_{i+1} is discarded (from the list of vertices of P).

◆ Edge e_i is inside H. Then point p_{i+1} is kept.

◆ Edge e_i crosses L and p_{i+1} is inside H. Then point p_{i+1} is kept, and the intersection point I between L and e_i is added to the list of vertices of P.

◆ Edge e_i crosses L and p_{i+1} is outside H. Then point p_{i+1} is discarded, and the intersection point I between L and e_i is added to the list of vertices of P.

The algorithm consists of two nested loops. The outer loop scans the edges of the clipping rectangle. At each step, an edge defines the "clipping half-plane" H_i, $i \in \{1, 2, 3, 4\}$. The inner loop scans the polygon edges and clips them against the current half-plane H_i: for each scanned edge, one of the previously listed actions is performed, and part of the polygon is clipped, a segment of the borderline L becoming a new edge. The resulting (clipped) polygon is in the next step then clipped again against another rectangle edge.

ALGORITHM   CLIPPING (P: polygon, r: rectangle): a polygon

```
begin
  Copy P into P′
  for (each edge rᵢ of r) do
    l = the straight line that contains rᵢ
    for (each edge eᵢ of P′) do
      if (l intersects eᵢ) then // Cases 3 and 4
        l = eᵢ ∩ l
        result ← l
      endif
      if (pᵢ₊₁ is on the left of rᵢ) then
        result ← pᵢ₊₁ // Case 3
      endif
    end
    Copy result into P
  end
end
```

Figure 5.25 shows the four steps of the outer loop on the example in Figure 5.23b. At the end of step 4 we obtain only one connected

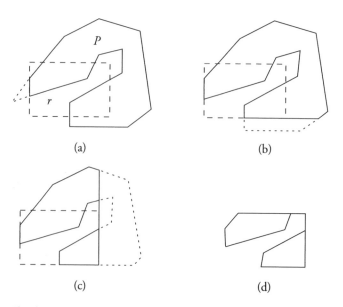

(a)   (b)

(c)   (d)

Figure 5.25 The four main steps of the simple polygon clipping: step 1 (a), step 2 (b), step 3 (c), and step 4 (d).

component, which is *not* a simple polygon. If a set of simple polygons is the expected result, this algorithm might be considered irrelevant. There exist (see bibliographic notes) clipping algorithms that yield a set of simple polygons.

The performance analysis is similar to that detailed for the windowing operation. The previous clipping operation, whose result is a single connected component, is $\Theta(n)$.

5.6   BIBLIOGRAPHIC NOTES

The following are bibliographic notes regarding general sources related to this chapter, as well as sources specific to the subject of algorithms.

5.6.1   *General Sources*

A basic methodology for the design and analysis of algorithms was first established in the fundamental work of [Knu73]. Similar material can be found in many other classic books, such as [AHU74, Sed83]. There also exist several textbooks on computational geometry, among which [PS85] served as a reference in the domain for a long time. More recent interesting references include [Ede87, Mul94, O'R94, dBvKOS97, BY98, SU00]. [Mul94] explores the recent development of randomized algorithms, whereas [O'R94] gives a simple presentation of many useful problems, along with some implementation guidelines, including the formulas for computing the area of a triangle or a polygon. The handbook [GO97] is an exhaustive presentation of the domain.

Some computational geometry topics interesting for GIS applications have not been addressed in this chapter. For instance, we did not discuss the representation and manipulation of *elevation data*. Other fundamental topics of computational geometry that go beyond the scope of this book and that have some application in spatial databases (for instance, the Voronoi diagrams and its dual Delaunay triangulation) can be found in any of the general sources previously cited, as well as in [vKNRW97, FPM00].

A major problem is the floating-point round-off error due to the finite precision of computer systems. As soon as a program manipulates and compares floating-point numbers (as, for example, for the intersection of two segments), numerical errors are unavoidable and can lead to a serious lack of robustness. A discussion on this topic can be found in [Sch97a].

5.6.2   Sources on Algorithms

Our presentation of the INCREMENTALCONVEXHULL algorithm is based on that of [O'R94]. Another version of the algorithm, proposed by [Pre79], stresses keeping the *dynamic* feature of the incremental algorithm, which does not require prior knowledge of the entire input and relies heavily on specialized data structures. Using these structures, seeking a tangency point becomes an $O(\log n)$ operation, and thus the global $O(n \log n)$ complexity is reached. This algorithm is actually a *real-time* algorithm, because the update complexity is optimal. See [Pre79] or, equivalently, [PS85], pages 119–124.

The recurrence formula for the divide-and-conquer analysis can be found in [Sed83], along with some other useful formulas. The half-plane intersection algorithm is sketched in [PS85]. The RECTANGLEIN-TERSECTION algorithm is from [BW80].

The simple triangulation algorithm was proposed in [GJPT78]. The optimality of the algorithm has been an open issue for a long time because it was not proved that $O(n \log n)$ is a lower bound. Actually, it is not, as shown by the $O(n \log \log n)$ algorithm proposed by [TvW88]. The problem was then conjectured to be linear. One way to prove it was to find a $\Theta(n)$ algorithm. This was done in [Cha91]. However, although this represents an important theoretical achievement, this optimal algorithm is hardly implementable. Candidate algorithms for a good trade-off between time complexity and implementation considerations can be found, for instance, in [KKT92, Sei91].

The bound on the number of convex components in a simple polygon is from [CD85], which also provides a complete analysis of the problem. There exists an algorithm proposed in [Kei85] that gives the optimal number of convex components. Unfortunately, in addition to being rather complex, this algorithm is expensive. Its complexity is $O(r^2 n \log n)$, where r is the number of notches. The suboptimal algorithm presented in this chapter is from [HM83].

There exist other algorithms for the point-in-polygon test, reported, for instance, in [Sed83]. The algorithm previously described seems to be the most robust.

The plane-sweep algorithm for testing segment intersection was first proposed in [SH76]. The variant for reporting all intersections is borrowed from [BO79]. Our presentation follows that of [PS85]. The red-blue intersection algorithm is from [MS88]. Another optimal algorithm for the same problem is reported in [Cha94]. An optimal, although far more complex, algorithm for the general problem of reporting pairwise intersections among a set of segments can be found in [CE92].

As far as the intersection of convex polygons is concerned, we chose the classical algorithm of [OCON82] (also in [PS85]). A quite detailed description and an implementation in C can be found in [O'R94].

For the intersection of simple polygons, we used the algorithm proposed in [MK89], whose implementation is simple. An important issue for the robustness of this algorithm is the correct computation of intersection points that are subject to floating-point errors. Some other references on the same topic are [NP82, CW83, Zub88]. We presented the polygon clipping algorithm of [SH74], which seems to be the most widely implemented. Another classical algorithm can be found in [LB83]. These algorithms are analyzed and compared in [HP92]. An algorithm that gives a "correct" answer (i.e., that avoids degenerated polygons) can be found in [FNTW90].

6

Spatial Access Methods

"The wolf took a short cut out of the woods, and soon came to the cottage of Red Riding Hood's grandmother."

Red Riding Hood
Illustrated by R. Andre (New York, McLoughlin Bros., 1888)

CONTENTS

In order to efficiently process spatial queries, one needs specific access methods relying on a data structure called an *index*. These access methods accelerate the access to data; that is, they reduce the set of objects to be looked at when processing a query. Numerous examples of queries selecting or joining objects were discussed in Chapter 3. If the selection or join criteria are based on descriptive attributes, a classical index such as the B-tree can be used. However, we shall see that different access methods are needed for spatial queries, in which objects are selected according to their location in space.

Point and *window queries* are examples of spatial queries (see Figure 1.7). In such queries, we look for objects whose geometry contains a point or overlaps a rectangle. *Spatial join* is another important example. Given two sets of objects, we want to keep pairs of objects satisfying some spatial relationships. Intersection, adjacency, containment, and North-West are examples of spatial predicates a pair of objects to be joined must satisfy.

As seen in Chapter 5, processing a spatial query leads to the execution of complex and costly geometric operations. For common operations such as point queries, sequentially scanning and checking whether each object of a large collection contains a point involves a large number of disk accesses and the repeated expensive evaluation of geometric predicates. Hence, both the time-consuming geometric algorithms and the large volume of spatial collections stored on secondary storage motivate the design of efficient spatial access methods (SAMs), which reduce the set of objects to be processed. With a SAM, one expects a time that is logarithmic in the collection size, or even smaller. In most cases, the SAM uses an explicit structure, called a *spatial index*. The collection of objects for which an index is built is said to be *indexed*.

We restrict our attention to objects whose spatial component is defined in the 2D plane. We will show some SAMs for points, but we focus on the indexing of lines and polygons. In this case, instead of indexing the object geometries themselves—whose shape might be complex—we usually index a simple approximation of the geometry. The most commonly used approximation is the minimum bounding rectangle of the objects' geometry, or *minimal bounding box*, denoted *mbb* in the following. By using the *mbb* as the geometric key for constructing spatial indices, we save the cost of evaluating expensive geometric predicates during index traversal (a geometric test against an *mbb* can be processed in constant time). A second important motivation is to use constant-size entries, a feature that simplifies the design of spatial structures.

A spatial index is built on a collection of *entries*; that is, on pairs [*mbb, oid*] where *oid* identifies the object whose minimal bounding box is *mbb*. We assume that *oid* allows us to access directly the page that contains the physical representation of the object; that is, the values of the descriptive attributes and the value of the spatial component.

An operation involving a spatial predicate on a collection of objects indexed on their *mbb* is performed in two steps. The first step, called *filter step*, selects the objects whose *mbb* satisfies the spatial predicate. This step consists of traversing the index, applying the spatial test on the *mbb*. The output is a set of *oids*.

An *mbb* might satisfy a query predicate, whereas the exact geometry does not. Then the objects that pass the filter step are a superset of the solution. In a second step, called *refinement step*, this superset is sequentially scanned, and the spatial test is done on the actual geometries of objects whose *mbb* satisfied the filter step. This geometric operation is costly, but is executed only on a limited number of objects. The objects that pass the filter step but not the refinement step are called *false drops*. In this chapter, we will not look at the refinement step, which is the same whatever the SAM is. The geometric operations in the refinement step have been studied in Chapter 5. We concentrate here on the design of efficient SAMs for the filter step.

In off-the-shelf database management systems, the most common access methods use B-trees and hash tables, which guarantees that the number of input/output operations (I/Os) to access data is respectively logarithmic and constant in the collection size, for exact search queries. A typical example of exact search is "Find County (whose name=) San Francisco." Unfortunately, these access methods cannot be used in the context of spatial data. As an example, take the B-tree. This structure indexes a collection on a *key;* that is, an attribute value of every object of the collection. The B-tree relies on a total order on the key domain, usually the order on natural numbers, or the lexicographic order on strings of characters. Because of this order, interval queries are efficiently answered.

A convenient order for geometric objects in the plane is one that preserves object proximity. Two objects *close* in the plane should be close in the index structure. Take, for example, objects inside a rectangle. They are close in the plane. It is desirable that their representation in the index also be close, so that a window query can be efficiently answered. Unfortunately, there is no such total order. The same limitation holds for hashing. Therefore, a large number of SAMs were designed to try as much as possible to preserve object proximity. The proposals are based on some heuristics, such as rectangle inclusion.

We present in this chapter two families of indices representative of two major trends; namely, the *grid* and the *R-tree*. These structures are simple, robust, and efficient, at least on well-behaved data. The bibliographic notes at the end of the chapter mention a variety of other structures. For each family, we successively study the following operations:

◆ *Index construction:* Insertion of one entry or of a collection of entries.
◆ *Search operations:* Point and window queries. The *search space* is assumed to be a rectangular subset of the 2D plane with sides parallel to the x and y axes.

The design of efficient SAMs is crucial for optimizing not only point and window queries but spatial operations such as join. We postpone the discussion of spatial join to Chapter 7.

The chapter is organized as follows. Section 6.1 discusses the main issues involved in the design of multidimensional access methods. We provide the assumptions on which the design of access methods is based, specify what we require from SAMs, and describe a simple classification. Grid-based structures are presented in Section 6.2, and the R-tree in Section 6.3. A variety of other structures and some more advanced material is discussed in the bibliographic notes of Section 6.4.

6.1   ISSUES IN SAM DESIGN

The design of SAMs relies on the same fundamental assumptions that originated the development of B-trees or hashing techniques for accelerating data access in classical databases. First, the collection size is much larger than the space available in main memory. Second, the access time to disks is long compared to that of random access main memory. Finally, objects are grouped in *pages*, which constitute the unit of transfer between memory and disk. Typical page sizes range from 1K to 4K bytes. Reading/writing one page from/to disk is referred to as an input/output operation, or I/O for short.

Once a page has been loaded into main memory, it is available for a further query unless the memory utilized for this page has been in the meantime reused for reading another page from disk. Then when accessing a particular object, two cases may happen: either the page containing the object is already in main memory or there is a *page fault* and the page has to be loaded from disk.

In traditional database indexing, central processing unit (CPU) time is assumed to be negligible compared to I/O time. The efficiency of the SAM is therefore measured in number of I/Os. In spatial database indexing, the CPU time should be taken into account in some situations. However, we still keep the assumption that it is negligible compared to I/O time. In addition, we do not take into account the caching of pages in main memory and assume the worst-case conditions. This means that each time a page is accessed, it is *not* present in main memory and a page fault occurs.

6.1.1   *What Is Expected of a SAM?*

Given these assumptions, a SAM should fulfill the following requirements:

◆ *Time complexity.* It should support exact (point) and range (window) search in sublinear time.
◆ *Space complexity.* Its size should be comparable to that of the indexed collection.

The first requirement states that accessing with the SAM a small subset of the collection must take less time than a sequential scan whose complexity is linear in the collection size. The space complexity criterion serves to measure how well the structure maps onto the physical resources of the underlying system. Indeed, if the indexed collection occupies n pages, the index size should be of the order of n.

Another important aspect of a SAM is *dynamicity*. It must accept insertions of new objects and deletions of existing ones, and adapt to any growth or shrink of the indexed collection (or to a nonuniform distribution of objects) without performance loss. It is a difficult task to get a structure robust enough to support any statistical distribution of rectangle shape, size, or location. For most of the structures studied in the following, on average, the index traversal is efficient. That is, its access time (measured in number of I/Os) is logarithmic in the collection size. However, there always exists some worst case in which the index is not performing.

The requirement that the structure adapts smoothly to dynamic insertions is important but less essential. One can design efficient structures that only support a *static* construction on a collection of objects known in advance.

6.1.2   *Illustration with a B+Tree*

The following is a concrete illustration of these properties using the classical variant of a B-tree, called a *B+tree*. Figure 6.1a depicts a B+tree index built on the set of keys {2, 3, 7, 9, 10, 13, 15}. It is a balanced tree in which each node is a disk page and stores *entries*, which are pairs of [*key, ptr*] values, where *ptr* points either to an object whose key attribute has for a value *key* (leaf nodes) or to a child node (internal nodes). Here, we assume that each page stores at most four entries. All entries in a node are ordered; for each entry *e*, subtrees on the left index objects *o* such that $o.key \leq e.key$, and subtrees on the right index objects such that $o.key > e.key$.

Given a key value *val*, an exact search is performed by traversing the tree top-down, starting from the root and, at each node, choosing the subtree left to the smallest entry *e* such that $val \leq e.key$. If *val* is greater than the largest entry in the node, then the rightmost subtree is chosen. In such a tree, all leaves are at the same depth (it is balanced).

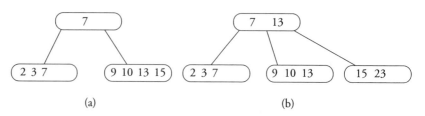

(a)   (b)

Figure 6.1   B-trees: A B+tree before (a) and after insertion of [23, *oid*] (b).

Then, the number of pages that must be read is equal to the depth of the tree, which is logarithmic in the size of the indexed data set.

Now consider the insertion of an entry $e = [23, oid]$. The insertion occurs in the second leaf (see Figure 6.1b). This leaf is full and must be split. Half the entries (the leftmost part) are kept in the page, the remaining half and e are inserted in a new leaf (in a new page), and a new entry with key 13 is inserted in the parent node. The result is shown in Figure 6.1b. The tree is still balanced and, in spite of the split, each node is still half full.

In summary, the B+tree is a nice illustration of the properties to be expected from a secondary memory structure. First (*time complexity*), the number of I/Os to access an object is logarithmic in the collection size. It is the length of a path from the root to a tree leaf. Second (*space complexity*), at least half the space needed to store the index is actually used. This ensures that the size of the index is comparable to the size of the indexed collection (it is smaller in most cases, because the key used to construct the B-tree is much smaller than an entire record in the data set). Finally (*dynamic updates*), the structure preserves its properties through random insertions and deletions, and adapts itself to any distribution.

6.1.3   *Space-Driven Versus Data-Driven SAMs*

All properties of the B-tree that permit efficient indexing rely on the existence of a total order on the key values. There is no simple adaptation of the technique to spatial data. We must use a different construction principle, which is not based on the ordering of objects on their coordinates. A large number of SAMs exist that follow one of two approaches:

◆ *Space-driven structures:* These are based on partitioning of the embedding 2D space into rectangular cells, independently of the distribution of the objects (points or *mbb*) in the two-dimensional plane. Objects are mapped to the cells according to some geometric criterion.

◆ *Data-driven structures:* These structures are organized by partitioning the set of objects, as opposed to the embedding space. The partitioning adapts to the objects' distribution in the embedding space.

We choose to present well-known families of SAMs for each category. Some of them have recently been implemented in commercial systems. The first SAM to be presented includes the *grid file* and *linear structures*. These are both space-driven methods.

The second set of SAMs presented in this chapter belongs to the data-driven family of R-trees. Similar to the B-tree, the R-tree is balanced, provides restructuring operations that allow one to reorganize the structure locally, and adapts itself to nonuniform distributions. We present the original R-tree structure and two variants, called R*tree and R+tree.

The lack of robustness of SAMs with respect to the statistical properties of the objects in the two-dimensional plane is true for all SAMs presented here, whether they are space driven or data driven. When the rectangle distribution is not too skewed, their behavior is satisfactory and the response time is close to optimal. Unfortunately, one can always find a skewed distribution for which the performance drastically degrades. In other words, although the B-tree is a worst-case optimal structure, this is not true anymore for the common multidimensional access methods.

Finally, recall that in the case of one-dimensional and two-dimensional objects, SAMs only accelerate the access to the objects's *mbb;* that is, they allow a fast filter step, which must be followed by a refinement step in which the exact geometry of the object (line or polygon) is checked against the query predicate. This issue is addressed in Chapter 7.

6.2   SPACE-DRIVEN STRUCTURES

Two families of SAMs are presented in this section: the *grid file* and *linear structures*. The *grid file* is an improvement of the *fixed grid* initially designed for indexing points. We will successively present in Section 6.2.1 both structures for points and their adaptation to rectangle indexing. The grid file was initially designed for indexing objects on the value of several attributes. Unlike the B-tree, it is a *multikey index* that supports queries on any combination of these attributes. *Linear structures* enable a simple integration with the B+tree of existing database management systems. Such a technique has been used in spatial extensions of commercial relational DBMSs (e.g., Oracle, Chapter 8). Two linear structures will be successively presented: the linear quadtree (Section 6.2.2) and the *z*-ordering tree (Section 6.2.3).

6.2.1   *The Grid File*

We start with the description of the grid file structure for point indexing, and then look in detail at its adaptation to indexing *mbb* (rectangles). We first present a simple variant, called *fixed grid.*

THE FIXED GRID

The search space is decomposed into rectangular *cells.* The resulting regular grid is an $n_x \times n_y$ array of equal-size cells. Each cell c is associated with a disk page. Point P is assigned to cell c if the rectangle $c.rect$ associated with cell c contains P. The objects mapped to a cell c are sequentially stored in the page associated with c.

Figure 6.2 depicts a fixed grid indexing a collection of 18 points. The search space has for an origin the point with coordinates $(x0, y0)$. The index requires a 2D array $DIR[1 : n_x, 1 : n_y]$ as a *directory.* Each element $DIR[i, j]$ of the directory contains the address $PageID$ of the page storing the points assigned to cell $c_{i,j}$. If $[S_x, S_y]$ is the 2D size of the search space, each cell's rectangle has size $[S_x/n_x, S_y/n_y]$. We sketch in the following the algorithms for point insertion and window query (the algorithm for point deletion is straightforward):

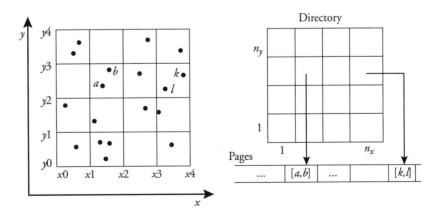

Figure 6.2   Fixed grid.

- *Inserting $P(a, b)$:* compute $i = (a - x_0)/(S_x/n_x) + 1$ and $j = (b - y_0)/(S_y/n_y) + 1$, and then read page $DIR[i, j].PageID$ and insert P.
- *Point query:* given the point argument $P(a, b)$, get the page as for insertion, read the page, scan the entries, and check whether one is P.
- *Window query:* compute the set S of cells c such that $c.rect$ overlaps the query argument window $W;$[23] read, for each cell $c_{i,j}$ in S, page $DIR[i, j].PageID$ and return the points in the page that are contained in the argument window W.

Point query is efficient in this context. Assuming the directory resides in central memory, a point query requires a single I/O. The number of I/Os for a window query depends on the number of cells the window intersects; that is, it is proportional to the area of the window.

The grid resolution depends on the number N of points to be indexed. Given a page capacity of M points, one can create a fixed grid with at least N/M cells. Each cell contains, on the average, less than M objects. A cell to which more than M points are assigned overflows. *Overflow pages* are then chained to the initial page. For instance, assuming that each page can store at most four entries, points satisfying a skewed distribution will be indexed as illustrated in Figure 6.3. $k, l, m,$ $n,$ and o are assigned to a cell that overflows. $k, l, m,$ and n are stored

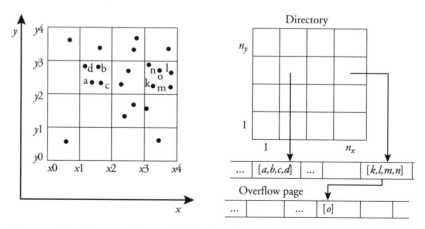

Figure 6.3   Page overflow in the fixed grid.

---

23. Algorithm GF-WINDOWQUERY (see p. 218) explains how this set can be computed.

in page p. o is stored in an overflow page linked to p. Then a point query might take up to q I/Os if the point is stored in the qth page of an overflow chain.

If the points are uniformly distributed in the search space, the phenomenon previously described seldom occurs and the overflow chains are not long. This is obviously not the case with skewed point distributions. In the worst case, all points fall into the same cell and the structure is a linear list of pages. Searching a point then takes linear time, and the structure fails to meet the basic requirement of sublinear time complexity. Overflows also occur when the data set size varies significantly. Even if the point distribution stays uniform, repeated insertions of new points result in a large number of overflow pages. Conversely, deletions might result in almost empty pages. In summary, under certain types of distribution, the fixed grid fails to satisfy the requirements expected of an index in secondary memory.

POINT INDEXING WITH THE GRID FILE

In the grid file, as in the fixed grid, one page is associated with each cell, but when a cell overflows, it is split into two cells and the points are assigned to the new cell they fall into. Then cells are of different size and the partition adapts to the point distribution. Three data structures are necessary (see Figure 6.4):

- The *directory DIR* is a 2D array that references pages associated with cells. The structure is similar to that of the fixed grid, the important difference being that two adjacent cells can reference the same page. In Figure 6.4, the directory is not explicitly represented. Pointers to disk pages are overlaid on the corresponding cells of the grid.
- Two *scales* S_x and S_y are linear arrays describing the partition of a coordinate axis into intervals. Each value in one of the scales (say, S_x) represents a boundary in the partition of the search space along the related dimension (here, the x axis).

The construction of the structure is best described using an example. Figure 6.4 illustrates four steps in the construction of a grid file on a collection of points. For the sake of clarity, we assume that M, the capacity of a page, is 4.

In step A, the structure contains four objects only. The directory is a single cell associated with page $p1$. In step B, points a, b, and c are

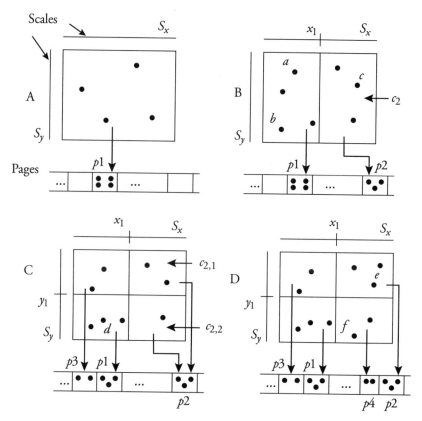

Figure 6.4 Insertions into a grid file.

successively inserted. When inserting a, $p1$ overflows: a vertical split is performed, a new data page $p2$ is allocated, and the five points are distributed among $p1$ and $p2$. The vertical split is reported in scale S_x as value x_1. a and b are inserted in $p1$, and c in $p2$.

In step C, point d is inserted. It should be stored in page $p1$, but $p1$ is full. A horizontal split is performed, reported on scale S_y as a value y_1. The five points are then distributed among pages $p1$ and $p3$.

Observe that the split also implies splitting all cells in the same S_y interval as y_1, although those cells do not overflow. However, the nonoverflowing split cells keep referencing the same pages. Cell c_2 is replaced by two new cells, $c_{2,1}$ and $c_{2,2}$, which both point to $p2$ (Figure 6.4c).

Finally, in step D, e and f are inserted. Page $p2$ overflows and a new page ($p4$) must be allocated. No interval split is necessary in this case, because a division was already defined in the *DIR* structure at value y_1. The points of cell $c_{2,1}$ are stored in $p2$, whereas the points of cell $c_{2,2}$ are stored in the new page $p4$. In summary, when inserting point P, three cases must be considered:

- *No cell splits.* This is the simplest case: point P falls into a page that is not full. Then the page is read and the point is inserted into it in sequence.
- *Cell split and no directory splits.* The point P to be inserted falls into cell c, and page p associated with c is full *but* referenced by several (at least two) distinct cells. In that case, a new page p' is allocated and assigned to c, and objects in p contained in $c.rect$, as well as the point to be inserted, are moved to p'. The directory entry corresponding to c is updated with p' (see step D).
- *Cell split and directory split.* This is the most complex case. Page p referenced by cell $c_{i,j}$ into which P falls is full, and there are no other cells referencing p. Then $c_{i,j}.rect$ is split along either x or y.

  Assume, without loss of generality, that the split is done along the x axis. Then the cell projection on S_x is split into two intervals and a new abscissa is inserted in S_x, with rank $i + 1$.[24] The old $c_{i,j}$ cell generated two half-size cells $c_{i,j}$ and $c_{i+1,j}$. A new page p' is created and assigned to $c_{i+1,j}$. It remains to distribute the points of the full page between page p (points that fall into $c_{i,j}.rect$) and page p' (points falling into $c_{i+1,j}.rect$).

  All previous columns in *DIR* with rank l, $l > i$ are switched to $l + 1$, and a new column with index $i + 1$ is created. Now, for all $k \neq j$, the new cell $c_{i+1,k}$ is assigned the same page as $c_{i,k}$ (see step C).

The grid file overcomes major limits of the fixed grid. A point search can always be performed with two disk accesses (one for accessing the page p referenced in the directory and one for the data page associated with one entry in p). In addition, the structure is dynamic, and it presents a reasonable behavior with respect to space utilization (although degenerate cases may occur). However, a shortcoming of the method is that for large data sets the number of cells in the direc-

---

24. The simplest choice is to split the x interval into two equal parts.

tory might be so large that the directory does not fit anymore in main memory.

RECTANGLE INDEXING WITH GRIDS

We now turn to the more complex case of rectangle (*mbb*) indexing. The simplest way of mapping rectangles to cells is to assign the rectangles to the cells that overlap the rectangles. Three cases may happen. The rectangle either contains the cell, intersects it, or is contained in it. In the two former cases, the rectangle is assigned to several neighbor cells, leading to an index size increase and therefore to an efficiency degradation.

An example of a fixed grid built on a collection of 15 rectangles is shown in Figure 6.5, whereas Figure 6.6 shows a grid file for the same collection. In both cases, the page capacity is 4.

The insertion and deletion of objects is the same as for points. As a consequence of object duplication in neighbor cells (see, for example, object 6 in Figure 6.5), cell split is likely to occur more often. Figure 6.7 illustrates a first case of cell split. Starting with the grid file of Figure 6.6, the insertion of object 14 in cell $DIR[1, 3]$ triggers the overflow of page $p5$. A new boundary is created at value $x3$ in order to divide cell $DIR[1, 3]$ along the x axis. $x3$ has been inserted in S_x, and the directory now consists of $3x(2 + 1) = 9$ cells. Cells $DIR[2, 1]$ and $DIR[2, 2]$ reference existing pages (respectively, $p1$ and $p3$), each being

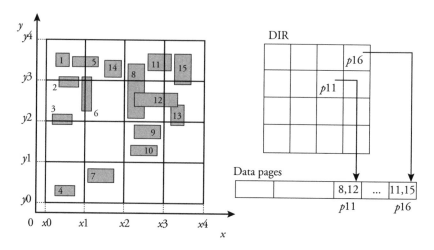

Figure 6.5   A fixed grid for rectangle indexing.

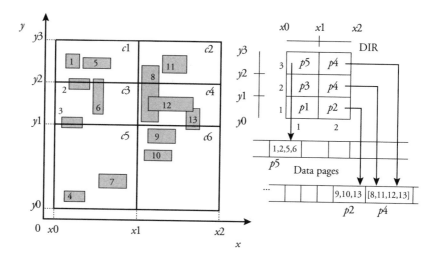

Figure 6.6   A grid file for rectangle indexing.

now assigned to two cells. The objects in $p5$ have been distributed among pages $p5$ and $p6$, respectively referenced by cells $DIR[1, 3]$ and $DIR[2, 3]$. Observe the duplication of objects 5 and 6.

A cell split without directory split is shown in Figure 6.8: when inserting object 15, page $p4$ overflows. The new page $p7$ is allocated, and the cells $DIR[3, 2]$ and $DIR[3, 3]$ are updated in the directory.

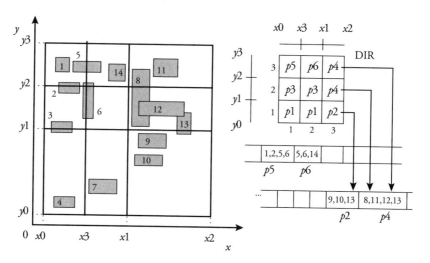

Figure 6.7   Insertion of object 14.

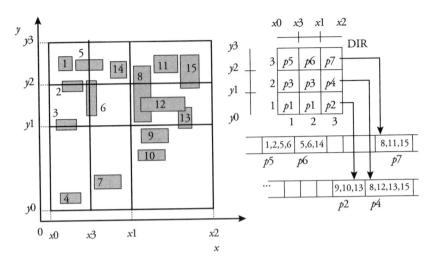

Figure 6.8   Insertion of object 15.

POINT AND WINDOW QUERIES

The point query algorithm works as follows. Given the point coordinates $P(a, b)$, one looks for the single cell containing P. In the case of the fixed grid, this can be done in constant (CPU) time, and in logarithmic time with the grid file by using a dichotomic search on the scales. One disk access is necessary to read the page referenced by the cell. One obtains a collection of entries[25] E. It remains, for each entry e in E, to test whether $e.mbb$ contains P. In a third step (refinement step), the object with identifier $e.oid$ is fetched in order to test for the inclusion of P in the actual geometry of the spatial object (see Chapter 5).

The algorithm follows. It returns the set of object identifiers for objects whose bounding box contains the point argument P. RANK(v, S) returns an integer, which is the rank of the interval in array S containing v (this can be implemented as a linear search or as a dichotomic search) whereas READPAGE(p) brings a page to main memory.

---

25. Recall that an index entry is a pair (mbb, oid), where mbb is the bounding box of an object with identifier oid.

ALGORITHM	GF-PointQuery ($P(a, b)$: point): set(oid)

begin
   $result = \emptyset$
   // Compute the cell containing P
   $i = $ Rank(a, S_x); $j = $ Rank(b, S_y)
   $page = $ ReadPage ($DIR[i,j].PageID$)
   for each e **in** $page$ **do**
     if ($P \in e.mbb$) **then** $result$ += {$e.oid$}
   end for
   return $result$
end

An example of a point query on the grid file is shown in Figure 6.9.
Cell $DIR[3, 2]$ is retrieved, and page $p4$, containing four entries, is
loaded. The sequential test on the four entries yields entries 8 and 12
containing P.

The window query algorithm works as follows. The first step consists
of computing all cells that overlap the window argument. In a second
step, each of them is scanned, as in the point query algorithm. Because
the result is likely to have duplicates, they need to be removed. This is
performed by sorting.

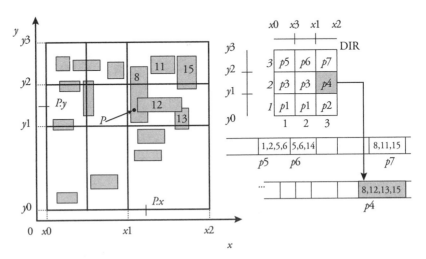

Figure 6.9 Point query with the grid file.

ALGORITHM	GF-WINDOWQUERY $(W(x_1, y_1, x_2, y_2)$: rectangle): set(oid)

```
begin
  result = Ø
  // Compute the low-left cell intersecting W
  i₁ = RANK (x₁, Sₓ); j₁ = RANK (y₁, Sᵧ)
  // Compute the top-right cell intersecting W
  i₂ = RANK (x₂, Sₓ); j₂ = RANK (y₂, Sᵧ)
  // Scan the grid cells
  for (i = i₁; i ≤ i₂; i++) do
    for (j = j₁; j ≤ j₂; j++) do
      // Read the page, and test each entry
      page = READPAGE (DIR[i,j].PageID)
      for each (e in page) do
        if (W ∩ e.mbb ≠ Ø) then result += {e.oid}
      end for
    end for
  end for
  // Sort the result, and remove duplicates
  SORT (result); REMOVEDUPL (result);
  return result
end
```

Two points are noteworthy:

◆ Removing duplicates can be costly and space consuming. Its time complexity is superlinear in the size of the result.

◆ Loading several pages can be accelerated if they are consecutive on the disk (a sequential scan of n pages is far more efficient than n random accesses).

It is easy to see that a point query can be carried out in constant I/O time (the two disk accesses principle holds), whereas the number of I/Os for the window query is proportional to the window area.

DISCUSSION

The grid structure for rectangle indexing seems to meet most of the requirements discussed in Section 6.1. Nevertheless, several problems remain. First, the object duplication in neighbor cells increases the number of entries in the index, and therefore the index size. This effect becomes more and more significant as the data set size increases and as the cell size decreases down to the *mbb*'s size. Second, removing duplicates from the result is expensive when the result size is large. Last, but not least, the efficiency of the SAM relies on the assumption that the directory is resident in central memory. For very large data sets, experiments show that this is impossible. If the directory has to be partly on disk, its management becomes complex and the response time is degraded, in that supplementary I/Os are necessary to access the directory. There have been some proposals to improve this situation, which render the SAM much more complex.

6.2.2   *The Linear Quadtree*

The SAMs presented in this section and in the next enable a simple extension of DBMSs using their B-tree as an index. Rectangles to be indexed are mapped to cells obtained by a recursive decomposition of the space into quadrants, known as *quadtree decomposition*. Cells (and associated rectangles) are indexed by a B-tree using the cell rank as a key. The scheme presented in this section and called *linear quadtree* relies on the *mbb* of spatial objects, whereas the structure (called a *z-ordering tree*) presented in the following section approximates the object geometry not by its *mbb* but by cells from its quadtree decomposition. We first describe the *quadtree* on which all SAMs are based.

THE QUADTREE

This main memory data structure is commonly utilized for accelerating the access to objects in the 2D plane because of its simplicity. In the following we sketch a variant for indexing a collection of rectangles (the *mbb* of objects) stored on disk. The search space is recursively decomposed into quadrants until the number of rectangles overlapping each quadrant is less than the page capacity. The quadrants are named North West (NW), North East (NE), South West (SW), and South East (SE). The index is represented as a quaternary tree (each internal node has four children, one per quadrant). With each leaf is associated a disk page, which stores the index entries, as defined in Section 6.2.1. As in the case of the grid file, a rectangle appears in as many leaf quadrants as it overlaps. Figure 6.10 shows a partitioning of the search collection for the collection of Figure 6.7 and its associated tree. The leaves are labeled with their corresponding rectangles. We assume in this example a page capacity of four entries.

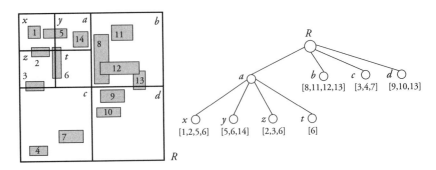

Figure 6.10 A quadtree.

Point query is simple with the quadtree. A single path is followed from the tree root to a leaf. At each level, one chooses among the four quadrants the one that contains the point argument. The leaf is read and scanned, as for the grid. Figure 6.11 illustrates a point query and the path followed from the root to a leaf, with rectangle 5 as a result. For the window query, one has to find all leaf quadrants that intersect the window argument. Because this SAM is not central to our study, we will not detail the algorithm, which is a bit more complex than for the grid. However, we shortly describe the dynamic insertion of rectangles.

A rectangle will be inserted in every leaf quadrant it overlaps. To insert the rectangle, as many paths as there are leaves that overlap the rectangle will be followed. The page p associated with each leaf is read. Then two cases may happen: either p is not full (a new entry is inserted) or it is full. Then the quadrant is subdivided into four quadrants. Three new pages are allocated. The entries of the old page as well as the new one are distributed among the four pages. An entry e is added to each

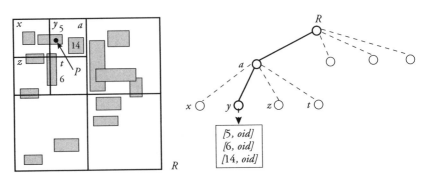

Figure 6.11 A point query on a quadtree.

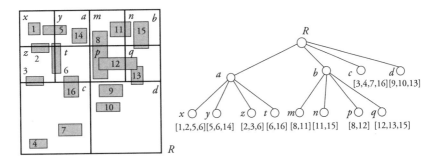

Figure 6.12   Insertion in a quadtree.

of the four pages, whose quadrants intersect *e.mbb*. Figure 6.12 shows the index obtained after the insertion of rectangles 15 and 16. The insertion of 15 leads to the split of *b* into quadrants *m*, *n*, *p*, and *q*. 15 is added to leaves *n* and *q*. The insertion of 16 does not lead to any split. 16 is added to leaves *c* and *t*.

This variant of a quadtree does not meet several of the requirements of a SAM. The essential reason for this mismatch is the small number of children (the node *fan-out*) fixed to 4, which occupies only a small part of a page. Then it is not easy to map a quadtree to disk pages. Tree structures with large node fan-out (such as the B-tree or R-tree, discussed in the following) allow one to efficiently map a node to a disk page and are thus more appropriate for secondary memory access methods.

The quadtree query time is related to the tree depth, which might be large. In the worst case, each internal tree node is in a separate page, and the number of I/Os is equal to the tree depth. If the collection is static, there exist efficient packings of the tree nodes onto pages, but the performance degrades in the dynamic case. Furthermore, like the grid file, the quadtree previously described suffers from object duplication in several leaves. When the collection size is so large that the quadrant size is of the order of the size of the rectangles to be indexed, the duplication rate (and therefore the index size) is exponentially increasing, and the SAM is not effective anymore.

SPACE-FILLING CURVES

A *space-filling curve* defines a total order on the cells of a 2D grid. This order is useful because it partially preserves proximity; that is, two cells close in space are likely to be close in the total order. Even though this is not always the case, some curves provide a reasonable approximation of this proximity property. The order should also be stable with respect to the resolution of the grid.

We describe two popular space-filling curves using, as an underlying grid, an $N \times N$ array of cells where $N = 2^d$. The grid can be seen as a complete quadtree with depth d.

The first variety (see Figure 6.13a), known as *z-order* or *z-ordering*, is generated as follows. A label is associated with each node of the complete quadtree, chosen among strings over the alphabet (0, 1, 2, 3). The root has for a label the empty string. The NW (respectively, NE, SW, SE) child of an internal node with label k has for a label $k.0$ (respectively, $k.1$, $k.2$, $k.3$), where "." denotes string concatenation. Then the cells are labeled with strings of size d. We can sort the cells according to their labels (in lexicographic order). For example, choosing a depth $d = 3$ and ascendent order, cell 212 is before cell 300 and after cell 21. The ordering NW, NE, SW, SE justifies its *z-order* name.[26] This order is also called Morton code.

The Hilbert curve is also a one-dimensional curve, which visits every cell within a 2D grid. The shape is not a Z but a Π. Unlike *z*-ordering,

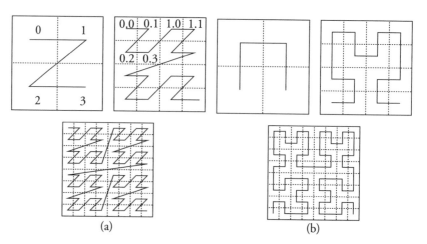

(a)   (b)

Figure 6.13   Space-filling curves: *z*-ordering (a) and Hilbert curve (b).

---

26. As a matter of fact, the original *z*-order (see bibliographic notes) has an "N" shape: the order between quadrants is SW, NW, SE, NE.

the Hilbert curve consists of segments of uniform length; that is, we never have to "jump" to a distant location while scanning the cells (Figure 6.13b). It is easy to see that in both cases there exist some unavoidable situations in which two objects are close in the 2D space, but far from one another on the space-filling curve.

QUADTREE LABELING

Now take a quadtree of depth d. It can be embedded in a grid with $N = 2^d$, as previously described. Any leaf quadrant can be labeled with a string of size $\leq d$. Figure 6.14 shows an example of such a quadtree. Observe (1) that the order of the leaves corresponds to a left-to-right scan of the leaves, and (2) that the labels are not of the same size. The size of the label is the depth of the leaf in the tree. The label of a leaf can also be seen as the label of a path from the root to the leaf.

Note also that if a leaf L contains a grid cell C, then the label l of L is a *prefix* of the label c of C, and we have $l < c$, where the order $<$ is the ascendent lexicographic order on strings. For example, $3 < 31 < 312$.

LINEAR QUADTREE

The key observation is that once the entries [mbb, oid] have been assigned (as for a regular quadtree) to a quadtree leaf with label l, and stored in a page with address p, then we index in a B+tree the collection of pairs (l, p) keyed on the leaf label l (Figure 6.15).

Such a structure provides a nice packing of quadtree labels into B+ tree leaves. The packing is dynamic; that is, it persists when inserting and deleting objects in the collection. For example, entries corre-

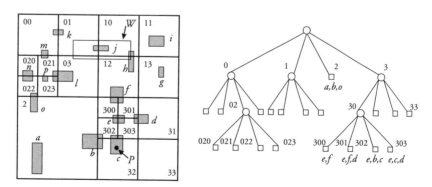

Figure 6.14 A quadtree labeled with z-order.

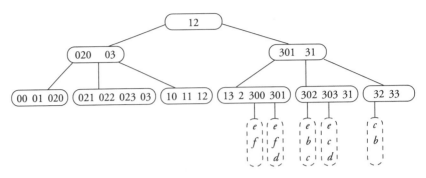

Figure 6.15   The leaves of the quadtree indexed with a B+tree.

sponding to leaves with labels 13, 2, 300, and 301 are in the same page. However, such a scheme has the same redundancy problem as the variant of the quadtree previously presented: *mbb*s that overlap several quadtree leaves are duplicated in pages associated with these leaves. As an example, *e* is stored in four pages. We will see in the following another linear structure that avoids duplication of *mbb*s.

POINT QUERY WITH A LINEAR QUADTREE

Retrieving identifiers of objects whose *mbb* contains a point P necessitates three steps:

◆ *Step 1: point label computation.* Compute the label l (a string of length d) of the grid cell containing P. This is performed by function POINTLABEL.

◆ *Step 2: quadtree leaf retrieval in the B+tree.* Let L be the label of the quadtree leaf that contains P. Then either $L = l$, the quadtree leaf is at depth d, or L is a prefix of l: its length is less than d and the leaf quadrant contains the grid cell including P. More precisely, this quadrant corresponds to the entry in the B+tree whose key L is the largest value less than or equal to l. Looking for such an entry is not a basic function provided with B+trees. We call such a function MAXINF (l). Although simple, it requires a slight modification of the code usually associated with this access method.

◆ *Step 3: leaf access and scan.* Once the B+tree entry $[L, p]$ has been found, one must as usual access the page with address p, scan all pairs $[mbb, oid]$ in this page, and check which $mbb(s)$ contains point P. The result is a list of object identifiers.

This algorithm is illustrated in Figure 6.14. From the coordinates of P, one finds that the grid cell containing P has for a label 320 (first step). One then retrieves in the B+tree, using function MAXINF, the maximal leaf label smaller than 320; that is, the leaf with label 32 (step 2). It remains (step 3) to access the page and scan the entries checking for each of them whether the *mbb* contains P: object c is found. The algorithm is summarized in the following.

ALGORITHM	LQ-PointQuery (P: point): set(*oid*)

```
begin
   result = ∅
   // Step 1: compute the label of the point
   l = POINTLABEL(P)
   // Step 2: the entry [L, p] is obtained by traversing the B+tree with key l.
   [L, p] = MAXINF (l)
   // Step 3: get the page and retrieve the objects
   page = READPAGE (p)
   for each e in page do
      if (e.mbb contains P) then result += {e.oid}
   end for
   return result
end
```

WINDOW QUERY WITH A LINEAR QUADTREE

The idea is to compute the interval I of labels covering all quadrants that overlap window W, and then to issue a range query on the B+tree with I. This is done in three steps.

◆ *Step 1.* Compute the label l of the NW window vertex, as in step 1 of the point query algorithm. Then compute MAXINF(l), as in step 2 of that algorithm. This yields [L, p], where label L is the lower bound of the interval. Then compute the label l' of the SE window vertex and MAXINF (l'). This gives [L', p'], where L' is the upper bound.

◆ *Step 2.* Issue a range query with interval [L, L'] on the B+tree, which retrieves all entries [l, p] whose label l lies in this interval.

◆ *Step 3.* For each B+tree entry $e = [l, p]$, compute the quadrant labeled by $e.l$ with function QUADRANT($e.l$). If QUADRANT($e.l$) overlaps the window, access the quadtree page $e.p$ and test each of the quadtree entries $[mbb, oid]$ for overlap with W.

Consider again the example of Figure 6.14 and the query window with argument W. The label of the NW vertex of W is 012, and the label of the SE vertex is 121. One then searches the B+tree of Figure 6.15 with function MAXINF for the largest quadtree labels less than 012 and 121, respectively. One obtains MAXINF(012) = 01 and MAXINF(121) = 12 (end of step 1).

Then (step 2) a range query on the B+tree of Figure 6.14 with interval [01, 12] is issued. For each entry e found during the scan (step 3), we access the page *only* if W overlaps QUADRANT($e.l$). This is not necessary, for instance, for the entries with labels 020–023 and 11. The algorithm is summarized in the following.

ALGORITHM　　　LQ-WINDOWQUERY $(W : \text{rectangle})$: set(oid)

---

begin
  result = ∅
  // Step 1: From the vertices *W.nw* and *W.se* of the window, compute
  // the interval $[L, L']$. This necessitates two searches through the B+tree.
  l = POINTLABEL (*W.nw*); $[L, p]$ = MAXINF (l)
  l' = POINTLABEL (*W.se*); $[L', p']$ =MAXINF(l')
  // Step 2: The set Q of B+tree entries $[l, p]$ with $l \in [L, L']$ is computed.
  Q = RANGEQUERY $([L, L'])$
  // Step 3: For each entry in Q whose quadrant overlaps W, access
  // the page
  for each q **in** Q **do**
    if (QUADRANT ($q.l$) overlaps W) **then**
      page = READPAGE ($q.p$)
      // Scan the quadtree page
      for each e **in** *page* **do**
        if (*e.mbb* overlaps W) **then** *result* += {*e.oid*}
      end for
    end if
  end for
  // Sort the result, and remove duplicates
  SORT (*result*); REMOVEDUPL (*result*);
  return *result*
end

The price to pay for mapping a 2D collection of quadrants onto a one-dimensional list of ordered cells is, as expected, an important clustering mismatch. In the interval $[L, L']$, there may be a large number of quadrants that do not overlap window W. Therefore, the range query might require more I/O than necessary. However, the pages associated with the quadrants that do not overlap W are not accessed.

INSERTION OF RECTANGLES

Two cases must be considered: either there is no split of the embedded quadtree, and the quadrant page is accessed and updated, or there is a split of the embedded quadtree. In this case, one entry of the B+tree must be deleted and replaced by four new entries (i.e., one per new quadtree page).

ANALYSIS

The number of I/Os for a point query has two components: (1) the number of I/Os for accessing a leaf of the B+tree (step 2), and (2) access to the quadrant page (step 3). Then the number of I/Os is $d + 1$, where d is the depth of the B+tree. We know that this is true even with skewed distributions, or in dynamic situations, because of the B+tree structure whose space and time performance is dependent on its size only. This efficient behavior, even in worst-case conditions, is at the origin of its use in the design of such a SAM.

The number of I/Os for a window query is more difficult to evaluate. Step 1 requires two accesses to the B+tree (i.e., $2d$ I/Os). Step 2 requires d I/O to reach the leaf corresponding to the lower bound of the interval, and then as many I/Os as there are chained B-tree leaves to be scanned. The number of I/Os of step 2 is dependent on the size of the interval (i.e., the size of the window). There exist more efficient algorithms, which avoid searching for quadrants that do not overlap the window argument, but the price to be paid is a serious increase in design complexity.

6.2.3   *The z-Ordering Tree*

In contrast to all SAMs studied in this chapter, the structure detailed in the present section does not use as an approximation of the object its *mbb*. Instead, the geometry of each object is decomposed into a quadtree of depth bounded by d, and one indexes the set of quadtree leaves that approximate the geometry. The leaves' labels (whose size is $\leq d$) are then inserted into a B+tree. The structure is known as a *z-ordering tree*.

The construction algorithm uses the following basic step. Given an object geometry o and a quadrant q, one checks whether o overlaps *all* leaves of the complete quadtree rooted at q. Then q is reported as an element of the resultant set. Otherwise, one decomposes o into as many pieces (≤ 4) as there are subquadrants of q overlapping o, and recursively applies the same process to each piece. The recursion stops when the maximal depth d is reached. The quadrant is then said to be *minimal*.

Alternately, the resulting set can be seen as a raster approximation of the object with a fixed grid of 4^d cells, in which sibling (NW, NE, SW, SE) cells, if any, have been recursively compounded.

Figure 6.16 illustrates the object decomposition and approximation. The object approximation is the list of quadrants with labels $\{023, 03, 103, 12, 201, 210, 211, 300, 301, 302\}$. All are minimal quadrants (or grid cells) at depth 3, except two quadrants at depth 2 with labels 03 and 12. The following algorithm summarizes the decomposition process. The operator $+$ denotes set union, whereas $\cup$ denotes geometric union. At the beginning, DECOMPOSE is called with q = search space.

ALGORITHM   DECOMPOSE (o: geometry, q: quadrant): set(quadrant)

```
begin
    decomp_NW, decomp_NE, decomp_SW, decomp_SE: set(quadrant)
    result = Ø
    // Check that q overlaps o, else do nothing
    if (q overlaps o) then
        if (q is minimal) then
            result = {q}
        else
            // Decompose o into pieces, one per subquadrant
            for each sq in {NW(q), NE(q), SW(q), SE(q)} do
                decomp_sq = DECOMPOSE (o, sq)
            end for
            // If each decomposition results in the full subquadrant, return q
```

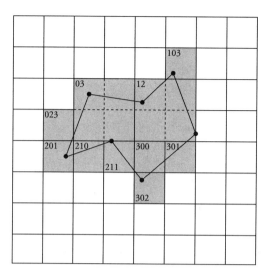

Figure 6.16 *z*-ordering and object decomposition.

```
        if (decomp_NW ∪ decomp_NE ∪ decomp_SW ∪ decomp_SE = q) then
            result = {q}
        else
            // Take the set union of the four decompositions
            result = decomp_NW + decomp_NE + decomp_SW + decomp_SE
        end if
      end if
    end if
    return result
end
```

A collection of eight objects, together with their *z*-ordering decomposition, is shown in Figure 6.17. The quadtree has a maximal depth

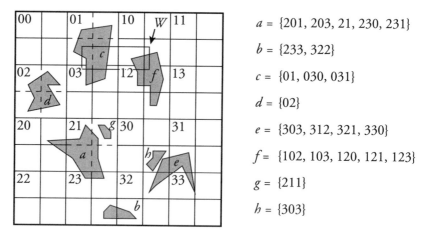

Figure 6.17   A set of objects with z-ordering decomposition.

$d = 3$. We obtain a set of entries $[l, oid]$, where l is a cell label and *oid* is the identifier of the object whose approximation contains or overlaps the cell with label l. For instance, object a in Figure 6.17 is represented by the following entries:

$$\{[201, a], [203, a], [21, a], [230, a], [231, a]\}$$

Obviously, this scheme, like the previous linear quadtree, implies duplication. An object's *id* is in as many entries as there are cells in its approximation. Conversely, there may be in the resulting collection several entries with the same l but with different *ids* when several object approximations share the same cell at the same level. This is the case for objects e and h, which share label 303. Finally, note that some objects may overlap the same cell, but at different decomposition levels (see objects a and g).

Entries are then inserted in a B+tree keyed on their label l. Figure 6.18 shows the B+tree obtained from the z-ordered data set of Figure 6.17. The *ids* are available in the B+tree leaf pages, whereas with the linear quadtree (see Figure 6.15), a supplementary page access from the B+tree leaf page is necessary. It is worth noting that the same object may be represented in two quite distant leaves of the B+tree, because of some unavoidable "jump" in the z-order. For example, object b is decomposed into two cells: the corresponding entries are stored in two distinct and non-neighbor pages of the B+tree.

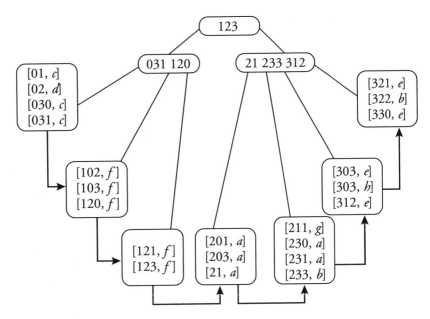

Figure 6.18   *z*-ordering tree.

The point and window algorithms are very similar to those for the linear quadtree. In the last step, one only needs to keep the *oid* of entries that overlap the window argument. The following is the WIN-DOWQUERY algorithm. The point query algorithm is left as an exercise.

ALGORITHM   ZO-WINDOWQUERY (*W :* rectangle): set(*oid*)

---

begin
   result = ∅
   // Step 1: From the vertices *W.nw* and *W.se* of the window, compute
   // the interval [*L, L'*]. This necessitates two searches through the B+tree.
   l = POINTLABEL (*W.nw*); [*L, p*] = MAXINF (*l*)
   l' = POINTLABEL (*W.se*); [*L', p'*] = MAXINF (*l'*)
   // Step 2: Compute the set *E* of entries [*l, oid*] such that *l* ∈ [*L, L'*].
   E = RANGEQUERY ([*L, L'*])
   // Step 3: For each entry in *E* that overlaps *W*, report the *oid*
   for each *e* in *E* **do**
      if (QUADRANT (*e.l*) overlaps *W*) **then** *result* += {*e.oid*}
   end for

```
// Sort the result, and remove duplicates
SORT (result); REMOVEDUPL (result);
return result
end
```

Examine window W in Figure 6.17. The labels of the minimal quadrants that contain $W.nw$ and $W.se$ are, respectively, 012 and 121. Function MAXINF gives, respectively, the entries [01, c] and [121, f], and the range query on the B+tree scans the first three leaves of the structure. Some entries are scanned, such as [02, d], which are not relevant to the query.

The number of I/Os for a window query depends on the window size. Step 1 requires one to access the B+tree twice ($2d$ I/Os, where d denotes the depth of the B+tree). Step 2 requires d I/Os to reach the leaf corresponding to the lower bound of the query interval, and then as many I/Os as the number of chained B+tree leaves to be scanned.

It is interesting to compare the linear quadtree to the z-ordering tree. With the latter structure, the B-tree depth, and therefore the number of I/Os, is likely to be larger because there are as many entries as there are cells in the decomposition of all objects. The finer the grid resolution, the better the objects' approximation but the larger the number of entries to be indexed in the B+tree.

With the linear quadtree, the number of B+tree entries is much smaller, because it is equal to the number of quadtree quadrants. However, a supplementary I/O is required per quadrant overlapping the window.

A RASTER VARIANT OF z-ORDERING (WITH REDUNDANCY)

A variant of the previous scheme consists of decomposing the object into elementary grid cells. The approximation is the set of minimal grid cells that contain, are contained by, or overlap the object. In other words, there is no gathering of sibling cells into larger quadrants, and the resulting set of cells is the *raster* representation of the object. This is shown in Figure 6.19 on the collection of objects of Figure 6.17. Object d, for instance, is now represented by four cells instead of one (see the difference on object a in Figure 6.17, for instance). All labels have the same size, equal to the depth $d = 3$.

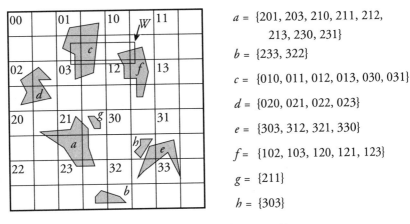

$a = \{201, 203, 210, 211, 212,$
$\qquad\quad 213, 230, 231\}$

$b = \{233, 322\}$

$c = \{010, 011, 012, 013, 030, 031\}$

$d = \{020, 021, 022, 023\}$

$e = \{303, 312, 321, 330\}$

$f = \{102, 103, 120, 121, 123\}$

$g = \{211\}$

$h = \{303\}$

Figure 6.19   A set of objects with raster decomposition.

In this particular case, the redundancy is worse, and the number of entries in the B+tree is larger. However, the algorithms for point and window queries (as well as spatial joins, Chapter 7) are much simpler. In particular, for the window query, the interval bounds are grid cell labels computed with function POINTLABEL. Because all cells are minimal, we do not need function MAXINF and therefore can use the B+tree existing code implemented in each DBMS without any modification. Figure 6.20 shows a B+tree for the raster decomposition. Given the same window W, with point labels 012 and 121, we can now directly issue a range query on the interval [012, 121]. Indeed, any object o overlapping the cell with label 012 is represented by an entry [012, o]. The WINDOWQUERY algorithm follows.

ALGORITHM   ZR-WINDOWQUERY (W: rectangle): set(oid)

begin
   result = ∅
   // Step 1: From the vertices $W.nw$ and $W.se$ of the window, compute
   // the interval $[L, L']$. This necessitates two searches through the B+tree.
   L = POINTLABEL ($W.nw$); L' = POINTLABEL ($W.se$)
   // Step 2: Compute the set E of entries $[l, oid]$ such that $l \in [L, L']$.
   E = RANGEQUERY ($[L, L']$)
   // Step 3: For each entry in E that overlaps W, report the oid
   for each e in E **do**
      if (QUADRANT ($e.l$) overlaps W) **then** *result* += {$e.oid$ }

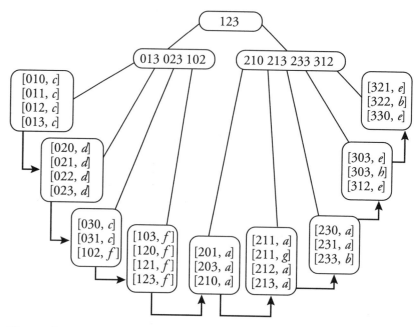

Figure 6.20 *z*-raster tree.

end for
// Sort the result, and remove duplicates
SORT (*result*); REMOVEDUPL (*result*);
return *result*
end

---

z-ORDERING WITHOUT REDUNDANCY

We end the presentation of linear SAMs with a variant of the *z*-ordering scheme without redundancy. The idea is the following. An object is not assigned to all quadrants it overlaps, but to the *smallest* quadrant that contains it.

In Figure 6.21, *b* is assigned to the initial search space with an empty label (_). Objects *c*, *d*, and *g* are, respectively, assigned to quadrants with labels 0, 02, and 211. The advantage of this SAM is that there are no duplications of objects into several quadrants. A drawback, however, is that the ratio between the object size and the assigned quadrant size might be small. In the case, such as for *b*, where the quadrant is close to the root, this implies that the object appears—as a false drop—in a

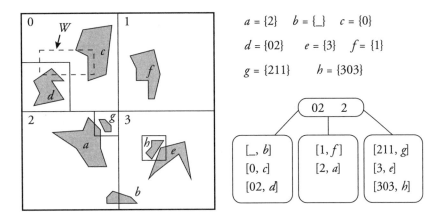

Figure 6.21 Z-ordering without redundancy.

large number of queries. Whatever the position of the point or window query, b is part of the candidate set of *all* queries, and thus will be processed during the refinement step.

The structure itself is a simple variant of the z-ordering tree. With each quadtree node, whether internal or leaf, is associated a list of objects contained in this quadrant. Each quadrant is assigned a label, as previously defined, which is a string over $\{0, 1, 2, 3\}$ or the empty string ($\_$) for the root. For each indexed object, there is an entry $[l, oid]$, where l is the label of the quadrant the object has been assigned to, and oid is the id of the object. As for the z-ordering tree, the entries are stored in a B+tree keyed on the label (see Figure 6.21). In contrast to the z-ordering scheme, there is a single entry per object. Thus, the B+tree is significantly less deep.

The following is an algorithm for the window query. We leave as an exercise the algorithm for a point query. The algorithm requires a function MINSUP(v), which looks for the smallest entry in the B+tree whose key is larger than or equal to v. PREFIX(k) is the set of labels that are prefix strings of k, including k. As an example, PREFIX(0312) yields $\{\_, 0, 03, 031, 0312\}$. NEXT(k) is the next entry in sequence in the B+tree leaf (or in the next chained B+tree leaf), after the entry k. The window argument W is also assigned the smallest quadtree quadrant containing W, with label $W.l$.

ALGORITHM   ZN-WINDOWQUERY (W: rectangle): set(*oid*)

---

begin
   result = ∅
   // Access the B-tree for each prefix of *W.l*
   for each *v* in PREFIX(*W.l*) **do**
      // *k* is the first entry whose label is greater than or = *v*
      k = MINSUP(*v*)
      // Scan the entries with label *v* if any, or (only for the last B-tree
      // access: *v* = *W.l*), the entries whose key is a suffix of *W.l*
      while (*k.l* = *v*) **or** (*v* = *W.l* and *W.l* in PREFIX(*k.l*)) **do**
         // Keep the *oid* of an entry
         result +={*k.oid*}
         k =NEXT(*k*) // Next entry in sequence
      end while
   end for
   return *result*
end

The B+tree is accessed $n + 1$ times if n is the size of the label $W.l$ of the window argument. For each prefix v of $W.l$ (each of the first n times), one accesses the B-tree and looks for the smallest entry k whose label is larger or equal to v. It might happen that the label of k is larger than v. Then we go to the next v. Otherwise ($k.l = v$), one keeps the entry *oid* and goes to the next entry in sequence. During the last B-tree access (quadrant with label $W.l$), one takes not only the objects assigned to the quadrant with label $W.l$, if any, but the objects assigned to the subquadrants (i.e., such that $W.l$ is a prefix of $k.l$).

In regard to the algorithm, examine Figure 6.21. The window argument is assigned to the quadrant with label 0. The first B+tree access with key value $v = '\_'$ yields entry [_, b]. The second, and last, access, with key value 0, gives [0, c], and scans the leaves of the B-tree until a label that is not a suffix of 0 is found. In this case, the scan stops at label 1. Entry d is found. The candidate set is $\{b, c, d\}$. In the refinement step, object geometries are accessed and checked against the window argument.

Note that the geometric representation of b will be accessed, although this is clearly unnecessary. Then many objects represented by small-size labels (close to the root of the quadtree) are likely to be accessed in a systematic way, whatever the query. Such a situation should deteriorate the query performance.

A simple optimization is to store in the entries of the B+tree the *mbb* of each object, in addition to its *oid*. Then a test with the *mbb* prior to the insertion of an object in the result set avoids a lot of false drops.

6.2.4   *Remarks on Linear SAM*

To conclude, by introducing a mapping from a two-dimensional partitioning of the plane into a one-dimensional list of cells, we enable the use of a B+tree, which is dynamic and efficient in terms of memory space and response time, even in worst-case conditions. More importantly, because commercial DBMSs use as an access method a B+tree, it is then easy to extend the system to handle spatial data. Indexing spatial data through the DBMS B+tree not only provides reasonably efficient access but allows one to benefit from other system features, such as concurrency control, recovery, access from the query language, and so on. Another advantage is that such a technique shown on a quadtree can be used with other space-partitioning SAMs.

There are several disadvantages, however. First, as discussed at length earlier on, the mapping of two-dimensional data sets onto a one-dimensional order leads to a clustering loss, which in turn leads to less efficient window queries. However, the main drawback of these structures, except for the last linear SAM, is the duplication of objects in neighbor cells. This increases the index size, decreases the access performance, and leads to a possibly expensive sort of the result for duplicate removal.

6.3   DATA-DRIVEN STRUCTURES: THE R-TREE

The SAMs of the R-tree family belong to the category of data-driven access methods. Their structure adapts itself to the rectangle distribution in the plane. Like the B-tree, they rely on a balanced hierarchical structure, in which each tree node, whether internal or leaf, is mapped onto a disk page. However, whereas B-trees are built on single-value keys and rely on a total order on these keys, R-trees organize rectangles according to a containment relationship. With each node is associated a rectangle, denoted the *directory rectangle* (*dr*) in the following, which is the minimal bounding box of the rectangles of its child nodes.

To access one rectangle of the indexed collection, one typically follows a path from the R-tree root down to one or several leaves, testing each directory rectangle at each level for either containment or overlap. Because, like the B-tree, the depth *d* of an R-tree is logarithmic in the number of objects indexed, and each node is mapped onto a disk page, the number of I/Os in nondegenerated situations is logarithmic in the collection size, and therefore the SAM is quite time and space efficient.

We first present the R-tree structure as originally proposed. Because in some situations the search time degrades, several variants have been proposed. Two of them, called R∗tree and R+tree, are described in subsequent sections.

6.3.1 The Original R-Tree

An R-tree is a depth-balanced tree in which each node corresponds to a disk page. A *leaf node* contains an array of *leaf entries*. A leaf entry is a pair (*mbb*, *oid*), with the usual meaning. *mbb* is of the form $(x_1, y_1, \ldots x_d, y_d)$, where *d* is the search space dimension. Although the R-tree structure can handle data with arbitrary dimensions, we limit the presentation to the 2D case. A *non-leaf node* contains an array of node entries. The structure satisfies the following properties:

- For all nodes in the tree (except for the root), the number of entries is between *m* and *M*, where $m \in [0, M/2]$.
- For each entry (*dr*, *nodeid*) in a non-leaf node *N*, *dr* is the directory rectangle of a child node of *N*, whose page address is *nodeid*.
- For each leaf entry (*mbb*, *oid*), *mbb* is the minimal bounding box of the spatial component of the object stored at address *oid*.
- The root has at least two entries (unless it is a leaf).
- All leaves are at the same level.

Figure 6.22 shows an R-tree with *m* = 2 and *M* = 4. The indexed collection *C* contains 14 objects. The directory rectangles of leaves *a*, *b*, *c*, and *d* are represented by a dotted line.

The properties previously listed are preserved under any dynamic insertion or deletion. Observe that the structure, while keeping the tree balanced, adapts to the skewness of a data distribution. A region of

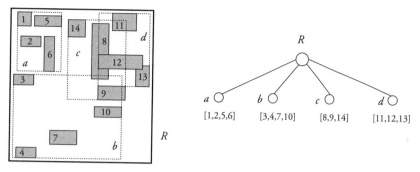

Figure 6.22 An R-tree.

the search space populated with a large number of objects generates a large number of neighbor tree leaves. This is not the case with space-partitioning trees, such as the quadtree. With the latter, some branches in the tree might be long, corresponding to regions with a high density of rectangles, whereas others might be short, the depth of the final tree corresponding to the region with highest density.

Figure 6.23b shows the directory rectangles of the leaves of an R-tree built on the hydrography data set of the state of Connecticut (Figure 6.23a). The rectangles' overlapping is obviously more important in dense areas than in sparse areas.

M, the maximal number of entries in a node, depends on the entry size $Size(E)$ and the disk page capacity $Size(P)$: $M = \lfloor Size(P)/Size(E) \rfloor$. Note that M might differ for leaf and non-leaf nodes,

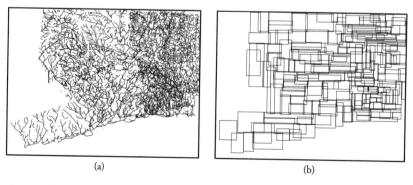

Figure 6.23 Indexing the hydrography network of Connecticut: TIGER data (simplified) (a) and R-tree (leaf level) (b).

because the size of an entry depends on the size of *nodeid* (non-leaf nodes) and *oid* (leaf nodes). *oid*, an object address inside a page, is generally longer than *nodeid*, which is a page address. The tuning of the minimum number of entries per node m between 0 and $M/2$ is related to the splitting strategies of nodes, discussed further in the following.

Given M and m, an R-tree of depth d indexes at least m^{d+1} objects and at most M^{d+1} objects. Conversely, the depth of an R-tree indexing a collection of N objects is at most $\lfloor \log_m(N) \rfloor - 1$ and at least $\lfloor \log_M(N) \rfloor - 1$. The exact value depends on the page utilization.[27]

To illustrate the R-tree time efficiency, assume the page size is 4K, the entry size is 20 bytes (16 bytes for the *mbb*, 4 bytes for the *oid*), and m is set to 40% of the page capacity. Hence, $M = 204$ and $m = 81$. An R-tree of depth 1 can index at least 6561 objects, whereas an R-tree of depth 2 can index at least 531,441, and up to 8,489,664, objects. Then, with a collection of one million objects, it takes three page accesses to traverse the tree, and a supplementary access to get the record storing the object. This example shows that even for large collections only a few page accesses are necessary to get down the tree in order to access the objects.

Unlike the space-partitioning SAMs seen previously, an object appears in one, and only one, of the tree leaves. However, the rectangles associated with the internal nodes do *not* constitute an exact partition of the space, and hence may overlap. In Figure 6.22, rectangles *b*, *c*, and *d* (which correspond to distinct leaves) overlap (see also Figure 6.23).

SEARCHING WITH R-TREES

This section presents a detailed algorithm for a point query. The algorithm for window queries is almost identical. The function RT-POINTQUERY is performed in two steps. First, one visits all children of the root whose directory rectangle contains the point P. Recall that because several directory rectangles may overlap, it might happen that the point argument falls into the intersection of several rectangles. All subtrees rooted at the intersecting rectangles then have to be visited.

---

27. The page utilization is defined as the ratio $[NbEntries \times Size(E)]/[NbPages \times Size(P)]$ between the space actually occupied by all entries (number of entries multiplied by the entry size) over the index space; that is, the number of pages (nodes) multiplied by the page capacity.

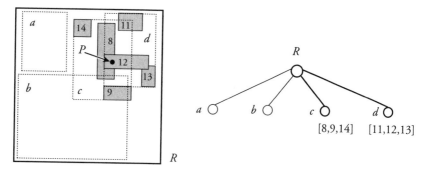

Figure 6.24   Point queries with R-trees.

The process is repeated at each level of the tree until the leaves are reached. For each visited node N, two situations may occur:

♦ At a given node, no entry rectangle contains the point, and the search terminates. This can occur even if P falls into the directory rectangle of the node. P falls into the so-called *dead space* of the node.

♦ P is contained by the directory rectangle of one or several entries. One must visit each associated subtree.

Hence, unlike the space-partitioning SAMs (i.e., the grid file or linear SAMs), several paths from the root to the leaves might be traversed. In a second step, the set of leaves produced in the first step is sequentially scanned: each leaf's entry whose *mbb* contains P is kept.

Figure 6.24 shows an example of a point query with P, which belongs to objects 8 and 12, as an argument. The query leads to the access of three nodes; namely, R, c, and d. A point query on the South-East corner point of object 8 would involve accessing four nodes; namely, R, b, c, and d.

The POINTQUERY algorithm with an R-tree follows.

ALGORITHM   RT-POINTQUERY (P: point): set (*oid*)

---

begin
  result = ∅
  // Step 1: Traverse the tree from the root, and compute *SL*, the
  // set of leaves whose *dr* contains *P*
  SL = RTREETRAVERSAL (*root*, *P*)

```
// Step 2: scan the leaves, and keep the entries that contain P
for each L in SL do
   // Scan the entries in the leaf L
   for each e in L do
      if (e.mbb contains P) then result + = {e.oid}
   end for
end for
return result
end
```

The algorithm for traversing the tree is given by the function RTREE-TRAVERSAL (see the following algorithm). It implements a left and depth-first traversal of the R-tree through recursive calls. The function is initially called with the root page address as the first argument.

ALGORITHM   RTREETRAVERSAL (*nodeid:* PageID, *P:* point): set of leaves

```
begin
   result = ∅
   // Get the node page
   N = READPAGE (nodeid)
   if (N is a leaf) return {N}
   else
      // Scan the entries of N, and visit those that contain P
      for each e in N do
         if (e.dr contains P) then
            result += RTREETRAVERSAL (e.nodeid, P)
         end if
      end for
   end if
   return result
end
```

It should be stressed that this algorithm is simplified from a memory management viewpoint. Keeping a set of leaves in memory would imply a large and unnecessary buffer pool. In an actual implementation, a one-page-at-a-time strategy should be used. We consider this issue in more detail in Chapter 7.

If the point falls into only one rectangle at each level, the point query necessitates d page accesses, where d is the depth of the tree, logarithmic in the number of indexed rectangles. Even if this seldom happens, one expects in practical situations that only a small number of paths are followed from root to leaves, and the expected number of I/Os is still logarithmic. Unfortunately, there are degenerated situations in which this number is not logarithmic anymore. In the worst case, it may occur that all directory rectangles of the leaves have a common intersection into which the point argument P falls. In this case, the entire tree must be scanned. However, despite its bad worst-case behavior, the R-tree is efficient in most practical situations.

The fact that the number of nodes visited is closely related to the overlapping of directory rectangles gave rise to numerous variants of the R-tree that intend to minimize this overlapping. You will see two of them at the end of the chapter.

The window query algorithm is a straightforward generalization of the point query in which the "contains P" predicate is replaced by the "intersect W" predicate, where W is the window argument. The larger the window, the larger the number of nodes to be visited.

INSERTION AND DELETION IN AN R-TREE

To insert an object, the tree is first traversed top-down, starting from the root (function INSERT). At each level, either one finds a node whose directory rectangle contains the object's *mbb* and then gets down the node subtree or there is no such node. Then a node is chosen such that the enlargement of its *dr* is minimal (function CHOOSESUBTREE). We repeat the process until a leaf is reached.

If the leaf is not full, a new entry [*mbb, oid*] is added to the page associated with the leaf. If the leaf directory rectangle has to be enlarged, the corresponding entry in the parent's node must be updated with the new value of *dr* (function ADJUSTENTRY). Note that this might imply the parent's directory rectangle in turn be enlarged. Thus, a leaf enlargement propagates up the tree, in the worst case up to the root (function ADJUSTPATH).

If the leaf l in which the object has been inserted is full, a *split* occurs. A new leaf l' is created, and the $M + 1$ entries are distributed among l and l'. How to split the leaf (function SPLIT) is the tricky part of the algorithm (explained later).

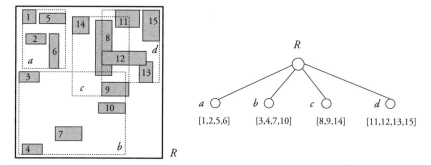

Figure 6.25   Insertion of object 15.

When the split is over, it remains to update the entry of the old leaf *l* in its parent node *f*, and to insert a new entry in *f* corresponding to the new leaf *l'*. If *f* itself is full because of this new insertion, the same splitting mechanism is applied to the internal node. In the worst case, this splitting process propagates up the tree to the root (function SPLITANDADJUST). The tree depth is incremented by 1 when the root is split.

We illustrate this process by inserting two new objects in the tree of Figure 6.22. For the sake of illustration, we assume that $M = 4$.

Object 15 (Figure 6.25) has first been inserted in leaf *d*. The *dr* of *d* must be enlarged to enclose this new object, and the *d* entry in the root must be adjusted. Object 16 (Figure 6.26) is to be inserted in leaf *b*. Because *b* already contains the four entries {3, 4, 7, 10}, a node overflow occurs (recall that the capacity *M* is 4), *b* is split. A new leaf, *e*, is then created, and the five entries are distributed among *b* and *e*.

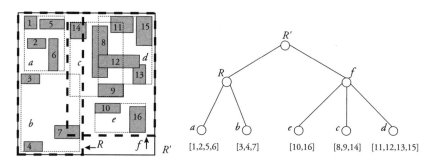

Figure 6.26   Insertion of object 16.

Entry 10 is moved to *e* (where entry 16 had already been inserted). Entries 3, 4, and 7 remain in *b*.

Now a new entry must be inserted in the parent of *b*, *R*. Because *R* already contains four children, it must in turn be split. The process is similar to that described for leaf *b*. A new node *f* is created, *a* and *b* stay in *R*, and *e*, *c*, and *d* are attached to *f*. Finally, a new root *R'* is created, whose two children are *R* and *f*. The insertion algorithm follows.

ALGORITHM   INSERT (*e:* LeafEntry)

---

begin
  // Initializes the search with root
  node = root
  // Choose a path down to a leaf
  while (*node* is not a leaf) **do**
    node = CHOOSESUBTREE (*node, e*)
  end while
  // Insert in the leaf
  INSERTINLEAF (*node, e*)
  // Split and adjust the tree if the leaf overflows, else adjust the path
  if (*node* overflows) **then**
    SPLITANDADJUST (*node*)
  else
    ADJUSTPATH (*node*)
  end if
end

Function CHOOSESUBTREE (*node, e*), which is not described here, picks the entry *ne* of *node* such that *ne.dr* either contains *e.mbb* or needs the minimum enlargement to include *e.mbb*. If several entries satisfy this, choose the one with smallest area.

Function ADJUSTPATH propagates the enlargement of the node's *dr* consecutive to an insertion. The process stops when either the *dr* does not require any adjustment or the root has been reached.

ALGORITHM   ADJUSTPATH (*node:* Node)

---

begin
  if (*node* is the root) **return**

```
  else
    // Find the parent of node
    parent = GETPARENT (node)
    // Adjust the entry of node in parent
    if (ADJUSTENTRY (parent, [node.mbb, node.id])) then
      // Entry has been modified: adjust the path for the parent
      ADJUSTPATH (parent)
    end if
  end if
end
```

ADJUSTENTRY (*node, child-entry*) is a Boolean function that looks for the entry *e* corresponding to *child-entry.id* in *node* and compares *e.mbb* with *child-entry.mbb*. If *e.mbb* needs to be updated because the *dr* of the child has been enlarged or shrunken, it is updated, and the function returns **true** (and **false** otherwise).

Function SPLITANDADJUST handles the case of node overflow. It performs the split and adjusts the path. It uses functions ADJUSTPATH and ADJUSTENTRY (already described), and can be recursively called in the case of propagated overflows.

ALGORITHM   SPLITANDADJUST (*node:* Node)

```
begin
  // Create a new node and distribute the entries
  new-node = SPLIT (node)
  if (node is the root) then
    CREATENEWROOT (node, new-node)
  else
    // Get the parent of node
    parent = GETPARENT (node)
    // Adjust the entry of node in its parent
    ADJUSTENTRY (parent, [node.id, node.mbb])
    // Insert the new node in the parent.
    INSERTINNODE (parent, [new-node.mbb, new-node.id])
    if (parent overflows) then
      SPLITANDADJUST(parent)
    else
      ADJUSTPATH (parent)
    end if
```

end if
end

CREATENEWROOT(*node, new-node*) allocates a new page p and inserts into p two entries: one for *node* and one for *new-node*. Observe that the root is the only node that does not respect the minimal space utilization fixed by m.

Once the entries have been distributed among the two nodes, the entry of *node* must be adjusted in *parent* (call of function ADJUSTENTRY). Then the new node is inserted into the parent node. Two cases may occur. Either the parent node overflows—in which case it must be split and adjusted—or it is only adjusted.

An important part of the algorithm is the *split* of a node. Recall the constraint of a minimal number of entries m in a node. Any solution with $m + i$ entries in one node and $M + 1 - m - i$ in the second, with $0 \leq i \leq M - 2m + 1$, is acceptable.

There are many ways of splitting a node. A well-designed splitting strategy should obey the following requirements:

♦ Minimize the total area of the two nodes.
♦ Minimize the overlapping of the two nodes.

Unfortunately, these two requirements are not always compatible, as illustrated in Figure 6.27. In the following, we focus on the first criterion.

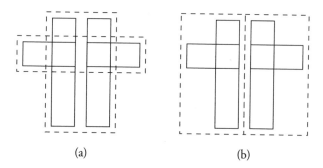

(a)   (b)

Figure 6.27   Minimal area and minimal overlap: a split with minimal area (a) and a split with minimal overlap (b).

A brute-force method is to exhaustively look at all possible distributions of rectangles among the two nodes and choose the one that minimizes the total area. Because M is of the order of 100 for common page sizes, this is clearly too expensive, the cost of this method being exponential in M.

Therefore, a trade-off between computation time and quality of the result has to be found. We now present two algorithms along these lines. The first, known as a *quadratic split* algorithm, has a computation time quadratic in M. It relies on the following heuristic. Two groups of entries are first initialized by "picking" two "seed" entries e and e', far away from each other, and more precisely such that the dead space is maximal. The dead space is defined as the area of the *mbb* of e and e' minus the sum of the areas of e and e'.

Then the remaining $M - 2$ entries are inserted in one of the two groups as follows. We call *expansion* of a group for an entry the dead space that would result from inserting the entry in this group. Then at each step we look for the entry e for which the difference in group expansions is maximal. We choose to add e to the group "closest" to the entry (for which the expansion is the smallest). In the case of equality, the following secondary criteria can be used: (1) choose the group with the smallest area, and (2) choose the group with the fewest elements.

ALGORITHM	QUADRATICSPLIT (E: set of entries)

```
begin
    MBB J; integer worst = 0, d1, d2, expansion = 0
    // Choose the first element of each group,
    // E' is the set of remaining entries
    for each e in E do
        for each e' in E do
            J = mbb(e.mbb, e'.mbb)
            if ((area(J) − area(e.mbb) − area(e'.mbb)) > worst) then
                worst = (area(J) − area(e.mbb) − area(e'.mbb))
                G₁ = {e}
                G₂ = {e'}
            end if
        end for
    end for
```

```
// Each group has been initialized. Now insert the remaining entries
E' = E − (G₁ ∪ G₂)
while (E' ≠ ∅) do
   // Compute the cost of inserting each entry in E'
   for each e in E' do
      d1 = area (mbb(e.mbb, G₁.mbb) − e.mbb)
      d2 = area (mbb(e.mbb, G₂.mbb) − e.mbb)
      if (d2 − d1 > expansion) then
         best-group = G₁; best-entry = e; expansion = d2 − d1
      end if
      if (d1 − d2 > expansion) then
         best-group = G₂; best-entry = e; expansion = d1 − d2
      end if
   end for
   // Insert the best candidate entry in the best group
   best-group = best-group ∪ best-entry
   E' = E' − {best-entry}
   // Each group must contain at least m entries.
   // If the group size added to the number of remaining
   // entries is equal to m, just add them to the group.
   if (|G₁| = m − |E'|) then G₁ = G₁ ∪ E'; E' = ∅
   if (|G₂| = m − |E'|) then G₂ = G₂ ∪ E'; E' = ∅
end while
end
```

The two parts of the algorithm (group initialization and insertion of entries) are both quadratic in M. In the last part of the algorithm, if it turns out that one of the groups (say, G_1) has been preferred to the other (say, G_2), the set of remaining entries E' must be assigned to G_2 independently from their location. This might lead to a bad distribution in some cases. Obviously, this depends on the parameter m, which defines the minimal cardinality of a group. It seems that $m = 40\%$ is a suitable value for this algorithm.

There exists a linear algorithm that consists of (1) choosing the seeds such that the distance along one of the axes is the greatest, and (2) assigning each remaining entry to the group whose *mbb* needs the least area enlargement. The algorithm is simpler and faster. However, as reported in several experiments, its result often suffers from an important overlap.

The deletion of an entry e from an R-tree is carried out in three steps: (1) find the leaf L that contains e, (2) remove e from L, and

(3) reorganize the tree if needed. Steps 1 and 2 are similar to the window query previously presented. The reorganization of the tree is the difficult part of the algorithm. It occurs when, after removal of an entry from a node N, N has less than m entries.

A simple approach is to delete the node and to insert the remaining $m - 1$ entries. The deletion algorithm follows.

ALGORITHM   DELETE (*e:* LeafEntry)

---

begin
  // Find the leaf containing e
  L = FindLeaf (e)
  // Remove entries and reorganize the tree, starting from L and e
  // The result is a set Q of nodes
  Q = Reorganize (L, e)
  // Reinsert entries in the nodes of Q
  Reinsert (Q)
end

The Reorganize function removes nodes that contain less than m entries. In the worst case, this can involve all levels of the tree. The function returns the set of removed nodes whose entries must be reinserted.

ALGORITHM   REORGANIZE (*N:* node, *e:* entry): set of node entries

---

begin
  Q: set of nodes, initially empty
  // Remove e from N
  N = N − {e}
  if (N is not the root) **then**
    if (|N| < m) **then**
      Q = Q ∪ {N}
      // Get the parent and reorganize it
      F = GetParent (N)
      Q = Q ∪ Reorganize (F, entry of N in F)
    else
      AdjustPath (N) // N has been modified: adjust the path
    end if
  end if

return *Q*
end

Once all nodes to be reinserted have been collected in *Q* by recursive calls (function REORGANIZE), the elements of *Q* are reinserted (function REINSERT). Reinserted elements may be either leaf entries or node entries, which must be inserted at the appropriate level in the tree.

The reinsertion process during deletion allows one to obtain a better clustering of rectangles and thus a better spatial organization of the R-tree. However, the overall quality highly depends on the insertion order. An initial creation of the tree with randomly distributed rectangles often results in an important overlapping of nodes. Indeed, once assigned to a node, an entry remains forever in the same part of the tree, although it could possibly be better located later on.

Consider the example in Figure 6.28. In step *a*, four objects are stored in a compact node *u*. Upon insertion of object 5, a split occurs. There is no good choice for the distribution of objects between node *u* and the new node *v*. Any distribution results in a large dead space in node *v*. In Figure 6.28 (step *b*), object 4 has been assigned with object 5 to node *v*. The subsequent insertions (objects 6 and 7, step *c*) do not change the situation, although a better distribution could then be possible.

The following explores two constructions that intend to overcome the poor spatial organization of R-trees due to random insertions. The R*tree relies on entry reinsertion to improve the clustering of *mbbs*, whereas *packed R-trees* pre-process a given set of rectangles to get the best insertion order.

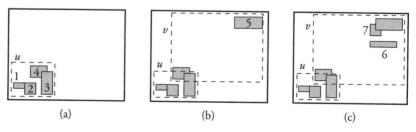

(a)   (b)   (c)

Figure 6.28   A bad insertion order.

6.3.2 The R*Tree

The R*tree is a variant of the R-tree that provides several improvements to the insertion algorithm. Essentially, these improvements aim at optimizing the following parameters: (1) node overlapping, (2) area covered by a node, and (3) perimeter of a node's directory rectangle. The latter is representative of the shape of the rectangles because, given a fixed area, the shape that minimizes the rectangle perimeter is the square.

There are no well-founded techniques to simultaneously optimize these three parameters. Thus, the design approach consists of considering each module of the insertion algorithm and experimenting with several heuristics. The following presents two variants that bring the most significant improvement with respect to the original R-tree. The first improves the split algorithm. Recall that when a node of capacity M overflows, a new page must be allocated, and the $M + 1$ entries have to be distributed among the two nodes. Because the size of the solution space (i.e., the number of possible solutions) is exponential in M, one cannot exhaustively look at all solutions for finding the best distribution.

The R-tree split algorithm first initializes the two groups with the two entries that are as far as possible from each other, then assigns each of the remaining entries to a group. The R*tree approach is different in the sense that it assumes the split to be performed along one axis (say, horizontal), and explores all possible distributions of objects above or below the split line.

The expected advantages of this method are illustrated in Figure 6.29 (assuming $M = 4$ and $m = 2$). The R-tree split algorithm chooses A and B as "seeds" for groups G_1 and G_2, respectively. Because A is much

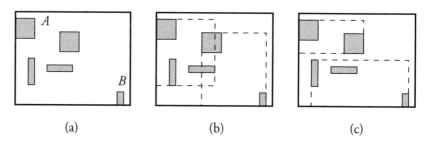

(a)   (b)   (c)

Figure 6.29   Splitting strategies: overflowing node (a), a split of the R-tree (b), and a split of the R*tree (c).

larger than B, subsequent insertions will tend to favor the group of A, G_1. However, when three rectangles have been assigned to G_1, the remaining entries are put in G_2, whatever their position. This results in a clearly non-optimal split.

On the other hand, the R*tree chooses the x axis and finds a partition in two nodes without overlapping. In order to find the best axis, one can sort on the upper or lower value of each rectangle. This yields $2(2(M - 2m + 2))$ computations. Now the best axis is the one such that S, the sum of perimeters, is minimal.

ALGORITHM   R*TREECHOOSEAXIS (E: set of entries)

```
begin
  Set variable min-perimeter to the maximum possible value
  for each axis a do
    sort E with respect to a
    S = 0
    // Consider all possible distributions
    for k = 1 to (M − 2m + 2) do
      G₁ = E[1, m + k − 1]; G₂ = E[m + k, M + 1]
      // The first m + k − 1 entries are stored in G₁, the remaining in G₂.
      Mg = perimeter (mbb(G₁)) + perimeter (mbb(G₂)) // Perimeter value
      S = S + Mg // Compute the sum of the perimeters for the current axis
    end for
    // If S is the minimal value encountered so far, then a becomes the best
      axis
    if  (S < min-perimeter) then
      best-axis = a
      min-perimeter = S
    end if
  end for
  return best-axis
end
```

Given the best axis, one chooses the distribution with minimal overlap. If two distributions share the same minimal overlap, one chooses the one with minimal area. These indicators can be computed together with S in R*TREECHOOSEAXIS.

The second important improvement in the R*tree insertion algorithm is the forced reinsertion strategy. Indeed, as seen previously, the

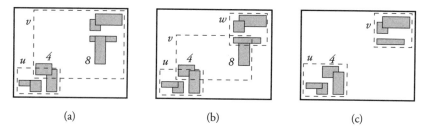

Figure 6.30   The R*tree reinsertion strategy: insertion of 8 (v overflows) (a), a split of the R-tree (b), and R*tree forced reinsertion of 4 (c).

insertion order can dramatically influence the quality of the R-tree organization. The R*tree tries to avoid the degenerated cases (such as those in Figure 6.28) by reinserting some entries whenever a node overflows.

Assume (see Figure 6.30a) that rectangle 8 is inserted in the tree of Figure 6.28c. Node v overflows, and the R-tree split algorithm will only perform a local reorganization with a rather important node overlapping (Figure 6.30b). The R*tree tries to avoid splitting by reinserting the rectangles in v for which the dead space in the node is the largest; here, rectangle 4. The reinsertion algorithm proceeds as follows:

◆ Remove 4 from v.
◆ Compute the new bounding box of v.
◆ Reinsert 4, starting from the root: the CHOOSESUBTREE algorithm assigns 4 to node u.
◆ Now entry 8 can be put into v, and no splits occur.

Because a node overflow might occur at any level of the tree, a removed entry must be reinserted at the same level it was initially inserted. This was already required by the DELETE function of the R-tree. However, we must avoid entering an infinite loop by reinserting the entries in their initial node. Hence, if we detect that a same node overflows a second time during the insertion of a given rectangle, the split algorithm must be carried out.

The entries to be reinserted are chosen as follows: compute the distance d between their centroid and the centroid of the node's *mbb*, sort in decreasing order on d, and take the p first entries from the sorted list. It seems that the best performance is obtained when $p = 30\%$ of the entries of an overflowing node are reinserted.

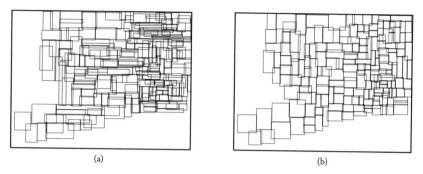

Figure 6.31   Comparison of R-tree (a) and R*tree (b) (state of Connecticut).

The improved split algorithm and the reinsertion strategy result in a much better organization of the R*tree with respect to the original R-tree, as illustrated in Figure 6.31, which gives both for the R-tree and the R*tree the *dr* of the leaves for the same collection of rectangles.

It is worth remembering that the data structures for the R-tree and R*tree are the same. Hence, the data retrieval operations defined for the R-tree remain valid with the R*tree. Due to the better organization of the R*tree, the performance of these operations is likely to be significantly improved.

6.3.3   R-Tree Packing

The algorithms presented so far for inserting entries in an R-tree (or an R*tree) are *dynamic* in the sense that they enable insertions and deletions in an already existing R-tree. However, the evolution of the structure with time does not allow one to optimize the space utilization and thus might lead to a performance degradation as the number of insertions and deletions grows.

In the *static* case, when the collection of rectangles is stable with time, one can pre-process the data before creating the R-tree. Several algorithms, called *packing algorithms*, have been proposed for the R-tree. The idea behind packing is best understood by looking at the B-tree case. If the data set to be indexed is known a priori, we can *sort* data, and construct the index bottom-up. First, the leaves are sequentially filled. The first M entries go to the first leaf, the M following to the second leaf, and so on. Once the leaf level has been created, the operation is recursively repeated on the following level up to the root. One obtains a B-tree with nearly 100% space utilization.

In the case of the R-tree, the pre-processing phase must sort the rectangles according to their location. We describe in the following a simple and efficient algorithm, called the Sort-Tile-Recusive (STR) algorithm.

The STR algorithm is as follows. Assume that the size of the data set is N. Then the minimal number of leaves is $P = \lceil N/M \rceil$, where M denotes, as usual, the node capacity. The idea is to organize the leaves as a "checkerboard" having vertical and horizontal slices. In addition, we require that the number of vertical slices be the same as the number of horizontal slices and equal to $\lceil \sqrt{P} \rceil$.

We first sort the source rectangles on the x coordinate of their centroid, and we partition the sorted list into $\lceil \sqrt{P} \rceil$ groups. This defines the vertical slices. Then the rectangles of each slice are loaded, sorted by y coordinate of their centroid, and grouped into runs of size M. This defines the leaves of the packed R-tree. Finally, we take the set of directory rectangles of the leaves and construct recursively the upper levels according to the same algorithm. The organization in horizontal or vertical slices is visualized in Figure 6.32, on the Connecticut hydrography data set.

All leaves (except those of the last vertical slice) are completely filled, so as to maximize space utilization. This may be a drawback if we want to allow subsequent dynamic insertions. Indeed, a split will occur at each level of the tree as soon as an object is inserted. Therefore, a space utilization lower than 100% should be chosen in an actual implementation.

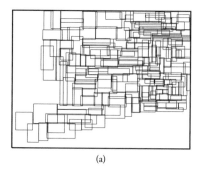
(a)

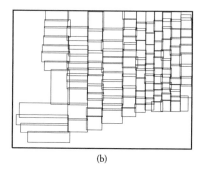
(b)

Figure 6.32   R-tree (a) and STR packed R-tree (b).

In spite of the optimized construction, there is still some (un-avoidable) overlapping among the nodes. We conclude the presentation of the R-tree with the R+tree variant, which generates no node overlapping.

6.3.4   The R+Tree

In the R+tree, the directory rectangles at a given level do not overlap. This has as a consequence that for a point query a single path is followed from the root to a leaf. Unlike the previous variants, the I/O complexity of this operation is thus bounded by the depth of the tree. The R+tree is defined as follows:

- The root has at least two entries, except when it is a leaf.
- The *dr* of two nodes at the same level cannot overlap.
- If node *N* is not a leaf, its *dr* contains all rectangles in the subtree rooted at *N*.
- A rectangle of the collection to be indexed is assigned to all leaf nodes the *dr*s of which it overlaps. A rectangle assigned to a leaf node *N* is either overlapping *N.dr* or is fully contained in *N.dr*. This duplication of objects into several neighbor leaves is similar to what we encountered earlier in other space-driven structures.

Figure 6.33 depicts an R+tree. Note that objects 8 and 12 are referenced twice. Object 8 is overlapping leaves *p* and *r*, whereas object 12 is overlapping leaves *p* and *q*. Note also that both at the leaf level and at the intermediate level, node *dr*s are not overlapping.

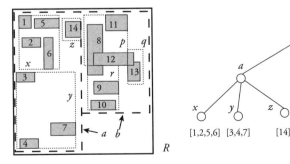

Figure 6.33   The R+tree.

The structure of an R+tree node is the same as that of the R-tree. However, because we cannot guarantee a minimal storage utilization m (as for the R-tree), and because rectangles are duplicated, an R+tree can be significantly larger that the R-tree built on the same data set.

The construction and maintenance of the R+tree are rather more complex than with the other variants of the R-tree. The following briefly outlines the dynamic insertion of an object.

At each level of the tree, a rectangle is inserted in all nodes the *drs* of which it overlaps. In order to achieve a zero overlap among the directory rectangles at the same level, the R+tree uses *clipping*. When a rectangle R to be inserted overlaps several directory rectangles $\{r_1, \ldots r_n\}$, R is split into subrectangles, one per r_i it overlaps, and inserted recursively in each of the paths starting at these r_is. Therefore, the same object will be stored in several leaves of the tree (duplication). For instance, in Figure 6.34a, R must be inserted in the subtrees rooted at r_1 and r_2.

If R is not fully contained in the union of the r_is it overlaps, one or several of the directory rectangles must be enlarged. This is similar to the R-tree insertion algorithm (see the ADJUSTPATH function), except that we must now prevent the enlarged nodes from overlapping. Unfortunately, this is not always possible (illustrated in Figure 6.34b), as none of the directory rectangles r_1, r_2, r_3, and r_4 can be enlarged without introducing some overlap. In that case, some reinsertion must be carried out.

Finally, when a node overflows, it has to be split. Once again, this is similar to the R-tree, except that the split must be propagated downward (see Figure 6.34c), still because of the nonoverlapping rule. This complicates the algorithms, and deteriorates the space utilization. For instance, in Figure 6.34c, the node A is split. Then the two children b and c must be split as well.

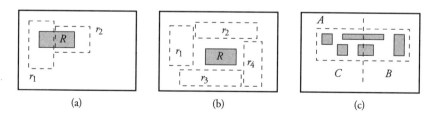

(a)   (b)   (c)

Figure 6.34 Operations on the R+tree: clipping in subrectangles (a), a deadlock (b), and a downward split propagation (c).

In summary, the point query performance benefits from the nonoverlapping of nodes. As for space-driven structures, a single path down the tree is followed, and fewer nodes are visited than with the R-tree. The gain for window queries is less obviously assessed. Object duplication not only increases the tree size, but potentially leads to expensive post-processing of the result (sorting for duplication removal).

6.3.5   Cost Models

We end the R-tree description with the presentation of a cost model. *Cost models* are useful for predicting the performance of an operation as a function of physical parameters of the spatial database, such as size of indices, size of records, selectivity of selection predicates, and so on. The following is a simple model for estimating the performance of operations on R-trees.

In order to simplify the presentation, we assume (without loss of generality) that the search space is a normalized unit square $[0, 1]^2$. Now consider a node N_i of an R-tree R, with a directory rectangle $N_i.dr$ of size $(s_{i,x}, s_{i,y})$, and assume that we execute point queries on the R-tree with uniformly distributed point arguments. Then the probability for a point query to fall into node N_i is

$$PQ(N_i) = s_{i,x} \times s_{i,y}$$

In other words, the probability is the ratio of the size of $N_i.dr$ and the size of the work space (which is equal to 1). Now the R-tree nodes visited during a point query are those whose dr contains the point argument. The number of visited nodes can be expressed as

$$PQ(R) = \sum_{i=1}^{n} PQ(N_i)$$

$$= \sum_{i=1}^{n} s_{i,x} \times s_{i,y},$$

where n denotes the number of nodes in R. These formulas can be extended to estimate the cost of window queries. Assume we are given a node N and a window w with size (w_x, w_y). The idea is to estimate the probability that $N.mbb$ intersects w as the probability of a point

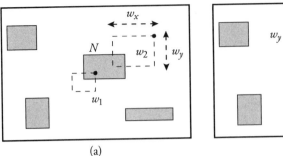 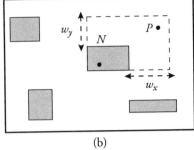

(a)   (b)

Figure 6.35 Estimating the cost of window queries: a window query (a) and its equivalent point query (b).

query with the upper-right corner of w. Indeed, two cases may happen (see Figure 6.35a):

- The upper-right corner of the window falls into $N.mbb$ (window w_1)
- The upper-right corner of w falls into an "inflation" of $N.mbb$, with w_x on the right and w_y above (window w_2)

It follows that a window w intersects $N.mbb$ if and only if its upper-right corner falls into the rectangle $W = (N.mbb.x_{min} + w_x, N.mbb.y_{min} + w_y)$. Because we assume that the window arguments are uniformly located in the search space, the cost can be estimated as for a point query over W (Figure 6.35b). In summary, the number $WQ(w)$ of nodes retrieved during a window query is

$$
WQ(w) = \sum_{i=1}^{n}(s_{i,x} + w_x) \times (s_{i,y} + w_y)
$$

$$
= \sum_{i=1}^{n} s_{i,x} \times s_{i,y} + w_y \times \sum_{i=1}^{n} s_{i,x}
$$

$$
+ w_x \times \sum_{i=1}^{n} s_{i,y} + n \times w_x * w_y
$$

This formula depends only on the properties of the R-tree, whatever its specific type (R-tree, R*tree) or construction mode (static or dynamic).

6.4   BIBLIOGRAPHIC NOTES

The design of 2D spatial structures for main memory was a flourish-ing research field in the computational geometry community in the 1970s. The need for external memory data structures, motivated by applications such as geographic applications, gave rise to an important research activity, both in the database and in the GIS communities (which started in the late 1970s). The classification of SAM is diffi-cult because of the large number of parameters involved. The space-driven versus data-driven classification of Section 6.1 is common, but too simple to take into account the large variety of structures proposed.

There exist a large number of comprehensive studies on SAM and related issues, among which [Sam90b, Sam90a] is one of the first text-books. It focuses, however, on space-driven access methods. Other gen-eral references of interest are [NW97, Aga97, GMUW00, MTT99]. A complete and recent survey of multidimensional access methods can be found in [GG98]. The latter reference distinguishes between point ac-cess methods (PAMs) and access methods for rectangles (SAMs). It also discusses transformation techniques that map a collection of rectangles onto a collection of 4D points that can then be managed by a point access method.

The B-tree proposed by Bayer and McCreight was first described in [BM72, Com82]. It has been utilized in numerous system designs, including all commercial relational DBMSs, because of its optimal per-formance. Lately, some extensions of the B-tree have been proposed for multidimensional access methods. The BV-tree [Fre95] is an attempt to generalize the B-tree to higher dimensions. A weight-balanced B-tree is proposed in [AV96]. The Cross-tree [GI99] is a multidimensional ver-sion of a B-tree that combines the B-tree data-driven partition of data with the quadtree space-driven partitioning.

PAMs index points and therefore do not need a decomposition in two steps: filter step and refinement step. In contrast, SAMs deal with lines and regions, approximated by rectangular *mbb*, and there is a clear division between the filter step that deals with *mbb* and the refinement step on the exact geometry. The approximation of lines by *mbb* is not appropriate in many applications. Although the *mbb* approximation of objects has been widely accepted, there have been a number of other proposals for region indexing (see [GG98]). In the polyhedral trees of

[Jag90b], for example, objects are approximated by a polygon rather than just a rectangle. Region objects have no polygonal approximation in the cell tree proposed by Günther [Gün89]. Instead, the search space is decomposed into disjoint convex subspaces. Convex components of the region to be inserted in the index are stored in the tree leaves.

The simplest space-driven SAM is the fixed grid, proposed by Bentley and Friedman [BF79]. The grid file was proposed for point indexing by Nievergelt, Hinterger, and Sevcik [NHS84]. There are a large number of extensions of the grid-based SAM (see [GG98]). Among them it is worth mentioning the multilayer grid file [SW88] and the BANG file [Fre87]. The latter is a PAM that partitions the search space in rectangular regions like the grid file, but allows the regions to overlap.

Finkel and Bentley [FB74] proposed one of the first variants of the quadtree for points. Another variant for points, called a region quadtree, is proposed by Samet [Sam90b]. There exist a large number of quadtrees for storing polygons and rectangles, described in [Sam90b].

A number of authors have proposed to map a simple space-driven index, most of the time a quadtree, onto a B+tree [Gar82, AS83, OM84, GR94, AS95, SGR96, FR89, Jag90b]. The linear order on cells in most proposals is based on *Peano curves* or *Morton code*, also referred to as *z-ordering* [OM84]. Some authors propose the use of different space-filling curves (not only for space-driven structures, see [GG98]), such as the Hilbert curve [FR89, Jag90b] or Gray codes [Fal86, Fal88]. The linear structures vary according to the assignment of objects to cells. The first scheme of Section 6.2.2, in which an object is assigned to all cells overlapping its *mbb*, is from [SGR96], where the linearized SAM is either a quadtree or a grid. The original SAM called *z-ordering* due to Orenstein and Merret, in which an object is approximated by a union of cells, was first described in [OM84] and further studied in [Ore86, OM88, Ore89, Ore90]. The redundancy of such a structure is analyzed in [Ore89, Gae95]. For clarity, our presentation of *z-ordering* uses a canonical quadrant numbering from 0 to 3. However, this coding allows us to gather only four sibling subquadrants into a single larger element, whereas the original *z-ordering* code for quadrants (based on bit interleaving) allows a finer grouping of two neighbor horizontal or vertical quadrants into a larger element. *z-ordering* is also used in [GR94].

The HHcode of the Oracle Spatial Data Option (SDO) [Sha99] is also a variant of z-ordering mapped onto the Oracle kernel B+tree. Two variants are proposed by Oracle SDO (see Chapter 8), among which one corresponds to the raster variant of z-ordering (see Section 6.2.3). The third scheme presented in Section 6.2.3, in which an object is assigned to the smallest quadtree quadrant containing it, is from [AS83]. As a matter of fact, in [AS83], *mbb*s rather than objects are indexed. This enables one to eliminate false hits prior to the refinement step.

The loss in clustering due to the mapping of cells onto a linear structure is important in range queries (see window query of the linear quadtree, Section 6.2.2). There have been several proposals for better performing, although more complex, window queries [AS95, SGR96]. [AS95] is based on *maximal quadtree blocks* [AS93]. [SGR96] maps a fixed grid and a quadtree (rectangles are assigned to each overlapping cell or quadrant) with optimized window querying onto a B+tree and compares their performance. Finally, [BKK99] proposes a scheme called XZ-ordering, a variant of z-ordering that allows a large resolution and thus a better approximation without performance degradation. Object duplication is avoided by enabling the overlap of cells, due to a new coding scheme for cells. Several improvements to the z-ordering technique are also surveyed in [BKK99].

The R-tree was introduced by Guttman [Gut84]. In this chapter, we closely followed the author's presentation for the insertion algorithm.

The R*tree variant was designed by Beckman, Kriegel, Schneider, and Seeger [BKSS90]. Section 6.3 illustrates the impact of the splitting algorithm on the R-tree performance. In [BKSS90], a performance comparison with several earlier versions of the R-tree (including the quadratic and linear R-tree) is made for several types of queries on a large range of data sets. The R*tree is shown to be steadily the best. It should be noted, however, that the R*tree construction is sometimes reported (for instance, in [HS92]) as being more costly than the R-tree construction with quadratic split, although the experiments in [BKSS90] did not show a significant overhead in I/Os.

The issue of R-tree node splitting has been revisited in [GLL98]. The paper proposes an optimal polynomial algorithm [in $O(n^d)$, where d is the dimension of the input] and a new dynamic insertion method.

Packing R-trees was successively proposed in [RL85], [KF94], and [LEL96]. The latter paper describes and experiments with the STR variant presented in Section 6.3. A new algorithm for fast bulk loading of the R*tree is described in [dBSW97]. Sellis, Roussopoulos, and Faloutsos proposed the R+tree variant [SRF87].

R-trees were primarily designed for supporting point and range (window) queries. Some authors consider other operations. [RKV95] studies the problem of reporting the nearest neighbors of a point P using R-trees. Given the *mbb* R of an object O, two distance functions of (R, P) are defined, which give, respectively, a lower and an upper bound of the distance from P to O. These functions are used during the traversal of the R-tree to explore the search space. An analytical study of the nearest neighbor problem is reported in [PM97]. Topological queries are considered in [PTSE95]. Topological information conveyed by the *mbb* of an R-tree is analyzed and used to optimize the processing of queries that involve one of the topological predicates of the 9-intersection model (see Chapter 3).

An analytical estimate of the search performance with R-trees was first proposed in [FSR87]. The formulas given in Section 6.3.5 are from [KF93], and were independently presented in [PSTW93]. They rely on the strong assumption that data is uniformly distributed. Subsequent works relaxed this assumption. See, for instance, [FK94] and [TS96]. Extensions of cost models to spatial joins can be found in [HJR97a, TSS98, PMT99].

Another class of tree structures for SAMs originated as modifications of the kd-tree [Ben75], suitable for secondary storage, such as the k-d-b-tree [Rob81] and the hB-tree [LS90].

Lately, external memory algorithms have again received considerable attention from the computational geometry community (see [Vit98] for a recent survey on external memory algorithms). This interest has two motivations. First, new nonstandard applications require efficient SAMs (as, for instance, spatio-temporal applications), in particular those dealing with *moving objects*, or network applications dealing with polyline objects and constraint databases requiring efficient access to constraint-based objects. The second motivation is to approach the optimal search time complexity. Consider first the latter objective. Getting, as in the one-dimensional case with B-trees, an optimal multidimensional access method is a real challenge. Recall an optimal SAM is such that its search complexity is $O(log_B(N) + T/B)$, where N is the collection size, B the buffer size, and T the result size; its update complexity is $O(log_B(N))$; and its space complexity is $O(N/B)$.

All SAMs proposed until now and discussed in this chapter are not optimal in worst-case conditions. Because the problem is not simple, most current theoretical studies provide close to optimal or optimal solutions for simpler problems, and queries such as the *stabbing query* (find all intervals of a line containing a point) [AV96]. The latter is a key component in the *dynamic interval management problem* (find all intervals that intersect a query interval on a given line; see [AV96, Vit98]). Because a large number of efficient main memory data structures have been designed for this problem and related issues, the trend has been in the past decade to adapt these techniques to multidimensional access methods. The range tree [Ben80], the segment tree [Ben77], the interval tree [Ede83], and the priority searchtree [McC85] are elegant main memory structures for 2D range searching. The previously cited theoretical work is justified by the three fields of application: moving objects, network applications, and constraint databases.

Network applications are common applications dealing with polyline objects. Approximating a polyline, even if it has been cut into smaller pieces, by a rectangle is not efficient, because most of the rectangle space is lost. Some classical SAMs have been adapted to line indexing [Sam90b]. Examples of SAMs dedicated to line segments are [Jag90a, KS91, BG94]. In the moving object application [SWCD97, WXCJ98, KGT99], a point is following a fixed trajectory (e.g., belonging to a road network) or a free line trajectory in the plane. A typical query is "Report the objects inside a rectangle within a given time interval."

Moving object applications are just one example of spatio-temporal applications that may require specific indexing techniques [TSPM98]. A recent work proposes an adaptation of the R-tree to moving object indexing [SJLL00]. The basic idea is that moving objects must be indexed by moving rectangles that at each moment enclose their entries. The parameter to minimize is then the sum of the areas (or, to better say, the integral) of the moving rectangles during their motion. The paper revisits the split algorithms of the R*tree in this context. There is a growing interest in the problem of moving point indexing. See, for instance, [NST99, KGT99, PJT00] and [TUW98], which attempts to use quadtrees. In order to support this research, some authors provide spatio-temporal data set generators [SM99, TSN99], following a trend initiated by [GOP$^+$98] with the *À la Carte* generator. This tool generates a set of rectangles according to a statistical model whose parameters (size, coverage, and distribution) can be specified.

Last, but not least, constraint databases motivated most of the theoretical work currently undertaken toward efficient SAMs for solving the interval management problem. Kanellakis, Ramaswamy, Vengroff, and Vitter [KRVV96] are at the origin of the work. They relate the problem of constraint indexing to the dynamic interval management problem and provide for this an index called the metablock tree. This work has initiated a large number of ongoing studies. [Ram00] is a comprehensive paper on the topic. See also [Vit98] for a survey on related external memory algorithms.

7

Query Processing

"One of Sherlock Holmes's defects—if, indeed, one may call it a defect—was that he was exceedingly loath to communicate his full plans to any other person until the instant of their fullfilment."

S IR A RTHUR C ONAN D OYLE
The Hound of the Baskervilles

CONTENTS

This chapter is devoted to the processing techniques for evaluating queries on spatial databases. We focus on the aspects specific to spatial data during the query evaluation process, although several of the issues addressed here are relevant to the area of query evaluation in general.

This chapter covers three topics. After an introduction, we provide (Section 7.2) a general discussion of *input/output (I/O) algorithms*, also called *external algorithms* or *physical operators*. Their common feature is to manipulate large volumes of objects stored on external devices. The bottleneck is the transfer of information from these devices to main memory, and this entails different techniques in comparison with the main memory algorithms investigated in Chapter 5. We illustrate the design and analysis of external algorithms on two examples that achieve a provable optimal worst-case bound.

The first example involves *external sorting*. The algorithm is not specific to spatial data but provides a nice insight on the mapping of well-known strategies (here, divide and conquer) to external memory computation requirements. The second example, called *distribution sweeping*, gives an equivalent of the plane-sweep paradigm (see Chapter 5) for external memory. We illustrate this strategy on the problem already used for plane sweep in main memory; namely, reporting the pairwise intersections in a set of rectangles. The size of this set is now assumed to be much larger than the available main memory. This algorithm can be used to solve an important subproblem of spatial join, the *filter step*.

We then describe (Section 7.3) some algorithms for implementing *spatial join*, a central operation in spatial query processing. We consider various cases, including joins based on linear structures and R-trees (see Chapter 6), and the strategies based on the existence of zero, one, or two SAMs. There is no better worst-case bound than the trivial $O(n^2)$ for these algorithms, which rely mostly on heuristics. However, they can be expected to perform correctly on well-behaved data.

Finally, we extend (Section 7.4) the discussion to the evaluation of queries involving several operations. We study how I/O algorithms can be combined to form a *query execution plan* (QEP).

7.1 AN INTRODUCTION TO QUERY PROCESSING

Algorithms on spatial (or geometric) data have already been studied in Chapter 5. There was, however, a fundamental hypothesis behind *all* computational geometry algorithms studied in that chapter. The data (polylines, polygons) were assumed to fit in main memory. In the Random Access Machine (RAM) model of computation used for estimating the algorithm complexity, each data access has a constant cost, whatever the actual location of this in main memory.

This assumption is not true here. As in Chapter 6, we consider that the database stores a large amount of data, which exceeds by far the size of the available main memory. Therefore, for each algorithm, the *key operation* (denoted I/O in the following) is now the transfer of a *page* from/to external memory (disk). The design of algorithms is based on the minimization of disk accesses, and the complexity is expressed as a function of the number of I/Os.

To illustrate the importance of taking into account the scheduling of page accesses during data manipulation, we will examine the display on the screen of a set of 40 items. We assume that a page holds 10 items at most, and that the main memory is reduced to three pages managed with a least recently used (LRU) replacement policy. Data is distributed among the four pages as shown in Figure 7.1. For each item, we display its identifier, an integer less than or equal to 40.

In order to print the items, a naive approach consists of reading in sequence; that is, item 1, item 2, item 3, and so on. To print item *i*, we need to access page *i* mod(4). When page 4 is accessed, page 1 must be flushed from main memory, according to the LRU policy that removes the least recently accessed page. The next item to be read is item 5, which resides in page 1. This page must be loaded again,

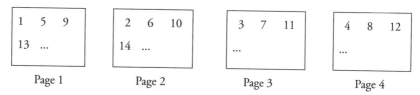

Page 1   Page 2   Page 3   Page 4

Figure 7.1 Scanning a set of items.

and page 2 is flushed. From now on, one page is accessed per item read. With this approach, 40 I/Os are necessary, whereas four I/Os are sufficient to get the entire data set if we do not need to print the items sorted on their identifier. Because a disk access typically takes a few milliseconds, whereas a main memory access takes a few nanoseconds, the ratio between the two strategies is on the order of millions.

The optimal cost (number of I/Os) for scanning the list of unsorted items is $40/10$. More generally, if N is the size of data and P the size of a page, the complexity must be expressed as a function of N/P and no longer as a function of N.

A general rule for query processing is that algorithms must take advantage of the organization of data on disk (see Chapter 6). If no convenient data structure is available, it often pays off to perform some pre-processing such as hashing or sorting.

The query execution engine tries to schedule the disk accesses required by the physical operators, in such a way that the number of I/Os is minimized. This is particularly important for the join operation, which involves a complex synchronization of two input relations. We spend a large part of the discussion on this topic.

A query evaluator (processor) utilizes a collection of efficient I/O algorithms for (1) evaluating the algebraic operators of the query language, and (2) accessing or pre-processing data. An important issue is how to choose and combine the various operators necessary for processing a complex query. Such a combination is usually called a *Query Execution Plan* (QEP). It describes how to compute the result of a given query. A QEP is represented (at least in a relational database context) as a tree that resembles closely the algebraic tree obtained from the translation of the end-user query expression. Each node in the algebraic tree is "expanded" as one or several nodes in the QEP, and the edges represent dataflows from one node to another. Figure 7.2 shows an example of an SQL query that selects for each state its counties, then an equivalent algebraic expression (join followed by a projection), and finally a possible QEP that uses a sort/merge join algorithm. States and counties are sequentially scanned and respectiveley sorted on the attributes *id* and *state*. The join is performed by merging the two sorted files, and the result is projected on attributes *sname* and *cname*.

A basic characteristic of relational query languages is that there exist many equivalent algebraic expressions for a given query. Moreover, for

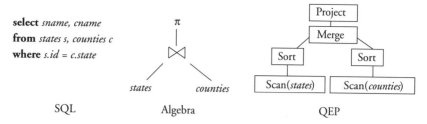

Figure 7.2 From the declarative query to the physical QEP.

a given algebraic expression, there are several QEPs, because there are several possible accesses to the data and many algorithms available for each operator. One of the essential tasks of the DBMS is to choose, among all these possible QEPs, the "best" (or nearly best) one according to certain criteria. A specific module, the *optimizer*, is in charge of this task. It relies on several characteristics of the DBMS, including the available algorithms; the expected cost of each possible QEP, estimated after a *cost model*; and some heuristics to reduce the number of candidate solutions to be looked at (search space). The execution of complex spatial queries and their optimization constitutes some of the most advanced topics studied in this book, which can be useful for the optimization of GIS or relational DBMS with spatial features.

7.2 TWO OPTIMAL I/O ALGORITHMS

Throughout this chapter we use a classical and simple execution model. We assume a single-disk, single-processor computer, and denote as n the size of the data set and as m the size of main memory (both expressed in *page* units). Each access to a page on the disk counts for one I/O. Hence, we do not distinguish between sequential and random I/O, although this is important in practice. All complexities are expressed in the number of I/Os.

7.2.1 *External Sort/Merge*

Sorting is a key operation in query processing. It is often used as a pre-processing step for algorithms that require the input(s) to be sorted. A well-known sorting algorithm is the *sort/merge join* algorithm used in relational databases to join two nonindexed relations. Because join can be done in linear time by *merging* two sorted relations, it is worthwhile to first sort each input [complexity $O(n \log_m n)$, as shown in the following]. One obtains an $O(n \log_m n)$ join algorithm, which performs much better than the naive $O(n^2)$ algorithm, called *nested loop*.

The most commonly used algorithm for external sorting is an adaptation of the sort/merge main memory algorithm, which relies on a classical divide-and-conquer strategy (see Chapter 5). First (sort phase), the input, which is an array, is recursively halved until one obtains pairs of elements that can be trivially sorted. This recursive partitioning defines a binary tree. In the second phase (merge phase), the sorted subarrays are recursively merged bottom-up, starting from the leaves of the tree. Because merging is performed in linear time, the standard analysis presented in Chapter 5 holds, and the algorithm reaches the optimal $O(N \log_2 N)$ complexity,[28] where N denotes the number of elements.

In the context of external memory, the binary tree structure is not convenient because it cannot easily be mapped to disk pages (this was already observed, for instance, for the quadtree structure in Chapter 6). Therefore, the algorithm is modified in such a way that at each node of the tree one manipulates data in chunks of pages rather than one record at a time.[29]

In the first phase, sorted subfiles, called "runs," are created from the data source. Each run occupies m pages and stores a sorted subset of the input. In order to create the runs, one repeats the following sequence of operations (Figure 7.3):

- The m buffer pages in main memory are filled with records from the data source.
- The records in the m pages are sorted with an internal memory algorithm (usually quicksort).
- The sorted blocks are written onto disk in a new run.

---

28. Although optimal, the sort/merge algorithm is not used in main memory because it necessitates a copy of the input to perform the merge operations. The *quicksort* algorithm, which does not require additional memory, is preferable.
29. We use here the term *record* to denote the elements to be sorted.

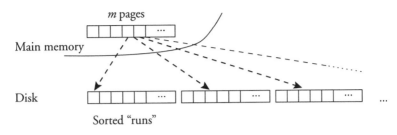

Figure 7.3   The creation of initial runs.

Note that except for the last run the space utilization (both in internal and external memory) is optimal because each page is filled with records.

Starting from the runs created in the first phase, the merge phase begins. Here, again, one tries to optimize memory utilization. One part of the m blocks in main memory is dedicated to the input runs (whose number is not restricted to two), and the remaining blocks are used to store the output of the merge. The simplest choice is to use one block in main memory for each run file: $m - 1$ runs are merged, $m - 1$ blocks are devoted to the input runs and the last block in main memory is allocated to the output run. The number of runs merged at one time is called the *merge fan-in*, the maximum fan-in being $m - 1$.

The process is illustrated in Figure 7.4. The merge phase can be represented by a tree, each node of the tree corresponding to a single

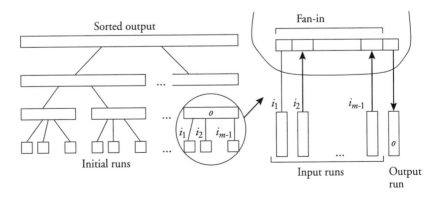

Figure 7.4   The merge phase.

merge operation, shown at right in the figure.[30] One reads the first page
of each input run $\{i_1, i_2, \ldots i_{m-1}\}$ in the main memory buffer (recall
that the input runs are sorted). The merge then begins on the data in
main memory. The smallest record is repeatedly picked in one of the
$m - 1$ blocks and stored in the output block. When all the records in
an input block, say, j, have been picked, one reads the following block
in run i_j. Once the output block is full, it is written in the output run.
Once an output run is full [$m \times (m-1)$ blocks have been written in the
run], it is ready to be merged at a higher level with other runs obtained
from the first-level merge operations, and so on. This scheduling of
blocked read/write operations is a crucial property that guarantees a
good behavior of the algorithm.

The merge of runs is performed in linear time. Each run is read
once, and the size of the output is the sum of the sizes of the input
runs. Therefore, at each level of the tree, one needs exactly $2n$ I/Os.
If the fan-in is $m - 1$, there are $O(\log_m n)$ levels in the tree, and one
obtains an $\Theta(n \log_m n)$ algorithm, which is optimal.

7.2.2   Distribution Sweeping (Rectangle Intersection)

The distribution sweeping technique was proposed as a generalization
of the plane-sweep paradigm combined with careful I/O management.
The technique can be used to achieve optimal worst-case bounds in
many computational geometry algorithms that necessitate I/O trans-
fers. In particular, an important subproblem of the *spatial join*, which
is reporting the pairwise intersections between two large sets of rectangles, can be handled by a distribution-sweeping-based algorithm. Indeed, the algorithm can be seen as an implementation of $R_1 \bowtie_o R_2$,
where $\bowtie_o$ denotes overlap join and R_1 and R_2 store large sets of rectangles. This algorithm is described in the following, and spatial joins are
more thoroughly discussed in the following section.

ORTHOGONAL LINE SEGMENTS

We first introduce the technique on a simpler problem. Given a set
of *orthogonal segments*, report their pairwise intersections. There is a

---

30. For the sake of clarity, the fan-in at higher levels of the tree in the figure is only 2,
although in reality it is still $m - 1$.

simple line-sweep algorithm to solve the problem in main memory (actually a variant of the line segment intersection algorithm, discussed in Chapter 5), which works as follows. First, sort the segments on their x_{min} coordinate, and then sweep the line from left to right, stopping as usual at each event. When a horizontal segment is met, it is stored in the active list (a binary search tree built on the constant y value of the segment). When a vertical segment $s(y_{min}, y_{max})$ is met, we just perform a range query $q(y_{min}, y_{max})$ on the active list. This reports all horizontal segments that intersect s. The algorithm runs in $O(N \log_2 N + K)$, where N denotes the number of segments and K the number of intersections.

In external memory, we seek an $O(n \log_m n + k)$ algorithm, where k is the size of the result and the parameters n, m, and k are expressed in pages. The distribution sweeping algorithm follows this general design. First, the segments are sorted by an external sort module—in $O(n \log_m n)$, as seen before—and then a plane sweep is performed to find solutions.

Assuming a buffer of m blocks (pages) is available in main memory, the set of segments is partitioned into m horizontal strips so that each strip contains approximately n/m objects. Each horizontal segment falls into exactly one strip, and as usual we maintain a list $\mathcal{L}_i$ of the active horizontal segments in each strip i. Each time a horizontal segment is met for the first time, it is entered in the active list. The choice of m strips ensures that we can maintain one block in the buffer for each list $\mathcal{L}_i$ and thus avoid random I/O. This is illustrated in Figure 7.5. Four strips are defined. For example, list $\mathcal{L}_2$, at position l_1, contains the segments h_1 and h_2.

When a vertical segment v is met during the sweep, we must report its intersections with horizontal segments in the active lists. A simple solution is to scan all lists associated with the strips that overlap v. However, if v does not span a strip completely, we cannot guarantee that an intersection is reported each time a horizontal segment is accessed.

For instance, when v_2 is met, we could scan list $\mathcal{L}_4$, which is partially covered by v_2. This implies loading the page that contains h_4, although no intersection is then reported. In the worst case, a list could be scanned without reporting any intersection, in which case we fail to reach the optimal complexity.

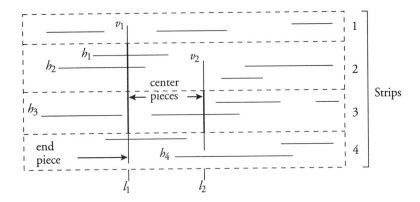

Figure 7.5 Distribution sweeping.

The solution is based on the intuitive fact that vertical segments can be decomposed into three parts: a part that lies completely within one or many strips and two parts that partially overlap a strip. More precisely, a vertical segment, say, v_1, can be partitioned into one *center piece* that spans completely one or several strips, and (at most) two *end pieces*, each of them being fully contained in one strip (see Figure 7.5). Each time a vertical segment is reached, all strips it completely spans are scanned. During this scan we know that each horizontal segment met will either be reported in the intersection or never be intersected (by another vertical segment with larger x coordinate) and can be removed from the list.

For instance, when the sweeping line reaches position l_1, the vertical segment v_1 is met. Its central piece spans strips 2 and 3. We perform two scans: one of strip 2 and one of strip 3. First, we scan list $\mathcal{L}_2$ to report the segments intersecting v_1. Horizontal segments h_1 and h_2 are met and reported in the intersection. Then list $\mathcal{L}_3$ is scanned. No horizontal segments are reported as intersecting v_1. h_3 is removed from the active list $\mathcal{L}_3$ because no further vertical segment can intersect it.

The active lists can be read in chunks of pages, and each access to a horizontal segment allows us to report an intersection, except in two cases: once when it is assigned to a strip and once when it is removed from the active list. Hence, the sweep takes $O(n + k)$ I/Os, where n is the size of the data set and $k = K/P$ is the number of pages needed to store the number of intersections found.

At the end of the sweep, we miss the intersections between horizontal segments and the vertical segments of the end pieces. Then the algorithm is called recursively for each strip, considered now as the entire search space. As an example, strip 1 is again divided into m strips, and we process all end pieces of vertical segments falling into strip 1.

The recursion terminates when the problem can be carried out in main memory; that is, after $O(\log_m n)$ steps. Because each step costs $O(n + k')$, where k' is the number of I/Os for the intersection reported in this step, the algorithm achieves the $\Theta(n \log_m n + k)$ optimal bound.

THE RECTANGLE INTERSECTION PROBLEM

The same technique can be applied to the rectangle intersection problem, with some modifications. The problem is stated as follows. Given two sets of rectangles, a blue set B and a red set R, we want to report all intersections between a red and a blue rectangle.

The algorithm starts, as usual, by sorting the rectangles of B and R on their x_{min} coordinate. A merger of the sorted lists yields the event list $\mathcal{E}$. As before, the space is partitioned into s horizontal strips, with a value of s to be discussed later. Each rectangle is cut into three pieces (end and center pieces) with respect to the strips it overlaps.

A simple modification of the previous algorithm is to maintain two active lists for each strip i: $\mathcal{L}_i^b$ for the blue rectangles intersecting the strip and $\mathcal{L}_i^r$ for the red rectangles. Now the same procedure as that for orthogonal line segments can be applied. When a new rectangle (say, a red one) r is introduced, we scan the blue list of all strips covered by the center piece (if any) of r and report all rectangles b in $\mathcal{L}_i^b$ such that $r.x_{min} < b.x_{max}$.

Unfortunately, this simple solution does not work because, unlike the horizontal segments in the previous algorithm, the rectangles in the active lists possibly span more than one strip. An intersection between two rectangles would be tested and reported more than once. In fact, the design of the active list structure must be such that a rectangle is stored in a single strip, and thus is accessed only once when an intersection needs to be reported.

To achieve this requirement, the algorithm maintains one list $\mathcal{L}_{i,j}$ for each possible pair (i, j), $0 \le i \le j \le s + 1$. A rectangle with its top-end portion falling into strip i and its bottom-end portion falling into strip j is stored in $\mathcal{L}_{i,j}$. See, for instance, Figure 7.6, where rectangle a

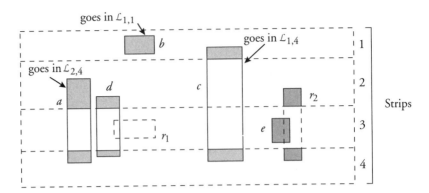

Figure 7.6   External rectangle intersection algorithm.

goes into $\mathcal{L}_{2,4}$. Similarly, b goes into $\mathcal{L}_{1,1}$, and c into $\mathcal{L}_{1,4}$. There are $(s+2) + (s+1) + \ldots 1 = (s+2)(s+3)/2$ possibilities. Because we must store separately the red and blue rectangles, we obtain a total of $(s+2)(s+3)$ lists $\mathcal{L}_{i,j}^b$ and $\mathcal{L}_{i,j}^r$. Now the process of inserting a new red rectangle r can be sketched as follows (the same procedure holds, of course, for the blue rectangles, by permuting r with b).

- If r consists of a single end portion contained in strip i, we scan the blue lists $\mathcal{L}_{h,k}^b$ such that $h < i < k$. In each list, *all* blue rectangles b with $r.x_{min} < b.x_{max}$ do intersect r. The bs such that $r.x_{min} > b.x_{max}$ can be removed from the list. In addition, r is inserted in $\mathcal{L}_{i,i}^r$.

  For instance, rectangle r_1 in Figure 7.6 is inserted in $\mathcal{L}_{3,3}^r$, and we scan the blue lists $\mathcal{L}_{h,j}^b$ for $h < 3$ and $j > 3$. The list $\mathcal{L}_{2,4}^b$ is scanned and an intersection with the blue rectangle d is reported.

- If r contains a center portion over the strips $i, \ldots j$, we scan all lists $\mathcal{L}_{h,k}^b$ with $i \le h, j \ge k$ and compute the intersections. In addition, r is inserted in $\mathcal{L}_{i-1,j+1}^r$.

  In Figure 7.6, rectangle r_2 has a center portion that spans strip 3. The list $\mathcal{L}_{3,3}^b$ must be scanned and the intersection with e is reported.

The end pieces of rectangles (in gray in Figure 7.6) are written onto disk and are involved in recursive subproblems, as in the orthogonal segments intersection algorithm. As a matter of fact, the same analysis holds. A rectangle is inserted into (and deleted from) a list exactly once, and produces an intersection each time it is accessed. Thus, we obtain the $\Theta(n \log_m n + k)$ optimal bound.

In order to read and write blocks instead of single rectangles, each list must be assigned at least one page in main memory. Because there are $O(s^2)$ lists, the number of strips should not exceed $\sqrt{m}$. Observe that this reduces the fan-out and thus increases the number of recursion levels. Because $\log_{\sqrt{m}} n = \log_m n / \log_m \sqrt{m} = 2 \log_m n$, the number of levels is doubled, which does not change the worst-case analysis.

7.3   SPATIAL JOIN

As seen in Chapter 3, the spatial join between relations R_1 and R_2 constructs the pairs of tuples from R_1 and R_2 whose spatial attributes satisfy a spatial predicate. There are several types of spatial predicates, among them *overlap*, *contain*, and other *topological*, *distance*, or *directional* predicates (see Chapter 3). We restrict our attention to *overlap* joins, which are useful for a large variety of queries.

We assume that each spatial attribute has for a value a pair (*mbb*, *spatial object representation*), where *mbb* is the minimal bounding rectangle of the spatial object. As explained in Chapter 6, the *mbb* is a convenient approximation of the actual geometry that allows us to perform a fast data pre-processing in order to eliminate those pairs that cannot qualify for the join predicate. A commonly accepted method consists of computing a spatial join in two steps:

- In the *filter step* the tuples whose *mbb*s overlap are selected. Due to the simple structure of rectangles, this step avoids the costly process of performing intersection algorithms on geometric data. The pairs that pass the filter step constitute the *candidate set*.
- During the *refinement step*, for each pair of the candidate set, the spatial object representations are retrieved and the geometric operation is performed.

In this section, we focus on the filter step. Algorithms for testing the overlap of two polygons have been discussed in Chapter 5. In Section 7.4, the importance of the refinement step on the overall query complexity is discussed.

There exist a large number of strategies and algorithms for spatial joins that rely on the SAM each relation is provided with (see Chapter 6). We successively consider the following cases:

♦ *Linear structures:* We first present an algorithm that assumes each relation to be indexed with a linear structure. We restrict our attention to z-ordering trees. However, there exist similar strategies for other linearized structures.

♦ *R-trees:* In the presence of two R-trees, a popular method is *synchronized tree traversal,* which carries out an efficient depth-first tree traversal of both trees.

♦ *Single index:* When only one relation is indexed, the simplest strategy is the indexed nested loop (INL) strategy, a variant of the relational nested loop algorithm. This algorithm scans the nonindexed relation and, for each of its tuples r, delivers to the index of the other relation a window query with $r.mbb$ as an argument.

♦ *No index:* In the case where no relation is indexed, several *partitioning* techniques have been proposed that partition the tuples into buckets and then use hash-based algorithms. We present a simple version of the relational *hash-join* strategy, adapted to spatial data.

Finally, the distribution sweeping algorithm presented in Section 7.2.2 offers another alternative in the case where no indices exist. In contrast to this optimal algorithm, no better worst-case bound than the trivial $O(n^2)$ can be shown for the methods previously discussed. However, they are expected to be efficient for well-behaved data.

7.3.1   z-Ordering Spatial Join

This first spatial join algorithm assumes that both relations are z-ordered; that is, they have a z-ordering tree as an index (see Section 6.2.3). The simple raster variant of the z-ordering tree (Section 6.2.3), which assumes an object decomposition (approximation) into minimal cells, leads to a very simple join algorithm used by the Oracle spatial extension, the details of which are provided in Chapter 8. However, such an approximation leads to a large object duplication. This is why we assume in the following the z-ordering variant in which cells of a decomposition are not necessarily minimal (Section 6.2.3). We further assume that the relations share the same space. This ensures a consistent encoding of the quadrants that approximate an object. The filter step consists of keeping as candidate pairs for the refinement step the pairs of object *ids* for which at least one pair of cells either is identical or is in a containment relationship. The corresponding spatial objects are likely to overlap.

The leaves of each z-ordering tree (see Section 6.2.3) scanned in sequence represent a list L of entries of the form $[z, oid]$, ordered on z, where oid is the id of an object whose approximation contains the cell with z-order value (key) z. One cell with key z is contained in (or identical to) a cell with key z' if z' is a prefix of z and we have $z' \leq z$.

The join algorithm can be sketched as follows. The lists of entries corresponding to the two relations, denoted L_1 and L_2, are merged. We keep one pair of entries from the two lists as a candidate for the refinement step if one key is a prefix of the other. Prior to the refinement step, the candidate pairs of object ids have to be sorted in order to remove duplicates. Recall that the redundancy is large with such a scheme, because an object approximation includes several cells.

In the example of Figure 7.7, the rectangles above (respectively, below) the z axis represent cells of list L_1 (L_2). The lowest value of a rectangle on the z axis is the key z associated with the cell c, whereas the largest z value of the rectangle represents the key z' of the smallest cell in the lower-right corner of c: $z' = scc(z)$. As an example, if $z = 30$, then assuming a maximal depth of 7 for the decomposition, $z' = 3033333$.

In the example of Figure 7.7, the filter step would report the candidate pairs (A, D), (A, E), (A, F), (B, E), (B, F), (C, H), and (C, I). Because some cells of a same list might be contained in one another, such as B and A in one list and F and E in the other, two stacks S_1 and S_2 are necessary. For instance, B is pushed onto S_1 on top of A, because B is contained in A. The rationale behind the use of stacks is that if

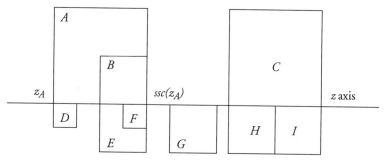

Figure 7.7   Example of a z-ordering join.

the top of one stack (say, B, on top of S_1) is to be joined with an entry of the other list (say, F), then all elements below in the stack must be joined with the same entry (A is also joined with F).

The two lists are scanned. This can be viewed as sweeping a vertical line along the z axis from left to right (see Figure 7.7), with the occurence of events of two types:

- *Entry* events occur each time a new entry, from either list L_1 or list L_2, is found (left bound of a rectangle). The entry is pushed onto the corresponding stack.
- *Exit* events occur when the right bound of a rectangle is reached by the sweeping line. A stack is popped, and some candidate pair is output.

To illustrate the algorithm, we run it on the example of Figure 7.7. The current elements in each list are *current*$_1$ and *current*$_2$. The state of the stacks is given after each event has been processed.

- *Step 1:* The first event is the entry of A. A is pushed onto stack S_1, and B becomes the current element in L_1. The other stack contains the entire space, and the current element in L_2 is D.

$$current_1 = B \qquad S_1 = \{A\} \qquad current_2 = D \qquad S_2 = \{\}$$

- *Step 2:* Entry of D, which is pushed onto stack S_2.

$$current_1 = B \qquad S_1 = \{A\} \qquad current_2 = E \qquad S_2 = \{D\}$$

- *Step 3:* The next z value met is the right border of D. This is an *exit* event, which is processed as follows. First, D is joined with all objects from the other stack S_1, and then it is removed from S_2. The pair $[A, D]$ is output, and we obtain the following situation:

$$current_1 = B \qquad S_1 = \{A\} \qquad current_2 = E \qquad S_2 = \{\}$$

- *Step 4:* Entry of B:

$$current_1 = C \qquad S_1 = \{B, A\} \qquad current_2 = E \qquad S_2 = \{\}$$

◆ *Step 5:* Entry of E:

$$current_1 = C \qquad S_1 = \{B, A\} \qquad current_2 = F \qquad S_2 = \{E\}$$

◆ *Step 6:* Entry of F:

$$current_1 = C \qquad S_1 = \{B, A\} \qquad current_2 = G \qquad S_2 = \{F, E\}$$

◆ *Step 7:* Exit of B, which is joined with the objects in S_2 and popped from S_1. $[B, E]$ and $[B, F]$ are output, and we obtain

$$current_1 = C \qquad S_1 = \{A\} \qquad current_2 = G \qquad S_2 = \{F, E\}$$

◆ *Step 8:* Exit of A, which is joined with the objects in S_2 and popped from S_1. $[A, E]$ and $[A, F]$ are output, and we obtain

$$current_1 = C \qquad S_1 = \{\} \qquad current_2 = G \qquad S_2 = \{F, E\}$$

The remainder of the process is left as an exercise. We provide in the following the pseudo-code for this algorithm. It assumes that the entire space is initially pushed onto each stack. By convention, the stack is empty if it contains only the entire space. CURRENT(L) denotes the current entry in list L, initialized to the first entry.

The algorithm processes in order the events coming either from the lists L_1 and L_2 or from the stacks S_1 and S_2. In the former case, the ENTRY (L, S) function pushes onto S CURRENT(L) and assigns to CURRENT(L) the next element in L. If the event comes from a stack, the function EXIT (S, S') (1) returns the set of pairs consisting of E, the top element of stack S, and each element of S', and (2) pops E from S.

ALGORITHM   ZORDERINGJOIN (L_1,L_2: list of *ids*): set of pairs of entries

---

begin
   result: Set of pairs of ids, initially empty
   while not (eof(L_1) **and** empty(S_1) **and** eof (L_2) **and** empty (S_2))
   begin
     event = MIN (CURRENT(L_1), SCC(top(S_1)),
                CURRENT(L_2), SCC(top(S_2)))
     if (*event* = CURRENT(L_1)) **then** // left bound of a rectangle
       ENTRY (L_1, S_1)
     else if (*event* = SCC(top(S_1))) **then** // right bound of a rectangle
       result += EXIT (S_1, S_2)

```
        else if (event = CURRENT(L₂)) then // left bound of a rectangle
            ENTRY (L₂, S₂)
        else if (event = SCC (top(S₂))) then // right bound of a rectangle
            result += EXIT (S₂, S₁);
    end while
    sort result; remove duplicates;
    return result
end
```

In the presence of well-behaved data, each z-ordering tree leaf is read only once. Assuming a main memory buffer of size three pages (one per z-ordering tree and one for the result), the number of I/Os is $n_1 + n_2 + k$, where n_1 and n_2 are the numbers of leaves of the z-ordering trees and k is the number of pages of the result. However, this requires each stack to always hold in main memory. In the worst case, this is no longer true, and the algorithm complexity is quadratic in the entry size (EXIT function). Recall also that in all cases, because of the z-ordering tree redundancy, a duplicate elimination is necessary whose complexity is $O(k \log k)$.

7.3.2   Joining Two R-Trees

We now describe the filter step of the STT algorithm for a spatial join $R \bowtie S$ when both relations are indexed with either an R-tree or an R*tree or any other variant. The algorithm attempts to minimize both the I/O and the CPU costs. This CPU cost optimization is justified by the large number of rectangle intersection tests. This operation is by far more costly than the simple scalar comparison necessary for a relational join, in which the CPU cost can be neglected in comparison to the I/O cost.

We present three variants of the algorithm. The simplest uses a depth-first tree traversal of both R-trees. Starting with the two roots, we compare at each step a node N_1 of one tree and a node N_2 of the other tree. We compute the pairs of overlapping entries (e_1, e_2), $e_1 \in N_1$ and $e_2 \in N_2$, and recursively call the procedure for the subtrees rooted at e_1 and e_2, respectively. When the leaf level is reached,[31]

---

31. We assume for the time being that both R-trees have the same depth.

the pairs of object *ids* are found. The basic algorithm is sketched as follows:

ALGORITHM   STT (Node N_1, Node N_2): set of pairs of *ids*

---

begin
   result: set of pairs of ids, initially empty
   for all e_1 in N_1 **do**
      for all e_2 in N_2 such that $e_1.mbb \cap e_2.mbb \neq \emptyset$ **do**
         if (the leaf level is reached) **then**
            result += {(e_1, e_2)}
         else
            N_1' = READPAGE ($e_1.pageID$); N_2' = READPAGE ($e_2.pageID$);
            result += STT (N_1', N_2')
         end if
      end for
   end for
   return *result*
end

Experiments show that although the scheduling of disk accesses yields a good I/O performance the CPU cost is high. In some situations, the CPU cost might even be larger than the I/O cost. The algorithm is said to be *CPU bound.* The CPU cost depends not only on the hardware but on the page size. The larger the page size, the larger the ratio of CPU cost over I/O cost, and the more impact the CPU computation has on the overall cost.

An obvious weakness of the previous algorithm is the nested loop over the entries of the nodes. The algorithm is simple, but it carries out a blind test of each candidate pair of entries, although we might sometimes know for certain entries that no overlapping can occur.

We present in the following two variants that refine this brute-force approach. The first one restricts the search space by considering only those entries in N_1 and N_2 that overlap the intersection $N_1.mbb \cap N_2.mbb$. The second optimization relies on a sweep-line technique that avoids the nested loop.

RESTRICTING THE SEARCH SPACE

This first optimization is based on a simple observation: the *directory rectangles* of two nodes N_1 and N_2 processed by the algorithm (i.e.,

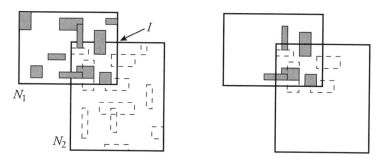

Figure 7.8 Space restriction when intersecting two nodes.

the *mbb* of the node's entries) do not cover the same space. This is illustrated in Figure 7.8, where I denotes the intersection $N_1.mbb \cap N_2.mbb$. Obviously, two entries can intersect only if both have a non-empty intersection with I.

Hence, we can eliminate all entries exterior to I from further consideration. This can significantly reduce the number of candidate entries (see Figure 7.8, right-hand side). Each node is first scanned to mark the candidate entries. The nested loop algorithm can then be processed on the marked entries.

SWEEP-LINE ALGORITHM

The second optimization relies on the plane-sweep technique. Recall that the technique was illustrated in Chapter 5 on the problem of reporting the pairwise intersections in a set of rectangles in main memory. The problem here is the same, except that we have *two* sets of rectangles (say, a blue one and a red one) and are only interested in the intersection between a blue rectangle and a red rectangle.

Although it is optimal, we will not use the algorithm of Chapter 5. Indeed, the interest of such an algorithm is that it guarantees optimal worst-case *asymptotic* I/O complexity $O(N \log_2 N + K)$, where N is the number of rectangles of the input, and K the number of pairs in the output. This is nice not only when the distribution is skewed but when the number of rectangles is extremely large. However, in the present case, the number of rectangles is *bounded* by the page size. For typical page sizes of 1K, 2K, or 4K, the number of entries is of the order of 50, 10, and 200, respectively.

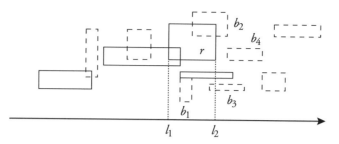

Figure 7.9   A simple plane sweep for rectangle intersection.

Therefore, although asymptotically optimal, the algorithm not only hides the constant that might represent an unacceptable overhead in a practical implementation but has an efficiency that depends on complex data structures. Then it is not necessarily better than a simpler algorithm that tries to minimize the number of passes over the data, and avoids the overhead of tricky algorithmic techniques. The plane-sweep algorithm presented here is a "greedy" variant of the algorithm of Chapter 5.

The idea is illustrated with the example in Figure 7.9. When the sweep line reaches position l_1, the red rectangle r is met,[32] and we look "forward" for *all* blue rectangles b that are likely to intersect r. We consider successively rectangles b_1, b_2, b_3, and b_4. Because $b_4.x_{min} > r.x_{max}$, the forward lookup stops. All the intersections with r have been reported, and we can get rid of r. The algorithm follows (compare it with the optimal version in Chapter 5):

ALGORITHM STT_{sweep} (Node N_1, Node N_2): set of pairs of *ids*

begin
  result: set of pairs of ids, initially empty
  $pos_1 = 1$, $pos_2 = 1$// current positions in N_1 and N_2
  Sort the entries e in N_1 and N_2 on $e.mbb.x_{min}$
  while ($pos_1 \leq |N_1|$ **and** $pos_2 \leq |N_2|$) **do**
  begin
    if ($N_1[pos_1].mbb.x_{min} < N_2[pos_2].mbb.x_{min}$) **then**

---

32. In the sweep-line algorithm of Chapter 5, r would be inserted in an active list and tested for intersection against the blue rectangles already present in this active list. The goal here is to avoid such a data structure.

```
      e = N₁[pos₁]; p' = pos₂; e' = N₂[p']
      while (e'.mbb.xₘᵢₙ ≤ e.mbb.xₘₐₓ) do
      begin
         if (e.mbb ∩ e'.mbb ≠ ∅) then result += {(e.oid, e'.oid)}
         p' = p' + 1; e' = N₂[p']
      end do
      pos₁ = pos₁ + 1 // next entry in N₁
   else
      Do as before, permuting the roles of entries of N₁ and N₂
   end if
  end while
  return result
end
```

The algorithm mixes plane-sweep and nested loop techniques.[33] Compared to the nested loop algorithm, except in unlikely situations, the line sweep limits the number of rectangles that must be tested against one another. In the previous example, r is tested against four blue rectangles and not against the entire set B. In the case in which all rectangles share more or less the same x interval, the algorithm costs $O(n^2)$, even if no intersections occur! With R*trees, we might expect to deal with regularly shaped rectangles; in which case, the algorithm can be considered both simple and efficient. Experiments show that the performance gain is considerable, even if a same page must be loaded (and thus sorted) several times.

In the case in which the two R-trees do not have the same depth, when the leaf level of the smallest R-tree is reached, pairs $[e_N, e_L]$ with an *internal node* entry e_N for the deepest R-tree and a *leaf* entry e_L for the other are delivered. A window query must then be carried out on the subtree of e_N, using $e_L.mbb$ as a window argument.

7.3.3 Spatial Hash Join

Spatial hash join is an application of the *hash-join* algorithm for spatial data. The method is applicable when no spatial index exists for the relations to be joined. It is an alternative to the external plane-sweep algorithm presented in Section 7.2.2.

---

33. The internal nested loop allows us to get rid of the active list of the algorithm (Chapter 5). That is, a rectangle can be removed as soon as it has been encountered.

We briefly recall the hash-join relational algorithm. Assume the smallest relation, say, R, fits in main memory. A hash table is built on R by a single scan of R. Then a simple scan is performed on the larger relation (say, S) such that each tuple t of S is probed against the hash table. We apply the hash function f to t and search the bucket assigned to $f(t)$ for the tuples in R that qualify with t. The algorithm is both efficient (a single scan of each relation) and simple.

The method is particularly effective when one of the inputs is small, whatever the size of the other. When, however, the smallest relation is larger than the available memory, some more complex techniques must be used. They usually try to keep as much as possible of the hash table in core, while flushing onto disk some of the hash buckets. Still, it is important that each bucket is small enough to fit in memory.

By hashing R and S with the *same* hash function, we obtain a simple one-to-one correspondence between the buckets in R and S. Things are not this simple with spatial data. There does not exist a function that easily maps a spatial object to a bucket, avoiding *simultaneous* overlapping and redundancy. Actually, this problem was studied in depth in Chapter 6. There, it led to two families of data structures: *space-driven structures* (with redundancy) and *data-driven structures* (with overlapping).

The same choice between redundancy and overlapping occurs for spatial hash join, as depicted in Figure 7.10, where the hash function partitions the search space into four buckets: A, B, C, and D. With each bucket is associated a rectangle, called *the bucket extent*.

In the first case (left-hand side), the search space is split into four buckets (A, B, C, and D), whose extents have the same size. This closely resembles the grid structure of Chapter 6, where the single-page cells are replaced by buckets. In that case, the "hash" function assigns

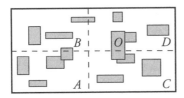 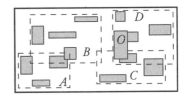

Figure 7.10 Alternatives for spatial hashing.

a rectangle r to *all* buckets whose extent intersects r. For example, rectangle O is assigned to buckets C and D (redundancy).

In the second case (right-hand side), closer to the R-tree approach, a rectangle is assigned a single bucket, and the bucket extent is such that it encloses all assigned rectangles. This implies a possible enlargement of a bucket extent when rectangles are inserted, and thus entails some bucket overlapping. Assume, for instance, that O is the last object to be inserted in the hash table: bucket D is chosen, and the enlargement of its extent gives rise to an important overlapping with the extent of C. We present in the following a spatial hash-join algorithm based on overlapping. The algorithm for the overlap spatial join $R \bowtie S$ requires three steps:

◆ *Step 1: initial partitioning.* First, R is partitioned: each rectangle is assigned to a single bucket, and the extent of a bucket is the *mbb* of all of its rectangles. At the end of this step, we obtain a situation similar to that of Figure 7.10 (right). The quality of this initial partition (of the hash function) is assessed according to the following criteria: (1) there should be roughly the same number of rectangles in each bucket, (2) each bucket should fit in main memory, and (3) the overlapping of bucket extents is minimized.

◆ *Step 2: second partitioning.* Any rectangle of S is assigned to any bucket of the initial R partition whose extent overlaps it. Note that this introduces some redundancy, as in Figure 7.10 (left). In addition, because the distribution of S might be completely different from that of R, the assignment of records in S is unpredictable, and the number of rectangles from S in a bucket might significantly vary from one bucket to the other.

◆ *Step 3: join phase.* We now have two sets of buckets, each with the same extent. Each bucket B_R from relation R must be joined with a single bucket B_S from S with the same extent. As for the relational hash join, it is required that at least one of the buckets (say, B_R) fits in main memory. This allows us to perform the join by a simple scan of B_S, which can be arbitrarily large. A very naive approach is to test each rectangle from B_S against all rectangles in B_R. This might be CPU time consuming. As for the join with R-trees, there exist techniques to speed up this process. A plane-sweep algorithm or an internal data structure can be used.

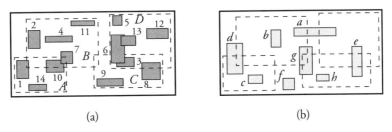

(a)   (b)

Figure 7.11   Illustration of spatial join: (a) initial partitioning (first data set) and (b) second partitioning (second data set).

By avoiding the introduction of redundancy in *both* partitions, the algorithm guarantees that the result contains no duplicate. An example is shown in Figure 7.11. The partitioning of the data set of Figure 7.10 yields four buckets with overlapping extents. The content of the buckets are

$$A = \{1, 14, 10\}, \qquad B = \{2, 4, 7, 11\},$$
$$C = \{3, 8, 9\}, \qquad D = \{5, 6, 12, 13\}$$

Next, we partition the second data set, which consists of the objects $\{a, b, c, d, e, f, g\}$. Keeping the bucket extents of A, B, C, and D for the buckets of the second data set, we obtain

$$A' = \{c, d\}, \qquad B' = \{a, b, d, g\},$$
$$C' = \{e, g, h\}, \qquad D' = \{a, e\}$$

Observe that some rectangles can be assigned to several buckets (a, d, e, and g) but that some rectangles might be "filtered" out during this step, because they do not overlap any bucket extent (as for rectangle f in the example). Finally, the following pairs of buckets must be joined:

$$[A, A'], [B, B'], [C, C'], [D, D']$$

The join of a pair of buckets consists of looking for the pairs of overlapping rectangles.

Recall that the hash function for the initial partitioning must be cautiously defined. As mentioned previously, the main goal is to obtain a balanced distribution of data among the buckets at the end of the process. This means that the initial definition of the bucket extents should take into account the distribution of the data sets; that is, there should be more buckets with small extents in the dense areas. Because the algorithm does not have an a priori knowledge of the input's statistical properties, a candidate solution is to estimate the distribution by randomly sampling the input data.

7.4   COMPLEX QUERIES

So far we have considered the implementation of single spatial operators (essentially, spatial joins). We turn now to the issue of evaluating complex queries that involve several spatial operators in sequence. The problem has been studied at length for relational databases. We present some peculiarities when dealing with spatial data.

We first describe a general query execution model that is suitable both for simple and complex queries, and that encompasses relational and spatial query processing. In this model, a query is described as a *query execution plan* (QEP).

We then investigate the execution of spatial queries and illustrate the problems with two typical situations: (1) the sequence *filter step/refinement step* for a spatial selection or join and (2) *multiway spatial joins* (i.e., the execution of several spatial joins in sequence).

7.4.1   Query Execution Plans

When a query is to be executed in a DBMS, it must be first transformed into a program that accesses data and processes the query. A typical sequence of steps for processing a query is depicted in Figure 7.12. First, the user query is translated into an equivalent algebraic expression by the *parser*. An algebraic expression is a composition of logical operations belonging to a given algebra. The *type checker* controls the

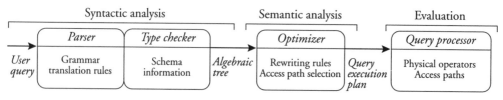

Figure 7.12   Evaluation of queries.

existence and consistent use of relation names, attribute names, and attribute types using schema information. The result can be represented as a tree in which each node corresponds to a logical operation such as a spatial join. The third step is the *optimization* of the query according to rewriting rules and access path selection. The optimizer delivers a QEP, which is evaluated. This QEP relies on a set of physical operators and access paths (e.g., indices and hash tables).

This set of operators can be seen as a *physical algebra* that provides an equivalent counterpart to the *logical algebra* defining the query language. There are some strong differences, however. First, there usually exist several physical operators for a single logical operator. As an example, take the (logical) spatial overlap join. We have seen many algorithms (i.e., physical operators) for this join. Second, there are physical operators (sorting, for instance) that do not have their counterpart in the logical algebra and that may be involved in several situations.

Any user query can be evaluated by assembling a subset of the available physical operators into a QEP. The optimizer creates the QEP by choosing the appropriate operators and by determining their execution order according to several factors, such as the size of data sets, the existence of indices, and the estimated cost of the many candidate solutions.

In the following, we concentrate on the last step of a query evaluation; that is, on the execution of QEPs. As a running example, we will consider the query **SPAT-ADM-LU1**: Display of all residential areas in the County of San Jose (see Chapter 3). We assume that two spatial indices—denoted, respectively, I_{states} and I_{LU}—exist on the relations *States* and *LandUse*.

A QEP is commonly represented as a binary tree that captures the order in which a sequence of physical operations is going to be executed. The leaf operations are executed first. Because the evaluation of a single logical operation often involves several physical operations (for instance, a join evaluated with a sort/merge algorithm, as in Figure 7.2), a QEP is often an "inflated" version of the algebraic tree of logical operations.

Figure 7.13 shows the logical tree and a first example of QEP for query **SPAT-ADM-LU1**. The QEP is evaluated bottom-up. The leaves in the QEP represent access to data files or indices. We perform a sequential scan of the relation *States* and access the index I_{LU}. The

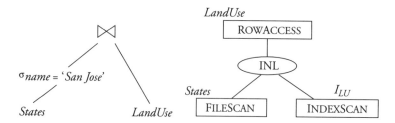

Figure 7.13　Logical and physical trees for query **SPAT-ADM-LU1**.

selection, a node in the logical tree, is in the QEP integrated with the
FileScan operator. Actually, selection is performed when the data is
accessed on the disk, through either a sequential scan or a random access. We represent data access with rectangular boxes.

Internal nodes usually represent physical algebraic operations, in
which case they are represented by ovals. The INL node is an *indexed
nested loop* join, which takes each state record coming from its left
input and performs a window query on the right input (the spatial
index I_{LU}), with the state geometry *mbb* as the window argument.
The *oid*s of all land-use parcels overlapping the state are obtained. By
convention, the left branches in a QEP are interpreted as outer inputs.

It may happen that an internal node represents a data access. This
is the case with the uppermost node of the QEP. Recall that an index
usually stores object *id*s (i.e., the physical address of an object on the
disk). The INL node delivers pairs of (1) state *records* for the *State*
relation and (2) *LandUse id*s from the I_{LU} index. It remains to get
LandUse records from these *id*s. A record access is performed by the
RowAccess operator.

The edge between a node and its parent node in the QEP represents dataflows between two operations in sequence. A query could be
naively executed as follows: (1) carry out one operator, and then store
the result in a temporary file, and (2) use this temporary file as an input for the next operator in sequence in the tree. However, because
intermediate results are usually too large to fit in main memory, and
because of the repeated flushing of intermediate results onto disk, such
a solution would be extremely time consuming.

A more appropriate model for executing a sequence of operations
J, I is not to wait until J is over before starting I. As soon as record
r has been delivered as an output of J, use it as an input for I. Then

we do not need to reserve much main memory space or flush intermediate results onto disk when this space overflows. As a matter of
fact, the process is implemented as a demand-driven process with *iterator functions*. This model allows for a *pipelined* execution of multiple
operations, thereby minimizing the system resources (memory space)
required for intermediate results: data consumed by an iterator, say, I,
is generated by its child(ren) iterator(s), say, J. Records are produced
and consumed one at a time. Iterator I asks iterator J for a record.
Therefore, the intermediate result of an operation is not stored in such
pipelined operations, except for some specific iterators (called *blocking
iterators*), such as sorting.

Consider the INL node of the QEP in Figure 7.13. Whenever its
parent, node RowAccess, initially requires a record, INL first asks
for a *State* record s from its left input, FileScan. It then initializes
a window query wq on its right source I_{LU}, with the *mbb* of s as an
argument, and gives the pair formed with s and the first *id* supplied
by wq to RowAccess. Now, each time a new record is demanded to
INL, the latter retrieves the next *id* from wq. Eventually, the window
query on I_{LU} is over; that is, all candidate land-use *ids* associated with
s have been retrieved. A new state record s' is then required to the
left input, and the process continues. Clearly, INL just maintains one
States record and the current status of the window query. Therefore,
the memory requirement is minimal.

Each iterator comes with three functions: Open, Next, and Close.
Open prepares each input source and allocates the necessary system
resources. Next runs one iteration step of the algorithm and produces
a new record. Close ends the iteration and relaxes resources. Consider the trivial example of the FileScan iterator, which sequentially
accesses a data file.[34] It is implemented as follows:

- *Step 1:* Open opens the data file, and sets a page cursor to the beginning of the file (first page).
- *Step 2:* Next accesses the current file page addressed by the page
  cursor, returns the current record to the parent node iterator, and sets

---

34. The initial data sources are not represented in the QEP, except as labels of rectangular nodes.

the record cursor to the next record. This possibly implies reading a new page if the current page records have all been scanned.

◆ *Step 3:* CLOSE closes the file.

Any query is executed by using the sequence OPEN, {NEXT}, CLOSE on the root of the QEP (iterator ROWACCESS), where {NEXT} denotes a sequence of iterations, each of them propagating down the tree a demand for a record. This design enables simple QEP creations by "assembling" iterators.

The previous query execution model is implemented in the core of several relational DBMSs. As shown previously, it adapts easily to spatial data processing. There are, however, at least two issues that need to be considered carefully in spatial databases. The first is the *refinement step*. Recall that the algorithms and spatial access methods are based on the *mbb* approximation and deliver a superset of the result. Hence, a further access to the full geometric description is necessary to complete the query.

The second issue is the high cost of spatial operations. Unlike relational query processing algorithms that deal with a set of simple predicates (largely the equality between two atomic values), a broad range of time-consuming operations must be supported for the manipulation of spatial data. For instance, a *window query* on an R-tree is more costly than the traversal of a B-tree, because a significant part of the structure must be traversed, and because of the repeated *overlap* predicate evaluation between rectangles. Thus, the cost of evaluating queries, which in the relational case is estimated by the number of I/Os, requires in the spatial case taking into account the CPU time as well. We investigate in the following the impact of these two issues on spatial QEPs.

7.4.2 Spatial Joins with Refinement Step

Consider the overlap join *LandUse* ⋈ *Roads*. In contrast to the QEP of Figure 7.13, assume now that each relation is spatially indexed with an R-tree (called, respectively, I_{LU} and I_{Roads}).

There is a simple way to model the sequence filter/refinement steps in the query execution framework previously presented. If we implement a standard join algorithm such as the synchronized tree traversal (STT) as an iterator, it must be followed by two ROWACCESS operators. They allow us to fetch the records containing the spatial

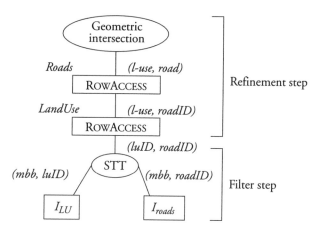

Figure 7.14 Filter and refinement steps.

description of objects of each relation. Indeed, STT delivers pairs of object *id*s.

The resulting QEP is depicted in Figure 7.14. The join algorithm (filter step) takes as inputs the two R-trees, each of them supplying entries of type (*mbb*, *o id*). Hence, the type of the records delivered by the join is (*luID*, *roadID*), where *luID* and *roadID* denote, respectively, the disk addresses of *LandUse* and *Roads* records.

The refinement step necessitates retrieval of objects on the disk. The first ROWACCESS gets the page of the *LandUse* physical relation with address *luID*, and the second gets the page of the *Roads* physical relation with address *roadID*. When both objects are in main memory, the geometric intersection test can be carried out.

Although quite simple, this QEP suffers from important shortcomings. It accesses randomly the records and results; in the worst case, in one I/O per retrieved tuple. As illustrated at the beginning of this chapter (see the example on scanning a set of items), this might lead to a very inefficient execution.

Moreover, in the case of joins, we are likely to get multiple accesses to a same record (and thus to a same page). This means that the refinement step, although quite simple from an algorithmic point of view (we just have to fetch records on the disk), is likely to be the most expensive part of the entire spatial join processing.

This drawback is illustrated in Figure 7.15. Part (a) of the figure shows the pairs of (*luID*, *roadID*) delivered by the STT join, together

lID 1 (u)	rID 1 (b)	lID 1 (u)	rID 1 (b)	l 1 rID 1 (b)	l 3 rID 3 (a)	
lID 2 (v)	rID 2 (c)	lID 1 (u)	rID 6 (d)	l 1 rID 6 (d)	l 5 rID 3 (a)	
lID 3 (w)	rID 3 (a)	lID 8 (u)	rID 1 (b)	l 8 rID 1 (b)	l 1 rID 1 (b)	
lID 4 (v)	rID 4 (d)	lID 2 (v)	rID 2 (c)	l 2 rID 2 (c)	l 8 rID 1 (b)	
lID 5 (w)	rID 5 (c)	lID 4 (v)	rID 4 (d)	l 4 rID 4 (d)	l 2 rID 2 (c)	
lID 1 (u)	rID 6 (d)	lID 3 (w)	rID 3 (a)	l 3 rID 3 (a)	l 5 rID 5 (c)	
lID 5 (w)	rID 3 (a)	lID 5 (w)	rID 5 (c)	l 5 rID 5 (c)	l 1 rID 6 (d)	
lID 8 (u)	rID 1 (b)	lID 5 (w)	rID 3 (a)	l 5 rID 3 (a)	l 4 rID 4 (d)	
	(a)		(b)	(c)	(d)	

Figure 7.15   Sequencing of row accesses.

with the page addresses. For instance, $lID1(u)$ denotes the *id* of record 1 in *LandUse*, which is stored in page u. Now assume that the LRU buffer in main memory holds four pages, and that each page can store up to two records (land-use or road records).

When the first two pairs are read, one must access pages u, v, b, and c, and thus the buffer is already full. When accessing the third pair [$lID3(w)$, $rID3(a)$], the pages u and b will be flushed, according to the LRU buffer policy. This should obviously be avoided, because both pages will be needed later in the join.

A better sequencing of page reads could save a significant amount of I/Os. The following algorithm, called *segmented sort*, partially avoids this random access to pages. It relies on a pre-processing of record *id*s based on sorting. The algorithm uses a dedicated buffer in main memory of size m pages, and can be sketched as follows (the join *LandUse* ⋈ *Roads* is used as illustration):

- *Step 1:* Compute the number k of pairs *(l-use, roadID)* that can fit in $m - 1$ pages.[35]
- *Step 2:* Load the buffer with k pairs *(luID, roadID)*.
- *Step 3:* Sort the buffer on *luID*.
- *Step 4:* Access relation *LandUse* and load records whose *id* is in the buffer. Now $m - 1$ pages in the buffer are full of records *(l-use, roadID)*.
- *Step 5:* Sort on *roadID;* load records from *Roads*, using the last page in the buffer; and perform the refinement step.
- *Step 6:* Repeat from step 2, until the entire join is processed.

---

35. *l-use* is the relation record and *not* the record *id luID*.

Consider again the example in Figure 7.15. We dedicate three pages of the buffer to the *LandUse* relation and, assuming that the size of an *id* is negligible, we compute $k = 3 \times 2 = 6$ as the number of land-use records that fit in the buffer. Hence, we first load in the buffer the pairs of record *id*s from Figure 7.15a, and sort them on the page *id* of the left attribute. We obtain the order shown in Figure 7.15b. Pages *u, v,* and *w* are read in sequence, and the six records $\{l_1, l_2, l_3, l_4, l_5, l_8\}$ of the *LandUse* relation are loaded (Figure 7.15c).

Then we sort on *roadID*, and obtain the sequence of Figure 7.15d. It now remains to read in sequence the pages *a, b, c,* and *d* of the *Road* relation, and to perform the refinement step on pairs of records. Each page need be accessed only once, by using the remaining page in the buffer, and we obtain an optimal execution that reads only once the seven pages involved in the join.

If the size of the left relation is *n* pages, the join needs n/m passes. Although a page *p* is never read twice in the same pass, it might happen that two distinct passes read *p*. Hence, the algorithm, although better than the brute-force version without sorting, does not yield an optimal scheduling of I/Os.

A more drastic solution, which allows us to completely avoid repeated accesses to the same page, is to sort the result of the STT join on the page *id*s. This external sort on the intermediate result introduces two new important issues.

- ◆ Sorting is expensive; its cost must be taken into account.
- ◆ The QEP requires the consumption of all input data before any output is possible. To sort the result, we need to wait until the join is over. Sorting is a blocking operator.

The ratio of sorting cost to random page-fetching cost depends on several factors, but largely on the size of the intermediate result (delivered by the STT join).

The QEPs considered so far were fully *pipelined* QEPs. Records are processed one at a time. To get the first record, we need not have processed the complete plan. The response time (i.e., the time required to get the first record) is reduced. Then getting the next record might need some time. Typically, time-consuming spatial computation, such as geometric intersection in the case of the overlap join, is part of the evaluation process. From the user point of view, such a slow but steady result output is often desirable and preferable to a solution in which the output flow is faster but the response time is much larger.

7.4.3 Multiway Joins

The evaluation of a QEP including a sequence of spatial joins raises some specific issues, discussed in this section. A sequence of pairwise joins $R_1 \bowtie R_2 \ldots \bowtie R_n$ is referred to in the following as a *multiway spatial join*. For the sake of simplicity, we initially restrict the discussion to 2-way joins $R_1 \bowtie R_2 \bowtie R_3$, and assume that each relation is indexed with an R-tree on its spatial attribute.

There are several meanings to these two-way joins. Without loss of generality, we restrict our attention to the so-called *chain joins*. "Finding the roads traversing forests (which forests are) crossed by rivers" is an example of a chain join query. Assume we would like to keep in the result the roads, as well as the forests traversed and the rivers crossed.

Figure 7.16 illustrates three possible QEPs for processing a two-way join, using indices I_1, I_2, and I_3. We do not consider the refinement step. Recall, however (as discussed in the previous section), that these QEPs should be completed by an access to spatial records in order to perform the refinement step.

The first QEP (Figure 7.16a) has the form of a *left-deep tree*. In such trees, the right operand of any join is always an index, as well as the left operand of the leftmost node. This QEP is fully pipelined. An STT join is first performed, taking as inputs indices I_1 and I_2 (filter step of $R_1 \bowtie R_2$); an INL join is then executed with inputs the result of the

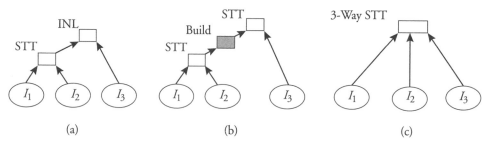

Figure 7.16 Two-way spatial joins: (a) a pipelined strategy, (b) a build-and-match strategy, and (c) generalized tree traversal.

first join and I_3 (filter step of $R_2 \bowtie R_3$). At each step, the STT node produces a pair of index entries ($[mbb_1, id_1]$, $[mbb_2, id_2]$), where id_1 (id_2) is the id of a record in R_1 (R_2), such that mbb_1 and mbb_2 overlap. Then mbb_2 is used as the argument of a window query for the INL join, which returns all entries $[mbb_3, id_3]$ such that mbb_3 overlaps mbb_2. The result of the execution of this QEP is a set of triples ($[mbb_1, id_1]$, $[mbb_2, id_2]$, $[mbb_3, id_3]$).

The approach is simple, and provides a short response time. It is also flexible, because it permits us to perform the refinement step prior to the completion of the entire query if it is expected that the candidate set delivered by STT contains a large number of false hits. By computing the refinement step in a lazy mode (i.e., after the QEP of Figure 7.16a), the cardinality of intermediate results is larger (because of false hits), but the size of records propagated up the tree is smaller than if the refinement step had been performed immediately after the filter step of the STT. In the latter case, the records propagated up the tree are R_1 and R_2 records.

A drawback of the pipelined execution of Figure 7.16a is the repeated application of window queries, one for each pair provided by the STT node. Then a given page p of the R-tree I_3 is likely to be loaded several times. Indeed, once p has been loaded, it is likely to be replaced by another page because the index is much larger than the available main memory. It is unfortunately likely that between the time p has been loaded and the time it is replaced that it is not accessed, because consecutive window queries are unlikely to cover the same part of the search space.

Avoiding repeated loading of the same index page would result in a significant performance gain. This is what the second QEP (Figure 7.16b) attempts, by following a *build-and-match* strategy. The idea is to pre-process the result of the STT (called R_{STT}) in order to create a structure that matches efficiently with the R-tree I_3. Of course, the building phase is implemented by a blocking iterator and requires memory space. However, the rationale of such an approach is that even though building the structure is time consuming, the join behind is so efficient that the overall time performance is better than using the INL algorithm.

One strategy is to build "on the fly" an R-tree on R_{STT}, followed by a regular STT join. Of course, creating the R-tree by inserting the

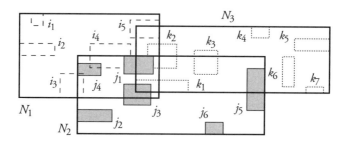

Figure 7.17   A 2-way join on R-tree nodes.

records one by one would be quite inefficient. Because the index is to be built only once on a fixed data set, bulk loading the R-tree is preferable.

Finally, the last approach (Figure 7.16c) consists of a 3-way STT; that is, a synchronized traversal of the three R-trees down to the leaves. The algorithm can be seen as a generalization of the STT method. The expected advantage here is that by considering simultaneously three (or more, generally n) nodes of the joined R-trees it becomes possible to drastically reduce the part of the indices that must be visited.

Consider the situation depicted in Figure 7.17, in which three nodes N_1, N_2, and N_3 from the respective R-trees I_1, I_2, and I_3 must be joined: we look for triplets of entries (i_a, j_b, k_c) such that the pairs $(i_a.mbb, j_b.mbb)$ and $(j_b.mbb, k_c.mbb)$ overlap. From the classical STT algorithm, we already know how to restrict the search space. During a pairwise join of two R-tree nodes N_1 and N_2, we are only interested in the entries whose *mbb* overlaps $N_1.mbb \cap N_2.mbb$. By performing simultaneously the two joins, the condition on the entries of node N_2 is further strengthened: it is enough to qualify those entries j_b of N_2 overlapping $N_1.mbb \cap N_2.mbb$, as well as $N_2.mbb \cap N_3.mbb$.

As a matter of fact, only the entries j_1 and j_3 satisfy this condition in Figure 7.17. Such a strategy saves, for instance, the join between the subtrees rooted at i_3 and j_4 that would have been performed in a regular pairwise join.

REFINEMENT STEP

The result of the filter step is a tuple $[i_1, i_2, \ldots i_n]$ of record *id*s. According to our execution model, the records must then be retrieved with RowAccess iterators (one for each relation) in order to perform the refinement step on the n-way join. However, the costs of this refinement step might be prohibitive. Indeed, the pair of record ids (i_j, i_{j+1}) may appear in several tuples. This means that not only the corresponding pages may be loaded several times but, worse, the expensive overlap test on the spatial objects themselves might be done several times for the same pair!

Imagine, for instance, that the sequence of triplets in the result of STT is (r_1, r_1', r_1''), (r_1, r_1', r_2''), (r_2, r_1', r_1''). Each triplet (o_1, o_2, o_3) is such that $o_1.mbb \cap o_2.mbb \neq \emptyset$ and $o_2.mbb \cap o_3.mbb \neq \emptyset$. In order to qualify the triplet for the final result of the join, we must perform an intersection test involving the exact geometry of each object. Therefore, given the previous sequence, we will perform this expensive operation twice for the pairs (r_1, r_1') and (r_1', r_1''). This overhead comes in addition to the already mentioned cost of accessing randomly the pages to fetch the records.

In the QEP of Figures 7.16a and 7.16b (pipelined and build-and-match QEP), the refinement step can be introduced at various places, depending on many parameters, such as the size of the relations, the size of intermediate results, the cost of the geometric operator, and the quality of the approximation of the *mbb* of the spatial object. The *n*-way generalized STT (Figure 7.16c) provides somewhat less flexibility because it delivers *n*-tuples of record *ids*. However, it is attractive because of its extremely efficient filter step in the presence of several R-trees.

The problem, raised previously, with multiway joins is to find a query execution strategy combining low memory requirements, an efficient filter step, and an optimal sequencing for the refinement step. There is as yet no comprehensive solution to this open problem.

7.5 BIBLIOGRAPHIC NOTES

[Gra93], [SKS98], and [YM98] are general references on query processing and optimization. [Ooi90] is specifically devoted to spatial query processing and optimization. A large part of it covers the design of the GEOQL system. The system consists of a classical relational database module and a spatial processor. Query optimization extends the classical relational techniques by considering separately spatial and non-spatial subqueries.

The external sort/merge algorithm is a classical illustration of I/O algorithms. Several improvements of the simple version presented in Section 7.2.1 are possible. For instance, instead of sorting the buffer with quicksort during the initial sort phase, one can use a replacement selection algorithm [LG98], which allows one to create larger initial runs and thus potentially reduce the number of merge levels. For a detailed analysis of the cost of external sorting, see [Gra93] and [SKS98], as well as [AV88].

The distribution sweeping technique was originally proposed in [GTVV93]. Since then, the technique has been applied successfully to many problems, including the red/blue line segment intersection problem [AVV95], for which an optimal internal memory algorithm has been given in Chapter 5. Two surveys on external algorithms for computational geometry are [Arg97] and [Vit98]. Our presentation of the algorithm for the orthogonal segment intersection problem in Section 7.2.2 is drawn from [Arg97].

The external sweep-line algorithm for reporting the pairwise intersections in a large set of rectangles of Section 7.2.2 is from [APR+98]. Although the algorithm achieves the optimal bound, the algorithmic analysis hides, as usual, the constant that might represent an unacceptable overhead in a practical implementation. Moreover, the worst-case optimality guarantees a robust behavior of the algorithm even for highly skewed data, but it should also be required that the algorithm behaves correctly on real-life data with average statistical properties. [APR+98] not only gives the theoretical worst-case optimal algorithm but describes an implementation that relies on simplified data structures and algorithms.

An interesting practical aspect is that the actual algorithm tries to exploit the so-called square-root rule. That is, it seems that in most practical situations the number of rectangles that intersect a given line is in $O(\sqrt{n})$, with a small constant [OW86]. Therefore, even for very large data sets, the number of rectangles that must actually fit in main memory at any time is expected to be relatively small. The algorithm exploits this optimistic assumption by carrying out a classical main memory algorithm, and relies on partitioning only when the size of the active lists becomes greater than the available memory. The experimental performance evaluation reported in [APR+98] shows that the practical behavior of the algorithm is comparable to that of the spatial hash-join algorithm of [PD96] on real-life data, and outperforms its competitors when the data set becomes highly skewed.

It should be noted that the extension of the plane-sweep technique to process large sets of rectangles in external memory has been initially presented in the early work of [GS87] and implemented in the GRAL system [BG92]. The algorithm of [GS87] is similar in spirit to that of [APR$^+$98], but follows a divide-and-conquer strategy: the active lists are halved whenever memory shortage is encountered, whereas a $\sqrt{m}$ splitting policy is used in [APR$^+$98].

Our presentation of the algorithm for joining two z-ordered relations in Section 7.3.1 (shown in Figure 7.7) is borrowed from [OM88]. This strategy (see also [Ore86, Ore89, Ore90]) is probably the first proposal of spatial join. The technique has been experimented in the PROBE system [OM88]. [GOP$^+$98] sketches an algorithm and reports an implementation for the join of two relations, indexed with a linear quadtree, and the comparison of its performance with other join strategies.

A potential problem of join strategies based on linear structures is the high redundancy in these structures, as explained in Section 7.3.1 and in Chapter 6. See also [Ore89, Gae95]. In Chapter 6 we presented a variant of linear structure without redundancy. To the best of our knowledge, no join strategies based on this index are reported in the literature. The join of two z-ordered relations is an example of a strategy that does not use the *mbb* of objects but a finer approximation. [ZS98] is another example of an algorithm using a raster approximation. [ZSI00] proposes a join of trapezoids. The algorithm can be used to evaluate spatial joins for polygons by decomposing the polygons into trapezoids.

The join algorithm with two R-trees given in Section 7.3.2 is from [BKS93]. The algorithm is acknowledged as being efficient; see, for instance, [TS96, LR96, PD96, HJR97b, PRS99]. The algorithm can be seen as an R-tree-specialized version of the general technique known as synchronized tree traversal (STT) for joining two tree-based structures, proposed in [G93]. The same idea can be applied to quadtrees, for instance, as advocated in [HS92].

The relational hash-join algorithm was shown during the 1980s to be an efficient alternative to the sort/merge join algorithm when no index is available. Early references include [DKO$^+$84, DG85], and detailed discussions can be found in [Gra93] and [SKS98]. The technique is commonly used in relational database systems [GBC98].

The adaptation of hash join to spatial data has been proposed simultaneously and independently by [LR96] and [PD96]. The algorithm described in Section 7.3.3 is essentially that of [LR96], which avoids duplicates in the output by a partitioning of the data set without redundancy. A difficulty of the algorithm is the initial definition of bucket extents that should reflect the spatial distribution of objects. This can be achieved with sampling techniques; see, for instance, [Ahr85, Vit84, LR95].

The partition-based spatial-merge (PBSM) join of [PD96] proposes a full spatial join implementation, including the refinement step, which is part of the query processor of the PARADISE system [PYK+97]. In contrast to the algorithm of Section 7.3.3, PBSM uses a fixed set of bucket extents and assigns an object o to *all* buckets whose extent overlaps $o.mbb$. An object can thus be assigned to several buckets (see Figure 7.10). The two data sets are partitioned with the same bucket extent, and the algorithm requires that the two buckets B_R and B_S with the same extent fit *both* in memory. A plane-sweep algorithm (similar to that of [BKS93]) is then performed to join objects from B_R and B_S.

The spatial partitioning function tries to create buckets of roughly equal size by using a specific assignment of objects to partitions. This is depicted in Figure 7.18. We assume that four buckets are sufficient to partition the entire data set. A naive assignment policy associates an entire rectangular area with each partition. If the distribution is not uniform, the buckets will have very different sizes. In Figure 7.18 (left),

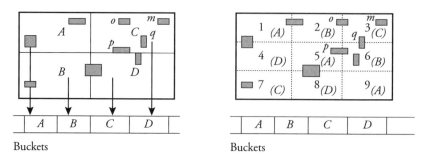

Figure 7.18 The PBSM partition function.

the four objects (m, o, p, q) are assigned to D because of the high density of the upper-right part of the working space.

The spatial partition of PBSM uses a decomposition of the space in n cells, with n larger than the number of buckets. Then each cell is mapped to a bucket independently of its location. This is illustrated in Figure 7.18 (right), in which nine cells are defined and ranked from 1 to 9. The assignment of a cell to one of the four buckets follows a round-robin scheme. Cells 1, 5, and 9 are assigned to bucket A, cells 2 and 6 to B, and cells 3 and 7 to C. Therefore, even in dense areas, objects will be distributed evenly in the buckets.

A potential problem with this algorithm is the storage of objects in several buckets. This might lead to a high redundancy factor and impact badly the algorithm efficiency. The issue is discussed in [APR+98], and an improvement is proposed in [KS97], which uses several layers to avoid replication.

Finally, we mention several algorithms that handle the case when only one R-tree exists. As discussed at length, this is a situation that frequently occurs, for instance, when one input comes from another operator in the query tree. The INL presented in this chapter is a simple but inefficient algorithm. It generates one window query for each record from the outer data set, and because the window arguments are randomly located, the same R-tree nodes must be loaded repeatedly. This results in large overhead as soon as the R-tree size is larger than the available buffer [LR98, PD96, MP99, PRS99].

The first attempt to overcome the problem is the *seeded tree join* (STJ) [LR98]. This technique consists of building from the existing R-tree, used as a *seed*, a second R-tree (called a *seeded R-tree*). The motivation behind this approach is that tree matching during the join phase should be more efficient than if a regular R-tree were constructed. During the *seeding phase*, the top k levels of the seed are copied to become the top k levels of the seeded tree. The entries of the lowest level are called *slots*. During the *growing phase*, the objects of the nonindexed source are inserted in one of the slots. A rectangle is inserted in the slot that contains it or needs the least enlargement.

When the source has been exhausted, the construction of the tree begins. For each slot, the objects inserted in the associated temporary files (as well as the objects remaining in the buffer) are loaded to build an R-tree.

Although the method looks appealing, subsequent experiments have shown that it suffers from several shortcomings. For instance, as mentioned in [MP99], the buffer must be large enough to provide at least one page to each slot. If this is not the case, the pages associated with a slot will be read and written during the growing phase, thus rendering the method ineffective. In addition, the CPU cost of the construction is still very high, due to the quadratic split algorithm of the R-tree [PRS99]. Finally, the method lacks flexibility, particularly in regard to large page sizes, because the number of slots cannot be tuned easily.

Two other candidate algorithms have been proposed recently for situations in which only one relation is indexed. The *sort-and-match* [PRS99] performs a preliminary sorting of the records from the non-indexed data set, and groups them in clusters. The *mbb* of each cluster is then used to perform a window query on the R-tree. Because of the sorting phase, two window queries are close to each other in the search space, which significantly limits buffer trashing. The *slot index spatial join* of [MP99] combines techniques from the seeded tree and from the spatial hash join. The idea is to use the upper nodes in the R-tree as bucket extents, and to hash the nonindexed data set using these extents. The buckets are then joined with the existing R-tree. This algorithm seems to be the most efficient proposed so far.

Other spatial join techniques include join with grid files; storing *mbbs*, which are seen as points in a 4D space [BHF93]; and techniques based on *join indices*, a specific type of index that stores pairs of record *ids* that qualify for a join. This structure was proposed and analyzed in [Val87], and its application to spatial join can be found in [Rot91].

Most of the effort has been devoted to the *overlap* spatial join, whereas other predicates are somewhat neglected. Some exceptions are [HS98, CMTV00], which study *distance* joins, and [GOP+98], which investigates direction predicates such as *North-East*. For such a join, the very low selectivity renders the simple nested loop solution an acceptable candidate. [GOP+98] also proposes some guidelines for benchmarking.

As seen previously, most of the effort so far has been devoted to the evaluation of spatial joins. The evaluation of complex queries and their optimization generated less interest, with the exception of some advanced prototypes, such as PROBE [OM88], GEOQL [Ooi90],

PARADISE [PYK+97], and GRAL [Güt89, BG92]. The latter paper investigates in depth the issue of extending an existing query processor and optimizer to handle spatial queries.

The design of query processors that encompass spatial and relational data is studied in [PRS99, MP99, PMT99]. It is still not clear which strategy, among the numerous strategies proposed for evaluating complex spatial queries, is the most general and efficient. For example, the evaluation of the refinement step in a query involving several spatial joins is an open issue. The sequencing filter/refinement deserves further investigation. A fast filter step that delivers a set of *id* pairs is not that useful if the refinement step is 100 times more costly.

The *segmented sort* technique presented in this chapter is from [Val87], and is not specific to spatial data. Several papers propose to introduce another step to reduce the number of false hits after the refinement step. See, for example, [BKSS94, HJR97c].

8

Commercial Systems

"So endeth this chronicle. It being strictly a history of a *boy*, it must stop here; the story could not go much further without becoming the history of a *man.* When one writes a novel about grown people, he knows exactly where to stop—that is, with a marriage; but when he writes for juveniles, he must stop where he best can.

Most of the characters that perform in this book still live, and are prosperous and happy. Some day it may seem worth while to take up the story of the younger ones again and see what sort of men and women they turned out to be; therefore it will be wisest not to reveal any of that part of their lives at present."

MARK TWAIN
The Adventures of Tom Sawyer,
Conclusion

CONTENTS

8.1 AN INTRODUCTION TO COMMERCIAL SYSTEMS

This chapter is devoted to the study of current commercial solutions for handling geographic information. It illustrates many concepts presented in the previous chapters that are often not trivially understandable from the documentation provided by vendors. In particular, the comparison with the theoretical concepts, techniques, and algorithms studied so far in the book shows how recent achievements slowly find their way into existing GISs and DBMSs.

Commercial GISs rely on a long-term development that depends heavily on technical choices made earlier on. This makes the introduction of new features a costly and delicate task. On the other hand, the management of spatial information is somewhat of secondary importance for DBMS products, whose main market is still primarily oriented toward business data management. In many cases, we will see in this chapter that recent evolution in commercial GIS results from a compromise between existing features and some of the most salient techniques proposed recently to handle spatial data.

Among several examples, the ArcInfo product is currently evolving toward a more declarative way of expressing queries, although it is still, under this perspective, one step behind more recent products such as ArcView or Smallworld. Querying with ArcInfo requires a much larger expertise than with a relational-like query language as advocated in Chapter 3. On the other hand, the Oracle DBMS—which had been a "pure" relational DBMS until a few years ago—proposes a spatial extension whose design exploits as much as possible the powerful query engine and query optimizer of the system. We will see that its indexing method is very close to the z-ordering tree presented in detail in Chapter 6.

8.1.1 How to Read This Chapter

In an ideal situation, this chapter would cover all functionalities expected from products available on the market. The major points to consider when looking at commercial off-the-shelf systems are the following (in addition to cost and distribution issues, such as the possible number of sites):

- *Data collection.* Do these systems allow one to easily input data, either from satellite images (raster) or from other systems (e.g., the World Wide Web)? How much effort would it take to incorporate such a module?

- *Data representation.* Can all relevant data of a given application be represented (e.g., non-connected regions or regions with holes) in the system? (See Chapters 2, 3, and 4.)

- *Data storage and fast access.* Is data stored efficiently with indices? (See Chapter 6.)

- *Data analysis and computation.* Is there a way to analyze the data and perform well-known computations (e.g., classification and allocation). Are such functions built in? If not, what is the complexity of plugging in such functionalities?

- *Concurrency and recovery.* Can users access the data in a concurrent and transparent manner (for instance, when editing maps)? Can the system recover after various types of failures, including disk crashes?

- *Query facility and optimization.* Are typical GIS queries (see Chapters 3 and 4) expressible? Is the interaction with the end user friendly? What levels of storage detail should be known when posing a query, even simple, against the system? Can the processing of these queries be optimized either by predefined techniques or by user-defined techniques?

In the following, we focus our attention largely on the study of data representation, modeling, and query facilities offered by these systems. In particular, we try, for each system, to extract from its functionalities those that can be closely related to the material found in the rest of the book. We believe that these explanations will bring to the reader, whether he is a geographer or a database specialist, two complementary aspects:

- *A concrete illustration of major concepts.* Consider some of the various illustration examples presented in this chapter. The topological model of ArcInfo is a detailed illustration of the topological representation of spatial objects (Section 2.3) and resembles closely the TIGER spatial model (Section 2.4.2). Spatial indexing and query processing in Oracle are respectively similar to the z-ordering tree (Section 6.2.3) and to the z-ordering join (Section 7.3.1), whereas

PostgreSQL relies on an R-tree (Section 6.3) and an indexed nested loop join (Section 7.3). By comparing with the strict, "theoretical" description of these techniques proposed earlier in this book, one can gain a better understanding of the practical applicability of research achievements in the context of a real system.

◆ *An insight on the inner features of commercial products.* It is often not trivial to understand the design of a system from its documentation. Clearly, a good understanding of a system is essential for using it more efficiently. From this point of view, the presentation we propose on each topic, completed with the relevant chapters of the book, should be considered a means of assessing more intelligently the strengths and weaknesses of current and future spatial database systems.

As discussed in Chapter 1, current GISs range from loosely coupled systems to integrated systems. The first GISs were *dedicated systems.* The lack of ability to develop new applications, the lack of general database functionalities such as query languages, along with the lack of functional extensibility, are among the limitations of such architectures, which are still used by several application-specific systems. Today, the available systems (from the second and third generation) rely on the following architectures:

◆ *Loosely coupled systems.* These systems (e.g., ArcInfo from ESRI or Tigris from Intergraph) separate spatial data management from thematic data management. For example, in ArcInfo the *Arc* module manages spatial data linked to nonspatial data handled either by the *Info* module or by coupled (relational) DBMS.

◆ *Integrated architecture.* More recent products, such as ArcView (from ESRI) or Smallworld (from Smallworld, Ltd.), provide a database-like approach to the modeling of geographic information. Such information is modeled as sets (relations) of geographic objects. Each geographic object has nonspatial attributes (description) and one spatial attribute.

In an orthogonal way, most of the general-purpose relational DBMS vendors now propose a spatial extension to their data management kernel. Such systems cannot really be called GISs, in that they lack a large number of functions a full-fledged GIS is able to offer. These are, for instance, data input and data analysis and visualization, which require special techniques with the presence of spatial data. Neverthe-less, this extension to spatial data management enables the application developer to add spatial types and spatial functions to be used with SQL. The basic set of spatial functionalities is not as rich as in GIS. However, (1) geospatial data and alphanumeric data are handled in a uniform way, and (2) well-known database techniques can be used. An illustration of database extensions to spatial data management is given in this chapter through the presentation of two systems: Oracle and PostgreSQL.

8.1.2   Interacting with a GIS or with a Spatial DBMS

Regarding the possible types of interaction with a GIS, there is an important distinction to be made among the categories of users who interact with such systems; namely, designers and end users. Design-ers develop applications and define "canned" actions in order to hide low-level details implemented by programmers. End users use these pre-programmed actions to interact with the system. It is clear that this interaction is more or less user friendly, depending on the system. However, the easier the interaction, the more limited the set of func-tionalities end users are able to use. Given these considerations, manip-ulating geographic information from a GIS user interface obeys one of the following approaches:

◆ *Data manipulation through a customized interface (end user).* End users have access to geographic information through a graphical user interface (GUI) customized for the application needs. Any evolution in the application, any change in some parameters of the end-user query is not simple and requires the designer to interact with the system.

◆ *Application development (designer).* Application developers use a pro-gramming language for customizing the system and the GUI to the application needs. This programming language includes a rich set of *primitives,* each implementing a spatial function. Access to geo-graphic information is directly programmed in the language with the spatial primitives. Usually, an end-user query requires the execu-tion of a sequence of primitives and the management of intermedi-ate results. Its preparation and programming require a deep knowl-edge of the system architecture. Then, by combining the primitives and choosing the right order of primitives, the expert can provide efficient end-user query facilities customized to specific needs. All commercial systems offer, more or less, the same set of primitives.

◆ *Access through a query language (end user and designer)*. A third way of manipulating geographic information is through high-level query languages, as discussed in Chapter 3. A high-level declarative query language enables the user to express what she needs without specifying how the system must operate to get the answer. This renders the query facility (1) accessible to nonexpert users, and (2) independent of the underlying software and platforms.

A closer look at a given system is necessary to get an idea of the actual power of its high-level query facility. Three criteria might be useful for that purpose. They can be formulated through the following interrogations:

◆ *Parameterization, genericity.* Is there a general GUI or textual language that enables us to parameterize a query with the theme(s), attributes, predicates, and functions to be applied? How much effort is necessary in order to modify a query or to create a new one?

◆ *Complex queries.* Does this high-level query facility enable complex queries involving more than two themes, mixing descriptive queries and spatial queries? How much architecture knowledge is required from the end user to sequence the simple operations necessary to pose a complex query?

◆ *Query optimization.* Is there an automatic system optimization for efficiently answering queries? How many low-level implementation details should end users be aware of in order to get a fast answer to their queries?

Today's trend of commercial GIS is to develop high-level query language facilities along the lines of the preceding list. Because a full automation of query optimization is a complex and only partially solved issue, no GIS is likely to provide in a short range the previously outlined (idealistic) powerful, efficient, implementation-independent, and easy-to-use query language.

These aspects are taken into account in the following study of three commercial GISs. The first, ArcInfo from ESRI, only provides a complete set of low-level efficient primitives. Complex queries can only be prepared by programmers who are expert in system architecture. Once a query has been prepared, it can be encapsulated in a friendly interface. Nevertheless, any change in the query requires an update by the expert. The second, more recent, system from ESRI, ArcView GIS, corresponds to a trend toward a high-level query facility. The Smallworld GIS provides a higher-level query language for simple queries that involve one or two themes. In the case of complex queries, the user has to explicitly specify the sequence of operations in the right order.

This chapter is organized as follows. Sections 8.2, 8.3, and 8.4 are dedicated to the study of, respectively, the ArcInfo, ArcView, and Smallworld systems. For each of these systems, we describe its major features as well as the provided spatial model. We then illustrate its query capabilities with a sample database and examples of queries as close as possible to those used in Chapter 3. Sections 8.5 and 8.6 are devoted, respectively, to the Oracle and PostgreSQL systems. Finally, Section 8.7 provides references to both systems presented here, as well as to further solutions available on the market.

8.2   ARCINFO

ArcInfo was first designed by ESRI in 1969, and has been available on the market since 1982. It is one of the most widely used GISs. It offers a rich set of spatial functions. ArcInfo was originally defined as a toolbox that could be enriched by the addition of new modules and functions. In this system, data is modeled and queried in a quite different way from that discussed in Chapter 3, as examined in the following sections.

In the following, we first give the general functionalities as well as the architecture of ArcInfo (Section 8.2.1). We then describe (Section 8.2.2) how data is internally represented in this GIS and define (Section 8.2.3) a sample database. Finally, we show (Section 8.2.4) how typical queries on this database can be answered with ArcInfo.

8.2.1   *Functionalities of ArcInfo*

ArcInfo offers a variety of capabilities in addition to the common data definition, access-right management, and data administration capabilities. It includes capabilities for data acquisition, exchange, and spatial analysis. Moreover, it offers more specific tools for topological structuring, among them powerful tools for thematic data distribution into coverages (a coverage is a set of spatial objects, to be more precisely defined later), entity extraction from coverages, fragmentation and fusion of coverages, and geometric correction. Spatial data querying, which will be illustrated using queries from Chapter 3, is enriched with several features:

- Querying external relational databases
- Tools for classification and statistical analysis
- Specific display tools, such as scale change or zooming
- Support for a large number of graphical formats

The functional power of ArcInfo is enriched with other tools for thematic analysis, network analysis, and terrain modeling, among others. The customization of these functions to a given application or user is possible by programming with AML, an interpreted programming language.

Two subsystems are in charge of data storage. The first, *Arc*, is dedicated to spatial data, whereas the second, *Info*, is the relational component in charge of thematic (or descriptive) information. Thus, a geographic object is split into a spatial component managed by *Arc* and a thematic component handled by *Info*, the internal object identifier (*ID*) being the link between the two components (Figure 8.1). A specific data structure is chosen for representing spatial data so as to permit efficient spatial queries.

The loose coupling between the two subsystems allows us to easily replace *Info* with another relational DBMS such as Oracle or Informix. Similarly, *Arc* may be replaced with *ArcScan*, a module for manipulating digital terrain data in triangular irregular network (TIN) format and for managing raster data (GRID) and converting data from raster to vector (and vice versa).

These modules represent the GIS kernel. On top of this kernel, applications can be written using a set of tools dedicated to a specific task and gathered in a module called *ArcTools* (Figure 8.1). The main tools available are

- Graphical display and interaction with the user (*Arcedit*)
- Map editing tools (*Arcplot*)
- Network management (*Network*); in particular, computation of optimal paths

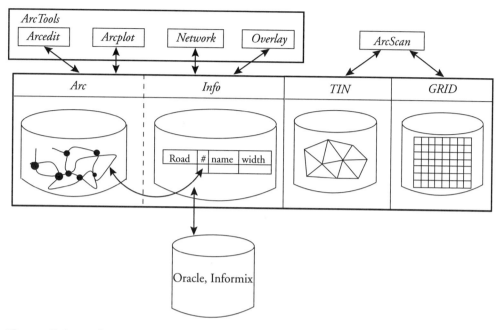

Figure 8.1   Architecture of ArcInfo.

◆ Tools for overlaying several layers (*Overlay*), map overlay being a
fundamental operation for thematic analysis

8.2.2   *Spatial and Topological Information in ArcInfo*

There exist three modes in ArcInfo for representing spatial data: the
vector mode, the raster or grid mode, and the TIN mode. We sketch
here the representation of grid and TIN data and focus on the vector
mode.

GRID AND TIN DATA REPRESENTATION IN ARCINFO
A *surface* in ArcInfo represents field-based data (see Chapter 2); that is,
functions such as elevation and temperature, having a value for every
point of the plane. To represent a surface, we use either the grid mode
or the TIN mode. With the grid mode, this function is not calculated
for each point of the plane but for each cell.[36] A single cell value is
stored for each cell. Descriptive attributes associated with a cell (e.g.,

---

36. Recall (see Chapter 2) that the space is divided into rectangular cells of equal size.

1	1	4	4	4
1	1	4	4	4
2	2	3	3	4
2	2	2	3	4
2	2	3	3	4

Value attribute table (VAT)

Value	Count	Owner
1	4	Agnes
2	7	Phil
3	5	Mike
4	9	Diana

Figure 8.2 An example of a grid with ArcInfo.

parcel owner) are stored in a table VAT (see Figure 8.2). There is one row in the VAT per cell value containing the cell value, the number of occurrences of this value in the grid, and possibly other attribute values.

Surfaces are alternately represented by TINs (see Chapter 2 for a definition of TINs). Each triangle is represented by an identifier, the list of node *id*s (triangle vertices), and the list of neighbor triangle *id*s. See Figure 8.3, in which the absence of a neighboring triangle is represented by a hyphen (-).

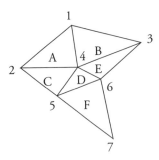

Triangle	Node list	Neighbors
A	1, 2, 4	-, B, C
B	1, 3, 4	-, A, E
C	2, 4, 5	-, A, D
D	4, 5, 6	C, E, F
E	3, 4, 6	-, B, D
F	5, 6, 7	-, -, D

Figure 8.3 An example of a TIN with ArcInfo.

VECTOR DATA REPRESENTATION IN ARCINFO

To create a geographic object, one starts from a spatial object, called a *feature* in ArcInfo. Upon creation, this feature receives a geometric identifier. The descriptive attributes associated with this feature are stored in separate files, the link between the feature and its descriptive attribute values being the geometric identifier. For instance, to create a stream, one first defines a feature of type arc and links it to a tuple in a separate file, with as attributes the arc identifier, the stream name, the width, and so on.

Data handled by *Arc* is in vector mode and limited to the 2D space. As previously mentioned, for manipulating 3D terrain data or raster data, *Arc* can be replaced by module *ArcScan* (Figure 8.1). ArcInfo uses the following three primitives: *point*, *arc*, and *polygon*.

◆ A *point* is represented by its coordinates; that is, a pair (x, y).
◆ An *arc* is a sequence of line segments. It is represented by a sequence of pairs of coordinates (one per arc vertex). It corresponds to the polyline, as defined in Section 2.1.1.
◆ A *polygon* is represented by a sequence of arcs.

A file is associated with each primitive.

◆ *File LAB contains the point description.* Each record corresponds to a point and has three fields: the point identifier and the point's x and y coordinates.

point#	x	y
22	25.1	53.2

◆ *File ARC contains the description of the arcs.* An arc is stored as a variable-length record in this file and has three fields: the internal arc identifier (arc#), the number of points in the arc, and the list of point coordinates.

arc#	number of points	x1	y1	x2	y2	⋯	x9	y9
212	9	20.3	12.3	21.4	13.5	⋯	22.5	14

◆ *File PAL contains the polygon description.* Each record has three fields; namely, the polygon identifier (polygon#), the number of arcs, and the list of arc identifiers. In order to specify that the arc must be scanned in inverse order with respect to the storage order, the arc identifier is prefixed by a minus sign.

polygon#	number of arcs	list of arcs
32	25	98, 54, −32, 83, ..., −65

THE TOPOLOGICAL MODEL OF ARCINFO

The *coverage* is the ArcInfo primary method for grouping and organizing spatial data in vector mode. Coverages are handled by the *ArcStorm* module. Typically, a database contains several coverages; one per theme, each representing a single set of geographic objects, such as roads, wells, and land use. More precisely, a coverage is (in an exclusive way) one of the following:

◆ A set of points.
◆ A *nonplanar graph;* that is, a set of (possibly intersecting) arcs.
◆ A *planar graph;* that is, a set of arcs and nodes with the following constraints: (1) the nodes must either start or end an arc, and (2) two arcs can only intersect each other at their ending nodes.
◆ A set of arcs, nodes, and polygons. As before, it is a planar graph in which the graph faces are also of interest. A polygon is a face of the graph. An arc has a left face and a right face.

Figure 8.4 shows examples of data types that can be found in a coverage. The cross inside a polygon represents the label point of the polygon, which will be defined further.

These strong constraints on primitives of a given coverage have as a consequence several limitations on the objects that can be represented in a given coverage. For example, one cannot represent in the same coverage a road network and a set of census zones. Then it might be necessary to store the objects in several coverages, each of them satisfying one of the four types previously listed. We will see in the following that some of the previously listed restrictions can be relaxed.

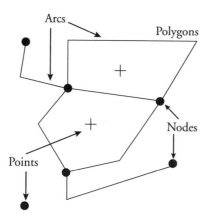

Figure 8.4   Various types of data in an ArcInfo coverage.

The first type of coverage is a set of points. The three other types of coverage correspond to one of the topological models studied in Chapter 2. These are called network or topological models, because topological relations such as an arc endpoint or common boundary between two polygons are explicitly represented. The representation of the topology in these coverages also resembles that of the TIGER format (Chapter 2).

The topology attributes are given in three tables handled by *Arc*; namely, AAT, NAT, and PAT (described in the following). Once a coverage has been created, descriptive attributes can be added to these three tables or through a module called *Tables* in *Info*. This is not mandatory, and therefore a coverage can exist without geographic objects (without descriptive attributes).

In each table, a tuple has two identifiers. The *geometric identifier* is a record identifier (point, arc, or polygon) in the corresponding geometric file LAB, ARC, or PAL. The *geographic identifier* identifies the geographic object managed by the *Info* module. For example, a road section has for a geometric identifier an arc identifier (in file ARC) and a road section identifier. The geographic identifier is an integer sometimes referred to as *User ID*. It has for a suffix -ID, whereas the geometric identifier is suffixed by #.

TABLE AAT

This table describes geographic objects whose geometry is of type "sequence of arcs." Each tuple in this table corresponds to an arc and has at least seven fields, as follows:

- The identifier of the initial node of the arc, called FNODE#.
- The identifier of the end node of the arc, called TNODE#.
- The left face identifier, called LPOLY#.
- The right face identifier, called RPOLY#.
- The length of the arc, called LENGTH.
- The geometric identifier of the arc. The attribute name is prefixed by the coverage name. For instance, if the coverage has for a name *Adm* (administrative boundaries), this field has for a name *Adm#*.
- The geographic identifier. With coverage *Adm*, this field has for a name *Adm-ID*.

The fields LPOLY# and RPOLY# are not mandatory if the coverage is of type network.

```
Table AAT
   FNODE#      : integer,
   TNODE#      : integer,
   LPOLY#      : integer,
   RPOLY#      : integer,
   LENGTH      : real,
   Adm#        : integer,
   Adm-ID      : integer
```

TABLE NAT

This table stores nodes. Nodes are objects whose geometry is of type point. Each record has at least three fields, as follows:

- An arc identifier ARC# having this point as a starting or ending node. This identifier is the smallest identifier of arcs starting or ending at this node.
- The geometric identifier of the node.
- The geographic identifier.

```
Table NAT
   ARC#        : integer,
   Adm#        : integer,
   Adm-ID      : integer,
```

ArcInfo distinguishes three types of nodes: normal nodes, pseudo-nodes, and dangling nodes. A normal node indicates the endpoints and intersections of arcs. In addition, normal nodes can represent geo-

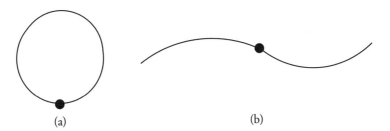

(a)   (b)

Figure 8.5   Examples of acceptable pseudo-nodes: an island (a) and a pseudo-node marking a stream type change (b).

graphic objects of type point, which connect geographic objects of type arc. For instance, it can be a valve connecting pipe segments. *Pseudonodes* are linked to two arcs, and two arcs only. Pseudo-nodes may indicate an error (e.g., a node inadvertently inserted, or a connection to another arc was missed) or not (e.g., point where an attribute value changes, such as a stream type changing from water supply canal to drainage ditch). Figure 8.5 shows two examples of acceptable pseudo-nodes.

A dangling node refers to the unconnected node of a dangling arc. Dangling nodes also either correspond to an error (e.g., a polygon that does not close properly) or are acceptable (e.g., a cul-de-sac, as in Figure 8.6).

TABLE PAT
The PAT table describes *label points*. A label point is one of the following:

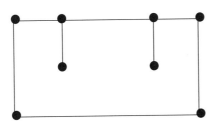

Figure 8.6   An acceptable dangling node.

♦ An isolated point disconnected from the graph.
♦ The centroid of a polygon.[37] The correspondence between the centroid and the polygon is done through the centroid (CNT) file.

point#	polygon#
22	12

Point# is the label point geometric identifier, whereas *polygon#* is the polygon geometric identifier. Each tuple in table PAT has at least four attributes, as follows:

♦ The polygon area AREA (set to zero if it is a label point)
♦ The polygon perimeter PERIMETER (set to zero if it is a label point)
♦ The geometric label point identifier
♦ The geographic object identifier

```
Table PAT
    AREA        : real,
    PERIMETER   : real,
    Adm#        : integer,
    Adm-ID      : integer,
```

Figure 8.7 indicates the dependencies between geometric files and topological files. Files AAT and NAT only exist if file ARC exists. A

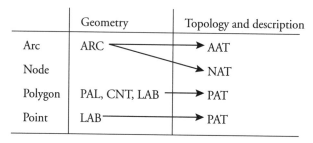

	Geometry	Topology and description
Arc	ARC	AAT
Node		NAT
Polygon	PAL, CNT, LAB	PAT
Point	LAB	PAT

Figure 8.7   Relevant files in ArcInfo coverages.

---

37. The centroid is a point located inside the polygon.

point coverage is described by a file LAB and a table PAT. Similarly, a coverage of polygons is described by a table PAT and files CNT, PAL, and LAB.

COMPLEX ENTITIES

The rather strong constraints imposed by the definition of a coverage lead to the use of several coverages for the same area. For instance, consider a transportation application. If we want to represent bus routes, we need two coverages: one for the street network and one for the bus routes. To avoid this artificial multiplication of coverages, some features have been added that allow us to define more complex entities constructed with the elementary primitives arc and polygon. This has as a consequence that we can not only create several sets sharing the same coverage but relax the constraint of the planar graph behind the coverage. The following are some of the major complex entities that can be created:

◆ *Routes* define paths along an existing set of arcs. They can be disconnected. Figure 8.8 depicts two examples of routes. In the first example (Figure 8.8a), the route starts and ends at an arc end node. However, routes may start/end at a point along an arc (Figure 8.8b). Routes are sequences of sections.

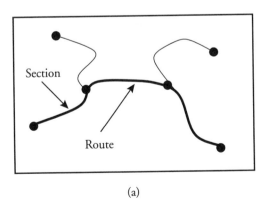
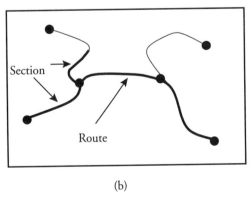

(a)   (b)

Figure 8.8   Examples of routes: route ending at arc end node (a) and route ending at a point along an arc (b).

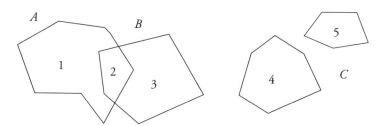

Figure 8.9   Examples of regions.

◆ A *section* is an arc or portion of an arc. A section cannot overlap two arcs. It is described by the arc identifier, the distance along the route the section represents, and what percentage of the arc is used.

◆ A *region* is a set of polygons that are not necessarily connected. Several regions may share the same faces (polygons). Then two regions of the same coverage may overlap. Figure 8.9 depicts five polygons and three regions. Region *A* is a composite of polygons 1 and 2. Region *C* consists of polygons 4 and 5. Regions can be used in a single coverage for representing geographic objects from different themes or composite objects (e.g., a state consisting of counties or a census tract consisting of census blocks).

8.2.3   Representation of Sample Schemas

For the purpose of illustrating the querying capabilities of ArcInfo, it was run on a French sample database whose schema is close to that described in Chapter 3. We show how to represent each of the four themes of this database with ArcInfo, and then how to answer a sample of queries similar to that of Chapter 3, using the primitives provided by ArcInfo.

ADDING DESCRIPTIVE DATA TO ARC
In principle, the descriptive attributes to represent the geographic object are represented in a separate relational table handled either by *Info* or by an external relational DBMS. The link is then made via a geographic object identifier in an *-ID* attribute in the *Arc* tables (AAT, NAT, and PAT). The problem is that in order to access a geographic

object, a join has to be performed between one or several relational tables and one or several files managed by *Arc*.

In order to avoid performing such a time-consuming join, both the spatial and descriptive attributes can be stored in *Arc* (tables AAT, NAT, and PAT), along with topological information. The consequences of this are the following:

♦ A faster data access, as a join with a relational table is avoided.

♦ Redundancy. If a road is described by several arcs, the same descriptive attributes are repeated (stored) in each arc.

♦ No "spatial sharing," as an arc represents a single geographic object (it has a single list of descriptive attributes). For instance, an arc in the same coverage cannot represent both a road and a river.

Figure 8.10 shows an example of road representation that uses descriptive information in the topological tables. *Highway 1* is described by four records, one per arc. Each arc is described by an arc identifier, two node identifiers, and a descriptive attribute (road name). Arc and node identifiers are geometric identifiers in the files storing the geometry (file ARC for the arcs, and file LAB for the nodes). For clarity, we have not represented in this example all attributes of table AAT.

It is noteworthy that a geographic object is split into several components and that these components are visible to the user, who hence needs to be aware of such implementation details when querying the GIS.

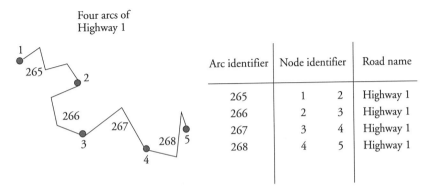

Figure 8.10   Representing a geographic object in ArcInfo.

FRENCH ADMINISTRATIVE UNITS

Adm is a set of three partitionings of the French territory of different granularities. *Communes* are gathered in *départements*, which in turn are gathered in *régions*.[38]

We assume that *régions* and *départements* have no spatial attributes. The geometry of a *région* (*département*) is computed from that of its *départements* (*communes*), as was done in Chapter 3 with State and Country. Then these entities are represented as in a regular relational DBMS, as shown in the following:

```
Région
    région-name        : string,
    capital            : string

Département
    num-département    : integer,
    département-name   : string,
    région-name        : string
```

Foreign key *région-name* (respectively, *num-département*) in entity *département* (*commune*) refers to the *région* key (*département* key).

Communes are described in table PAT. Communes have a spatial attribute that corresponds to the elementary polygonal parcels of the ArcInfo coverage. The descriptive attributes follow attribute *Adm-ID*, which is no longer useful, as there is no descriptive information in the relational modules.

```
PAT
    AREA               : real,
    PERIMETER          : real,
    Adm#               : integer,
    Adm-ID             : integer,
    commune-num        : integer,
    commune-name       : string,
    population         : integer,
    num-département    : integer
```

---

38. The American equivalent of a commune is a *county*. *Départements* and *régions* have no equivalent in the United States. The *région* entity in the schema must not be mistaken with the ArcInfo region concept, which was not used to build *départements* and *régions*.

Adm# is a pointer to a record of PAL describing the geometry of a polygon. The topology of the commune is not visible in PAT but is stored in table AAT, in which fields LPOLY# and RPOLY# are filled.

Had we decided to store the geometry of both *départements* and *communes*, then either ArcInfo regions would have been used for storing composite objects or three coverages would have been necessary, as well as three PAT tables for describing the three polygon partitionings of the French territory. This not only implies redundancy but introduces complexity in querying.

HIGHWAY NETWORK

Regarding the schema of Chapter 3, a *highway* has a number and a name. It consists of *sections* (not to be confused with ArcInfo sections, which were not used to represent highway sections). Each section has a number (*num-section*) and a number of lanes (*nb-lanes*). As in the case of *Adm*, the geometry of the road is not stored but computed on the fly from the geometry of its sections.

```
Highway
  road-number : string
  road-name   : string
```

The coverage of sections is a planar graph of arcs, one per section. Sections are described in table AAT, which follows.

```
AAT
  FNODE#      : integer,
  TNODE#      : integer,
  LPOLY#      : integer,
  RPOLY#      : integer,
  LENGTH      : real,
  Highway#    : integer,
  Highway-ID  : integer,
  num-section : integer,
  nb-lanes    : integer,
  road-number : integer
```

FNODE# and TNODE# are the initial and end nodes of a section. LPOLY# and RPOLY# are set to *nil*. LENGTH stores the section length, *Highway#* is the geometric identifier of the section, and

Highway-ID is its geographic identifier (referring to void). Attribute *road-number* is the link (foreign key) to table *Highway*.

GROUND OCCUPANCY

Coverage GO implements a planar graph of nodes, arcs, and faces. Each face corresponds to a ground occupancy ("go") parcel. As previously, parcels are stored in PAT. As for communes, the topology is not visible in this table but stored in file AAT.

```
PAT
  AREA      : real,
  PERIMETER : real,
  GO#       : integer,
  GO-ID     : integer,
  type      : string
```

The coverages queried in the following and that satisfy the schema previously presented have been extracted from the cartographic database *BDCarto* of the French National Geographic Institute IGN (*Institut Géographique National*), restricted to the *Haut-Rhin* département. They are displayed in Figures 8.11, 8.12, and 8.13.

8.2.4 Querying with ArcInfo

We illustrate the querying capabilities of ArcInfo on the previous coverages with most of the queries discussed in Chapter 3. For each query, we give the sequence of ArcInfo primitives (or the algorithm). For some of them, the result is displayed. Recall that once a query has been prepared it can be encapsulated in a friendly interface.

ALPHANUMERIC CRITERIA

The following are queries with alphanumeric criteria.

ALPHA-ADM1. Number of inhabitants in the Commune of Mulhouse.

This query can be answered either with module *Arcedit* or with a module called *Tables*, which allows us to create, query, display, and perform simplified analysis. We chose to present the answer to the query

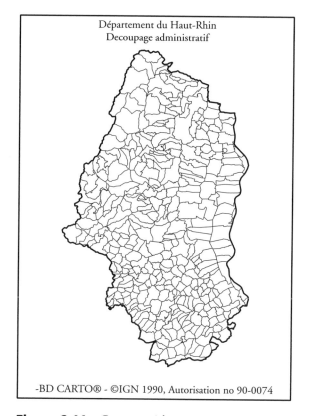

Département du Haut-Rhin
Decoupage administratif

-BD CARTO® - ©IGN 1990, Autorisation no 90-0074

Figure 8.11   Coverage *Adm.*

with *Arcedit*, as it is used extensively in the following queries. It allows us to edit geographic data and interact with the user.

Several steps are necessary to answer the query. An initialization step includes the choice of the coverage to be edited (command *editcoverage*) and the choice of the object type (polygon, arc, or node) to edit (command *editfeature*). Then the selection query is performed. Finally, the attributes to be displayed are chosen with the command *list*, as follows:

```
arcedit
editcoverage Adm
editfeature polygon
Arcedit: select nom = 'Mulhouse'
Arcedit: list population
```

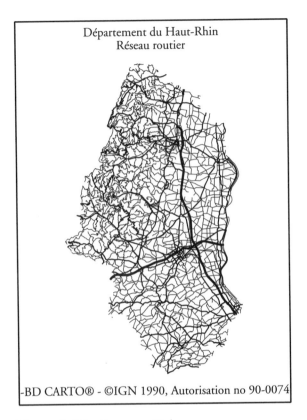

Département du Haut-Rhin
Réseau routier

-BD CARTO® - ©IGN 1990, Autorisation no 90-0074

Figure 8.12 Coverage *Highways*.

The result of this query is 112,157 inhabitants (according to the French 1982 census).

ALPHA-ADM2. List of the communes of the "Haut-Rhin" *département*.

Tables *Communes* and *Département* have to be joined (command *Joinitem* in *Arc*). The first two parameters are the entry tables. The third parameter is the result table. The join attribute is specified in the fourth argument. This attribute must have the same name in both entry tables. Finally, the fifth parameter specifies from which attribute in the result table the attributes resulting from the join must be added.

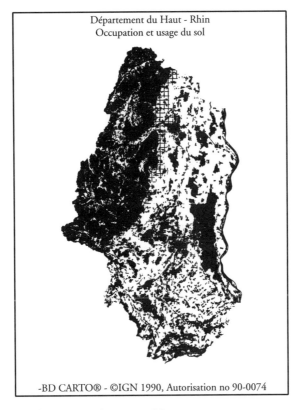

Département du Haut - Rhin
Occupation et usage du sol

-BD CARTO® - ©IGN 1990, Autorisation no 90-0074

Figure 8.13   Coverage *GO*.

The command in the following (step 1) adds in *Adm.PAT*, for each commune, the attributes of its département (*département* name and *région* name). It is run once. It will be useful not only for this query but for the following. Once the join has been performed, we can select the communes of the Haut-Rhin *département* and list their names (step 2).

◆ *Step 1:* Join

```
Joinitem Adm.PAT Département Adm.PAT num-département
num-département
```

◆ *Step 2:* Selection and projection

```
arcedit
Arcedit:editcoverage Adm
Arcedit:editfeature polygon
```

```
Arcedit:select département-name = 'Haut-Rhin'
Arcedit:list commune-name
```

The *département* of Haut-Rhin has 386 communes. If the entire carto-graphic database of the French territory had been stored, the join would have been performed over all French communes (about 50,000). Only after the join had been performed could one have selected the relevant communes (from the *département* of "Haut-Rhin"). This is prohibitive as too costly. The alternative is first to select the communes of Haut-Rhin (whose *département* number is 68) and then perform the join. This illustrates that in contrast to relational DBMSs that automatically choose the best strategy, users must have a deep knowledge of ArcInfo and the database they are manipulating, and optimize query processing by themselves.

ALPHA-ADM3. Number of inhabitants in the *département* of Haut-Rhin.

The *département*'s population is not stored in table *Département*. It has to be aggregated from its commune population. Recall that *Adm.PAT* now contains the join between *Communes* and *Département*. Once the *département* of Haut-Rhin has been selected (command *select*), command *statistics* aggregates the population of communes. *Statistics* computes simple aggregate functions such as sum, maximum, and average.

```
arcedit
Arcedit:editcoverage Adm
Arcedit:editfeature polygon
Arcedit:select département-name = 'Haut-Rhin'
Arcedit:statistics
Statistics:sum population
```

The result is 695,193 inhabitants (1982 French census).

ALPHA-R1. Number of lanes in the first section of Nationale 66 (or N66).

Tables AAT (highway sections) and Highway have first to be joined on *road-number*, as in query **ALPHA-ADM2** (command *Joinitem* of *Arc*). Then with *Arcedit*, the first section of Nationale 66 is selected.

ALPHA-R3. Draw Nationale 66.

Once the join has been performed (see previous query), highway Nationale 66 has to be selected. In order to display the highway, during the initialization step, two commands have to be run. Command *mapextent* specifies the rectangular area to be displayed (here, the default rectangle is chosen). Command *drawenvironment* chooses which types of objects in the coverage have to be drawn (arcs, nodes, faces). After selection, the display is performed with command *drawselect*.

```
arcedit
Arcedit:editcoverage Highway
Arcedit:mapextent default
Arcedit:drawenvironment arc
Arcedit:editfeature arc
Arcedit:select road-number='N66'
Arcedit:drawselect
```

SPATIAL CRITERIA

The following are descriptions of queries associated with spatial criteria.

SPAT-ADM4. Communes adjacent to the communes of Mulhouse in the same *département*.

This query requires one to program, using the programming language AML, a function testing the adjacency between polygons. Indeed, in table AAT, only the adjacency relation between an arc and a face is known with attributes RPOLY# and LPOLY#.

SPAT-ADM5. Display of the "Haut-Rhin" *département*.

Because the geometry of *département* is not stored, it has to be computed as an aggregation (a union) of the geometry of its communes. Using *Adm.PAT* as computed in **ALPHA-ADM2**, one selects all communes of "Haut-Rhin" and creates a new coverage (called *HR-Communes*) using command *reselect*. Then command *dissolve* performs the union of the geometries and deletes inner borders. This command creates a new coverage, called *Haut-Rhin*.

```
reselect Adm HR-Communes POLY
>: reselect département-name = 'Haut-Rhin'
dissolve HR-Communes Haut-Rhin département-name
```

The third parameter of *reselect* specifies that the type of objects in the coverage to be selected for the new coverage is *polygon*. Prompt > shows that the system is waiting for a selection criterion. Command *dissolve* allows for eliminating inner borders of adjacent communes having the same value for the attribute specified in the third parameter (here, same *département* name). Coverage *Haut-Rhin* is then displayed as in query **ALPHA-R3**.

SPAT-ADM6. Largest commune in the Haut-Rhin *département*.

Because the area is automatically computed and stored in attribute *AREA* of table PAT, the commune with maximum area is selected with command *Statistics*.

```
arcedit
Arcedit:editcoverage Adm
Arcedit:editfeature polygon
Arcedit:select département-name = 'Haut-Rhin'
Arcedit:Statistics
Statistics: maximum AREA
```

The result is *Colmar*, whose area is 66,567,968 m^2.

SPAT-R3. Length of Highway A35.

This query requires one to sum the length of the various sections of Highway A35 (the length of each section is stored in attribute *LENGTH* of table AAT). Recall from query **ALPHA-R1** that *Highway.AAT* includes the join between sections and highways for all highways of the *département*. One then has to select Highway A35 and compute its length with command *Statistics*.

```
arcedit
Arcedit:editcoverage Highway
Arcedit:editfeature arc
Arcedit:select road-number = 'A35'
Arcedit:Statistics
Statistics: sum LENGTH
```

In 1990, the length of Highway A35 was 67,932 *km*.

SPAT-ADMR1. All highways going through the *département* of Haut-Rhin.

One starts with tables *Adm.PAT* (join of communes and départements) and *Highway.AAT* (join of sections and highways). The geometry of Haut-Rhin is computed (i.e., a new coverage *Haut-Rhin* is computed, as in query **SPAT-ADM5**). Coverages *Highway.AAT* and *Haut-Rhin* are overlaid with command *Intersect* as follows.

```
Intersect Highway Haut-Rhin highways-Haut-Rhin # nojoin
```

The first two parameters are the coverages on which the overlay is performed. The coverage obtained after having performed an overlay is specified in the third parameter. The fourth parameter specifies the level of tolerance for the geometric intersection computation. # is the default tolerance. The last parameter (*nojoin*) specifies whether or not a join is performed when overlaying. In the case of a join, all attributes of both coverages are kept in the result.

SPAT-ADM-LU1. Display of all residential areas in the Commune of Mulhouse.

The commune of Mulhouse is first selected (creation of a coverage from coverage *Adm* with name Mulhouse). Living areas are then selected (attribute type = '01', creation of coverage *Living-areas* from coverage *GO*). Then the two coverages are overlaid (command *Intersect*). The result is displayed as in query **SPAT-DR1**:

```
Reselect Adm Mulhouse POLY
>: reselect commune-name = 'Mulhouse'

Reselect GO Living-areas POLY
>: reselect type = '01'

Intersect Living-areas Mulhouse Living-areas-Mulhouse POLY

arcedit
Arcedit:editcoverage Living-areas-Mulhouse
Arcedit:mapextent default
Arcedit:drawenvironment polygon on arc on
Arcedit:draw
```

INTERACTIVE QUERIES

The following are descriptions of queries associated with interactive criteria.

INTER-ADM7. Description of the commune pointed to on the screen (Figure 8.14).

After the usual initialization (see, for instance, queries **ALPHA-R3** and **SPAT-ADM6**), function *select ** selects the closest centroid to the point on the screen. These steps are outlined in the following. Command *list* displays all descriptive attributes of the commune.

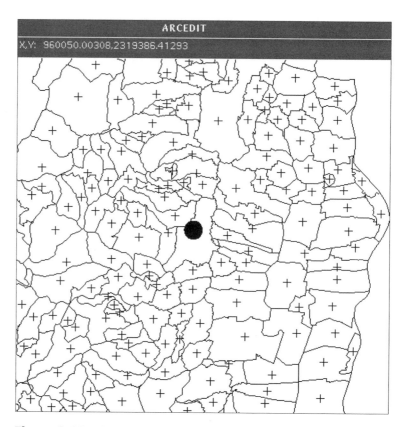

Figure 8.14   Commune display.

◆ *Step 1:* Initialization.

```
arcedit
Arcedit:editcoverage Adm
Arcedit:mapextent default
Arcedit:drawenvironment polygon on arc on
Arcedit:draw
```

◆ *Step 2:* Selection.

```
Arcedit:select *
Arcedit:list
```

The commune of Rouffach was selected. The following description of the commune is given.

```
AREA                =  29403012.000
PERIMETER           =     33162.137
ADM#                =  96
ADM-ID              =  95
COMMUNE-NUM         =     680000281
COMMUNE-NAME        =  ROUFFACH
POPULATION          =      4615
NUM-DEPARTEMENT     =  68
DEPARTEMENT-NAME    =  HAUT-RHIN
REGION-NAME         =  ALSACE
```

8.3   ARCVIEW GIS

ArcView GIS, also from ESRI, belongs to the category of *desktop GIS*. In that sense, it is easy to install and to use, and offers a set of predefined functionalities, although it does not provide the richness of ArcInfo. It is available on a large number of platforms, running under Apple Macintosh, Microsoft Windows, or UNIX-like operating systems.

ArcView provides a large set of tools for querying, displaying, and editing maps, as well as for data access and spatial analysis (*ArcView Spatial Analyst* and *ArcView Network Analyst* modules). Easy integration with applications, text editors, and databases is a key feature of ArcView. Map data and image data satisfying a large number of formats can be read directly (among them, ArcView shapefiles or ArcInfo coverages for spatial data, or TIFF, ERDAS, or Sun raster files for raster data). ArcView is connected to ESRI's *Spatial Database Engine* (SDE) and to a large number of relational DBMSs (such as Oracle, Postgres, Sybase, or Informix).

In terms of spatial analysis, it provides a powerful set of spatial operations, as well as statistical tools. However, as a desktop GIS, it is more oriented toward data integration and visualization than map production and querying. Its use is customized through scripts written in the programming language *Avenue*. To implement an end-user analysis function, a script calls spatial operations provided by the core. The most useful operations or simple queries are available through the interactive interface. However, as in ArcInfo, there is no high-level query language to interact with the system. When a complex query needs to be expressed, one of the following must occur:

- ◆ A script first has to be developed (which requires an expert knowledge of the system, with any change in the query implying a script update).
- ◆ The user has to carry out a sequence of interactive actions, which might be excessively large, even for some simple queries (as illustrated in the following). The use of the interactive interface also requires a good knowledge of the underlying system.

The following provides an overview of ArcView's spatial model. We then illustrate the querying capabilites of ArcView on a few examples taken from our sample queries in Chapter 3.

8.3.1   ArcView Spatial Model

A *theme* is, as defined in Chapter 1, a collection of geographic objects of the same type. A *view* is a map that gathers the spatial objects from one or several themes sharing the same geographic territory. It provides the means for displaying and querying themes. It is a type of document (document is a class of objects in ArcView) contained in a window that one can open, close, move, or resize.

A view is defined by a name, the sets of themes, a scale, and a coordinate system. A *project* gathers all objects, views, themes, tables, and scripts referred to within an ArcView session. Two projects cannot use the same view, but a project can have many views.

Spatial objects belong to one of the following four spatial types: *point, multipoint, line,* and *polygon*. An instance of *multipoint* is a set of points. An instance of type *line* is a set of *arcs* that are not necessarily connected and that possibly intersect. An arc is, as defined in Chapter 2 and according to ArcInfo, a sequence of connected segments. An instance of type *polygon* is a set of nonintersecting polygons. Polygons can share a vertex, but they are not allowed to share a segment. For all objects, except objects of type *point*, the minimal bounding rectangle (*mbr*) is also stored.

A theme is represented by two files. The first (Relation, shown in Figure 8.15) is a sequence of fixed-length records, one per geographic object, in which the descriptive attributes are stored. The second file (Geometry) stores in the same order the geometries of objects (record Rec_i of file Relation corresponds to record $Geom_i$ of file Geometry)

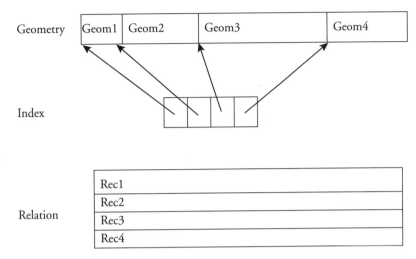

Figure 8.15   Theme implementation in ArcView.

represented by variable-length records, without any topological relation. It uses a spaghetti model. In order to link a tuple to its corresponding geometry, and vice versa, a third file (called *index*, Figure 8.15) is
required, which is a sequence of pointers to the geometries (offsets from
the beginning of the file storing the geometry). The index records are
in the same order as the records in the two other files.

A *VTab* stands for virtual table. It is a view built from one or more
physical tabular sources on disk (relations). Through the *VTab*, one
can, for instance, edit the values in a table (relation), extend the table
by joining other tables to it, and query the values in the table.

8.3.2   Querying with ArcView

There is no high-level query language offered in the environment. Instead, the user does one of the following:

◆ Uses the interactive query facility that allows him to carry out a sequence of steps, each of them corresponding to an Avenue script,
  which is interpreted.
◆ Develops her own script using Avenue.

Figure 8.16 shows an elementary ArcView screen with a view on the
right-hand side and the legend on the left-hand side.

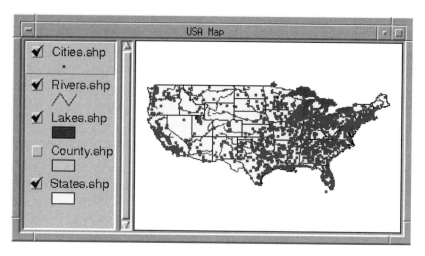

Figure 8.16   Example of a map displayed in ArcView.

Most of the queries of Chapter 3 can be answered using the ArcView environment. We show in the following the sequence of steps and the generated Avenue scripts for three typical queries. The theme used in the queries is *County,* and the view is *United States.*

QUERY I: COUNTIES THAT INTERSECT A GIVEN RECTANGLE (INTER-ADM8)

Assuming that the view containing the theme *County* is open, and that the relevant theme has been loaded, the steps are the following: choose the pattern "rectangle," draw a rectangle, and click on the selection button. The selected counties are displayed in some other color, and the table associated with counties is displayed. For this simple windowing query (see Chapter 1), the following Avenue statement is executed:

County.SelectByRect(MyRectangle,#VTAB_SELTYPE_NEW)

The spatial operation *SelectByRect* is applied to theme *County* with *MyRectangle* as a first argument. The second argument *#VTAB_SELTYPE_NEW* indicates that *VTab* contains the *County* table. The description of *all* counties is displayed, each selected row (counties overlapping the rectangle) being highlighted.

QUERY 2: DRAW THE STATE OF CALIFORNIA (SPAT-ADM5)

Assume that in the view *United States* there is no theme for the states and that the only theme in this view is *County*. One then proceeds as follows, using the query interface (the detailed actions in each step are not shown):

◆ *Step 1:* Open the view and load theme *County*.
◆ *Step 2:* Using the query builder, select the counties in theme *County* whose state name is California. *ThemeCalifornia* is created.
◆ *Step 3:* Apply spatial function *Union.Selected*. The result is an update of the theme, *ThemeCalifornia*, which contains a single row corresponding to the map of California (with no descriptive attributes).

The (simplified) Avenue script generated by this sequence of steps is the following:

UnitedStatesView av.FindDoc('United-States')
expr = ([name] = "California");
ThemeCalifornia = UnitedStatesView.FindTheme('County');
ThemeCalifornia.GetVtab.SetDefinition (expr);
ThemeCalifornia.GetVtab.UpdateDefbitmap;
ThemeCalifornia.Union.Selected

The first statement opens the view. *UnitedStatesView* is loaded with the view *United-States*, given as an argument of *av.FindDoc*. The second statement defines a selection criterion. *ThemeCalifornia* is created as a copy of theme *County* in statement 3. The two following statements (4 and 5) apply the selection. The result is the set of counties of California. Statement 6 computes the geometric union of counties (and automatically erases inner boundaries between counties).

Creating a theme *States* from theme *County*, with the name of the state as a descriptive attribute and the union of the geometries of its counties as a spatial attribute, is not possible with the current interactive query facilities. However, it should be possible using the Avenue language. Note that, in general, the query interface does not provide facilities for map production; that is, for queries whose result is a theme with new objects to be stored in the database. In this query, the result is no more than a display of the boundary of California, and no object is created.

QUERY 3: COUNTIES ADJACENT TO THE COUNTY OF SAN FRANCISCO
(SPAT-ADM4)

Finding counties adjacent to San Francisco County is obtained as follows:

◆ *Step 1:* Open the view, and load theme *County*.
◆ *Step 2:* Using the query builder, select the counties in theme *County* whose name is San Francisco.
◆ *Step 3:* Prepare the query: choose option "selection by theme" in the menu and set to zero the menu entry "within distance of."
◆ *Step 4:* Send the query to the system.

ArcView interprets adjacency as "spatial objects at a null distance." The result of this query includes San Francisco. To get rid of San Francisco County when selecting the counties (step 2), the criteria *name* ≠ "San Francisco" should be added. The previous steps generate the following Avenue script:

> *USAView = av.FindDoc*('United-States')
> *expr = ([name]* = "San Francisco")
> *ThemeSanFrancisco = USAView.FindTheme*('County')
> *ThemeSanFrancisco. GetVtab.SetDefinition(expr)*
> *ThemeSanFrancisco. GetVtab. UpdateDefbitmap*
> *ThemeCounties = USAView.FindTheme*('County')
> *ThemeSanFrancisco.SelectbyTheme(ThemeCounties,*
> > *#FTAB_RELTYPE_ISWITHINDISTANCEOF, 0,*
> > *#VTAB_SELTYPE_NEW)*

The first five statements select the county San Francisco. They are similar to the first five steps of Query 2. Statement 6 copies theme *County* into *ThemeCounties*. Statement 7 selects all counties whose geometry is within distance *0* of the geometry of San Francisco County. This spatial join between Theme *ThemeSanFrancisco* and *ThemeCounties* is done by applying function *SelectbyTheme* to *ThemeSanFrancisco*.

The first argument of *SelectbyTheme* is the second theme to be joined. The second and the third arguments indicate the spatial predicate to be checked against each pair of objects of each theme. Here, a theme has a single object, San Francisco, whose geometry is checked against the geometry of each object of the other theme. *#VTAB_SELTYPE_NEW* indicates that *VTab* contains the *County* table displayed with *all* counties, each adjacent county being highlighted. *Vtab* contains the result of the last *FindTheme* function (expressed in statement 6).

8.4 SMALLWORLD

Initially addressing the CAD market, then specializing in the market of geographic networks and utilities, Smallworld[39] has become a complete and powerful GIS with a rich versioning mechanism and a powerful object-oriented development language, called *Magik*. Smallworld manages both vector and raster data (grids and TINs). It also provides most of the facilities currently required from a GIS in terms of data analysis, conversion between raster and vector modes, data import/export tools, customization of interfaces, and so on.

8.4.1 *Smallworld Spatial Data Model*

Smallworld's vector spatial model enables the representation of topological relations between objects, as defined in the *topological* model of Chapter 2. The geometric primitives are called *points, chains*, and *areas*. They respectively correspond to the *point, arc, and polygon* primitives defined in Chapter 2. The corresponding topological primitives in Smallworld are called *nodes, links,* and *polygons*. Individual spatial topologically related objects are grouped in *manifolds*. A manifold comes with a set of topological rules to be enforced upon object insertion into the manifold. For example, the "connect-split-link" rule implies that when a point is placed on a chain the associated link will be split into two, having as an end node the node associated with the point.

Descriptive attributes are called in the Smallworld model *text* attributes. They are either atomic, as in the relational model, or *join fields*; that is, references to other objects, as in the object-oriented ODMG data model. A theme is called an *object type*.

Themes are displayed by selecting a *view* in the *graphic window*. Point and window spatial selections can be performed on such views. By probing one piece of an object geometry, one gets the descrip-

---

39. Smallworld is a registered trademark of Smallworld Systems Ltd., Cambridge, England.

tive attributes of the objects. Objects are also manipulated through an *object editor*, and queried through an *object browser*, described in the following.

8.4.2 *Querying with Smallworld Object Browser*

Object editors allow one to locate, display, and edit details of individual objects. For instance, to display many objects, a selective set of objects, or only part of the attributes of objects, one uses an object browser. The object browser facility is available through a window split into two subwindows. In the top subwindow, either a query is typed or each of its fields is filled out with the help of menus. After selection of the attributes to be projected (button "fields"), the query is run (button "apply"). It is interpreted in Magik. The result is displayed in the bottom subwindow. We now focus on the expression of queries. The purpose is not to give an exhaustive presentation of the query language but to illustrate its most salient features by means of examples.

A query is either a *selection* or a *complex query* including a sequence of selections and *assignments*. Let's first look at selections.

SELECTION

A *selection* is a unary operation taking as a source a unique set of objects and giving as a result a subset of these objects. A selection is a Boolean combination of atomic conditions. It has the form

source **where** *condition* **and/or** *condition...,*

where *source* denotes the source set of objects. It might be one of the object types in the view or other temporary sources. *Condition* has the form

[**not**] *attribute predicate value*

Attribute can be either a text attribute or a spatial attribute. An object type can have several spatial attributes. If the attribute is textual, the predicate is one of the usual comparators. If the attribute is spatial, the predicate is chosen among {*on, inside, surrounds, touches, crosses, connected-to, adjacent*}. The semantics of the spatial predicate depends on the type of the arguments (point, chain, area).[40] If the atomic condi-

---

40. For a definition of these predicates, see Section 3.3.3.

tion starts with **not**, then obviously the negation of the condition that follows must be satisfied in order to select the object. *Value* is either an attribute value, in the case of a textual simple attribute, or another condition, in the case of a join attribute on the referenced object. Following are two examples of selections on textual attributes, using the schemas defined in Chapter 1.

♦ Selection example 1 (**ALPHA-ADM1**):

  County **where** *county-name* = "San Francisco"

♦ Selection example 2 (**ALPHA-ADM2**):

  County **where** *State.state-name* = "California"

The first query selects San Francisco County; that is, the counties that statisfy the atomic condition stating that the county name is San Francisco. The second selection looks for all counties that belong to the state of California. It involves object type *County*, and has a single condition on attribute *State.state-name*. This attribute is a *join field;* that is, its value is an attribute of an object of another object type. In this example, it is the attribute *state-name* of a state (an object of object type *State*).

  This is convenient when manipulating one-to-many relationships; that is, when an object of a certain type A (here, *State*) is linked with many objects of type B (here, *County*). Note that the join is implicitly mentioned here.

  In the case of a spatial attribute, *value* is either *selected geometry* or *source.attribute*. This corresponds to a spatial (semi-) join, where we keep the source objects whose spatial component satisfies a predicate with the spatial component of an object drawn from another set. The latter is either the spatial component of a currently selected (set of) object(s) *selected-geometry* or the set specified by *source* (*attribute* in *source.attribute* specifying which spatial attribute has to be taken into account). This is illustrated in the following three queries.

SPATIAL SELECTIONS
  County **where** *geometry* **surrounds** *selected-geometry*
  County **where** *geometry* **crosses** *clipboard.coverage*
  Land-use **where** *type* = *"forest"* **and** *geometry* **inside** *City.geometry*

The first query selects counties surrounding one of the objects of the selected geometry (e.g., containing a selected park). The second selects counties intersecting the area described by a spatial attribute *coverage* of a working window called *clipboard*. The third query selects forests inside cities. The first condition checks for land parcels whose type is "forest," and the second condition checks whether or not the land parcel is inside the city. The result of a selection of any more complex query can be assigned to a temporary *scrapbook* to be used later. For example, the query

@temp<< (County **where** *geometry* **surrounds** *selected-geometry)*

assigns to a clipboard named *temp* the result of the query "Counties surrounding the selected object."

COMPLEX QUERY

A *complex query* can be recursively defined as

- A *selection* is a *(complex) query*.
- If *q* and *q′* are two queries, then *q;q′* is a query. In other words, one can run in sequence several queries separated by the semicolon (;) delimiter. Basically, the result of the first query is assigned to a scrapbook, which acts as the source of the second query *q′*.
- If *q* and *q′* are two queries, then *q* **plus** *q′*, *q* **minus** *q′*, and *q′* **intersect** *q′* are queries. In other words, the usual set operators can be applied to the set of objects obtained from subqueries.

Following is an example of a complex query combining the two complex query constructions:

Road **plus** *Trunk-road; current* **minus** *current* **where** *centreline* **crosses** *Restaurant.location*

In this query, we first perform the union of two sets of roads: the objects of object types *Road* and *Trunk-road*. The result is stored in the temporary object type *current*. The subquery, which starts after the semicolon (;) delimiter, deletes from the set of roads in *current* those roads on which there is a restaurant (*centreline* and *location* are the spatial attributes of, respectively, roads and restaurants).

8.4.3 *Discussion*

In contrast to GISs such as ArcInfo and ArcView, Smallworld provides to the user a high-level query language, thereby hiding implementation details. However, the query language used in Smallworld is still procedural. Except for simple selections involving a single source of objects, users have to express their queries as execution plans consisting of a sequence of operations. We would prefer, of course, a more global means of expressing queries, where the user does not have to decide which are the elementary operations to be performed, in which order the operations are to be performed, and where the intermediate results have to be assigned. Note that this is true even for simple queries involving a join between two sources. A *join* occurs in common situations in which a new object type is created from two existing object types (e.g., "restaurant with Chinese cuisine on a freeway with three lanes"). Currently, it seems that the only way is to decompose such a single operation into a sequence of selections, as follows:

- *Step 1:* Select a subset of one object type (e.g., select a subset of freeways with three lanes and assign it to scrapbook *temp*).
- *Step 2:* Select one subset of another object type (e.g., select the restaurants where the cuisine is Chinese and the location is on objects of *temp*).

It is not clear whether this approach provides the full power of a single join. In particular, one cannot join two object types on textual attributes unless one type appears in a reference attribute (join field) of the other; that is, one cannot create a new object type out of two source types. For example, one would like to overlay roads with places of interest, and keep as new objects the part of roads inside a place of interest, with as new textual attributes the road attributes as well as the place-of-interest attributes. Note also that the set of spatial functions available at the query language level is not complete. For example, clipping of areas with other areas or chains does not seem to be available at the language level (clipping of areas with chains is necessary for the overlay, for example, between places of interest and roads). As another example, *Buffer* queries (e.g., "give me the objects at distance *d* of some selected objects") are not available either.

This ends the examination of commercial GIS. We now turn to the description of spatial extensions to a relational DBMS.

8.5   ORACLE EXTENSION FOR HANDLING SPATIAL DATA

Most of the commercial DBMSs offer an extension for managing and querying multidimensional data. Some also provide a loosely coupled connection with one or several commercial GISs that goes beyond the usual facilities for importing/exporting descriptive data from/to a relational system. A characteristic of the commercial DBMS spatial extensions is to provide high-level query languages, capable of expressing complex queries mixing descriptive and spatial criteria.

Of course, the spatial functionalities of these systems are limited. They are not powerful enough to fulfill the numerous functional requirements expected of a GIS (such as raster/vector conversion, raster facilities, spatial analysis tools, and elaborate graphical user interfaces). They are more useful for simple applications dealing with 2D data. Although the trend is toward a more integrated approach between one-dimensional and two-dimensional data in the kernel of the DBMS, this is far from achieved in the current releases and, as a consequence, the optimization of complex queries is still an open problem. We now detail the extension *Oracle Spatial* of the Oracle DBMS, version Oracle8*i*, for handling spatial data.

8.5.1   *Introduction to Oracle Spatial*

Oracle Spatial completes the implementation of the OpenGIS Consortium RFP1-Simple Features guidelines. It is targeted to applications such as basic land management by government agencies, telephone/utilities infrastructure, energy exploration and distribution, and data warehousing.

Oracle Spatial is sold as an option to Oracle8*i*. It is fully compatible with applications written for spatial data stored using Oracle Spatial Cartridge, its predecessor. Oracle Spatial takes advantage of enhanced Oracle8*i* features and capabilities, such as expanded database size limits, high-performance maintenance utilities for large databases, replication, and faster backup and recovery techniques.

Oracle Spatial provides a spatial data type *SDO_GEOMETRY*. The standard SQL query language of Oracle is extended with functions/ operators on *SDO_GEOMETRY* so as to allow spatial queries, as well as queries mixing regular relational (descriptive) attributes and spatial attributes. To facilitate the evaluation of application-specific operators such as those provided by Oracle Spatial, Oracle8*i* server was extended to specialized index creation and manipulation. It was also extended with the ability to inform the optimizer of the evaluation cost and selectivity of specialized operators such as those incorporated in *SDO_GEOMETRY*. In the following, we successively describe the Oracle spatial data model, the expression of some typical queries using the extended SQL query language, and the spatial indexing capability.

8.5.2 Spatial Data Model

A table has a number of regular relational attributes and one spatial attribute of type *MDSYS.SDO_GEOMETRY*. Such a table represents a *theme;* that is, a collection of geographic objects of the same type, one per row (tuple). The spatial attribute of a tuple is called a *geometry.* The projection of a table onto its spatial column returns a collection of geometries called a *layer.* For example, one can create a table *Highway- Section* as follows:

Create Table *Section*
    (section-code **varchar** *(64)*
    section-name **varchar** *(64)*
    number-lanes **integer**
    city-start **varchar** *(64)*
    city-end **varchar** *(64)*
    geometry MDSYS.SDO_GEOMETRY)

A geometry consists either of a single *element* or of an ordered list of elements. An element is the atomic building block of the geometry. It is either of type *point, line string,* or *polygon.* Geometries consisting of a list of elements model complex geometries. For instance, (1) a set of islands is modeled by an ordered list of polygons, or (2) an island within a lake is represented by a list of two polygons (the exterior ring and the interior ring). The ordered list of elements in a geometry may be heterogeneous; that is, made of elements of different types.

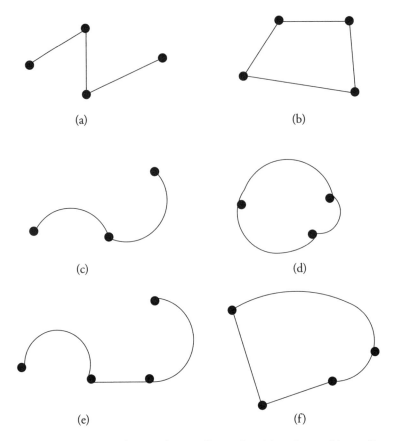

Figure 8.17 Oracle spatial types: line string (a), polygon (b), arc line string (c), arc polygon (d), compound line string (e), and compound polygon (f).

The point, line string, and polygon atomic types are depicted in Figure 8.17. A line string (polygon) is a sequence of *vertices*. Two adjacent vertices can be connected by either a straight line or a circular arc. A line string whose vertices are connected by a straight line was defined in Section 2.1.1 as a polyline (an arc in ArcInfo, as in Section 8.2.2). A *compound* line string (polygon) is one whose vertices are connected by a mix of straight-line and circular arc segments.

The insertion of a row (a highway section) in table *Section* created in the foregoing is done through the following standard SQL **insert** statement, which gives some insight into the internal structure used by Oracle Spatial for storing a geometry:

insert into *Section*
values *('1840233', 's33', 4, 'Huntington', 'Baker',*
      MDSYS.SDO_GEOMETRY (2, **null**, **null**,
      MDSYS.SDO_ELEM_INFO_ARRAY (1, 2, 1),
      MDSYS.SDO_ORDINATE_ARRAY (2, 2, 2, 3, 3, 3, 3, 4)));

The arguments of *MDSYS.SDO_GEOMETRY* represent the geometry to be inserted. The first argument, *2*, is an element type identifier indicating that it is a line string. The second and third values, set to **null**, represent, respectively, a spatial reference identifier and a label point location. The fourth value, *MDSYS.SDO_ELEM_INFO_ARRAY (1, 2, 1)*, is the element descriptor array that specifies that the element vertex ordinates can be found at offset 1 in the *SDO_ORDINATES* array, that the element type is a line string (code 2), and that vertices are connected by straight-line segments (indicated by code 1). The last argument of *MDSYS.SDO_GEOMETRY* is the ordered sequence of coordinate values that in this example specifies the vertices $(2, 2)$, $(2, 3)$, $(3, 3)$, and $(3, 4)$.

8.5.3   Spatial Operations

The spatial operations incorporated in the *MDSYS.SDO_GEOMETRY* data type can be classified into two categories:

◆ *Index-aware operators.* These are Boolean functions known from the optimizer. An SQL query containing one of these operators is evaluated using the associated spatial index. The optimizer is informed about the cost and selectivity of these operators.

◆ *Other spatial operators.* A query containing such an operator is evaluated on a row-by-row basis. The spatial operation is applied to each geometry using full table scans.

INDEX-AWARE OPERATORS

There are three operations in this category; namely, *SDO_RELATE*, *SDO_FILTER*, and *SDO_WITHIN_DISTANCE*. *SDO_RELATE* checks topological relationships between two spatial objects. Any of the relationships *contains, coveredby, covers, disjoint, equal, inside, overlap*, and *touch*[41] can be checked and specified as a value of the *SDO_RELATE* argument *mask*. Other relationships can be derived as a combination of these relationships. For example, the query for counties adjacent to San Francisco County (query **SPAT-ADM4** of Section 3.2) is formulated as

select	*c1.county-name*
from	*County c1, County c2*
where	*c2.county-name = 'San Francisco'*
and	*MDSYS.SDO_RELATE(c1.geometry,c2.geometry,* *'mask = TOUCH') = 'TRUE';*

Query "Counties that intersect a given window on the screen" (Query **INTER-ADM8**) is formulated as

select	*County.county-name*
from	*County, Windows*
where	*MDSYS.SDO_relate(County.geometry, Windows.geometry,* *'mask = OVERLAP') = 'TRUE';*

The window(s) drawn on the screen is (are) stored as one (several) rows in the *Windows* table. The other index-aware operations are *SDO_FILTER* and *SDO_WITHIN_DISTANCE*. *SDO_FILTER* performs only the filter step (see Section 8.5.4); that is, it uses only the index entries to find out which geometry pairs are likely to be non-disjoint. In some cases, this is sufficient and leads to a fast answer. For instance, a zoom query in a mapping application quickly returns a superset of the solution. Operator *SDO_WITHIN_DISTANCE (Geometry1, Geometry2, 'distance = d')* checks whether *Geometry1* is within *d* units of *Geometry2*. In order to do this, it first computes the buffer polygon of *d* units around *Geometry1*, and then checks for overlapping.

OTHER SPATIAL OPERATORS

The main operations of this category are *SDO_GEOM.SDO_BUFFER*, which returns the buffer polygon of a given distance around the speci-

---

41. See Section 3.3.3 for a description of these relationships. The Oracle relationship *touch* corresponds to the *meet* relationship of Section 3.3.3.

fied geometry, and set operations such as *UNION, DIFFERENCE,* and *INTERSECTION.* For instance, drawing the living areas in the county of San Francisco (query **SPAT_ADM-LU1**) is expressed as

select	*INTERSECTION (Land-use.geometry, County.geometry)*
from	*County, Land-use*
where	*County.county-name* = 'San Francisco'
and	*Land-use.land-use-type* = 'living area'
and	*MDSYS.SDO_RELATE(County.geometry, Land-use.geometry, 'mask = OVERLAP') = 'TRUE'*

Finally, *SDO_GEOM.AREA* computes the area of a 2D geometry and *SDO_GEOM.LENGTH* computes the length of a 1D geometry. The Boolean index-aware operators also exist as "functions" evaluated on a row-by-row basis.

8.5.4 *Spatial Indexing and Query Processing*

Oracle Spatial uses a *z*-ordering tree spatial index (see Section 6.2.3) and a two-step mechanism for query evaluation of index-aware operations. In the first step, called *filter step* (primary filter, to be precise), the operation is fast and is evaluated on an approximation of the geometry. This selects a small superset of the solution; that is, a small subset of the geometries on which the second step, called *refinement step* (secondary filter),[42] is performed. For a more detailed presentation of *z*-ordering indices and this two-step query evaluation, see Chapter 6. The Oracle Spatial indexing mechanism has the following characteristics:

◆ The rectangular coordinate space is decomposed into a grid of 4^n fixed-size cells, which are ordered using a variant of *z*-ordering, called *HHcode.* This corresponds to a complete quadtree decomposition in which all leaves are at the same level *n*.

◆ Oracle Spatial approximates the spatial object by the smallest set of grid cells that covers it; that is, it is the smallest set of adjacent cells that either are inside the geometry or intersect its boundary.

---

42. Recall that the refinement step consists in sequentially scanning the list of exact geometries resulting from the filter step and performing the spatial operation.

Cells are ordered according to a key. The index includes only non-empty cells; that is, cells overlapping at least one geometry. The index of a table A is a table whose name is $A\_SDOINDEX$, with two columns: SDO_CODE (cell key) and SDO_GID (geometry identifier). An index entry (i.e., a row in this table) corresponds to a geometry whose approximation includes the cell. This table is indexed with the Oracle B-tree on the cell key. The grid resolution level n is a parameter fixed by the user application. Figure 8.18 shows a fixed tiling with $n = 2$, a set of three geometries, and the resulting index. The polygon with identifier 705 is approximated by cells with keys c3, c4, c7, and c8. The line segment with identifier 80 is approximated by cell c5. The triangle 534 is approximated by cells c5, c6, c9, and c10.

The filter step is easily implemented using this scheme, referred to as *fixed-size tessellation*, which corresponds to the raster variant of z-ordering (defined in Section 6.2.3) by using existing relational joins, as shown in the following. However, as argued in Chapter 6, grid-based schemes present some limitations. This is why Oracle Spatial offers another scheme, called *hybrid tessellation*, in which two modes can coexist: a mode based on the foregoing fixed-resolution grid and a mode based on variable resolution grids. The latter assumes that variable-size cells form a better approximation of the geometry, depending on the size of the geometry. The user application specifies as a parameter a number ($SDO\_NUMTILES$) to set the number of cells to be used for approx-

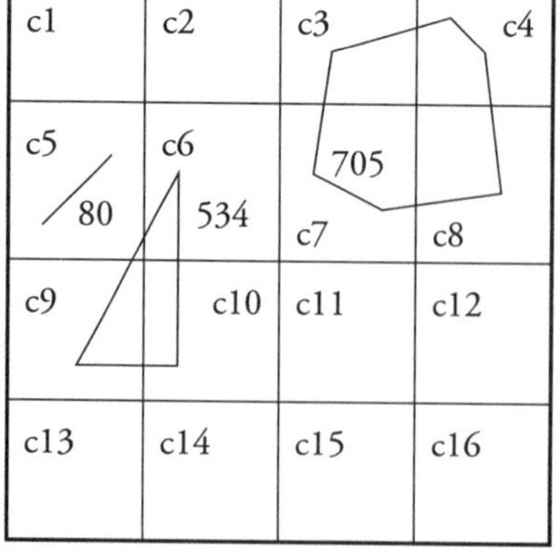

A_ SDOINDEX

SDO_CODE	SDO_GID
c3	705
c4	705
c5	80
c5	534
c6	534
c7	705
c8	705
c9	534
c10	534

Figure 8.18 Spatial indexing with Oracle.

imating each geometry. The underlying grid level, therefore, depends on the geometry size and shape and may vary from one geometry to the other. Although this obviously improves the querying performance, it makes the filter step much more complex.

Oracle Spatial queries can be classified into two categories: (1) window queries for which a single table is queried with the window as an argument, and (2) spatial joins involving two tables. We assume in the following that all tables are indexed and have the same index grid resolution (fixed-size tessellation mode). We consider in the following only the filter step.

WINDOW QUERY PROCESSING

Assume the execution of the following window query: "Return objects of table *A* overlapping window *w*." Table *A* is indexed by means of a table *A_SDOINDEX* having two columns: *SDO_CODE* (*cell key*) and *SDO_GID* (*geometry element key*). *A_SDOINDEX*, together with the B-tree on *SDO_CODE*, constitutes the spatial linear index. First, window *w* is tiled into cells of the fixed-size grid. Then, for each of these cells, say, *c*, we look at the corresponding index entries that give the geometries of objects of Table *A*, whose approximation contains *c*. This is formulated by the following standard SQL query:[43]

select	**distinct** *I.SDO_GID*
from	*A_SDOINDEX I, Windows_SDOINDEX J*
where	*I.SDO_CODE = J.SDO_CODE*

This query expresses an equi-join between the index of table *A* (table *A_SDOINDEX*) and the set of cells obtained from tiling window *w*. The join is on the cell keys (*SDO_CODE*). The result is a list of geometry identifiers. Such a query can efficiently be answered using standard optimization techniques provided by Oracle, taking advantage in particular of the existence of the B-tree index on *A_SDOINDEX*.

SPATIAL JOIN

Assume an SQL query involving two tables, *A* and *B*, and a spatial predicate expressed by the operator *SDO_RELATE* mask argument. Assume

43. The generated internal SQL query is more complicated. It is simplified here for the sake of clarity.

also that at least one table, say, *A*, has a spatial index.[44] Two algorithms are then possible.

- *Scan and index.* Sequentially scan table *B*. For each geometry *g*, generate a window query against table *A* with window *g* (an internal SQL query is generated, as shown previously).
- *Synchronized index traversal.* If table *B* is also indexed, both indices can efficiently be merged, keeping only the geometries of cells present in both indices.

8.6 POSTGRESQL

The Postgres system is perhaps the most notable, and pioneering, extended relational DBMS, now commonly called *object-relational* DBMS. This system provides a spatial extension to SQL. In 1996, the system became an open source project, its name changed to PostgreSQL, and some new geometric functionalities were added. The system is now widely used in the open software community, where it is regarded as the most complete, cost-free DBMS implementation.

In that one of the novel features of the initial Postgres system was its extensibility with new data types, it has been one of the first database systems to integrate geometric types and operations, together with spatial indexing. As to the design of its geometric features, the PostgreSQL model is quite close to the logical model presented in Section 3.3. These features can be summarized as follows:

- A set of common geometric types, similar to that discussed in Chapter 3, implementing a spaghetti-like spatial data model.
- Operations on these types.
- An extended SQL syntax, which integrates the previous operations.

Last, but not least, spatial indexing is achieved with an R-tree, based on the quadratic split algorithm discussed in Chapter 6.

---

44. If neither table *A* nor table *B* has a spatial index, the query is costly. The query algorithm is then as follows (nested loop): scan table *A* and, for each geometry, scan table *B*. Check the spatial predicate against each pair of geometries.

Table 8.1 Geometric types in PostgreSQL.

Geometric Type	Representation	Description
point	(x, y)	Point in space
line	$((x_1, y_1), (x_2, y_2))$	An infinite straight line defined by two points
lseg	$((x_1, y_1), (x_2, y_2))$	A line segment defined by its two endpoints
box	$((x_1, y_1), (x_2, y_2))$	A rectangle (rectangular box)
path	$((x_1, y_1), \ldots)$	A *closed* polyline (closed path)
path	$[(x_1, y_1), \ldots]$	A polyline (open path)
polygon	$((x_1, y_1), \ldots)$	Polygon
circle	$< (x, y), r >$	A circle (with center and radius)

8.6.1 Geometric Types and Operators

Table 8.1 lists and describes the geometric types of the PostgreSQL system. For clarity, the descriptions rely on the vocabulary used throughout this book, with the PostgreSQL terminology, if different, provided in parentheses.

PostgreSQL distinguishes *closed* from *open* polylines (called paths in PostgreSQL), the former being characterized at input by a pair of parentheses, ( ), instead of brackets, [ ]. In a closed polyline, the last point is connected with the first.

The syntax for creating a polygon is similar to that of closed polylines, as observed in Section 2.3.1. However, the storage is different, as well as the functions that can be applied. Because the syntax for defining a new geometric object might be ambiguous, PostgreSQL uses the *'(Representation)'::type* notation, which gives explicitly the type intended by *Representation*. For instance, *'((0, 0),(1, 1))'::box* creates a rectangle, whereas *'((0, 0),(1, 1))'::lseg* creates a line segment.

The spatial model of PostgreSQL does not include a *region* type (set of polygons), and consequently does not propose the computation of the intersection of polygons, as this operation potentially yields a set of polygons (see Section 3.3.2). The same comment holds for *lines*, which are represented by a list of connected segments. The intersection of a line and a polygon might result in a polyline consisting of several components, which cannot be handled by PostgreSQL. Due to these closure issues, thoroughly discussed in Chapter 3, the spatial operators of PostgreSQL are largely spatial predicates (as opposed to operations), and do not permit the construction of new objects.

Table 8.2 lists and describes the main geometric operators of PostgreSQL. In *translate* and *scale*, *point* is the vector of translation (scale). Some of these operators are *polymorphic*; that is, they apply to arguments of various types. For instance, *contain* takes as a first argument a point, and as a second argument any geometric type (polygon, circle, box, lseg, and so on). In such cases, we use the generic word *geom* to represent any geometric type.

Table 8.2 Spatial operators of PostgreSQL.

Operator	Description	Signature
+	Translates a rectangle.	$box \times point \rightarrow box$
⋆	Scales a rectangle.	$box \times point \rightarrow box$
#	Computes the intersection of two segments.	$lseg \times lseg \rightarrow point$
#	Number of vertices in polygon.	$polygon \rightarrow integer$
&&	Overlap of polygons.	$polygon \times polygon \rightarrow bool$
<<	Is left? Checks whether the rightmost point of the first argument is on the left of the leftmost point of the right argument.	$geom << geom$
>>	Is right of?	$geom >> geom$
<^	Is below?	$geom <\,\hat{}\,geom$
>^	Is above?	$geom >\,\hat{}\,geom$
?#	Intersection test of a pair of polylines, or of a polyline and a polygon.	$path \times geom \rightarrow bool$
?-	Tests whether two points define a horizontal segment.	$point \times point \rightarrow bool$
?—	Tests whether two points define a vertical segment.	$point \times point \rightarrow bool$
?-	Tests whether two segments are perpendicular.	$lseg \times lseg \rightarrow bool$
?||	Tests whether two segments are parallel.	$lseg \times lseg \rightarrow bool$
@	Tests whether a point belongs to a geometric object.	$point \times geom \rightarrow bool$
~=	Tests equality of polygons.	$polygon \times polygon \rightarrow bool$

In addition to the operators listed in Table 8.2, several functions can be used to perfom computations from geometric objects. Among these functions are *area*, which computes the area of a surfacic object, and *length*, which computes the length of a linear object.

8.6.2 Creating the Database

Given these types, using the standard SQL syntax, a table can be created with geometric attributes. The following is a review of part of the example schema of Chapter 3.

```
Create Table LandUse (
        regionName   varchar (15),
        landUseType  varchar (10),
        geometry   polygon,
        PRIMARY KEY (regionName));

CREATE TABLE Highway (
    highwayCode integer,
    highwayName char (4),
    highwayType char (2),
    PRIMARY KEY (highwayCode));

CREATE TABLE Section (
    sectionCode integer,
    sectionName varchar (40),
    numberLanes integer,
    geometry     path,
    PRIMARY KEY (sectionCode));

CREATE TABLE HighwaySection (
    sectionCode integer,
    sectionNumber integer,
    highwayCode integer,
    PRIMARY KEY (sectionCode, highwayCode),
    FOREIGN KEY (sectionCode) REFERENCES Section,
    FOREIGN KEY (highwayCode) REFERENCES Highway);
```

Finally, the schema should be completed by creating an R-tree on the spatial attribute of each table having a geometric attribute, as follows:

```
Create Index RtrLandUse On LandUse using  RTREE (geometry);
```

PostgreSQL will automatically maintain the R-tree during insertions, updates, and deletions. The query optimizer will consider using an

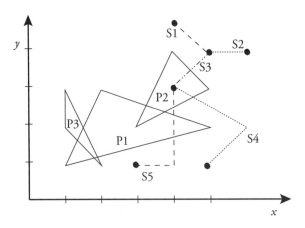

Figure 8.19   A sample data set.

R-tree index whenever an indexed attribute is involved in a comparison using one of the following: << *(left of)*, >> *(right of)*, @ *(point-in-polygon test)*, ˜ = *(polygon equality)*, or && *(polygon overlap)*.

8.6.3 *Expressing Queries*

For concreteness, we will use a very simple data set (Figure 8.19) to populate our schema. It contains three simple parcels (P1, P2, and P3), which, for the sake of illustration, overlap. The data set also features two highways:

- Highway I99 consists of sections S1, S3, and S5.
- Highway I100 consists of sections S2, S3, and S4.

As we can see in the figure, section S3 is shared by both highways. Data is inserted with the standard SQL **insert** clause. The following commands show some examples for our sample data set.

```
Insert Into LandUse (regionName, landUseType,geometry)
Values ('P1', 'Wheat', '((1,1), (2,3), (5,2))');
Insert Into LandUse (regionName, landUseType,geometry)
Values ('P2', 'Corn', '((2,2), (3,2), (5,3))');

Insert Into Section (sectionCode, sectionName,
numberLanes, geometry)
Values      (1, 'S1', 1, '((4,5), (5,4))');
Insert Into Section (sectionCode, sectionName,
```

```
numberLanes, geometry)
Values      (4, 'S4', 1, '[(4,3),(6,2),(5,1)]');
```

Such queries are run using the interactive SQL monitor of PostgreSQL. However, they could as well be embedded in a programming language or a graphical interface. This monitor prompts *SpatialDB ->* at the beginning of each line (*SpatialDB =>* at the beginning of the query), where *SpatialDB* is the name of the database. We express some queries of Section 3.2 using the extended SQL language of PostgreSQL. Some queries are only variants of queries discussed in Section 3.2, where counties have been replaced by land parcels to adapt to our simple sample database.

The reader will note that the syntax is quite similar to that presented in Chapter 3 for extended relational databases.

QUERIES WITH ALPHANUMERIC CRITERIA

ALPHA-R2. Name of sections that constitute Interstate 99.

This query also returns the number of lanes.

```
SpatialDB=> Select sectionName, numberLanes
SpatialDB-> From  HighwaySection h1, Highway h2, Section s
SpatialDB-> Where h2.highwayCode = h1.highwayCode
SpatialDB-> And   h1.sectionCode =  s.sectionCode
SpatialDB-> And   highwayName = 'I99';

sectionname|numberlanes
-----------+-----------
S1         |          1
S3         |          2
S5         |          1
```

This is standard SQL querying, and PostgreSQL follows closely the SQL ANSI specification. Any of our queries based on alphanumeric criteria can be expressed.

QUERIES INVOLVING SPATIAL CRITERIA

SPAT-R3. Length of Interstate 99.

This query is expressed as follows:

```
SpatialDB=> Select sum(length(geometry))
SpatialDB-> From  HighwaySection h1, Highway h2, Section s
SpatialDB-> Where h2.highwayCode = h1.highwayCode
```

```
SpatialDB-> And    h1.sectionCode = s.sectionCode
SpatialDB-> And    highwayName = 'I99';


                sum
----------------
5.82842712474619
```

SPAT-ADMR1 (variant). Highways going through parcel P1.

The predicate *?#* tests for intersection between a polygon and a polyline. This query is expressed as follows:

```
SpatialDB=> Select highwayName
SpatialDB-> From    LandUse l, HighwaySection h1, High-
way h2, Section s
SpatialDB-> Where  h2.highwayCode = h1.highwayCode
SpatialDB-> And    h1.sectionCode = s.sectionCode
SpatialDB-> And    l.regionName = 'P1'
SpatialDB-> And    l.geometry ?# s.geometry;


highwayname
-----------
I99
```

Section S5, which belongs to Highway I99, intersects the polygon P1 (see Figure 8.19).

SPAT-ADM-LU1 (variant). Display of the pairs of intersecting parcels.

The intersection test is &&. This query is expressed as follows:

```
SpatialDB=> Select l1.regionName, l2.regionName
SpatialDB-> From   LandUse l1, LandUse l2
SpatialDB-> Where  l1.geometry && l2.geometry
SpatialDB-> And    l1.regionName < l2.regionName;

regionname|regionname
----------+----------
P1        |P2
P1        |P3
```

PostgreSQL offers other spatial join predicates. For instance, one can select polygons that are "left of" (respectively, "right of") another polygon. The semantics is that the rightmost point of the left polygon should be on the left of the leftmost point of the right polygon. This is the case for parcels (P3, P2). (See Figure 8.19.) The query is expressed as follows:

```
SpatialDB=> Select 11.regionName, 12.regionName
SpatialDB-> From   LandUse 11, LandUse 12
SpatialDB-> Where  11.geometry << 12.geometry;

regionname|regionname
----------+----------
P3        |P2
```

INTERACTIVE QUERIES

INTER-ADM7 (variant). Description of the parcel pointed to on the screen.

The point-in-polygon test is expressed with the @ operator. This query is expressed as follows:

```
SpatialDB=> Select *
SpatialDB-> From LandUse
SpatialDB-> Where '(2,2)'::point @ geometry;

regionname|landusetype|geometry
----------+-----------+-------------------
P1        |Wheat      |((1,1),(2,3),(5,2))
```

An explicit cast with the double colon (::) syntax is required to convert the coordinates (2, 2) into a point. The coordinates (2, 2) can be obtained by use of a graphical interface.

INTER-R5. Description of the section pointed to on the screen.

The @ operator is polymorphic, and can be used for polylines. This query is expressed as follows:

```
SpatialDB=> Select *
SpatialDB-> From   Section
SpatialDB-> Where  '(4,3)'::point @ geometry;

sectioncode|sectionname|numberlanes|geometry
-----------+-----------+-----------+-------------------
          3|S3         |          2|((5,4),(4,3))
          4|S4         |          1|((4,3),(6,2),(5,1))
          5|S5         |          1|((4,3),(4,1),(3,1))
```

Of course, one can easily add joins with relations *Highway* and *HighwaySection* to express queries such as *Description of the highway(s) whose one section is pointed to on the screen* (**INTER-R6**).

INTER-ADM8 (variant). Parcels that intersect a given rectangle on the screen.

Windowing is expressed with the overlap operator, and requires converting the rectangle to a polygon. This query is expressed as follows:

```
SpatialDB=> Select *
SpatialDB-> From   LandUse
SpatialDB-> Where  '((1,1),(1,2),(2,2),(2,1))'::polygon &&
geometry;

regioname|landusetype|geometry
---------+-----------+-------------------
P1       |Wheat      |((1,1),(2,3),(5,2))
P3       |Rice       |((1,2),(1,3),(2,1))
```

There is no clipping with PostgreSQL. Recall that the result of a clipping on a polygon or a polyline can potentially result in several components, which cannot be handled by PostgreSQL. That is, the result of an operation must be a single object of the predefined geometric types.

WHAT CANNOT BE EXPRESSED WITH POSTGRESQL

Many of our reference queries cannot be expressed with PostgreSQL. In addition to what we saw in Section 8.6.1, the system lacks *topological operators* (such as adjacency). It should be noted that it is possible to extend the set of operators by adding new functions, but the absence of topological information in the spatial representation would make such an implementation difficult, error prone due to geometric approximation, and inefficient. Another important operation that is not expressible is *map overlay*, because there is no way to compute the intersection of two polygons.

8.7   BIBLIOGRAPHIC NOTES

The Canadian Geographic Information System, intended for collection of information on natural resources of Canada (1965), was the first full-fledged GIS. During the same decade, cartography benefited from the development of computer graphics systems, influenced in particular by research at the Harvard Graphics laboratory. In the 1970s, many companies started developing products for automated map production and for urban planning (ESRI) or public utilities (e.g., Intergraph). In the early 1980s, a few companies provided complex software used only by a few agencies who had acquired the knowledge required to use it profitably. In the meantime, numerous organizations built their own systems to fit their particular needs. In the 1990s, the offer of GIS products was diversified from general-purpose complex GISs offered by only a few vendors to simpler systems provided for special markets. This short panorama on GIS is drawn from [Fra95]. A history of GIS can also be found in [CR91].

The *second-generation* of *GIS*s (e.g., ArcInfo from ESRI) separates the spatial data management from thematic data management (see Figure 8.20). The rationale behind this choice is mostly historical. Most vendors first mastered map production and developed an efficient technology for handling spatial data (first-generation of GISs). Each spatial object on a map was then linked to nonspatial attribute values. Later, coupling with relational data was added. Although such *loosely coupled* GISs evolved with time toward more general systems, the ability of customizing the GIS to users' needs has some limitations. In particular, as discussed in depth in Section 8.2, there is no high-level query language. The ArcInfo GIS spatial model is discussed in [Mor85, Mor89]. We presented version 7 of the product. However, the queries were run on ArcInfo version 6.1.2. Our presentation is drawn from [SVP+96], [ESR96], and more recent ArcInfo manuals. Tigris from Intergraph [Her87] is another widely used GIS.

Influenced by the spatial database research community, more recent products model geographic information as collections of geographic objects. Each geographic object incorporates nonspatial attributes and one spatial attribute, which is an abstract data type. Some systems following this approach, such as ESRI's ArcView [Dan94], do not have a high-level query language. Instead, they offer intermediate-level primitives through an application development platform (Avenue language). Our presentation is drawn from the ArcView manuals. Information about ArcView can be found at [ESR01]. Other systems, such as MapInfo [DW96], offer a high-level SQL-like query language, but the actual expressive power of the language is still limited.

(a)

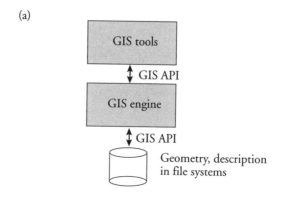

(b)

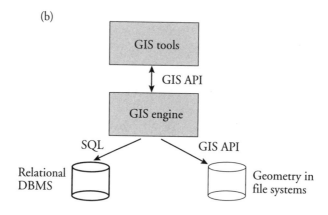

(c)

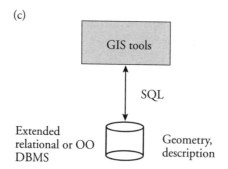

Figure 8.20 Three GIS generations: first generation (a), second generation (b), and third generation (c).

Information on Smallworld can be found at [SML00]. Our presentation is taken from the Smallworld manuals and more particularly from the user guide [SML94].

Most of the general-purpose DBMS vendors now offer a spatial extension. This extension allows the application developer to add spatial types and spatial functions to be used with SQL, but the integration with the DBMS is rather loose. In particular, the optimization of queries involving spatial as well as nonspatial attributes is limited. Our presentation of the Oracle version 8*i* extension to spatial data is from [Sha99]. [Ash99] describes the current effort toward an extension of SQL called SQL/MM Spatial, for querying spatial data. *Oracle8i Spatial User's Guide and Reference* can be found at [Ora00].

Postgres design and implementation began in 1986 at the University of California at Berkeley. For many years, Postgres was used as a platform for experimenting with advanced database techniques, including the extension of the relational data model with classes, inheritance, types and functions, triggers and rules, and extendable optimization. Early design and development of the Postgres system is reported in [SR86, SRH90]. The paper [vOV91] presents an experience on using Postgres in a GIS environment. Our presentation is based on the latest version of PostgreSQL (V7.0). [Mom00] covers all aspects of the new PostgreSQL system.

Spatial Database Engine (SDE) from ESRI is a software that enables spatial data to be stored, managed, and retrieved from commercial DBMSs such as Oracle, Microsoft SQL Server, Sybase, IBM DB2, and Informix. It is meant to be used by the GIS community as well as the DBMS community who wish to extend their own products with spatial technology. Information on SDE can be found at [ESRb]. [ESRa] is a technical white paper that describes its main features in a comprehensive way (note that the last version of SDE is named ArcSDE 8).

From a GIS viewpoint, SDE provides a solution for managing and providing access to spatial data. It is fully integrated with ESRI applications, including ArcInfo, ArcView GIS, and ArcExplorer (ESRI's Internet browser technology). It provides a single interface between end users and possibly many collections of geographic data.

From a database point of view, SDE provides an open solution for storing, managing, and using spatial data. It uses a three-tier architec-

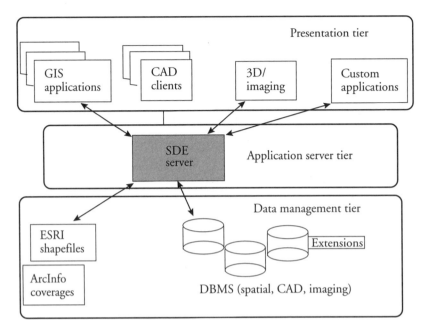

Figure 8.21   The SDE three-tier architecture.

ture to run distributed applications. It extends a two-tier implementation by adding a middle application server to support distributed computed services. SDE is, then, a spatial application server that provides functionalities such as spatial query processing, map projections, GIS database loading, and administration tools. This is illustrated in Figure 8.21.

SDE enables one to develop custom applications within its Open Development Environment (ODE), which includes a C API and the extended SQL API. They can also be created with ArcInfo using ODE or ArcView using Avenue software. SDE can also be used in conjunction with selected database environments. It can, for instance, read and write data in Oracle's Spatial Data Option (SDO) and Spatial Cartridge formats. It was also licensed as a spatial extender to IBM DB2 DataJoiner.

Bibliography

[ABCK91]   J. C. Antenucci, K. Brown, P. L. Croswell, and M. J. Kevany. *Geographic Information Systems: A Guide to the Technology*. Van Nostrand Reinhold (International Thomson Publishing), New York, 1991.

[Abe89]   D. Abel. "SIRO-DBMS: A Database Toolkit for Geographical Information Systems." *Intl. Journal of Geographical Information Systems (IJGIS)*, 3(2):103–116, 1989.

[AG97]   N. R. Adam and A. Gangopadhyay. *Database Issues in Geographic Information Systems*. Vol. 6 of *Advances in Database Systems*. Kluwer Academic Publishers, New York, 1997.

[Aga97]   P. K. Agarwal. "Geometric Range Searching." In *CRC Handbook of Discrete and Computational Geometry*. CRC Press, Boca Raton, 1997.

[Ahr85]   J. H. Ahrens. "Sequential Random Sampling." *ACM Trans. on Mathematical Software*, 11(2), 1985.

[AHU74]   A. V. Aho, J. E. Hopcroft, and J. D. Ullman. *The Design and Analysis of Computer Algorithms*. Addison-Wesley, Reading, MA, 1974.

[AHV95]   S. Abiteboul, R. Hull, and V. Vianu. *Foundations of Databases*. Addison-Wesley, Reading, MA, 1995.

[AO93]   D. Abel and B. C. Ooi, editors. *Proc. Intl. Symposium on Large Spatial Databases (SSD)*. Vol. 692 of *Lecture Notes in Computer Science*, Singapore. Springer-Verlag, Berlin/Heidelberg/New York, 1993.

[APR+98]   L. Arge, O. Procopiuc, S. Ramaswami, T. Suel, and J. Vitter. "Scalable Sweeping Based Spatial Join." In *Proc. Intl. Conf. on Very Large Data Bases (VLDB)*, 1998.

[Arg97]   L. Arge. "External Memory Algorithms with Applications in GIS." In [vKNRW97], pages 213–249, 1997.

[Arm90]   M. A. Armstrong. *Basic Topology.* Springer-Verlag, Berlin/Heidelberg/New York, 1990.

[AS83]   D. Abel and J. L. Smith. "A Data Structure and Algorithm Based on a Linear Key for a Rectangle Retrieval Problem." *Computer Vision, Graphics and Image Processing,* 24:1–13, 1983.

[AS93]   W. G. Aref and H. Samet. "Decomposing a Window into Maximal Quadtree Blocks." *Acta Informatica,* 30:425–439, 1993.

[AS95]   W. G. Aref and H. Samet. "A Window Retrieval Algorithm for Spatial Databases Using Quadtrees." In *Proc. ACM Intl. Symp. on Geographic Information Systems (ACM-GIS),* 1995.

[Ash99]   M. Ashworth. *Information Technology, Database Languages, SQL Multimedia, and Application Packages, Part 3: Spatial, ISO/IEC 13249-3,* 1999.

[AV88]   A. Aggarwal and J. S. Vitter. "The Input/Output Complexity of Sorting and Related Problems." *Communications of the ACM,* 31(9):1116–1127, 1988.

[AV96]   L. Arge and J. S. Vitter. Optimal Interval Management in External Memory. In *IEEE Conf. on Foundations of Computer Science,* pages 560–569, 1996.

[AVV95]   L. Arge, D. E. Vengroff, and J. S. Vittter. "External-Memory Algorithms for Processing Line Segments in Geographic Information Systems." In *European Symposium on Algorithms (ESA),* 1995.

[Bau72]   B. G. Baumgart. "Winged Edge Polyhedron Representation." Technical Report CS-TR-72-320, Stanford University, Department of Computer Science, 1972.

[BBC98]   A. Belussi, E. Bertino, and B. Catania. "An Extended Algebra for Constraint Databases." *IEEE Transactions on Knowledge and Data Engineering (TKDE),* 10(5):686–705, 1998. A shorter version appeared in SSD'97.

[BD98]   P. A. Burrough and R. A. McDonnell. *Principles of Geographical Information Systems.* Oxford University Press, Oxford/New York, 1998.

[BDK92]   F. Bancilhon, C. Delobel, and P. C. Kanellakis, editors. *Building an Object-Oriented Database System: The Story of O₂.* Morgan Kaufmann, San Francisco, 1992.

[BDQV90]   K. Bennis, B. David, I. Quilio, and Y. Viémont. "GÉOTROPICS: Database Support Alternatives for Geographic Applications." In *Proc. Intl. Symp. on Spatial Data Handling (SDH),* 1990.

[Ben75]   J. L. Bentley. "Multidimensional Binary Search Trees Used for Associative Searching." *Communications of the ACM,* 18(9):509–517, 1975.

[Ben77]   J. L. Bentley. "Algorithms for Klee's Rectangle Problems." Technical Report, Carnegie Mellon University, Department of Computer Science, 1977.

[Ben80]   J. L. Bentley. "Multidimensional Divide and Conquer." *Communications of the ACM,* 23:214–229, 1980.

[Ber97]   P. Bergougnoux. "Bridging the Gap Between Computer Science and Geography." *GeoInformatica*, 1(1): 1997.

[BF79]   J. L. Bentley and J. H. Friedman. "Data Structures for Range Searching." *ACM Computing Surveys*, 11(4), 1979.

[BG92]   L. Becker and R. H. Güting. "Rule-Based Optimization and Query Processing in an Extensible Geometric Database System." *ACM Transactions on Database Systems*, 17(2):247–303, 1992.

[BG94]   G. Blankenagel and R. H. Güting. "External Segment Trees." *Algorithmica*, 12:498–532, 1994.

[BGSW89]   A. Buchmann, O. Günther, T. R. Smith, and Y.-F. Wang, editors. *Proc. Intl. Symposium on Design and Implementation af Large Spatial Databases (SSD)*. Vol. 409 of *Lecture Notes in Computer Science*, Santa Barbara. Springer-Verlag, Berlin/Heidelberg/New York, 1989.

[BHF93]   L. Becker, K. Hinrichs, and U. Finke. "A New Algorithm for Computing Joins with Grid Files." In *Proc. IEEE Intl. Conf. on Data Engineering (ICDE)*, 1993.

[BHG87]   P. A. Bernstein, V. Hadzilacos, and N. Goodman. *Concurrency Control and Recovery in Database Systems*. Addison-Wesley, Reading, MA, 1987.

[BKK99]   C. Boehm, G. Klump, and H. P. Kriegel. "XZ-Ordering: A Space-Filling Curve for Objects with Spatial Extension." In [GPL99], pages 75–90, 1999.

[BKS93]   T. Brinkhoff, H. P. Kriegel, and B. Seeger. "Efficient Processing of Spatial Joins Using R-Trees." In *Proc. ACM SIGMOD Intl. Symp. on the Management of Data*, 1993.

[BKSS90]   N. Beckmann, H. P. Kriegel, R. Schneider, and B. Seeger. "The R*Tree: An Efficient and Robust Access Method for Points and Rectangles." In *Proc. ACM SIGMOD Intl. Symp. on the Management of Data*, pages 322–331, 1990.

[BKSS94]   T. Brinkhoff, H. P. Kriegel, R. Schneider, and B. Seeger. "Multi-Step Processing of Spatial Joins." In *Proc. ACM SIGMOD Intl. Symp. on the Management of Data*, pages 197–208, 1994.

[BM72]   R. Bayer and C. McCreight. "Organization and Maintenance of Large Ordered Indexes." *Acta Informatica*, 1(3):173–189, 1972.

[BM91]   B. P. Buttenfield and R. B. MacMaster, editors. *Map Generalization: Making Rules for Knowledge Representation*. Longman Scientific and Technical, London, 1991.

[BO79]   J. L. Bentley and T. A. Ottmann. "Algorithms for Reporting and Counting Geometric Intersections." *IEEE Trans. on Comp.*, C(28), 1979.

[BS97]   A. Brodsky and V. E. Segal. "The C^3 Constraint Object-Oriented Database System: An Overview." In *Proc. Intl. Workshop on Constraint Database Systems*, LNCS 1191, pages 134–159, 1997.

[BTAPL99] C. Bonhomme, C. Trépied, M.-A. Aufaure-Portier, and R. Laurini. A Visual Language for Querying Spatio-temporal Databases. In *Proc. ACM Intl. Symp. on Geographic Information Systems (ACM-GIS)*, pages 34–39, 1999.

[Buc94]   H. Buchanan. "Geographic Information: The Source Book for GIS." In D. R. Green, D. Rix, and J. Cadoux-Hudson, editors, *Standards for Spatial Data Transfer*, pages 254–261. Taylor and Francis, London, in cooperation with the Association for Geographic Information, 1994.

[Bur94]   P. A. Burrough. "Accuracy and Error in GIS." In D. R. Geen and D. Rix, editors, *The AGI Source Book for Geographic Information Systems*, pages 87–91. Association for Geographic Information, London, 1994.

[BW80]   J. L. Bentley and D. Wood. "An Optimal Worst Case Algorithm for Reporting Intersections of Rectangles." *IEEE Transactions on Computers*, 29, 1980.

[BW88]   K. E. Brassel and R. Weibel. "A Review and Conceptual Framework of Automated Map Generalization." *Intl. Journal on Geographical Information Systems*, 2(3):229–244, 1988.

[BY98]   J.-D. Boissonnat and M. Yvinec. *Algorithmic Geometry*. Cambridge University Press, New York, 1998.

[Cat95]   R.G.G. Cattell. "Object Databases and Standards." In *Proc. British National Conference on Databases*, pages 1–11, 1995.

[CD85]   B. Chazelle and D. P. Dobkin. "Optimal Convex Decomposition." In G. T. Toussaint, editor, *Computational Geometry*, pages 63–133. North Holland, Amsterdam, 1985.

[CE92]   B. Chazelle and E. Edelsbrunner. "An Optimal Algorithm for Intersecting Line Segments in the Plane." *Journal of the ACM*, 39, 1992.

[Cha91]   B. Chazelle. "Triangulating a Simple Polygon in Linear Time." *Discrete and Computational Geometry*, 6:485–524, 1991.

[Cha94]   T. M. Chan. "A Simple Trapezoid Sweep Algorithm for Reporting Red/Blue Segment Intersections." In *Proc. Canadian Conf. on Computational Geometry*, 1994.

[CL93]   J.-P. Cheylan and S. Lardon. "Towards a Conceptual Data Model for the Analysis of Spatio Temporal Processes: The Example of the Search for Optimal Grazing Strategies." In *Proc. Intl. Conf. on Spatial Information Theory (COSIT)*, LNCS 716, pages 158–176. Springer-Verlag, Berlin/Heidelberg/New York, 1993.

[Clu98]   S. Cluet. "Designing OQL: Allowing Objects to Be Queried." *Information Systems*, 23(5):279–305, 1998.

[CMTV00]   A. Corral, Y. Manolopoulos, Y. Theodoridis, and M. Vassilakopoulos. "Closest Pair Queries in Spatial Databases." In *Proc. ACM SIGMOD Intl. Symp. on the Management of Data*, 2000.

[Com82]   D. Comer. "The Ubiquitous B-Tree." *ACM Computing Surveys*, 11(2):121–137, 1982.

[CR91]   J. T. Coppock and D. W. Rhind. *Geographical Information Systems: Principles and Applications*. Vol. 1: Principles (chapter: "The History of GIS"). Longman Scientific and Technical, London, 1991.

[CR99]   J. Chomicki and P. Revesz. "A Geometric Framework for Specifying Spatio-temporal Objects." In *Proc. Intl. Workshop on Time Representation and Reasoning*, 1999.

[CW83]   F. Chin and C. A. Wang. "Optimal Algorithms for the Intersection and the Minimum Distance Problems Between Planar Polygons." *IEEE Transactions on Computers*, 32:1203–1207, 1983.

[Dan94]   J. Dangermond. "ArcView Status and Direction." *ESRI ArcNews*, 16(2):1–6, 1994.

[dBSW97]   J. Van den Bercken, B. Seeger, and P. Widmayer. "A Generic Approach to Bulk Loading Multidimensional Index Structures." In *Proc. Intl. Conf. on Very Large Data Bases (VLDB)*, pages 406–415, 1997.

[dBvKOS97]   M. de Berg, M. van Kreveld, M. Overmars, and O. Schwarzkopf, editors. *Computational Geometry: Algorithms and Applications*. Springer-Verlag, Berlin/Heidelberg/New York, 1997.

[DG85]   D. J. DeWitt and R. H. Gerber. "Multiprocessor Hash-Based Join Algorithms." In *Proc. Intl. Conf. on Very Large Data Bases (VLDB)*, 1985.

[DGVV97]   F. Dumortier, M. Gyssens, L. Vandeurzen, and D. Van Gucht. "On the Decidability of Semi-Linearity for Semi-Algebraic Sets and Its Implications for Spatial Databases." In *Proc. ACM Intl. Symp. on Principles of Database Systems (PODS)*, 1997.

[DKO+84]   D. J. DeWitt, R. H. Katz, F. Olken, L. D. Shapiro, M. Stonebraker, and D. A. Wood. "Implementation Techniques for Main Memory Database Systems." In *Proc. ACM SIGMOD Intl. Symp. on the Management of Data*, 1984.

[DPS98]   T. Devogele, C. Parent, and S. Spaccapietra. "On Spatial Database Integration." *International Journal of Geographical Information Science*, 12(4), 1998.

[DRSM93]   B. David, L. Raynal, G. Schorter, and V. Mansart. "GeO2: Why Objects in a Geographical DBMS?" In [AO93], pages 264–276, 1993.

[DSS98]   T. Dalamagas, T. K. Sellis, and L. Sinos. "A Visual Database System for Spatial and Non-spatial Data Management." In *Proc. Intl. Conf. on Visual Database Systems (VDB)*, pages 105–122, 1998.

[Dum97]   P. Dumolard. "Multiscale Statistical Spatial Data Bases." In I. Bowler and C. Laurent, editors, *Common Agriculture Policy and the Regions*. INRA Editions, Paris, 1997.

[DW96]   L. Daniel and A. Whitener. *Inside Map Info Professional*. OnWord Press, Santa Fe, 1996.

[Ede83]   H. Edelsbrunner. A New Approach to Rectangle Intersections. *Int. J. Computer Mathematics*, 13:209–229, 1983.

[Ede87]   H. Edelsbrunner. *Algorithms in Combinatorial Geometry*. Springer-Verlag, Berlin/Heidelberg/New York, 1987.

[EF91]   M. Egenhofer and R. D. Franzosa. "Point-Set Topological Spatial Relations." *International Journal of Geographical Information Systems*, 5(2):161–174, 1991.

[Ege89]   M. Egenhofer. "A Formal Definition of Binary Topological Relationships." In *Proc. Intl. Conf. on Foundations of Data Organization and Algorithms (FODO)*, pages 457–472, 1989.

[Ege94]   M. Egenhofer. "Spatial SQL: A Query and Presentation Language." *IEEE Transactions on Knowledge and Data Engineering (TKDE)*, 6:86–95, 1994.

[Ege96]   M. Egenhofer. "Spatial-Query-by-Sketch." In *Proc. IEEE Intl. Symposium on Visual Languages (VL'96)*, 1996.

[Ege97]   M. Egenhofer. "Consistency Revisited." *GeoInformatica*, 1(4), 1997.

[EGSV98]   M. Erwig, R. H. Güting, M. Schneider, and M. Vazirgiannis. "Abstract and Discrete Modeling of Spatio-temporal Data Types." In *Proc. Intl. Symp. on Geographic Information Systems*, pages 131–136, 1998.

[EGSV99]   M. Erwig, R. H. Güting, M. Schneider, and M. Vazirgiannis. "Spatio-temporal Data Types: An Approach to Modeling and Querying Moving Objects in Databases." *GeoInformatica*, 3(3):269–296, 1999.

[EH90]   M. Egenhofer and J. R. Herring. "A Mathematical Framework for the Definition of Topological Relationships." In *Proc. Intl. Symp. on Spatial Data Handling (SDH)*, vol. 2, pages 803–813, 1990.

[EKS97]   M. Ester, H. P. Kriegel, and J. Sander. "Spatial Data Mining: A Database Approach." In [SV97], pages 47–66, 1997.

[EN94]   R. Elmasri and S. Navathe. *Fundamentals of Database Systems*, 2d Ed., Benjamin/Cummings, Redwood City, CA, 1994.

[ESRa]   ESRI, Inc. "Getting Started with SDE Version 3.0." URL: *www.esri.com/software/sde/pdfs/getstart.pdf*.

[ESRb]   ESRI, Inc. URL: *www.esri.com/software/arcinfo/arcsde/index.html* (SDE home page).

[ESR96]   ESRI. *ArcInfo Version 7 Manual*, Redwood, CA, 1996.

[ESR01]   ESRI, Inc. URL: *www. esri.com/software/arcview/* (ArcView home page).

[Fal86]   C. Faloutsos. "Multiattribute Hashing Using Gray Codes." In *Proc. ACM SIGMOD Intl. Symp. on the Management of Data*, 1986.

[Fal88]   C. Faloutsos. "Gray Codes for Spatial Match and Range Queries." *IEEE Transactions on Software Engineering*, 14(10), 1988.

[FB74]   R. A. Finkel and J. L. Bentley. Quad-Trees: A Data Structure for Retrieval on Composite Keys. *Acta Informatica*, 4:1–9, 1974.

[FB97]   S. Faïz and P. Boursier. "Geographic Data Quality: From Assessment to Exploitation." *Cartographica*, 33(1):33–40, 1997.

[FGNS00]   L. Forlizzi, R. H. Güting, E. Nardelli, and M. Schneider. "A Data Model and Data Structures for Moving Object Databases." In *Proc. ACM SIGMOD Intl. Symp. on the Management of Data*, 2000.

[FK86]   A. Frank and W. Kuhn. "Cell Graphs, a Provable Correct Method for the Storage of Geometry." In *Proc. Intl. Symp. on Spatial Data Handling (SDH)*, 1986.

[FK94]   C. Faloutsos and I. Kamel. "Beyond Uniformity and Independence: Analysis of R-Trees Using the Concept of Fractal Dimension." In *Proc. ACM Intl. Symp. on Principles of Database Systems (PODS)*, 1994.

[FNTW90]   K. Y. Fung, T. M. Nicholl, R. E. Tarjan, and C. J. Van Wyck. "Simplified Linear-Time Jordan Sorting and Polygon Clipping." *Information Processing Letters*, 35(2):85–92, 1990.

[FP95]   L. De Floriani and E. Puppo. "Hierarchical Triangulation for Multiresolution Surface Description." *ACM Transactions on Graphics*, 14(4):363–411, 1995.

[FPM00]   L. De Floriani, E. Puppo, and P. Magillo. "Applications of Computational Geometry to Geographical Information Systems." In J. R. Sack and J. Urrita, editors, *Handbook of Computational Geometry*, pages 333–388. Elsevier Science, 2000.

[FR89]   C. Faloutsos and S. Roseman. "Fractals for Secondary Key Retrieval." In *Proc. ACM Intl. Symp. on Principles of Database Systems (PODS)*, pages 247–252, 1989.

[Fra82]   A. Frank. "Mapquery: Data Base Query Language for Retrieval of Geometric Data and Their Graphical Representation." *ACM Computer Graphics*, 16(3):199–207, 1982.

[Fra92]   A. Frank. "Qualitative Spatial Reasoning About Distances and Directions in Geographic Space." *Journal of Visual Languages and Computing*, 3(4):343–371, 1992.

[Fra95]   A. Frank, editor. *Geographic Information Systems: Materials for a Post-graduate Course*. Vols. 4–6 of *GeoInfo*. Technical University of Vienna, Department of Geoinformation, 1995.

[Fre87]   M. Freeston. "The BANG File: A New Kind of Grid File." In *Proc. ACM SIGMOD Intl. Symp. on the Management of Data*, 1987.

[Fre95]   M. Freeston. "A General Solution of the *n*-dimensional B-Tree Problem." In *Proc. ACM SIGMOD Intl. Symp. on the Management of Data*, 1995.

[FSR87]   C. Faloutsos, T. Sellis, and N. Roussopoulos. "Analysis of Object Oriented Spatial Access Methods." In *Proc. ACM SIGMOD Intl. Symp. on the Management of Data*, pages 426–439, 1987.

[FT94]   A. Frank and S. Timpf. "Multiple Representations for Cartographic Objects in a Multi-Scale Tree: An Intelligent Graphical Zoom." *ACM Computer Graphics*, 18(6):823–829, 1994.

[G93]   O. Günther. "Efficient Computation of Spatial Joins." In *Proc. IEEE Intl. Conf. on Data Engineering (ICDE)*, pages 50–59, 1993.

[Gae95]   V. Gaede. Optimal Redundancy in Spatial Database Systems. In [HE95], No. 951 in LNCS, pages 96–116, 1995.

[Gar82]   I. Gargantini. "An Effective Way to Represent Quadtrees." *Communications of the ACM*, 25:905–910, 1982.

[GB90]   O. Günther and A. Buchmann. "Research Issues in Spatial Databases." *SIG-MOD Record (ACM Special Interest Group on Management of Data)*, 19(4):61–68, 1990.

[GBC98]   G. Graefe, R. Bunker, and S. Cooper. "Hash Joins and Hash Teams in Microsoft SQL Server." In *Proc. Intl. Conf. on Very Large Data Bases (VLDB)*, pages 86–97, 1998.

[GEFK99]   M. Goodchild, M. Egenhofer, R. Fegeas, and C. Kottman, editors. *Interoperating Geographic Information Systems.* Kluwer Academic Publishers, New York, 1999.

[GG89]   M. Goodchild and S. Gopal, editors. *Accuracy of Spatial Databases.* Taylor and Francis, London, 1989.

[GG98]   V. Gaede and O. Günther. "Multidimensional Access Methods." *ACM Computing Surveys*, 30(2), 1998.

[GI99]   R. Grossi and G. F. Italiano. "Efficient Cross-Trees for External Memory." In J. Abello and J. S. Vitter, editors, *External Memory Algorithms and Visualization.* DIMACS, Series in Discrete Mathematics and Theoretical Computer Science. American Mathematical Society, 1999.

[GJ98]   M. Goodchild and R. Jeansoulin, editors. *Data Quality in Geographic Information: From Error to Uncertainty.* Hermes, Paris, 1998.

[GJPT78]   M. R. Garey, D. S. Johnson, F. P. Preparata, and R. E. Tarjan. "Triangulating a Simple Polygon." *Information Processing Letter*, 7(4):175–180, 1978.

[GK96]   D. Goldin and P. Kanellakis. "Constraint Query Algebras." *Constraints*, 1(1/2):45–83, 1996.

[GKS00]   R. Güting, M. Koubarakis, and T. Sellis, editors. *Spatiotemporal Databases: The Chorochronos Approach.* Springer-Verlag, Berlin/Heidelberg/New York, 2000. *(http://www.dbnet.ece.ntua.gr/˜choros/).*

[GLL98]   Y. J. Garcia, M. A. Lopez, and S. T. Leutenegger. "On Optimal Node Splitting for R-Trees." In *Proc. Intl. Conf. on Very Large Data Bases (VLDB)*, 1998.

[GM95]   S. C. Guptill and J. L. Morrison, editors. *Elements of Spatial Data Quality.* Elsevier Science, Amsterdam, 1995.

[GMUW00]   H. Garcia-Molina, J. D. Ullman, and J. Widom. *Database System Implementation.* Prentice Hall, Englewood Cliffs, NJ, 2000.

[GO97]   J. E. Goodman and J. O'Rourke. *Handbook of Discrete and Computational Geometry.* CRC Press, Boca Raton, 1997.

[GOP⁺98]   O. Günther, V. Oria, P. Picouet, J.-M. Saglio, and M. Scholl. "Benchmarking Spatial Joins *à la Carte*." In *Proc. Intl. Conference on Scientific and Statistical Database Management (SSDBM)*, 1998.

[GPL99]   R. H. Güting, D. Papadias, and F. H. Lochovsky, editors. *Proc. Intl. Symposium on Large Spatial Databases (SSD)*. Vol. 1651 of *Lecture Notes in Computer Science*, Hong Kong. Springer-Verlag, Berlin/Heidelberg/New York, 1999.

[GR93]   O. Günther and W. F. Riekert. "The Design of GODOT: An Object-Oriented Geographic Information System." *IEEE Data Engineering Bulletin*, 16(3):4–9, 1993.

[GR94]   V. Gaede and W. F. Riekert. "Spatial Access Methods and Query Processing in the Object-Oriented GIS GODOT." In *Proc. of the AGDM'94 Workshop*, pages 40–52. Netherlands Geodetic Commission, 1994.

[Gra93]   G. Graefe. "Query Evaluation Techniques for Large Databases." *ACM Computing Surveys*, 25(2):73–170, 1993.

[GRS98a]   S. Grumbach, P. Rigaux, and L. Segoufin. "Spatio-temporal Data Handling with Constraints." In *Proc. ACM Intl. Symp. on Geographic Information Systems (ACM-GIS)*, 1998.

[GRS98b]   S. Grumbach, P. Rigaux, and L. Segoufin. "The DEDALE System for Complex Spatial Queries." In *Proc. ACM SIGMOD Intl. Symp. on the Management of Data*, pages 213–224, 1998.

[GRS00]   S. Grumbach, P. Rigaux, and L. Segoufin. "Manipulating Interpolated Data Is Easier Than You Thought." In *Proc. Intl. Conf. on Very Large Data Bases (VLDB)*, 2000.

[GRSS97]   S. Grumbach, P. Rigaux, M. Scholl, and L. Segoufin. "DEDALE: A Spatial Constraint Database." In *Proc. Intl. Workshop on Database Programming Languages (DBPL)*, pages 38–59, 1997.

[GRS00]   S. Grumbach, P. Rigaux, M. Scholl, and L. Segoufin. "The DEDALE Prototype." In [KLP00], 2000.

[GS87]   R. H. Güting and W. Schilling. "A Practical Divide-and-Conquer Algorithm for the Rectangle Intersection Problem." *Information Sciences*, 42:95–112, 1987.

[GS91]   O. Günther and H.-J. Schek, editors. *Proc. Intl. Symposium on Design and Implementation af Large Spatial Databases (SSD)*. Vol. 525 of *Lecture Notes in Computer Science*, Zurich. Springer-Verlag, Berlin/Heidelberg/New York, 1991.

[GS93]   R. H. Güting and M. Schneider. "Realms: A Foundation for Spatial Data Types in Database Systems." In [AO93], 1993.

[GS95]   R. H. Güting and M. Schneider. "Realm-Based Spatial Data Types: The ROSE Algebra." *The VLDB Journal*, 4(2):243–286, 1995.

[GS97a]   S. Grumbach and J. Su. "Finitely Representable Databases." *Journal of Computer and System Sciences*, 55(2), 1997.

[GS97b]   S. Grumbach and J. Su. "Queries with Arithmetical Constraints." *Theoretical Computer Science*, 171(1), 1997.

[GST94]   S. Grumbach, J. Su, and C. Tollu. "Linear Constraint Query Languages: Expressive Power and Complexity." In *Logic and Computational Complexity*, 1994. LNCS 960.

[GTVV93]   M. T. Goodrich, J.-J. Tsay, D. E. Vengroff, and J. S. Vitter. "External-Memory Computational Geometry." In *Proc. IEEE Intl. Symp. on Foundations of Computer Sciences*, pages 714–723, 1993.

[Gün88]   O. Günther. *Efficient Structures for Geometric Data Management.* Springer-Verlag, Berlin/Heidelberg/New York, LNCS 337, 1988.

[Gün89]   O. Günther. "The Design of the Cell Tree: An Object-Oriented Index Structure for Geometric Databases." In *Proc. IEEE Intl. Conf. on Data Engineering*, pages 598–605, 1989.

[Gün98]   O. Günther. *Environmental Information Systems.* Springer-Verlag, Berlin/Heidelberg/New York, 1998.

[Gut84]   A. Guttman. "R-Trees: A Dynamic Index Structure for Spatial Searching." In *Proc. ACM SIGMOD Intl. Symp. on the Management of Data*, pages 45–57, 1984.

[Güt88]   R. H. Güting. "Geo-relational Algebra: A Model and Query Language for Geometric Database Systems." In *Proc. Intl. Conf. on Extending Data Base Technology (EDBT)*, pages 506–527, 1988.

[Güt89]   R. H. Güting. "Gral: An Extensible Relational Database System for Geometric Applications." In *Proc. Intl. Conf. on Very Large Data Bases (VLDB)*, 1989.

[Güt94]   R. H. Güting. "An Introduction to Spatial Database Systems." *The VLDB Journal*, 3(4), 1994.

[GW87]   O. Günther and E. Wong. "A Dual Space Representation for Geometric Data." In *Proc. Intl. Conf. on Very Large Data Bases (VLDB)*, 1987.

[GY86]   D. H. Greene and F. F. Yao. "Finite-Resolution Computational Geometry." In *IEEE Conf. on Foundations of Computer Science*, pages 143–152, 1986.

[HE95]   J. R. Herring and M. Egenhofer, editors. *Proc. Intl. Symposium on Large Spatial Databases, (SSD).* Vol. 951 of *Lecture Notes in Computer Science*, Portland, Maine. Springer-Verlag, Berlin/Heidelberg/New York, 1995.

[Her87]   J. R Herring. "TIGRIS: Topologically InteGRated Information System." In *Proc. Intl. Symp. on Computer-Assisted Cartography (Auto-Carto 8)*, pages 282–291, 1987.

[HJR97a]   Y.-W. Huang, N. Jing, and E. A. Rundensteiner. "A Cost Model for Estimating the Performance of Spatial Joins Using R-Trees." In *Proc. Intl. Conference on Scientific and Statistical Database Management (SSDBM)*, 1997.

[HJR97b]   Y.-W. Huang, N. Jing, and E. A. Rundensteiner. "Spatial Joins Using R-Trees: Breadth-First Traversal with Global Optimizations." In *Proc. Intl. Conf. on Very Large Data Bases (VLDB)*, 1997.

[HJR97c]   Y.-W. Huang, M. C. Jones, and E. A. Rundensteiner. "Improving Spatial Intersect Joins Using Symbolic Intersect Detection." In [SV97], 1997.

[HM83]   S. Hertel and K. Mehlorn. "Fast Triangulation of Simple Polygons." In *Proc. Intl. Conf. on Foundations of Computer Theory*, LNCS No. 158, pages 207–218. Springer-Verlag, Berlin/Heidelberg/New York, 1983.

[HP92]   E. Horowitz and M. Papa. "Polygon Clipping: Analysis and Experiences." In J. D. Ulmann, editor, *Theoretical Studies in Computer Sciences*. Academic Press, New York, 1992.

[HS92]   E. G. Hoel and H. Samet. "A Qualitative Comparison Study of Data Structures for Large Line Segment Databases." In *Proc. ACM SIGMOD Intl. Symp. on the Management of Data*, pages 205–214, 1992.

[HS93]   Z. Huang and P. Svensson. "Neighborhood Query and Analysis with GeoSAL, a Spatial Database Language." In [AO93], pages 413–436, 1993.

[HS98]   G. R. Hjaltason and H. Samet. "Incremental Distance Join Algorithms for Spatial Databases." In *Proc. ACM SIGMOD Intl. Symp. on the Management of Data*, 1998.

[HT97]   T. Hadzilacos and N. Tryfona. "An Extended Entity-Relationship Model for Geographic Applications." *SIGMOD Record (ACM Special Interest Group on Management of Data)*, 26(3), 1997.

[ISO00]   ISO. URL: *www.statkart.no/isotc211/*, 2000.

[Jag90a]   H. V. Jagadish. "On Indexing Line Segments." In *Proc. Intl. Conf. on Very Large Data Bases (VLDB)*, pages 614–625, 1990.

[Jag90b]   H. V. Jagadish. "Spatial Search with Polyhedra." In *Proc. IEEE Intl. Conf. on Data Engineering (ICDE)*, pages 311–319, 1990.

[Jea99]   R. Jeansoulin. "Uncertainty Handling and Revision of the Geographic Information." In *Proc. of the 5th EC-GIS Workshop*, 1999.

[JM95]   R. Jeansoulin and C. Mathieu. "A Modal Logic for Spatial Hypothesis." In *Proc. Joint European Conference on GIS*, 1995.

[Kei85]   J. M. Keil. "Decomposing a Polygon into Simpler Components." *SIAM Journal of Computing*, 14(4):799–817, 1985.

[KF93]   I. Kamel and C. Faloutsos. "On Packing R-Trees." In *Proc. Intl. Conf. on Information and Knowledge Management (CIKM)*, 1993.

[KF94]   I. Kamel and C. Faloutsos. "Hilbert R-Tree: An Improved R-Tree Using Fractals." In *Proc. Intl. Conf. on Very Large Data Bases (VLDB)*, 1994.

[KGT99]   G. Kollios, D. Gunopulos, and V. J. Tsotras. "On Indexing Mobile Objects." In *Proc. ACM Intl. Symp. on Principles of Database Systems (PODS)*, 1999.

[KH95]   K. Koperski and J. Han. "Discovery of Spatial Association Rules in Geographic Information Databases." In [HE95], pages 47–66, 1995.

[Kin93]   L. C. Kinsey. *Topology of Surfaces*. Springer-Verlag, Berlin/Heidelberg/New York, 1993.

[Kir95]   P. Kirschenhofer. "The Mathematical Foundation of Graphs and Topology for GIS." In [Fra95], 1995.

[KKR90]   P. C. Kanellakis, G. Kuper, and P. Z. Revesz. "Constraint Query Languages." In *Proc. ACM Intl. Symp. on Principles of Database Systems (PODS)*, pages 299–313, 1990.

[KKR95]   P. Kanellakis, G. Kuper, and P. Revesz. "Constraint Query Languages." *Journal of Computer and System Sciences*, 51(1):26–52, 1995. A shorter version appeared in PODS'90.

[KKT92]   D. G. Kirkpatrick, M. M. Klawe, and R. E. Tarjan. "Polygon Triangulation in $O(n \log \log n)$ Time with Simple Data Structures." *Discrete and Computational Geometry*, 7:329–346, 1992.

[KLP00]   G. Kuper, L. Libkin, and J. Paradaens, editors. *Constraint Databases*. Springer-Verlag, Berlin/Heidelberg/New York, 2000.

[KN96]   E. Knorr and R. Ng. "Finding Aggregate Proximity Relationships and Commonalities in Spatial Data Mining." in *IEEE Transactions on Knowledge and Data Engineering (TKDE)*, 8:884–896, 1996.

[Knu73]   D. E. Knuth. *The Art of Computer Programming*, vol. 1. Addison-Wesley, Reading, MA, 1973.

[Kou97]   M. Koubarakis. "The Complexity of Query Evaluation in Indefinite Temporal Constraint Databases." *Theoretical Computer Science*, 171(1/2), 1997.

[KPJE95]   M. Kavouras, D. Paradissis, J. Jansa, and R. Ecker. "Data Sources for GIS." In [Fra95], 1995.

[KPV95]   B. Kuijpers, J. Paredaens, and J. Van den Bussche. "Lossless Representation of Topological Spatial Data." In [HE95], pages 1–13, 1995.

[KPV97]   B. Kuijpers, J. Paradaens, and J. Van den Bussche. "On Topological Elementary Equivalence of Spatial Databases." In *Proc. Intl. Conf. on Database Theory (ICDT)*, pages 432–446, 1997.

[KRSS98]   G. Kuper, S. Ramaswamy, K. Shim, and J. Su. "A Constraint-Based Spatial Extension to SQL." In *Proc. ACM Intl. Symp. on Geographic Information Systems (ACM-GIS)*, 1998.

[KRVV96]   P. C. Kanellakis, S. Ramaswamy, D. E. Vengroff, and J. S. Vitter. "Indexing for Data Models with Constraints and Classes." *Journal of Computer and System Sciences*, 52(3), 1996.

[KS91]   C. P. Kolovson and M. Stonebraker. "Segment Indexes: Dynamic Indexing Techniques for Multi-dimensional Interval Data." In *Proc. ACM SIGMOD Intl. Symp. on the Management of Data*, pages 138–147, 1991.

[KS97]   N. Koudas and K. C. Sevcik. "Size Separation Spatial Join." In *Proc. ACM SIGMOD Intl. Symp. on the Management of Data*, 1997.

[KV99]   B. Kuijpers and J. Van den Bussche. "On Capturing First-Order Topological Properties of Planar Spatial Databases." In *Proc. Intl. Conf. on Database Theory (ICDT)*, pages 187–198, 1999.

[Lan92]   G. Langran. *Time in Geographic Infomation Systems.* Taylor and Francis, London, 1992.

[Lau98]   R. Laurini. "Spatial Multidatabase Topological Continuity and Indexing: A Step Towards Seamless GIS Data Interoperability." *International Journal of GIS*, 12(4), 1998.

[Lau00]   R. Laurini. *Information Systems for Urban Planning: A Hypermedia Cooperative Approach.* Taylor and Francis, London, 2000.

[LB83]   Y-D Liang and B. A. Barsky. "An Analysis and Algorithm for Polygon Clipping." *Communications of the ACM*, 26(11):868–877, 1983.

[LEL96]   S. Leutenegger, J. Edgington, and M. Lopez. "STR: A Simple and Efficient Algorithm for R-Tree Packing." In *Proc. IEEE Intl. Conf. on Data Engineering (ICDE)*, 1996.

[LG98]   P.-A. Larson and G. Graefe. "Memory Management During Run Generation in External Sorting." In *Proc. ACM SIGMOD Intl. Symp. on the Management of Data*, pages 472–483, 1998.

[LP86]   G. E. Langran and T. K. Poiker. "Integration of Name Selection and Name Placement." In *Proc. Intl. Symp. on Spatial Data Handling (SDH)*, pages 50–64, 1986.

[LPL97]   F. Lecordix, C. Plazanet, and J.-P. Lagrange. "A Platform for Research in Generalization: Application to Caricature." *GeoInformatica*, 1(2), 1997.

[LPV93]   T. Larue, D. Pastre, and Y. Viémont. "Strong Integration of Spatial Domains and Operators in a Relational Database System." In [AO93], pages 53–72, 1993.

[LR95]   M.-L. Lo and C. V. Ravishankar. "Generating Seeded-Trees from Data Sets." In [HE95], 1995.

[LR96]   M.-L. Lo and C. V. Ravishankar. "Spatial Hash-Joins." In *Proc. ACM SIGMOD Intl. Symp. on the Management of Data*, pages 247–258, 1996.

[LR98]   M.-L. Lo and C. V. Ravishankar. "The Design and Implementation of Seeded Trees: An Efficient Method for Spatial Joins." *IEEE Transactions on Knowledge and Data Engineering (TKDE)*, 10(1), 1998. First published in SIGMOD'94.

[LS90]   D. B. Lomet and B. Salzberg. "The hB-Tree: A Multiattribute Indexing Method with Good Guaranteed Performance." *ACM Transactions on Database Systems*, 15(4):625–658, 1990.

[LT92]   R. Laurini and D. Thompson. *Fundamentals of Spatial Information Systems.* No. 37 in the A.P.I.C. series. Academic Press, New York, 1992.

[Mai95]   M. Mainguenaud. "Modeling the Network Component of a Geographical Information System." *International Journal of Geographical Information Systems*, 9(6), 1995.

[McC85]   E. McCreight. "Priority Search Trees." *SIAM Journal of Computing*, 14:257–276, 1985.

[MGR99]   D. Maguire, M. Goodchild, and D. Rhind. *Geographic Information Systems.* 2d ed., 2 vols. Longman Scientific and Technical, London, 1999.

[MK89]   A. Margalit and G. D. Knott. "An Algorithm for Computing the Union, Intersection, or Difference of Two Polygons." *Computers and Graphics,* 13(2):167–183, 1989.

[MKB94]   M. Molenaar, O. Kufoniyi, and T. Bouloucos. "Modeling Topologic Relationships in Vector Maps." In *Proc. Intl. Symp. on Spatial Data Handling (SDH),* 1994.

[MLW95]   J.-C. Muller, J.-P. Lagrange, and R. Weibel, editors. *GISs and Generalization: Methodological and Practical Issues.* Taylor and Francis, London, 1995.

[MO86]   F. Manola and J. Orenstein. "Toward a General Spatial Data Model for an Object-Oriented DBMS." In *Proc. Intl. Conf. on Very Large Data Bases (VLDB),* 1986.

[Mol95]   M. Molenaar. "Spatial Concepts as Implemented in GIS." In [Fra95], 1995.

[Mom00]   B. Momjian. *PostgreSQL, Introduction and Concepts.* Addison-Wesley, Reading, MA, 2000. See *http://postgresql.org.*

[Mor85]   S. Morehouse. "ArcInfo: A Geo-Relational Model for Spatial Information." In *Proc. Intl. Symp. on Computer-Assisted Cartography (Auto-Carto 7),* pages 388–397, 1985.

[Mor89]   S. Morehouse. "The Architecture of ARC/INFO." In *Proc. Intl. Symp. on Computer-Assisted Cartography (Auto-Carto 9),* pages 266–277, 1989.

[MP78]   D. E. Muller and F. P. Preparata. "Finding the Intersection of Two Convex Polyhedra." *Theoretical Computer Science,* 7(2):217–236, 1978.

[MP90]   M. Mainguenaud and M. A. Portier. "CIGALES: A Graphical Query Language for Geographical Information Systems." In *Proc. Intl. Symp. on Spatial Data Handling (SDH),* 1990.

[MP94]   C. Bauzer Medeiros and F. Pires. "Databases for GIS." *SIGMOD Record (ACM Special Interest Group on Management of Data),* 23(1):107–115, 1994.

[MP99]   N. Mamoulis and D. Papadias. "Integration of Spatial Join Algorithms for Joining Multiple Inputs." In *Proc. ACM SIGMOD Intl. Symp. on the Management of Data,* 1999.

[MPS+00]   I. Mirbel, B. Pernici, T. K. Sellis, S. Tserkezoglou, and M. Vazirgiannis. "Checking the Temporal Integrity of Interactive Multimedia Documents." *VLDB Journal,* 9(2):111–130, 2000.

[MS88]   H. G. Mairson and J. Stolfi. "Reporting and Counting Intersections Between Two Sets of Line Segments." *Theoretical Foundations of Computer Graphics and CAD,* F40. NATO ASI Series. Springer-Verlag, Berlin/Heidelberg/New York, 1988.

[MTT99]   Y. Manolopoulos, Y. Theodoridis, and V. Tsotras. *Advanced Database Indexing.* Kluwer, Academic Publishers, New York, 1999.

[Mul94]   K. Mulmuley. *Computational Geometry: An Introduction Through Randomized Algorithms.* Prentice Hall, Englewood Cliffs, NJ, 1994.

[NCG00]   NCGIA URL. *www.ncgia.org*, 2000.

[NH94]   R. Ng and J. Han. "Efficient and Effective Clustering Methods for Spatial Data Mining." In *Proc. Intl. Conf. on Very Large Data Bases (VLDB)*, pages 144–155, 1994.

[NHS84]   J. Nievergelt, H. Hinterger, and K. C. Sevcik. "The Grid File: An Adaptable Symmetric Multikey File Structure." *ACM Trans. on Database Systems*, 9(1):38–71, 1984.

[NP82]   J. Nievergelt and F. P. Preparata. "Plane-Sweep Algorithms for Intersecting Geometric Figures." *Communications of the ACM*, 25(10):739–747, 1982.

[NST99]   M. A. Nascimento, J. R. O. Silva, and Y. Theodoridis. "Evaluation of Access Structures for Discretely Moving Points." In *Intl. Workshop on Spatio-Temporal Database Management (STDBM)*, LNCS 1678, 1999.

[Num95]   J. Numes. "General Concepts of Space and Time." In [Fra95], 1995.

[NW97]   J. Nievergelt and P. Widmayer. "Spatial Data Structures: Concepts and Design Choices." In [vKNRW97], pages 153 and 198, 1997.

[OCON82]   J. O'Rourke, C.-B. Chien, T. Olson, and D. Naddor. "A New Linear Algorithm for Intersecting Convex Polygons." *Computer Graphics and Image Processing*, 19:384–391, 1982.

[OGD00]   OGDI. URL: *www.ogdi.org/faq/faq-web.asp*, 2000.

[OGI00]   OGIS. URL: *www.ogis.com*, 2000.

[OM84]   J. Orenstein and T. H. Merrett. "A Class of Data Structures for Associative Searching." In *Proc. ACM Intl. Symp. on Principles of Database Systems (PODS)*, pages 181–190, 1984.

[OM88]   J. Orenstein and F. Manola. "PROBE: Spatial Data Modeling and Query Processing in an Image Database Application." *IEEE Transactions on Software Engineering*, 14(5):611–628, 1988.

[O'N94]   P. E. O'Neil. *Database: Principles, Programming, Performance.* Morgan Kaufmann, San Francisco, 1994.

[Ooi90]   B. C. Ooi. *Efficient Query Processing in a Geographic Information System.* LNCS No. 471. Springer-Verlag, Berlin/Heidelberg/New York, 1990.

[O'R94]   J. O'Rourke. *Computational Geometry in C.* Cambridge University Press, New York, 1994.

[Ora00]   Oracle. URL: *oradoc.photo.net/ora81/doc/inter.815/a67295/toc.htm*, 2000. *Oracle8i Spatial User's Guide and Reference, Release 8.1.5.*

[Ore86]   J. A. Orenstein. "Spatial Query Processing in an Object-Oriented Database System." In *Proc. ACM SIGMOD Intl. Symp. on the Management of Data*, pages 326–336, 1986.

[Ore89]   J. A. Orenstein. "Redundancy in Spatial Databases." In *Proc. ACM SIGMOD Intl. Symp. on the Management of Data*, 1989.

[Ore90]   J. A. Orenstein. "A Comparison of Spatial Query Processing Techniques for Native and Parameter Spaces." In *Proc. ACM SIGMOD Intl. Symp. on the Management of Data*, 1990.

[OSDD89]   B. C. Ooi, R. Sack-Davis, and K. J. McDonell. "Extending a DBMS for Geographic Applications." In *Proc. Intl. Conf. on Data Engineering*, pages 590–597, 1989.

[OW86]   T. Ottmann and D. Wood. "Space-Economical Plane Sweep Algorithms." *Comp. Vision Graphics and Image Processing*, 34, 1986.

[P86]   C. H. Papadimitriou. *The Theory of Database Concurrency Control.* Computer Science Press, Rockville, MD, 1986.

[PBR98]   C. Plazanet, N.-M. Bigolin, and A. Ruas. "Experiments with Learning Techniques for Spatial Model Enrichment and Line Generalization." *GeoInformatica*, 2(4), 1998.

[PD96]   J. M. Patel and D. J. DeWitt. "Partition Based Spatial-Merge Join." In *Proc. ACM SIGMOD Intl. Symp. on the Management of Data*, pages 259–270, 1996.

[PE97]   D. Papadias and M. Egenhofer. "Hierarchical Spatial Reasoning About Direction Relations." *GeoInformatica*, 1(3), 1997.

[Peu84]   D. J. Peuquet. "A Conceptual Framework and Comparison of Spatial Data Models." *Cartographica*, 21(4):66–113, 1984.

[PJT00]   D. Pfoser, C. S. Jensen, and Y. Theodoridis. "Novel Approaches in Query Processing for Moving Objects." In *Proc. Intl. Conf. on Very Large Data Bases (VLDB)*, 2000.

[Ple97]   B. Plewe. *GIS On-Line: Information Retrieval, Mapping, and the Internet.* On-Word Press, (Delmar, Publishers, Albany NY), 1997.

[PM97]   A. Papadopoulos and Y. Manolopoulos. "Performance of Nearest Neighbor Queries in R-Trees." In *Proc. Intl. Conf. on Database Theory (ICDT)*, 1997.

[PMT99]   D. Papadias, N. Mamoulis, and Y. Theodoridis. "Processing and Optimization of Multi-Way Spatial Joins Using R-Trees." In *Proc. ACM Intl. Symp. on Principles of Database Systems (PODS)*, 1999.

[Pre79]   F. P. Preparata. "An Optimal Real-Time Algorithm for Planar Convex Hulls." *Communications of the ACM*, 22:402–405, 1979.

[PRS99]   A. Papadopoulos, P. Rigaux, and M. Scholl. "A Performance Evaluation of Spatial Join Processing Strategies." In [GPL99], 1999.

[PS85]   F. P. Preparata and M. I. Shamos. *Computational Geometry: An Introduction.* Springer-Verlag, New York, 1985.

[PS94]   D. Papadias and T. K. Sellis. "Qualitative Representation of Spatial Knowledge in Two-Dimensional Space." *VLDB Journal*, 3(4), 1994.

[PS95]   D. Papadias and T. K. Sellis. "A Pictorial Query-by-Example Language." *Journal of Visual Languages and Computing*, 6(1):53–72, 1995.

[PSTW93]   B. Pagel, H. Six, H. Toben, and P. Widmayer. "Toward an Analysis of Range Query Performance." In *Proc. ACM Intl. Symp. on Principles of Database Systems (PODS)*, pages 214–221, 1993.

[PSV99]   C. H Papadimitriou, D. Suciu, and V. Vianu. "Topological Queries in Spatial Databases." *Journal of Computer and System Sciences*, 58(1):29–53, 1999.

[PTSE95]   D. Papadias, Y. Theodoridis, T. K. Sellis, and M. Egenhofer. "Topological Relations in the World of Minimum Bounding Rectangles: A Study with R-Trees." In *Proc. ACM SIGMOD Intl. Symp. on the Management of Data*, pages 92–103, 1995.

[PVV94]   J. Paredaens, J. Van den Bussche, and D. Van Gucht. "Toward a Theory of Spatial Database Queries." In *Proc. ACM Intl. Symp. on Principles of Database Systems (PODS)*, pages 279–288, 1994.

[PYK+97]   J. M. Patel, J. Yu, N. Kabra, K. Tufte, B. Nag, J. Burger, N. E. Hall, K. Ramasamy, R. Lueder, C. Ellman, J. Kupsch, S. Guo, D. J. DeWitt, and J. F. Naughton. "Building a Scalable Geo-spatial DBMS: Technology, Implementation, and Evaluation." In *Proc. ACM SIGMOD Intl. Symp. on the Management of Data*, pages 336–347, 1997.

[Qua98]   T. Quatrani. *Visual Modeling with Rational Rose and UML.* Addison-Wesley, Reading, MA, 1998.

[Ram97]   R. Ramakrishnan. *Database Management Systems.* McGraw-Hill, New York, 1997.

[Ram00]   S. Ramaswamy. "Theory and Practice of I/O-Efficient Algorithms for Constraint Databases." In [KLP00], 2000.

[RBP+91]   J. Rumbaugh, M. Blaha, W. Premerlani, F. Eddy, and W. Lorensen. *Object-Oriented Modeling and Design.* Prentice Hall, Englewood Cliffs, NJ, 1991.

[RKV95]   N. Roussopoulos, S. Kelley, and F. Vincent. "Nearest Neighbor Queries." In *Proc. ACM SIGMOD Intl. Symp. on the Management of Data*, 1995.

[RL85]   N. Roussopoulos and D. Leifker. "Direct Spatial Search on Pictorial Databases Using Packed R-Trees." In *Proc. ACM SIGMOD Intl. Symp. on the Management of Data*, pages 17–26, 1985.

[Rob81]   J. T. Robinson. "The K-D-B-Tree: A Search Structure for Large Multidimensional Dynamic Indexes." In *Proc. ACM SIGMOD Intl. Symp. on the Management of Data*, pages 10–18, 1981.

[Rot91]   D. Rotem. "Spatial Join Indices." In *Proc. IEEE Intl. Conf. on Data Engineering (ICDE)*, 1991.

[RS95]   P. Rigaux and M. Scholl. "Multi-scale Partitions: Application to Spatial and Statistical Databases." In [HE95], pages 170–183, 1995.

[RSHN97]   L. Relly, H.-J. Schek, O. Henricsson, and S. Nebiker. "Physical Database Design for Raster Images in Concert." In [SV97], 1997.

[Rua98]   A. Ruas. "A Method for Building Displacement in Automated Map Generalization." *International Journal of Geographical Information Science*, 12(8), 1998.

[Sam90a]   H. Samet. *Applications of Spatial Data Structures*. Addison-Wesley, Reading, MA, 1990.

[Sam90b]   H. Samet. *The Design and Analysis of Spatial Data Structures*. Addison-Wesley, Reading, MA, 1990.

[Sch97a]   S. Schirra. "Precision and Robustness in Geometric Computations." In [vKNRW97], pages 255 and 287, 1997.

[Sch97b]   M. Schneider. *Spatial Data Types for Database Systems: Finite Resolution Geometry for Geographic Information Systems*. Vol. 1288 of *Lecture Notes in Computer Science*. Springer-Verlag, New York, 1997.

[SDMO87]   R. Sack-Davis, K. J. McDonell, and B. C. Ooi. "GEOQL: A Query Language for Geographic Information Systems." In *Australian and New Zealand Association for the Advancement of Science Congress*, 1987.

[SE89]   J. Star and J. Estes. *Geographic Information Systems: An Introduction*. Prentice Hall, Englewood Cliffs, NJ, 1989.

[Sed83]   R. Sedgewick. *Algorithms*. Addison-Wesley, Reading, MA, 1983.

[Sei91]   R. Seidel. "A Simple and Fast Incremental Randomized Algorithm for Computing Trapezoidal Decompositions and for Triangulating Polygons." *Computational Geometry*, 1(1), 1991.

[SEM98]   A. R. Shariff, M. Egenhofer, and D. Mark. "Natural-Language Spatial Relations Between Linear and Areal Objects: The Topology and Metric of English-Language Terms." *Intl. Journal of Geographical Information Science*, 12(3), 1998.

[SGR96]   M. Scholl, G. Grangeret, and X. Réhsé. Point and Window Queries with Linear Spatial Indices: An Evaluation with O_2." Technical Report CS/TR-007, Cedric/CNAM, 1996. Available at *ftp://sikkim.cnam.fr/reports/*.

[SH74]   I. E. Sutherland and G. W. Hogdman. "Reentrant Polygon Clipping." *Communications of the ACM*, 17(1):33–42, 1974.

[SH76]   M. I. Shamos and D. Hoey. "Geometric Intersection Problems." In *IEEE Conf. on Foundations of Computer Science*, 1976.

[Sha99]   J. Sharma. "Oracle8*i* Spatial: Experiences with Extensible Databases." An Oracle technical white paper, Oracle Corp., Redwood City, CA, May 1999.

[SJLL00]   S. Saltenis, C. S. Jensen, S. T. Leutenegger, and M. A. Lopez. "Indexing the Positions of Continuously Moving Objects." In *Proc. ACM SIGMOD Intl. Symp. on the Management of Data*, 2000.

[SKS98]   A. Silberschatz, H. F. Korth, and S. Sudarshan. *Database System Concepts*. McGraw-Hill, New York, 1998.

[SL95]   S. Servigne and R. Laurini. "Updating Geographic Databases Using Multi-Source Information." In *Proc. ACM Intl. Symp. on Geographic Information Systems (ACM-GIS)*, 1995.

[SM99]   J.-M. Saglio and J. Moreira. "Oporto: A Realistic Scenario Generator for Moving Objects." In *Proc. Intl. Conf. on Databases and Expert Applications (DEXA)*, pages 426–432, 1999. Extended version to appear in *GeoInformatica*.

[SML94]   SmallWorld, Ltd. *SmallWorld GIS 2*, London, 1994.

[SML00]   SmallWorld, Ltd. URL: *www.smallworld-systems.co.uk/*, 2000. SmallWorld presentation.

[SPV00]   S. Spaccapietra, C. Parent, and C. Vangenot. "GIS Databases: From Multiscale to Multirepresentation." In *Intl. Symp. on Abstraction, Reformulation, and Approximation (SARA)*, 2000.

[SR86]   M. Stonebraker and L. A. Rowe. "The Design of Postgres." In *Proc. ACM SIGMOD Intl. Symp. on the Management of Data*, pages 340–355, 1986.

[SRF87]   T. Sellis, N. Roussopoulos, and C. Faloutsos. "The R+Tree: A Dynamic Index for Multi-dimensional Objects." In *Proc. Intl. Conf. on Very Large Data Bases (VLDB)*, pages 507–518, 1987.

[SRG83]   M. Stonebraker, B. Rubenstein, and A. Guttman. "Application of Abstract Data Types and Abstract Indices to CAD Data Bases." In *Proc. ACM/IEEE Conf. on Engineering Design Applications*, pages 107–113, 1983.

[SRH90]   M. Stonebraker, L. Rowe, and M. Hirohama. "The Implementation of Postgres." *IEEE Transactions on Knowledge and Data Engineering (TKDE)*, 2(1):125–142, 1990.

[Sto86]   M. Stonebraker. "Inclusion of New Types in Relational Data Base Systems." In *Proc. Intl. Conf. on Data Engineering*, pages 262–269, 1986.

[SU00]   J.-R. Sack and J. Urrutia, editors. *Handbook of Computational Geometry*. Elsevier Science, Amsterdam, 2000.

[SUPL00]   S. Servigne, T. Ubeda, A. Puricelli, and R. Laurini. "A Methodology for Spatial Consistency Improvement of Geographic Databases." *GeoInformatica*, 4(1):7–34, 2000.

[SV89]   M. Scholl and A. Voisard. "Thematic Map Modeling." In [BGSW89], pages 167–192. Springer-Verlag, Berlin/Heidelberg/New York, 1989.

[SV92]   M. Scholl and A. Voisard. "Object-Oriented Database Systems for Geographic Applications: An Experiment with O_2." Chapter 28 of [BDK92].

[SV97]   M. Scholl and A. Voisard, editors. *Proc. Intl. Symposium on Large Spatial Databases (SSD)*. Vol. 1262 of *Lecture Notes in Computer Science*, Berlin. Springer-Verlag, Berlin/Heidelberg/New York, 1997.

[SV98]   L. Segoufin and V. Vianu. "Querying Spatial Databases via Topological Invariants." In *Proc. ACM Intl. Symp. on Principles of Database Systems (PODS)*, 1998.

[SVP+96]   M. Scholl, A. Voisard, J.-P. Peloux, L. Raynal, and P. Rigaux. *SGBD Géographiques*. International Thomson Publishing, Paris, 1996.

[SW88]   H. Six and P. Widmayer. "Spatial Searching in Geometric Databases." In *Proc. IEEE Intl. Conf. on Data Engineering (ICDE)*, pages 496–503, 1988.

[SWCD97]   A. P. Sistla, O. Wolfson, S. Chamberlain, and S. Dao. "Modeling and Querying Moving Objects." In *Proc. IEEE Intl. Conf. on Data Engineering (ICDE)*, pages 422–432, 1997.

[TC200]   The CEN TC287 Standard. URL: *forum.afnor.fr/afnor/work/afnor/gpn2/z13c/public/web/english/pren.htm*, 2000.

[TIG00]   TIGER. URL: *www.census.gov/geo/www/tiger/*, 2000.

[Til80]   R. B. Tilove. "Set Membership Classification: A Unified Approach to Geometric Intersection Problems." *IEEE Transactions on Computers*, C-29(10), 1980.

[TJ99]   N. Tryfona and C. S. Jensen. "Conceptual Modeling for Spatiotemporal Applications." *GeoInformatica*, 3(3):245–268, 1999.

[Tom90]   C. D. Tomlin. *Geographic Information Systems and Cartographic Modeling*. Prentice Hall, Englewood Cliffs, NJ, 1990.

[TS96]   Y. Theodoridis and T. K. Sellis. "A Model for the Prediction of R-Tree Performance." In *Proc. ACM Intl. Symp. on Principles of Database Systems (PODS)*, 1996.

[TSN99]   Y. Theodoridis, J.R.O. Silva, and M. A. Nascimento. "On the Generation of Spatiotemporal Datasets." In [GPL99], 1999.

[TSPM98]   Y. Theodoridis, T. Sellis, A. N. Papadopoulos, and Y. Manolopoulos. "Specifications for Efficient Indexing in Spatiotemporal Databases." In *Proc. Intl. Conference on Scientific and Statistical Database Management (SSDBM)*, 1998.

[TSS98]   Y. Theodoridis, E. Stefanakis, and T. K. Sellis. "Cost Models for Join Queries in Spatial Databases." In *Proc. IEEE Intl. Conf. on Data Engineering (ICDE)*, 1998.

[TUW98]   J. Tayeb, O. Ulusoy, and O. Wolfson. "A Quadtree Based Dynamic Attribute Indexing Method." *Computer Journal*, 41:185–200, 1998.

[TvW88]   R. E. Tarjan and C. J. van Wyk. "An $O(n \log \log n)$ Time Algorithm for Triangulating a Simple Polygon." *SIAM Journal of Computing*, 17(1):143–178, 1988.

[Ull88]   J. D. Ullman. *Principles of Database and Knowledge-Base Systems*, Vol. 1. Computer Science Press, New York, 1988.

[Ull89]   J. D. Ullman. *Principles of Database and Knowledge-Base Systems*, Vol. 2. Computer Science Press, New York, 1989.

[Val87]   P. Valduriez. "Join Indices." *ACM Trans. on Database Systems*, 12(2):218–246, 1987.

[Vck99]   A. Vckovski, editor. *Proc. Intl. Workshop on Interoperating Geographic Information Systems (INTEROP)*. Vol. 1580 of *Lecture Notes in Computer Science*, Springer-Verlag, Berlin/Heidelberg/New York, 1999.

[VD01]   A. Voisard and B. David. "A Database Perspective on Geospatial Data Modeling." *IEEE Transactions on Knowledge and Data Engineering*, 2001. To appear.

[VGV95]   L. Vandeurzen, M. Gyssens, and D. Van Gucht. "On the Desirability and Limitations of Linear Spatial Database Models." In [HE95], pages 14–28, 1995.

[VGV96]   L. Vandeurzen, M. Gyssens, and D. Van Gucht. "On Query Languages for Linear Queries Definable with Polynomial Constraints." In *Proc. Intl. Conf. on Principles and Practice of Constraint Programming*, LNCS 1118, pages 468–481, 1996.

[Vit84]   J. S. Vitter. "Faster Methods for Random Sampling." *Communications of the ACM*, 27(7), 1984.

[Vit98]   J. S. Vitter. "External Memory Algorithms." In *Proc. ACM Intl. Symp. on Principles of Database Systems (PODS)*, 1998.

[vK97]   M. van Kreveld. "Digital Elevation Models and TIN Algorithms." In [vKNRW97], pages 37–78, 1997.

[vKNRW97]   M. van Kreveld, J. Nievergelt, T. Roos, and P. Wiedmayer, editors. *Algorithmic Foundations of Geographic Information Systems*. No. 1340 in LNCS. Springer-Verlag, Berlin/Heidelberg/New York, 1997.

[Vko98]   A. Vckovski, editor. *Intl. Journal of Geographic Information Science*, Vol. 12. Taylor and Francis, London, 1998. Special issue on interoperability in GIS.

[vOV91]   P. van Oosterom and T. Vijlbrief. "Building a GIS on Top of the Open DBMS Postgres." In *Proc. Eur. Conf. on Geographic Information Systems (EGIS)*, pages 775–787, 1991.

[vOvdB89]   P. van Oosterom and J. van den Bos. "An Object-Oriented Approach to the Design of Geographic Information Systems." In [BGSW89], pages 255–270, 1989.

[VTS98]   M. Vazirgiannis, Y. Theodoridis, and T. K. Sellis. "Spatio-temporal Composition and Indexing for Large Multimedia Applications." In *ACM Springer Multimedia Systems*, 6(4):284–293, 1998.

[Wei85]   K. Weiler. "Edge-Based Data Structures for Solid Modeling in Curved-Surface Environments." *IEEE Computer Graphics and Applications*, 5(1):21–40, 1985.

[WHM90]   M. Worboys, H. Hearnshaw, and D. Maguire. "Object-Oriented Data and Query Modelling for Geographical Information Systems." In *Proc. Intl. Symp. on Spatial Data Handling (SDH)*, 1990.

[WJ98]   R. Weibel and C. B. Jones. "Computational Perspectives on Map Generalization." *GeoInformatica*, 2(4):307–314, 1998.

[Wor94]   M. F. Worboys. "A Unified Model of Spatial and Temporal Information." *Computer Journal*, 37(1), 1994.

[Wor95]   M. Worboys. *GIS: A Computing Perspective.* Taylor and Francis, London, 1995.

[WXCJ98]   O. Wolfson, B. Xu, S. Chamberlain, and L. Jiang. "Moving Object Databases: Issues and Solutions." In *Proc. Intl. Conference on Scientific and Statistical Database Management (SSDBM)*, 1998.

[XEKS98]   X. Xu, M. Ester, H.-P. Kriegel, and J. Sander. "A Distribution-Based Clustering Algorithm for Mining in Large Spatial Databases." In *Proc. IEEE Intl. Conf. on Data Engineering (ICDE)*, pages 324–331, 1998.

[YdC95]   T. S. Yeh and B. de Cambray. "Time as a Geometric Dimension for Modeling the Evolution of Entities: A 3D Approach." In *Proc. Intl. Conf. on Integrating Geographical Information Systems and Environmental Modeling*, 1995.

[YM98]   C. T. Yu and W. Meng. *Principles of Database Query Processing for Advanced Applications.* Morgan Kaufmann, San Francisco, 1998.

[ZC95]   K. Zeitouni and B. de Cambray. "Topological Modeling for 3D GIS." In *Intl. Conf. on Computers in Urban Planning and Urban Management*, 1995.

[ZS98]   G. Zimbrao and J. M. Souza. "A Raster Approximation for the Processing of Spatial Joins." In *Proc. Intl. Conf. on Very Large Data Bases (VLDB)*, 1998.

[ZSI00]   H. Zhu, J. Su, and O. H. Ibarra. "Toward Spatial Joins for Polygons." In *Proc. Intl. Conference on Scientific and Statistical Database Management (SSDBM)*, 2000.

[Zub88]   R. B. Zubiaga. "On the Intersection of Two Planar Polygons." *Computers and Graphics*, 12:401–403, 1988.

Index

About the Authors

Philippe Rigaux   holds a Master's in mathematics and a Master's in computer science from the University of Paris VII. From 1986 to 1992, he was a software engineer in private industry. From 1992 to 1995, he was a research assistant in the database group of the *Conservatoire National des Arts et Métiers* (CNAM) in Paris, where he obtained his Ph.D. in 1995. He is currently an assistant professor in the CNAM database group. He has conducted research in the area of database management, strongly oriented toward spatial applications. His research interests include the design of query languages and query evaluation techniques. He has been involved in the program committee of various conferences in the field, such as SSD, ACM-GIS, and SSDBM.

Michel Scholl   received his Ph.D. in computer science from the University of California at Los Angeles in 1977, and his French *Thèse d'état* from the University of Grenoble in 1985. He was with INRIA (*French Institut National de Recherche en Informatique et en Automatique*) for twelve years, where he headed the Verso database group, prior to joining the faculty of the *Conservatoire National des Arts et Métiers* (CNAM). Since 1989, he has been a full professor of computer science at CNAM. He manages the database group in the research laboratory CEDRIC of CNAM and has a joint position at INRIA in the Verso database group. His background includes computer-assisted instruction, packet-switched radio networks, data structures, and databases. His current research interests include spatial databases and digital libraries. He has served as program chair for the 5th International Symposium on Spatial Databases (SSD'97) and as program committee member of many conferences, including ACM SIGMOD, VLDB, and EDBT.

Agnès Voisard received her Master's and Ph.D. degrees in computer science from the University of Paris at Orsay (Paris XI) and INRIA (*French Institut National de Recherche en Informatique et en Automatique*) in 1989 and 1992, respectively. During the academic year 1991–92 she was a research assistant in the database group of the *Conservatoire National des Arts et Métiers* (CNAM) in Paris. In 1992–93 she was an INRIA postdoctoral fellow at Ludwig Maximilian University in Munich. In 1993, she was appointed assistant professor of computer science at the Free University of Berlin, where she obtained her *Habilitation* in 1999. In January 2001, she joined Kivera, Inc. (Oakland, California) as a system architect. Her areas of expertise include geographic information systems, object-oriented databases, data modeling, graphical user interfaces, navigation systems, and interoperability in information systems. She has participated in several program committees, and was general chair of the 5th International Symposium on Spatial Databases (SSD'97).